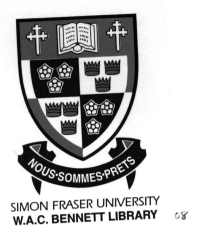

POSTMODERNISM AND THE ETHICAL SUBJECT

POST-MODERNISM AND THE ETHICAL SUBJECT

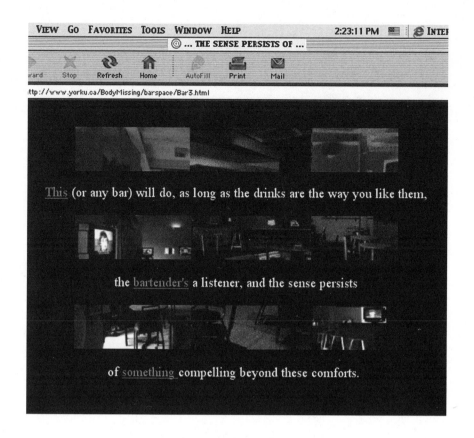

Edited by Barbara Gabriel

and Suzan Ilcan

McGill-Queen's University Press

Montreal & Kingston • London • Ithaca

©McGill-Queen's University Press 2004

ISBN 0-7735-2701-x (cloth)
ISBN 0-7735-2702-8 (paper)

Legal deposit third quarter 2004
Bibliothèque nationale du Québec

Printed in Canada on acid-free paper.

This book has been published with the help of funds from Carleton University and the University of Windsor.

McGill-Queen's University Press acknowledges the support of the Canada Council for the Arts for our publishing program. We also acknowledge the financial support of the Government of Canada through the Book Publishing Industry Development Program (BPIDP) for our publishing activities.

David Clark's chapter, pages 41-74, is copyright 1997 from *Becoming Beast: Discourses of Animality from the Middle Ages to the Present,* edited by Jennifer Ham and Matthew Senior. Reproduced by permission of Routledge/Taylor & Francis Books, Inc.

National Library of Canada Cataloguing in Publication

Postmodernism and the ethical subject / edited by Barbara Gabriel and Suzan Ilcan.

Includes bibliographical references.
ISBN 0-7735-2701-X
ISBN 0-7735-2702-8

1. Ethics, Modern—20th century. 2. Postmodernism. I. Gabriel, Barbara, 1944- II. Ilcan, Suzan M.

BJ319.P68 2004 170   C2004-901741-1

Design and typesetting by David LeBlanc
Frontispiece: "The sense persists of something compelling beyond these comforts."
Frame capture from the Body Missing web site, http://www.yorku.ca/BodyMissing.
Vera Frenkel, 1995 and continuing. ©CARCC 2004

Ethics is articulated through effective operations, and it defines a distance between what is and ought to be. This distance designates a space where we have something to do.

Michel de Certeau

Contents

Contributors

Deborah Burrett Independent scholar, Toronto

Brenda Carr Department of English, Carleton University

David L. Clark Department of English, McMaster University

Bina Freiwald Department of English, Concordia University

Barbara Gabriel School Studies in Art and Culture,
Carleton University

Suzan Ilcan Department of Sociology and Anthropology,
University of Windsor

Phyllis Lambert Canadian Centre for Architecture, Montreal

Francesco Loriggio School of Humanities, Carleton University

Daniel O'Connor Department of Sociology and Anthropology,
University of Windsor

Lynne Phillips Department of Sociology and Anthropology,
University of Windsor

Ruth Phillips School Studies in Art and Culture,
Carleton University

Barry Rutland Adjunct professor, Carleton University

Leandro Urbina Chilean-Canadian novelist, Washington, DC

PART ONE

INTRODUCTORY

"Writing against the Ruins":
Towards a Postmodern Ethics of Memory

BARBARA GABRIEL

You walk through a glass-enclosed hall with high-domed ceilings, making your way up a long ramp, and turn to the room on the right. Once there, you find yourself in the familiar space of a bar with other patrons milling around. The bar itself is arranged with small round tables, chairs, bar-stools and, along with a piano that seems to be playing itself and newspapers in many languages posted for reading, video monitors mounted to the wall and on the bar. Finally, you spot the suitcases, clues that this particular bar is located in the migratory space of an airplane or train station, reminders that you are just passing through.

A succession of faces, speaking languages that you cannot make out, are trying to tell you something in images flashed on the monitors positioned throughout the room. The subtitles promise some help. They are in alternating English, German, and French, languages that you can recognize. The screen to your left blinks again and its enigmatic message catches your eye: THE STORY IS ALWAYS PARTIAL. The bartender sets up his drinks at the counter and, for the moment, a sense of ordinariness returns.

The scene I am describing is Canadian multi-media artist Vera Frenkel's installation ... *from the Transit Bar*, a reconstruction at the National Gallery of Canada, from 9 May to 27 October 1996, of the work first shown four years earlier at documenta IX in Kassel, Germany. In its blurring of the boundaries of the artwork and the "real," Frenkel's installation inhabits a postmodern space that extends many of the conceptual problems posed earlier in the century by the Duchamps ready-made. This time round, however, they are folded into a scenic framework intensely saturated with social concerns. "*Whose* story?" the viewer is impelled to ask. And, even at the very moment when we are promised only partial narrative, the foreclosure of "full truth," the reply on the screen moves over into the register of encounter and desire. *Partial to what, you ask.*

This is, after all, a bar, the scene of casual stagings of the self that risk little and promise nothing. Yet, above all, it is a space of narrative desire, that yearning for story that Walter Benjamin sees as first taking place in oral tale. In Benjamin's *The Storyteller*, the archaic types of the teller of tales are the

Traveller who returns home and an Other who is rooted in his place – in a regularized grammar that obtains cross-culturally throughout much of human history. Yet we have only to consider the impossibility of these coordinates in our present moment of transnational migrations and diaspora to understand our vertigo before the video monitors of the transit bar, those faces compelling us to hear their stories in a babel of unknown languages. Here, the once stable markers of language, "race," and national identity are scrambled in a whole range of contradictory codes. An African-American tells his story with French subtitles, but the voice-over is in Polish; in turn, an Asian man speaks with an unfamiliar voice-over in Yiddish, while the subtitles are in German. Stereotypical identities collapse in a dissonant landscape of sound and image.

In the spacing that marks the division between those faces on the monitors of the transit bar and the ideal figures of Benjamin's own *ur*-narrative, we can chart the threshold of difference, the very moment when the *traveller* turns into the *foreigner*. In the global population movements and displacements of the contemporary West, stories are more important than ever, individual and collective memories breaking up authorized histories and changing them beyond recognition. Within this transformed field meaning no longer has even the illusion of transparency, foregrounding questions of value. Whose memories count – and why? Frenkel deliberately chose dominant European languages for the printed texts of her subtitles, but the voice-overs of the characters on-screen are made to speak the lost languages of her own grandparents. These video performances operate in a tension between *information* and *interference* that reminds us of the radical contingency of these two frame-bound terms. Yet this undecideability at the level of the signifier is no mere exercise in postmodern play. Frenkel draws from this controvertibility of signs an urgent ethical imperative – one that speaks to our own historical moment of heterogeneous national identities. "*We are all foreigners*" announces the special edition of *The Transit Bar* newspaper.

The overturning of the high modernist episteme of purity is one of the most striking characteristics of postmodern ontologies as well as cultural practices. A new ethical imperative of contamination and *im*purity is the signal marker of our moment, and if it refuses us a place to stand that reflects the shifting tectonic plates beneath our feet, then that is because space itself has been radically reconfigured. At the same time as the old maps no longer suffice and we have learned to question the operations that construct boundaries altogether, the reconceptualizing of space is more important than ever, informing a widespread critique of totalizing knowledge.

Long before those shock-images of 9/11 flashed across television screens, Michel de Certeau (1984, 92) had uncannily invoked the World Trade Center buildings as offering the very type of the panoramic *view from nowhere*.

To be lifted to the summit of the World Trade Center is to be lifted out of the city's grasp. One's body is no longer clasped by the streets that turn and return it according to an anonymous law; nor is it possessed, by the rumble of so many differences or by the nervousness of New York traffic. When one goes up there, he leaves behind the mass that carries off and mixes up itself any identity of authors or spectators ... His elevation transfigures him into a voyeur. It puts him at a distance. It transforms the bewitching world by which one was possessed into a text that lies before one's eyes. It allows one to read it, to be a solar Eye, looking down like a god. The exaltation of the scopic and Gnostic drive: the fiction of knowledge is related to this lust to be a viewpoint and nothing more.

Behind de Certeau's reading of the solar Eye lies Bataille and a longer tradition of French anti-Cartesianism. This time round, however, the critique of Western desire for mastery is provoked by "the nervousness of New York traffic, the rumble of so many differences below." Reframed by the intervention of historical event and aftermath, de Certeau's reading of this prospect is clearly more prescient than ever. What started out as a symbolic assault on American and Western hegemony turned out, soon enough, to mark a shift that was also epistemic and ethical, creating an endless spiral of insider and outsider in Fortress America. In ways strikingly anticipated by Melvin Charney's images in this volume, this was architectural space reconfigured as *disaster*. Whatever else, the God's-eye view was gone forever.

Transnational perspectives and global population movements have confirmed new ways of reconfiguring history as a discontinuous field, one that increasingly insists on recovering the forgotten in official narratives. What interests me here are the ways in which a work like ... *from the Transit Bar* dissolves some of our habitual ways of talking about postmodernism, a term whose slipperiness is in no small part due to the uneven development of the concept of modernism, itself, across both disciplinary and national boundaries. Though our concerns in this volume are frequently with a body of contemporary theoretical frameworks often aligned with poststructuralism as well as postcolonialism, this more inclusive understanding of postmodern theory is both situated in postmodernity as periodizing frame and bound up with a range of cultural practices. Rosalind Krauss (1994, 292) reminded us some time ago that much of what now goes by the name of postmodern theory is really a form of *paraliterature* (292). In turn, postmodern cultural practices operate to perform theory. It is the heightened self-conscious register of the postmodern that helps to explain its penchant for the performative – in a reciprocity of theory and cultural practice that is symptomatic of its redrawing of boundaries (Gabriel 1994).

Can we separate out these representational and discursive practices from the urgency of Foucault's (1982, 216) putting of the question first suggested by Kant: "What's going on just now? What's happening to us? What is this world, this period, this precise moment in which we are living?" It is a question that has only intensified in the decades since he asked it, suggesting that what we may really be doing is settling down into something that looks more and more like *long modernity*. Arjun Appadurai (1996, 2–3) argues for a thinking of "The global Now," a historical moment of rupture in which media and migration are the central axes in the making of a transformed subjectivity. To what extent, then, does this break connect up with the new ways of configuring knowledge we have come to think of as the postmodern? Unlike Lyotard (1979), whose reading of the demise of the grand foundational narratives of Enlightenment modernism marks the inaugural scene of contemporary discussions of the postmodern, Foucault eschewed the term altogether. Nor was this nomination important to the framework of those French thinkers around *Tel Quel* who were, themselves, engaged in a quarrel with Marx in the aftermath of the student revolutions of 1968 and who were drawing on a wider continental line of inheritance that included Freud and Nietzsche as well as Bataille and the phenomenological tradition. But the epistemic shift that they mark shares in a widespread suspicion of totalizing narratives, one inseparable from the legacy of the twin historical totalitarianism of fascism and Stalinism.

In order to understand something of the mistranslation that often occurred in their passage across the Atlantic, it is important to remember the embeddedness of this thinking in the traumatic historical frames of the postwar period. Without the same burden of history (the complicity of Vichy as well as the shadow of the Holocaust and the failure of classical Marxism), it was easy to read the primacy of the signifier in the critique of Saussurean linguistics as an abdication of meaning and value altogether. Instead, what much of late twentieth-century French thinking shared was a return to the Western metaphysical tradition to find out what went wrong – and, insofar as a thinker like Heidegger had gone before them, to find out what had gone wrong with this German philosopher who had, himself, ended up in the camp of National Socialism (Lyotard 1990, 51ff). Though structuralism continued to provide an important model for mapping synchronic relations of meaning, it stood accused, by the critics around *Tel Quel*, of introducing its own metaphysics by the back door. In a radical shift, the categories of history and the subject, which had been left out of the structuralist paradigm, now gained renewed urgency. Although this expanded framework introduced new sites of overdetermination, it also put pressure on ethical and political questions.

It is some indication of the protean character of the term whose contours we are tracing that "postmodernism" remains, in many quarters, associated with both ethical abandon and the total evacuation of history. Whose postmodernism, then? Frederic Jameson's (1984) now classic reading of a postmodernism that is the cultural logic of late capitalism laments the disappearance of history and the slide into a perpetual present that wipes out sedimented tradition. Yet if Jameson's Marxist critique unwittingly echoes T.S. Eliot here, it is important to recall the ways in which the postmodern dislocations of time and space collapse back into modernism. David Harvey (1994, 273) calls to mind Nietzsche's warnings about the disappearance of space in "newspapers (in place of daily prayers), railway, telegraph," while Marx read his historical moment as one characterized by the "annihilation of space by time" (Friedberg 1993, 55). It is unlikely that either could have imagined the dramatic implosion of both time and space brought about by the new global technologies of the twenty-first century.

This assault on the "real," with its flattening out of past, present, and future, has provoked a sense of history and memory as radically discontinuous. Still, there is evidence that even this crisis of memory spirals back to a prior moment, provoked by the revolutionary political and economic events of the early nineteenth century. It was history, argues Richard Terdiman (1984, 19), that was called upon to close the gap opened up by the loss of habitual meanings, becoming, by default, "the discipline of memory." In *The Eighteenth Brumaire of Louis Bonaparte* Marx (1978) had famously declared: "The tradition of all the dead generations weighs like a nightmare on the brain of the living" (qtd. in Terdiman 1984, 24). But could this panicked pressure on the recording of the past as historical narrative compensate for the shock brought about by the disappearance of stable communal memories? The rapid development of new cultural technologies could not help but accelerate the sense of crisis at new and different sites. Yet, as Anne Friedberg (1993, 2) reminds us, the shifting ground of habitual frameworks produced by the introduction of cinema and photography was inaugurated even earlier by social activities, such as walking and travel, that constructed a new *"mobilized gaze."*

Once again, it is Benjamin who operates as a prophetic guide to the unfolding century, writing "The Work of Art in the Age of Mechanical Reproduction" while he was in the midst of his monumental study of the Paris Arcades of the nineteenth century. The *Passagen-werk* introduces a number of the themes that appear in Frenkel's ... *from the Transit Bar*, the liminal space of transitoriness crossed with the memory-trace of the objects on display. *Andenken* translates as souvenir, Friedberg (1993, 49) reminds us, "but also as memory; memory was the commodity-fetish retailed in the arcade, a 'world in miniature.'" The seemingly fragmentary and random piecing-together of objects and things that interested Benjamin was caught by an eye already educated by the modernist practices of collage and montage. But here they were immersed in a non-reproducible as well as a temporal moment. "The passage," Friedberg adds, " (and here it is important to retain the word *passage*-not arcade) was an architectural monument to *time* and its passing" (49). Yet the ethical injunction to narrative memory that haunts Frenkel's postmodern installation folds in something of Benjamin's own fate in a tragic irony of history: in the background of the faces on the video screen, railway trains cross and recross. Though Benjamin's own suitcases were packed and ready for his attempt to cross the Pyrenees and so to escape the Nazis, he would take his own life at the border: a man without papers for passage.

The contemporary preoccupation with history and memory can be seen as operating in direct reaction to the amnesiac tendency of our era, the inscription of newly imagined communities and locations a response to the loss of shared ritual and national identities in a West increasingly characterized by shifting zones of cultural hybridization. However, it would be misleading to frame these gestures against forgetting as merely nostalgic and compensatory. New modes of theorizing questions of knowledge and the subject within the postmodern also mark important re-framings of the past – and in ways that work to expand rather than to diminish our ethical horizons.

Nowhere are these epistemological shifts more plainly on display than in the discipline and practice of history itself, which has undergone a sea change both in terms of what it perceives as its proper sphere and how it defines and weighs evidence. The reason for this is not hard to find. A more supple definition of evidence has gone hand in hand with an enlarged understanding of history. Until the *Annales* school in France in the 1930s, most history was conceived from the top-down, supported by those evidentiary materials that were likely to be preserved. There were occasional exceptions to this, but with the pioneering work of the *Annales* these departures became the rule. With this levelling, if not turning upside-down, of traditional objects of study, those subjects previously relegated to the sidelines of historical narrative – women, the lower orders, ethnic and racial minorities, dissident sexualities – have now moved to centre stage. Their arrival has necessitated a broader as well as a more self-conscious use of evidence: oral tradition, diaries, slave narratives, juridical accounts, daily practices and jokes, the evidence scored on the human body.

This shift is simultaneously an important marker of pervasive cultural changes and a provocation to a whole new set of questions, some of which are closely connected to the postmodern emphasis on enunciation (Hutcheon 1988b, 74–5). *Who*, in short, is speaking? Emile Benveniste draws the distinction between *discours* and *histoire*; the difference between them lies "in the fact that in the discursive form the source of the enunciation is present, whereas in the historical it is suppressed" (Nowell-Smith 1990, 234). Uncovering the forgotten of this suppression may be seen as an indispensable feature of the postmodern landscape, inseparably linked with what Cornel West (1990) has called "the new cultural politics of Difference," in which templates of race, gender, sexual orientation, empire, age, nation, and region construct new categories of investigation across all traditional domains of knowledge. Symptomatic of this new alertness to the position of the subject in language is the proliferation of spatial metaphors that has dominated contemporary theory for some time now, enabling a radically revised grid for mapping the uneven developments of historical narratives, which can no longer be read on a purely diachronic stage. Starting with the pioneering work of Marxist philosopher Henri Lefebvre, a new understanding of the social production of space emerged within postmodern geographies. Edward Soja (1989, 6) reminds us that we must become alert to the ways in which "space can be made to hide consequences from us, how relations of power and discipline are encircled into the apparently innocent spatiality of social life." Foucault, whose work became central to the *un*hiding of space came to understand retrospectively that geography lay at the "heart of (his) concerns" (26). Yet, whether articulated as Foucauldian micropolitics, local knowledge (Geertz 1983), microhistory (Ginzburg 1993), or ways of belonging (Grossburg 1996; Probyn 1996), a newly configured grid of space and time has become central to postmodern and postcolonial theory and practice. Alert to the ways in which partial and minority histories challenge and interrupt dominant narratives, we can no longer think of culture as a historically continuous space.

This shuttle movement back and forth between history and geography is exemplary of the testing of boundaries that is characteristic of a postmodern episteme, breaking up traditional frames of knowledge in new ways. Yet if, as Lynn Hunt (1987–8, 103) suggests, "history (is) an ongoing tension between stories that have been told and stories that might be told," then what room is there for the traditional historians hungering after "truth"? In turn, are these new ways of reconfiguring knowledge separable from questions of value and hierarchy? Hunt suggests that it might be more useful to think of history as an "ethical and political practice than as an epistemology with a clear ontological status." This is an insight that mirrors the widespread recognition throughout the human sciences that hermeneutic self-consciousness places *more* pressure, not less, on questions of value. De Certeau reminds us that the very attempt to construct an opposition of history/fiction within a stable dyad is misguided. For proponents of history as science, "fiction defines exactly what history is *not*; it fulfills the function of 'other' discourse in a proleptic gesture that diverts and forestalls judgment by casting it elsewhere"(qtd. in Ungar 1992, 67). We must learn, de Certeau insists, to recognize in "historiographical discourse … the struggle of reason with time, but of reason which does not renounce what it is as yet incapable of comprehending, a reason which is, in its fundamental working, *ethical*" (qtd. in Ungar 1992 68, emphasis added). This increased attention to modes of making meaning in history-writing is inseparable from a subject whose overdetermination is a legacy of Marxist and psychoanalytic models. Yet the characteristically postmodern refusal of the positivist model of a rational subject and an inert object of study also spirals back to earlier tensions in Western philosophy.

Though it is impossible to imagine the epistemological break that marks most accounts of the postmodern without the sundering of categories of subject and object traced in the trajectory from Descartes through to Kant, it is Nietzschean perspectivism that most famously opens out into shifts around conceptualizing knowledge in a self-reflexive operation that redefines the subject as much as the object. In *The Genealogy of Morals* Nietzsche (1956, pt. 3, 12) insisted that there is no such thing as "contemplation without interest … There is *only* perspective seeing, only a perspective 'knowing'; and the *more* affects we allow to speak about one thing, the *more* eyes, different eyes, we can use to observe one thing, the more complete will our 'concept' of this thing, our 'objectivity,' be."

History for Peter De Bolla (1986, 57) is always "disfigurative" work; the only certain thing is that the historian "cannot leave the historical record in the same condition in which he finds it." In turn, Dominick La Capra calls for a transferential model of history, evidence of the growing importance of psychoanalytic discourses in the postmodern turn to a fully theorized subject (qtd. in De Bolla 1986, 57). Inevitably, the recognition of the fallibility of memory itself, in the secondary processes of revision, has begun to play an increasingly important part in historical reassessments of eyewitness and documentary accounts. Yet recent historiography has gone even further than this, taking as its primary object of study the logic of memory – work itself. In his study of history-writing and the Second World War, R.J.B. Bosworth (1993, 5) suggests that, for more than a generation now, "the politics and culture of society after society has been underpinned by interpretations of the long Second World War, 'Auschwitz' and 'Hiroshima.'" In turn, these conflicting memories of the postwar period are impelled forward into the present, played out as rival histories in a newly reunited Germany after the collapse of the Wall or staged murderously in the killing fields of Bosnia-Herzogovina. But it is Vichy-France that has provided the almost text-book case of the logic of memory-work at the level of the nation-state. Bosworth suggests that "the problem for the French, before and after 1944, was to find a usable past and usable historians to relate to it" (112). De-Gaulle's ringing speech on 25 August 1944 to a newly liberated Paris established the framework for a myth-history in which the city had been "freed by itself, freed by its own people with the support of the armies of France which fights, of the only France, of the true France, of the eternal France" (112). His conscious and deliberate designs on the postwar memories of France were made explicit in an unguarded comment to an erstwhile ally: "Vichy was always and has remained null and void; it did not happen" (112).

It was French cinema that first broke through the national amnesia, exposing this usable past as a site of profound ethical failure. Yet the complicity of Vichy under the occupation was only one part of the story for historians. What became equally interesting now was the route by which national memories were constructed in the first place, how it came to be that a whole dark chapter from the past "did not happen." This is the story of Russo's *The Vichy Syndrome* (1991), whose title metaphor, drawn from medical discourses, provides a model for history-as-memory at the level of the nation-state, subject to the secondary processes of revision that mark the work of the unconscious but also, thereby, calling for an expanded archive – one that moves outward to include the oral and popular tradition.

This hermeneutic self-consciousness does not so much mark a retreat from history-writing as a return to it across the disciplines in ways that confront the historicity of text and the textuality of history – a double gesture that is signalled in the postmodern turn to what Linda Hutcheon (1988a, 61–77) first called "historiographic metafiction." Yet this insistence on writing and textuality also has a profoundly ethical dimension across cultural practices. It was Bakhtin who first reminded us that memory is the precondition for both intertextuality and dialogism. In turn, this possibility of a dialogical relation *enabled* by memory inaugurates a pre-eminently ethical opening when it moves over to questions of the writing of Other: "The word in language is half someone else's" (Bakhtin 1981, 293). This model is implicit in Lacan's (1968) template for a psychoanalysis informed by a radical critique of traditional ethnography. Refusing the behaviourist notion that the patient can be read as a human object, he stresses the "intrasubjective topography" of all analysis (69). If the only intermediary the analyst – like the reader – has to work with is the patient's word, then *"there is no word without a reply"* (9, emphasis added).

"Purposes," as sociologist Zygmunt Bauman (1994, 202) suggests, "can no longer be substantiated *monologically*; having become perforce subjects of a *dialogue*, they must now refer to principles wide enough to command authority of the sort *that belongs solely to ethical values"*(emphasis added). For the postmodern sociologist, the integration of Heideggerian, Wittgensteinian, Gadamerian, and other hermeneutical discourses constructs a transformed disciplinary field redefined as pre-eminently interpretive, and that, in itself, is enough to foreclose the option of "business as usual" (105). Bauman's postmodern sociological framework has always been explicitly ethical; his 1995 study, *Life in Fragments*, is subtitled "Essays in Postmodern Morality." Following the Adorno-Horkheimer critique of instrumental reason, which, like his own, is traced over the world of the concentration camp, Bauman sees the universals of modernism as masking an impulse to domination, one which refuses "the alterity of the Other" (29).

This double-edged preoccupation with questions of meaning and intersubjectivity is even more integral to the contemporary poetics and politics of ethnography. What is at stake, once again, is the putative transparency of the text, in which the actual process of writing is occluded. Instead, what a pioneering volume such as *Writing Culture: The Poetics and Politics of Ethnography*, edited by Clifford and Marcus (1986), foregrounded was the way in which writing had emerged as critical to what anthropologists do both in the field and in their presentation of their findings. Their introductory statement of intent can serve as a model for the way in which postmodern ontologies and epistemologies are inescapably implicated in an ethical field: "They assume that the poetic and the political are inseparable, that science is in, not above, historical and linguistic processes. They assume that academic and literary genres interpenetrate and the writing of cultural descriptions is properly experimental and ethical"(2).

If I emphasize this statement of intent in an exemplary early text of postmodern ethnography, it is because of the centrality of the critique of ethnography to much of what goes by the name of French theory, bridging both its structuralist and poststructuralist moments as well as its opening out to contemporary postcolonial theory. More overtly implicated in a Western colonial structure of domination than other academic discourses, it also found itself caught up earlier in ethical dilemmas, fraught with a hermeneutic self-consciousness that came only belatedly to other disciplines. No sooner had anthropology sought validation as a legitimate field of inquiry than it came face to face with the problematic status of the scientific "object" as both same and other. This dark double would come to be narrativized in Imperial fiction as much as in the growing body of travel and ethnographic accounts that flowed from the Western colonial adventure.

The increasingly widespread conviction among contemporary postmodern anthropologists is that any confrontation with an Other is also always a construction of a self. Vincent Crapanzano (1977, 70) suggests that "the 'moment' of field-work can be seen as a movement of self-dissolution and reconstitution" that poses a radical crisis for a subject always "constructed through a complex dialectical moment, mediated and hypostacized by language in relation to an other." He retells the remarkable account given by Malinowski in *A Diary in the Strict Sense of the Term* of his return from Brisbane. Far from being an easy passage from the *unheimlich* to the *heimlich*, what the ethnographer experiences is "the shock of return," haunted by dreams of an uncanny double.

> He is, after all, returning *home*. What he forgets of course is that the confrontation with the other – his informants – has had its effect upon him. His sense of self has been altered. He is other than he was, even if his relation to fieldwork has been conservative – a stubborn refusal to go native. At home he must be his old self again, must adopt the standpoint of those significant within his "own" socio-historical horizon. He requires re-affirmation–reconstitution – and this he tries to accomplish in many ways, including most notably the *writing* of ethnography. (Crapanzano 1977, 71)

The moral troubling of the ethnographic adventure that became pervasive in the immediate postwar period was inseparable from the dissolution of empire that accelerated in the 1950s and 1960s. Yet the emerging self-consciousness around the Imperial project, particularly in France, during these decades also hearkens back to the artistic revolution of modernism, in which a revaluing of the non-Western Other, alternately romanticized and wrested from a lived social and historical context, gave rise in at least one instance to explicit colonial critique. In 1931 a major exhibition around the French colonies was held in Paris, to which key Surrealists (Louis Aragon, Paul Eluard, and Yves Tanguy) responded with their own counter-exhibition:

"The Truth about the Colonies" (Foster 1986, 213). Though still complicit with a European Imaginary that identified the non-Western Other with an earlier or less highly developed stage, it nevertheless turned colonial notions of "primitivism" and "fetishism" on their head, relocating them in the European unconscious itself.

What can such spiralling backwards to exemplary modernist moments tell us about the terms put into play here? Are we dealing with concepts that serve a merely heuristic function, putting pressure on fractures and breaks at the expense of continuities? Within art-historical discourses, Surrealism itself, of course, represents a dissident strand in the epistemic purity of High Modernism. But it can serve us as an object-lesson here in another important way, a sobering reminder that even the strands of unreason in twentieth-century Western discourses are caught up in values and assumptions historically associated with Enlightenment reason. This attempt to recover what has been insufficiently thought through is central to a line of postmodern and deconstructive discourses that spirals back to central Hegelian themes. The *Phenomenology* traces crises of identity that arise from what the identity of mind is compelled to leave out or marginalize. Yet, unlike Hegel's teleological narrative, in which a growing self-identical rational consciousness paves the way for a march towards a single truth, postmodern readings refuse this grand design (Yeatman 1994, viii). Instead, they work to remind us that identity is always only achieved through a drawing of boundaries that constructs antinomies of inclusion/exclusion, self/other, in which the second term occupies the site of the *forgotten*.

To become a subject, as Judith Butler (1993, 3) reminds us, is to take up a position secured by an identification that has a discursive history, one that is structurally contingent upon a foreclosure of other identifications: "This exclusionary matrix by which subjects are formed thus requires the simultaneous production of a domain of abject beings, those who are not yet 'subjects,' but who form the constitutive outside to the domain of the subject." This refusal of older models of insides and outsides, centres and margins, has radically transformed our understanding of the ways in which boundaries are constructed at the level of ethnicity, race, and national identity as well as gender. Like dissident gender-identifications and sexualities, national "foreign bodies" have historically operated to secure a norm, one that is, paradoxically, central to the very domain that has marked them as "marginal." To understand this structure of disavowal and fetishism as opening outwards from a logic of subject-formation to a structure of alterity and even danger for the Other is to enter a postmodern terrain of theorizing that dramatically extends our ethical horizons (Gabriel, Chapter 9, this volume).

The contemporary emancipatory movements that belong historically to our postmodern moment can be seen as expanding the domain of entitlements that belong to Enlightenment ideals of reason and equality. Yet, if we attempt to make good on these promises today within demonstrably enlarged theoretical frames, we do so in terms unthought of by the eighteenth-century *philosophes*: we are, in effect, enabled by the radical critiques of representation and the subject that are integral to the epistemologies and ontologies of the postmodern.

To emphasize the continuities as well as breaks and fractures between the postmodern and the modern is to remember that, from the start, postmodernism has been a *meta*-modernism, retaining the suggestiveness of the Greek prefix "*meta*," which means both "with" and "after" as well as signifying change. Recovering this field of overdetermination moves us into a postmodern logic of return in which repetition refuses the meaning of the same. Yet what have we forgotten of a long modernity now being played out anew against the backdrop of what feels increasingly like an unfinished traumatic century?

"Try to Remember."
Waiting for Godot

On a barren stage, with only a tree, those two quintessential tramps of modernist drama play out their vaudeville routine, waiting for the unknowable in what Lyotard would later call the ruins of ethics of the postmodern moment. The date is 1954, and this production of Beckett's (1954) *Waiting for Godot* is being staged by prisoners at San Quentin who, having had more experience at waiting than most of us, immediately grasped its meaning. As for the more academic commentators, who still clung to the metaphysical vocabulary of an Absurd cut off from social meaning and history, Beckett was declared a writer who believed in nothing at all. But the Irish emigré who lived in Paris for much of his life was an ambulance driver in the resistance under the French occupation, and his theatre, like his fiction, resounds with the moral crisis of the immediate postwar period. In Beckett's (1960) later *Krapp's Last Tape*, his now familiar clown-like protagonist sorts out his ends and days on a tape-recorder. The only other characters on stage are the technological traces of his former self on tape, which he plays back at intervals in a vain attempt to capture a selfhood strung together only through failing memory.

Each age finds its own metaphor for memory. In a figure that later become central to Derrida's revisiting of Freud's scene of writing, Freud himself compared memory to a mystic writing pad. A much more recent essay, published in translation in 1995 but first delivered on 5 June 1994 in London during a conference sponsored by the International Society for the History of Psychiatry on Memory, "Archive Fever: A Freudian Impression," takes this notion further. It is one of Derrida's most intensely autobiographical texts, a meditation on his own "deferred obedience" to the tradition of his father(s) that weaves in and out of a consideration of Freud's own repression of his personal history. Where it takes the reader, in the process, is through a complex meditation on psychoanalysis and memory – memory understood and constituted as *archive*. But Derrida begins by reminding his reader how much the archive has changed with the new technologies of television, the Internet, the Xerox machine, and e-mail. If writing with pen and paper constituted the limits of the archival imagination in Freud's day, the bounded terrain in which questions of psychoanalysis and memory might be thought through, how much different the whole history of psychoanalysis might have been, he suggests, within a postmodern moment of proliferating memory-machines.

Derrida's interest in this question is framed by three over-arching assumptions. The first is that psychoanalysis is, above all, a science of memory and the archive. The second is that no discipline today remains untouched by what goes under the proper name of Freud. The third is that remembering is pre-eminently an ethical act. Any project of archeology would, he explains have to include psychoanalysis, which is, above all else, a general science of the archive, of everything that can happen to the economy of memory" (Derrida 1995, 26). Repression itself, he reminds us, is an archivization, a means "to archive otherwise" (43). If any disciplinary field or history, not to mention historiography itself, thinks it remains untouched by these insights, or believes that it can fail to take them into account, forgetting them or effacing them, it will have confirmed (thus archived) this repression or suppression. Like Derrida's essay on *The Postcard*, this text makes explicit the extent of deconstruction's debt to psychoanalysis as well as its fundamentally ethical character (Critchley 1992). Alongside Derrida's writing on questions of justice and the law, it also confirms his belief that the ethics of memory is fundamental to his concerns: "the task of a historical and interpretive memory is at the heart of deconstruction" (Derrida 1995, 19). Yet, in this intensely personal text on the archive, acknowledging its debt to the law of his father(s), the convergence of these concerns is clearer than ever before: "Is it possible that the antonym of 'forgetting' is not 'remembering' but *justice?*" (49).

How much of postmodern theory and cultural practice can be read as a lesson *against forgetting*? The injunction to memory is inevitably charged in this new century with the moral shock of mass genocides and annihilations, echoing Toni Morisson's "re-memory" as much as Elie Wiesel's writing against silence. It is at the centre of Milan Kundera's *The Book of Laughter and Forgetting* (1999) as well as the fiction of W.G. Sebald or Mavis Gallant (Gabriel 2003) or the postwar German sculpture and painting of Joseph Beuys and Gerhard Richter. It resounds in cultural practices that range from Frenkel's "… *from the Transit Bar*" installation to international projects that archive accounts of Holocaust survivors, to Japanese post-Hiroshima Butoh dance, AIDS quilts, and memorials or international film practices (Marks 2000) and practices of pedagogy (Simon 2000). In turn, the genre of the testimonial records events that range from Latin-American accounts of torture regimes to narratives of mass rapes and genocides in Bosnia, Palestinian narratives of diaspora, and the "Scar" literature of the Chinese Cultural Revolution. Meanwhile, feminist diaries, journals, and fictions, along with critical revaluations of women's writing and place in already-existing frameworks, have transformed the landscape of literary studies forever. Like Aboriginal visual culture, African-American slave narratives, ethnic and migrant fiction, or the new museology, these sites operate to recover the forgotten in frameworks heightened by emerging transnational and global identities.

How can these shared openings out into narrative and cultural representation be read as anything other than ethical acts? And, if they are characteristic of a postmodernism that defines itself against that strand of modernism that sought to empty out historical content, are we not, then, witnessing a radical return of the repressed? What interests me here are the ways in which this widespread injunction against forgetting permeates contemporary critical theory in a historical moment that magnifies both the technological crisis of the modern and the ethical shock posed by that earlier encounter with an ethnographic and colonial other. Though it shares many of the values and assumptions that belong to existing humanistic and Enlightenment frames in the West, a contemporary ethics of memory proceeds from a new constellation of discourses.

What has not been sufficiently remarked, perhaps, is the persistence of a thematics of remembering and forgetting at sites that, at first glance, have different genealogies. Deconstruction shares with psychoanalysis the radical insight that self-identity and presence can only be achieved at the cost of an economy of forgetting that is foundational to the subject. Yet how does this family narrative connect up, in turn, with another discursive cluster that enjoins against forgetting: one that works to uncover relations of power in the social field? A reconfigured nexus of psychoanalysis, deconstruction, and ideology critique is increasingly central to a theoretical turn in which Marx is contaminated by the spectre of Freud. The post-Marxist theorizing of hegemony in Laclau and Mouffe (1990) has its counterpart in Derrida's spectral Marxism or Judith Butler's theorizing of abjection as much as in the Lacanian revisiting of the phantasms of the nation-state in Slavoj Zizek's (1989) work. This turn is exemplified in more recent dialogues and debates on the Left (Butler, Laclau, and Zizek 2000).

To uncover a historically informed line of inheritance for some of the most influential strands of postmodern theory we need only turn to the master genealogist himself – to a Nietzsche who is also the forgotten in Freud. The insistence on the problematic of forgetting is pervasive in Nietszche in ways that implicitly cross questions of power with insights into unconscious processes and a logic of desire. Nietzsche's insistence in the *Genealogy of Morals* that what are frequently taken as facts are the products of earlier and forgotten values and interpretations lies at the heart of his attempt to recover their always contingent and interested nature. For Nietzsche (1956, 112), genealogy is not so much a new method of doing history as an attempt "to find it where it has least been expected to be." What starts out as a morality, ends up dominating as a law: "it is part of its development that its origin should be forgotten – That is a sign that it has become master" (Nietzsche qtd. in Nehemas 1985, 33). In *The Order of Things* Foucault (1970, 279) rewrites this insight over a model of language that "forms the locus of tradition, of the unspoken habits of thought, of what lies hidden in a people's mind; it accumulates an irreducible memory which does not even know itself as memory." In turn, Nietzsche's injunction to find memory where "it has least been expected to be" finds a direct echo in Foucault's chronicler of effective history, who "must seek history out in the most unpromising places, in what we tend to feel is without history" (139). What is uncovered in such work is not the memory of a unified tradition but, rather, a counter-memory (160).

Pierre Bourdieu, in turn, repeatedly returns to a discourse of remembering and forgetting in his attempt to situate artistic works within the social conditions of their production, circulation, and consumption. In *The Historical Genesis of a Pure Aesthetic*, Bourdieu (1993, 256) reminds us that "what is forgotten in self-reflexive analysis is the fact that although appearing to be a gift from nature, the eye of the twentieth-century art lover is a product of history." He outlines his own project of a genetic sociology as one that recovers the value and meaning of the artwork in the entire set of agents and institutions involved in its transmission and reception. The mythic "pure gaze" of idealist aesthetics represents, for Bourdieu, a kind of *genesis amnesia*

(262). In its place, he proposes "reappropriating through historical *anamnesis*, the product of the entire historical operation of which consciousness, too, is (at every moment) the product" (256). Despite Bourdieu's distancing of himself from deconstruction and Foucault's own quarrels with classical psychoanalysis, what Derrida shares with both figures is a widespread postmodern injunction against forgetting. Moving beyond a traditional humanist vocabulary, this postmodern ethics of *anamnesis* not only comes from a different place but it also gives us work to do.

Freud's own account of the dialectic of remembering and forgetting in the economy of the subject came to be foundational to the new science of psychoanalysis in ways that provide an uncanny echo of Nietzsche. "Forgetting," writes the author of the *Genealogy of Morals*, "is an active and, in the structural sense, positive faculty of repression. Active forgetfulness ... is like a doorkeeper, a preserver of psychic order" (Nietzsche 1956, 58). Like postmodernism's representational model of a copy without an original in the age of mechanical reproduction, Freud's theorizing of memory as *nachträglich* refuses the promise and plenitude of an originary "real"; instead, memory proceeds by the structure of a later event that is both traced over an earlier one and anterior to it in the logic of its formation. Yet both events are equally constitutive of the memory-trace. If it is true to say that "it always takes two traumas to make one trauma," or two distinct events to produce repression, as Jean Laplanche puts it, then we can never hope to arrive at a single scene of primary repression or trauma (Laplanche 1989, 88)

Freud's own interest in trauma, the shutting down of the subject's system in a death-defence against shock, was itself prompted by clinical experience with soldiers returning from the front in the First World War (Foster 1991, 81ff). During the years of the Great War of 1914–18, European civilization experienced the first wave of those shocks that would characterize a whole century, registered and remembered in unprecedented new ways by the rapidly expanding technologies of photography, radio, and television. A litany of place names ensued that signalled the ethical crisis of the West, followed by the dissolution of the unitary nation-state in the era of global capital and the displacements and diasporas that marked the collapse of European empire and the redrawing of maps in the postcolonial era. As early as 1962, Paul Ricoeur (1965, 278) understood that "the discovery of the plurality of cultures is never a harmless experience":

When we discover that there are several cultures instead of just one and consequently at the time when we acknowledge that end of a sort of cultural monopoly, be it illusory or real, we are threatened with the destruction of our own discovery. Suddenly it becomes possible that there are just *others*, that we ourselves are an "other" among others. All meaning and every goal having disappeared, it becomes possible to wander through civilization as if through vestiges and ruins.

Against this cumulative trauma in the West, the dialectic of remembering and forgetting operates as a postmodern version of the Freudian *fort/da*: a Times Square billboard in which two separate images sharing neon space flicker, fade into each other, and gradually change places. Meanwhile, in the postmodern sites of cultural theory and practice, the compulsion to forget is followed by the ethical imperative to remember. Though we may no longer believe that historical events and their narrativization can ever fully coincide, the injunction to history and memory is stronger than ever before. Nor has the challenge to the *grands recits* tarnished the search for ethical frameworks newly reconstituted outside of the Western metaphysical tradition. "Philosophy as architecture is ruined," Lyotard (1990, 43) reminds us, but a "writing of the ruins, micrologies, graffiti can still be done."

The notion of ruins that permeates the contemporary critique of Western metaphysics resonates with Benjamin's Angel of History, that fiercely imagined figure who is quickly becoming the dissident memorial of a terrible century. Traced over Klee's "Angelus Novus," Benjamin's angel does not move ahead into the future but, instead, turns his face towards the past. A storm is blowing from paradise, which "irresistibly propels him into the future to which his back is turned, while the pile of debris before him grows skyward" (Benjamin 1969, 258). The potent symbol of Benjamin's angel, with its mix of Marxist and Messianic themes, may now seem too apocalyptic a figure for actually thinking through the still unfinished project of a radical democratic politics. Yet Benjamin anticipates productive postmodern motifs at a number of important points, and the relationship between "Art in the Age of Mechanical Reproduction" and the unfinished Arcades project remains central to a number of contemporary themes. The latter's preoccupation with memory found even earlier expression in Benjamin's *Berlin Childhood*, traced over Proustian themes drawn from his translation into German of *Remembrance of Things Past* (Szondi 1991, 20). Even more pertinent to my own argument here is the vocabulary that Benjamin invokes in this autobiographical text, one in which memories are preserved as a *"trail of shocks."* (qtd. in Szondi 1991, 20–1).

Yet it is in his interest in the fragment as a philosophical form that Benjamin most fully anticipates the postmodern impulse, and Lyotard's call for a micrological writing "in the ruins of ethics" resonates with Benjamin's own impulses (Lyotard 1990, 44). As Hannah Arendt (1969) reminds us, Benjamin had a life-long fascination with the miniature, part of a wider strategic interest in the detail and the partial in his sociological critique. His was an "attempt to capture the portrait of history in the most insignificant representations of reality, its scraps" (11). For Adorno, Benjamin's interest in the fragment constituted the key to his break with idealism and systematic philosophy. His "micrological gaze, the unmistakable hue of his manner of concretion, is directed towards the historical in direct opposition to *Philosophia perennis*" (Adorno qtd. in Smith 1989, 10). Just as Benjamin took his Marxism from the unorthodoxies of his old friend Brecht, so he confirmed his philosophy of the fragment in both the montage experiments of Eisenstein and the avant-garde cultural practices of the Surrealists and Dadaists:

> One made still lifes out of tickets, spools of cotton, cigarette butts, and mixed them with pictorial elements. One put a frame around the whole thing. And in his way one showed the public: Look, your picture frame explodes time; the smallest authentic fragment of everyday life says more than a painting. Just as a murderer's bloody fingerprint on a page says more than the book's text. (229)

A number of recognizable postmodern themes are in evidence here: the critique of the sign inaugurated by collage and bricolage, the emphasis on the partial and the "trace," the fascination with the detective novel. But Benjamin's subsequent emphasis on the revolutionary uses to which photomontage, in particular, could be put shows an alertness to just those avant-garde cultural practices that would be recovered for the politically engaged neo-avant-garde of a resistant postmodernism (see Buchloh 1982, 43ff).

In *The Return of the Real*, Hal Foster (1996) makes an important case for reading the neo-avant-garde as a deferred event in which, for the first time, we are fully able to comprehend the revolutionary insights of the first avant-garde. It was Benjamin's fate, too, to be fully valued and understood only posthumously. In her Introduction to *Illuminations*, Arendt tells the story of this fate in the fairy-tale terms of the "little hunchback," the *bucklicht Männlein* folklore figure drawn from German whose very presence causes the object of his gaze to bungle whatever he is doing. Benjamin himself wrote whimsically of this personage standing "before a pile of debris" – a description I am tempted to read as a carnivalesque version of his angel, the comic satyr-play counterpart to the full-blown tragedy of his *Angelus* (Arendt 1969, 7).

This little gnome, who seemed to dog Benjamin's step at every turn, was never more in appearance, Arendt suggests, than on that fateful day at the Franco-Spanish border when Benjamin took his own life. Without a French exit visa, he had fled with other refugees to a Spanish border town, only to learn that Spain had closed the border that same day. "One day earlier," as Arendt tells the story, "Benjamin would have gotten through without any trouble; one day later the people in Marseilles would have known that for the time being it was impossible to pass through Spain. Only on that particular time was the catastrophe possible" (18). Like the *nachträglich* of memory and the postmodern, Benjamin was always either too early or too late. Yet he stands before us at our own end of century as a remarkably prescient figure – his own work of quotations, fragments, and micrologies, along with the memory of his fate, a writing against the ruins.

Works Cited

Appadurai, Arjun. 1996. *Modernity at Large: Cultural Dimensions of Globalization.* Minneapolis: University of Minnesota Press.

Arendt, Hannah. 1969. "Introduction: Walter Benjamin: 1892–1940." In *Illuminations,* trans. Harry Zohn, 1–58. New York: Schocken.

Bauman, Zygmunt. 1989. *Modernity and the Holocaust.* Ithaca: Cornell University Press.

–1994. *Intimations of Postmodernity.* London and New York: Routledge.

–1995. *Life in Fragments: Essays in Postmodern Morality.* Oxford and Cambridge: Blackwell.

Bakhtin, M.M. 1981. *The Dialogical Imagination: Four Essays.* Ed. Michael Holquist. Austin: University of Texas Press.

Beckett, Samuel. 1954. *Waiting for Godot.* New York: Grove.

–1960. *Krapp's Last Tape and Other Dramatic Pieces.* New York: Grove.

Benjamin, Walter. 1969. "The Storyteller: Reflections on the Works of Nikolai Leskov." In *Illuminations,* ed. Hannah Arendt, trans. Harry Zohn, 83–110. New York: Schocken.

Bosworth, R.J.B. 1993. *Explaining Auschwitz and Hiroshima: History Writing and the Second World War, 1945–1990.* London and New York: Routledge.

Bourdieu, Pierre. 1993. "The Historical Genesis of a Pure Aesthetic." In *The Field of Cultural Production,* ed. Randal Johnson, 254–66. UK: Polity.

Buchloh, Benjamin H.D. 1982. "Allegorical Procedures: Appropriation and Montage in Contemporary Art." *Artforum* 21 (1): 43–56.

Butler, Judith. 1993. *Bodies that Matter: On the Discursive Limits of "Sex."* New York: Routledge.

Butler, Judith, Ernesto Laclau, and Slavoj Zizek. 2000. *Contingency, Hegemony, Universality: Contemporary Dialogues on the Left.* London and New York:Verso.

Clifford, James, and George E. Marcus. 1986. *Writing Culture: The Poetics and Politics of Ethnography.* Berkeley and Los Angeles: University of California Press.

Crapanzano, Vincent. 1992. *Hermes' Dilemma and Hamlet's Desire: On the Epistemology of Interpretation.* Cambridge and London: Harvard University Press.

-1977. "On the Writing of Ethnography." *Dialectical Anthropology* 2: 69–73.

Critchley, Simon. 1992. *The Ethics of Deconstruction: Derrida and Levinas*. Cambridge and Oxford: Blackwell.

De Bolla, Peter.1986."Disfiguring History." *Diacritics* 16(4): 49–58.

De Certeau, Michel. 1984. *The Practice of Everyday Life*. Los Angeles: University of California Press.

Derrida, Jacques. 1995. "Archive Fever: A Freudian Impression." *Diacritics* 25 (2): 9–63.

-1996. *The Return of the Real: The Avant-Garde at the End of the Century*. Cambridge, MA: MIT Press

Foster, Hal. 1991. "Armor Fou." *October* 56: 65–97.

Foucault, Michel. 1970. *The Order of Things: An Archeology of the Human Sciences*. London: Tavistock.

-1982. "The Subject and Power." In *Beyond Structuralism* and *Hermeneutics*. Ed. Hubert L. Dreyfus and Paul Rabinow, 208–26. Chicago: University of Chicago Press.

Friedberg, Anne. 1993. *Window Shopping: Cinema and the Postmodern*. Berkeley: University of California Press.

Gabriel, Barbara. 1994. "Performing Theory, Performing Gender: Critical Postscript." *Essays on Canadian Writing* 54 (1994): 237–60.

Geertz, Clifford. 1983. *Local Knowledge: Further Essays in Interpretive Anthropology*. New York: Basic.

Ginzburg, Carlo. 1993. "Microhistory: Two or Three Things That I know about It." Trans. John and Anne C. Tedeschi. *Critical Inquiry* 20 (Autumn): 10–35.

Grossberg, Lawrence. 1996. "Identity and Cultural Studies: Is That All There Is?" In *Questions of Cultural Identity*, ed. Stuart Hall and Paul du Gay, 87–107. London: Sage.

Harvey, David. 1994. *The Condition of Postmodernity*. Cambridge and Oxford: Blackwell.

Hunt, Lynn. 1987–8. "History as Gesture; or The Scandal of History." In *Consequences of Theory: Selected Papers from the English Institute, 1987–88*, ed. Jonathon Arac and Barbara Johnson, 91–107. Baltimore and London: Johns Hopkins University Press.

Hutcheon, Linda. 1988a. *A Poetics of Postmodernism: History, Theory, Fiction*. London and New York: Routledge.

-1988b. *The Canadian Postmodern: A Study of Contemporary English Canadian Fiction*. Toronto: Oxford University Press.

Jameson, Fredric. 1984."Postmodernism, or the Cultural Logic of Late Capitalism." *New Left Review* 146: 53–93.

Krauss, Rosalind E. 1994. *The Originality of the Avant-Garde and Other Modernist Myths*. Cambridge and London: MIT Press.

Kundera, Milan. 1999. *The Book of Laughter and Forgetting*. Trans. Aaron Asher. New York: Harper.

Kushner, Tony. 1993. *Angels in America: A Gay Fantasia on National Themes*. 1st ed. New York: Theatre Communications Group.

Lacan, Jacques. 1968. *Speech and Language in Psychoanalysis*. Trans. Anthony Wilden. Baltimore and London: Johns Hopkins University Press.

Laclau, Ernesto, and Chantal Mouffe. 2001. *Hegemony and Socialist Strategy: Towards a Radical Democratic Politics*. 2nd ed. London; New York: Verso.

Laplanche, Jean. 1989. *New Foundations of Psychoanalysis*. Trans. David Macey. London: Basil Blackwell.

Lyotard, Jean-Francois. 1979. *The Postmodern Condition: A Report on Knowledge*. Trans. Geoff Bennington and Brian Massumi. Manchester: Manchester University Press.

–1990. *Heidegger and "the Jews."* Minneapolis: University of Minnesota Press.

Marks, Laura. 2000. *The Skin of the Film: Intercultural Cinema, Embodiment, and the Senses*. Durham: Duke University Press.

Marx, Karl. 1978. "The Eighteenth Brumaire of Louis Bonaparte." In *The Marx-Engels Reader*, ed. Robert C. Tucker, 594–617. New York: W.W. Norton.

Nehemas, Alexander. 1985. *Nietzsche: Life as Literature*. Cambridge, MA: Harvard University Press.

Nietzsche, Friedrich Wilhelm. 1956. *The Birth of Tragedy and the Genealogy of Morals*. Garden City, New York: Doubleday.

Nowell-Smith, Geoffrey. 1981. "A Note on 'History/Discourse.'" In *Theories of Authorship*, ed. Caughie, John, 232–41. London and New York: Routledge and Kegan Paul.

Probyn, Elspeth. 1996. *Outside Belongings*. New York: Routledge.

Ricoeur, Paul. 1961. "Civilization and National Cultures." In *History and Truth*. Trans. Chas. A. Kelbley, 276–7. Evanston: Northwestern University Press.

Roger I. Simon, Claudia Eppert, and Sharon Rosenberg. 2000. *Between Hope and Despair: Pedagogy and the Rememberance of Historical Trauma*. Maryland: Rowand and Littlefield.

Russo, Henry. 1991. *The Vichy Syndrome: History and Memory in France since 1944*. Trans. Arthur Goldhammer. Cambridge and London: Harvard University Press.

Smith,Gary. 1989. *On Walter Benjamin: Critical Essays and Recollections*. Cambridge: MIT Press.

Soja, Edward W. 1989. *Postmodern Geographies: The Reassertion of Space in Critical Social Theory*. New York: Verso.

Szondi, Peter. 1991. "Walter Benjamin's City Portraits." In *On Walter Benjamin: Critical Essays and Recollections*, ed. Gary Smith, 18–32. Cambridge and London: MIT Press.

Terdiman, Richard. 1984. "Deconstructing Memory: On Representing the Past and Theorizing Culture in France since the Revolution." *Diacritics* 15 (4): 13–35.

Ungar, Steven. 1992. "Against Forgetting: Notes on Revision and the Writing of History." *Diacritics* 22 (2): 62–9.

West, Cornell. 1990. "The New Politics of Difference." In *Out There: Marginilization and Contemporary Cultures*, ed. Russell Fergusone, Martha Geyer, Trinh T. Minh-ha, and Cornel West, 19–29. Cambridge, MA: MIT Press.

Yeatman, Anna. 1994. *Postmodern Revisionings of the Political*. London and New York: Routledge.

Zizek, Slavoj. 1989. *The Sublime Object of Ideology*. London: Verso.

From Modernity to Postmodernity

SUZAN ILCAN

> Modernity belongs to that small family of theories that both declares and
> desires universal applicability for itself. What is new about modernity (or
> about the idea that its newness is a new kind of newness) follows from this
> duality. Whatever else the project of Enlightenment may have created, it
> aspired to create persons who would, after the fact, have wished to have
> become modern.
>
> Arjun Appadurai, *Modernity at Large*

It is not a coincidence that postmodernism and postcolonialism have materialized at the same time as objects of study in the human sciences: the one
is a function of the other. The collapse of the *grands récits* of the Enlightenment that Jean-François Lyotard (1986) identifies as the signifying mark
of postmodernity is contingent upon the end of the great European nation-
state empires and of capitalism grounded in nation-states. Trans- or multinational capitalism is a system that has outgrown the institutions that
created a space for its expansion, as it previously outgrew and disregarded
the centralized monarchies that fostered its development over against the
particular interests of the feudal estates. Extended periods of crisis, restruc-
turing, and reorganization – of "discontinuous change" – have, as Arrighi
(1994) reminds us, typically characterized the history of capitalism throughout the world. The flexible and geographical mobility of networks of capital, knowledge, and "knowledge capital" (Bauman 2002, 231; 1998) now
shape global economies at the same time that they generate new risks, new
fragmentations, and new forms of injustice that marginalize various groups
and populations. Grands récits are comic in the face of their fury. They are
not so much discredited as dispersed and disseminated among those others
who were never included in capital's project except as labour (i.e., as energetic bodies to be ordered and controlled). The idea and suggested possibility of such an orderly world is, however, not only a familiar feature of
modernism/colonialism but also a form of life bound up in Enlightenment
rationality and post-Enlightenment cosmopolitanism.

Enlightenment rationality promised to emancipate humanity from authoritarian dogma by supplying a natural basis for knowledge and spawning a

wealth of ideas in search of universal, rational "truths." Now a "cosmopoli-tanism of the Enlightenment" (Kristeva 1990, 126) lingers with us in the name of modernity. Modernity – with its stress on the purity of its project, the reduction of all Other(s) to the Western Same, and the sovereignty of Western culture as a whole – seeks its legitimacy not in the past but, as Lyotard sug-gests, in the future; it aims to observe, predict, and control the external world, without bias and prejudice, through the detached objectivity of scientific and technical knowledge. It wittingly embarks on a quest for epistemic purity or "epistemic violence" (Spivak 1990) in the totalizing standpoint demanded by a Euro-centred imperialism. As Bauman (2002, 28) argues in *Society under Siege*, modernity is bent on "making the world manageable, and on its daily management." The idea of order or control, as a goal, as a condition to be sus-tained and nurtured, is intrinsic to modernity (Smart 1993; Bauman and Tester 2001) and its styles of organizing reality in terms of the "freedom" of the indi-vidual (Rose 1999). But many writers have already claimed that such grand schemes of progress no longer seem feasible or even possible. Nevertheless, early twenty-first-century societies bear the marks of modernity's will to con-quest as contemporary deployments of knowledge have led to new forms of modernist subjugation (globalizing discourses and political powers, marginal-ized knowledges and groups across cultures and nations); colonialist represen-tations of indigenous peoples, objects, and geographies; and late modern schemes directed to create, in Escobar's (1995, 7) words, "a regime of objec-tivism." Late modern schemes to produce neutral knowledge are, however, pursued at the expense and exclusion of the situated knowledges of marginal and subaltern groups: women, indigenous populations, gays and lesbians, eth-nic minorities. Thus, the problem with modernity is that the crises it has forged are not solvable within its conceptual framework primarily because the idea of separating "*pouvoir-savior*," or that which goes together, is modernity's basic limitation.

As an attitude, movement, or condition of the contemporary culture of crises, postmodernism offers an implicit critique of the reign of Western objectivity and domination. It not only interrupts what was previously con-sidered constant and fragments what was thought integrated but it also reg-isters an emphasis on plurality, difference, and the marginal. This critique of and break with Western purity does not, however, make postmodernism necessarily negative; instead, it allows for a crossing of borders, a contami-nation of ideas, a "new configuration" of politics (Butler 1990, 149), and, overall – in Braidotti's (1994, 197) words – "positive openings." Moving beyond the reform principles of liberalism and their tie to purity movements (see Valverde 1991), postmodernism/postcolonialism, referring to a dialectical link between the modernity of the early twentieth century and Euro-imperialism, seeks to open the fractured or dislocated nature of totalities, explore the fluidity of boundaries and identities, and expose the potential for differences within situated knowledges. Not surprisingly, we now see a proliferation of critical reflections on the grand themes and promises of modernity, critiques of the traditional authority of "people in the know," and concerns with writing and de-scribing culture as a terrain of politics. Consequently, postmodernism/postcolonialism flees unequivocal definition and the (en)closures of meaning. It pursues the open spaces of dialogue and creativity (such as those "alternative geographies" [Shields 1991], rewritings "from the margins" [Fachinger 2001], or locations of "radical openness and possibility" [hooks 1990, 153]), and embraces new claims to alter habitual schemes and expectations grounded in the discourses of prohibition. Such transformations raise ethical questions for they experiment with limits and with levels of subversion (see Braidotti 2002, 145–6).

Already broached under the rubric of postmodernism, the issues of de-centred forms of knowledge and power, identity, subjectivity, and authorship are now ethical rather than "legislative" concerns. This ethical turn or re-turn is premised on an inquiry into the limits within which current forms of knowledges, practices, and modes of subjectivity are constituted. This ethical inquiry does not work to "rule" but, rather, seeks to energize and create, whether politically, culturally, or socially. Such new interrogations of the orders of modernity not only denaturalize modern/colonial relations of power but also offer critical perceptions of knowledge-power regimes. It is within this context that we are able to view postmodernism not only as the tension between the modern project and the repudiation of that project but also as a potential departure from the imposition of modern/colonial moralities and their efforts towards – in Bauman's (1993) expression – "the reduction of pluralism," the devaluation of multiple subjectivities, minority positions, and competing knowledges. Such radical breaks from the past, from an authorized history, give rise to the workings and effects of ethical relations.

Stimulated by postmodern/postcolonial imaginations and reflections, especially those generating alternative schemes for understanding and (un)learning, ethics is not a mere vision of things to come, an intent or goal (although no doubt these are some of its components); rather, it is a way of mediating and transforming hierarchical relations between ideas and things, self and others, so that they become interactive, resourceful, and creative. On this point, Spivak (1995, 202) reminds us that learning from below can only be "earned by the slow effect at ethical responding – a two way road – with the compromised other as teacher." Such a pedagogical coming-together indicates a "facing" up to modern/colonial limits and limitations, a navigation towards new directions and departures. Likewise, the specific interests in this volume attend to the processes and consequences of ethical relations, what they do and make, the linkages they establish, the alliances they forge, not what they mean, represent, or prohibit in Western universal language and discourses. Because "natural history" is of little concern, ethical encounters contain no previous impressions, no shallow nostalgia; they are dynamic, inspiring, celebratory. Without doubt, one can situate postmodern/postcolonial ethics in fluid, life-enhancing encounters rather than in transcendent moralities that dictate what is dutiful, what is resentful about the other, or what must not be forgotten about the endorsed past. With the potential to engender and transform, to intensify and become, ethical relations in this collection of essays are considered as ways of making changes.

Derived from a rediscovery of other voices and tensions found within those long-standing appeals made to secure foundations, metanarratives, or law-like propositions, the contributions in this interdisciplinary collection (including linguistic, literary-critical, film studies, feminist, environmentalist, anthropological, sociological, museological, historiographical, philosophic, and psychoanalytic) present ethics within a diverse range of social, cultural, and literary innovations to a succession of engagements with modern/colonial projects. The chapters of *Postmodernism and the Ethical Subject*, while explicating their authors' individual interests and specialization, offer no neat or universal definition of ethics; rather, they offer an understanding of ethics as a "potentiality" that entails change and movement (not repetition, stratification, hierarchization) and that can be actualized in a number of different relations, times, and places. No matter how this potential is conveyed – whether it is articulated in specific face-to-face activities, forms of encounter, representations of the Other, or in postcolonial reflexivities – it calls to the forefront the need for new modes of dealing with the "crises" of modernity and their derangements. As such, this ethical potency highlights innovative ways of relating to self and others by expanding our sensibilities for the "other" and for the "other" in ourselves.

The chapters that follow reflect the range of disciplinary and cross-disciplinary frameworks that are mobilized by the thinking together of postmodernism and that fraught category of the ethical subject. The opening chapter in Part 2, "Spectres of the Modern: Philosophical Reflections," is David L. Clark's "On Being 'the Last Kantian in Nazi Germany': Dwelling with Animals after Levinas," which raises some radical questions suggested by French philosopher Emmanuel Levinas's encounter with the unexpected Other of the dog "Bobby" in a Nazi slave-labour camp. This creature who greeted him affectionately, restoring to him the human status otherwise denied him in his captivity was, Levinas muses, "the last Kantian." In the face of the exclusionary logic by which humans abject each other through animalizing tropes, Levinas scandalously asks what the danger might be of animalizing *animals*. The ethical duty we owe to animals as being apart from humans is not a simple question; the stakes of raising it are high, posing a challenge to categories and frameworks that normally go unquestioned. Clark distinguishes between Heidegger's "careless" analogy between the instrumentalized technology of the food industry and Levinas's and Lyotard's ethically nuanced attention to the *difference* between the machinery of the Holocaust and the obligation to animals.

Yet Clark's chapter takes another turn to reflect upon what it means to kill and eat the animal Other (questions Derrida, in turn, takes up), to raise wide-ranging questions about symbolic and other forms of carnivorous violence. What happens, Levinas seems to be asking, "when the reach of the ethical question who is my *neighbour* is widened to include non-human acquaintances?" And what ensues, in turn, with the potential gradation of refusals that increase the evolutionary scale one looks? Clark notes how Levinas's move through a complex and layered argument inevitably falters where "the perimeter marking the human from the non-human, the faced from those without faces, is unstable, disrupted, subjected to differences that cannot be contained." Clark concludes that Bobby is closer to a cyborg than to a sentient creature, an animal robot who, nevertheless, commands affection. In the end, Bobby is excluded from the neighbourhood of human freedom and rationality: only in the most temporary mode is he "*mon semblable – mon frère.*" Yet what does this tell us both about "Bobby" and about ourselves?

Chapter 4, Barry Rutland's "The Transject: The Ethical Subject of Postmodernity," explores the potency of the Levinasian Face and our relation to it in the context of textuality and alterity and through the writings of Lacan, Derrida, Lyotard, and Bakhtin. What defines our relation and responsibility to alterity is considered primarily in response to the Face. The primordial, prediscursive potentiality of the face, and the responses it provokes, establishes a presence that haunts all discursive transformations. The emanations of the modern, sovereign, or patriarchal face constitute various regimes of power that serve both to position subjectivity and to secure its being within the frameworks and boundaries of modern projects (*grands récits*). Cultural performances that show "good form" are considered authorized or prescribed replies to the sovereign face. These emanations

legislate the settled ways, customary practices, and habits of modern society. Acquiring this cultural competence is accomplished by internalizing the
power emanating from the face – a relation of absorbing the other into itself
(a reduction to identity). Here, the subject becomes a mere agent of the
other and brings contractual closure to the immanent potentiality of the
Face. The author argues that the ethicality of the facial encounter is also the
effacement of the sovereign gaze/voice. The subject, however, far from
being originary and authentic, is constituted as the stopgap of lack. Previous cultures, including that of modernity, concealed this within authoritative discourses. With the collapse of such discourses, postmodernity reveals
the subject in its contingency and frangibility. The face-to-face encounter
of postmodern ethics calls for an immediate and unauthorized performa-
tivity rather than an authorized, discursively mediated response. These
impromptu acts are responses by an agency that seeks neither to loose itself
in the other nor to absorb the other into itself. In this way the ethical
encounter seeks again to pry open, or at least to prevent closure of, the
immanent dialogical potency of the Face.

Contemporary debates around museums and memorials provide evidence of both the hunger for memory in our particular moment and the
need to revisit traditional ways of marking history. Yet, though institution-
alized memory would seem, on the face of it, to be a good thing, the stories
that unfold in the chapters in Part 3, "Museum and Memory," show that it
can also be a considerably fraught ethical exercise. Chapter 5, "Salvador
Allende and the Construction of a Harmless Icon: Museums and Memory,"
is by the Chilean emigré novelist Leandro Urbina, who has lived both in
Canada and the United States since going into exile with a whole generation
of left-wing artists and intellectuals in the aftermath of the Allende coup. Yet,
when a Salvador Allende Museum and a statue of Allende are both instituted in the 1990s, he worries about what is being covered over in this prema-
ture institutional gesture of memorializing the Marxist president overthrown
in the heyday of Cold War politics. Is the plan to consecrate a museum to
Allende also another way of forgetting the dark reign of Augusto Pinochet?
"Are we, ourselves, the Pinochet Museum? All of us who have donated our
passport pictures, our police photos?" Urbina's chapter raises radical questions about what it means to institutionalize the memory of a figure in the
name of national "reconciliation." Does such a museum serve only to foreclose both the idea and the memory of Allende, "its four walls an architecture of ruins" (Urbina, this volume)?

In Chapter 6, "Commemoration/(de)Celebration: Super-Shows and the
Decolonization of Canadian Museums, 1967–1992," Ruth Phillips focuses
on the conflicts between traditional museum discourses around colonial

artifacts and the response to them by Canadian Aboriginal peoples in a moment of shifting power and knowledge relations. As both a curator and an academic centrally involved in the staging of important Aboriginal exhibitions during the period under consideration, she experienced first-hand the range of ethical issues at stake in the representation and display of the objects and Aboriginal cultures at hegemonic institutional sites. Phillips highlights the controversy over four Canadian exhibitions displaying indigenous objects, which implicitly authorized interpretations of Aboriginal heritage and offered representations of Aboriginal cultures. Through an analysis of these late twentieth-century show times, Phillips argues that such public commemorations comprise a mini-history of decolonization that is both politically significant and incomplete. She demonstrates that an increasingly liberalized public opinion and Aboriginal activism mobilized both shifting museum representations and Parliamentary politics in the period. The twenty-five-year history recounted in this chapter surveys a progressive and unfolding history during which colonized indigenous nations affirmed their right "to remember the past and to represent the present according to other measures of value and importance" (Phillips, this volume).

In Chapter 7, "'Into the Heart of Africa': Curatorship, Controversy, and Situated Knowledges," Deborah Burrett is concerned with the representation and controversy of museum artifacts, especially the way in which these artifacts delineate and register the weapons of colonialism. She offers an inquiry into the curatorial vision, representation, and situated knowledges of the *Into the Heart of Africa* exhibition held at the Royal Ontario Museum in Toronto, 1989–90. Through a detailed analysis of the creation and installation of the exhibition, the author documents the curator's use of a wide range of different approaches to contextualize both the display and the history of colonial violence. Burrett then provides a detailed, ethnographic account of the content and spatial organization of the exhibit's illustrations, texts, and objects. In highlighting several ethical controversies around the African collection – including the diverse readings of museum artifacts by different groups, the exhibition's omission of African voices and stories from explanatory texts, and the racist allegations voiced by demonstrators to the exhibition – Burrett asserts that the history of ethnographic collections cannot be separated from the history of imperialism and its situated knowledges. Of critical significance here is that both colonizers and colonized are connected to one another through their histories – histories that cannot be forgotten even in the face of attempts to diminish the powerful, textual narrations of Empire. Unpacking the imperial past, as Burrett does, involves the recognition and the re-vision of contestatory memory. Like Ruth Phillips's account, Burrett's chapter confirms the close connection between postmodern epistemic shift and postcolonial discourses. In this regard, postmodernity and postcoloniality are virtually coterminous in that a defining feature of the former is the collapse of old imperial centres and hegemonic Western ideologies.

Part 4, "Visual Culture," focuses on a growing body of visual theory that has shown the extent to which both figures of vision and visual practices are implicated in modernist regimes of knowing which, in turn, construct shifting grounds of subjectivity. In Chapter 8, "The Unbearable Strangeness of Being: Edgar Reitz's Film-Chronicle *Heimat*," Barbara Gabriel revisits one of the most important cultural events in Germany in the 1980s to uncover a much more uncanny film-text than has been read to date. Though Reitz's film was a huge success both at home and at international film festivals such as Cannes, a number of critics have challenged its responsibility to history, charging it with covering over the darkest events of the National Socialist era and repeating the pastoral idyll of the national genre of the Heimat-film. Gabriel argues that, far from idealizing Heimat (a term that means not only regional and national home, but also a place of belonging), Reitz's sixteen-hour film-chronicle draws self-consciously on Freud's classic 1919 essay *The Uncanny* (*The Unheimlich*) to deliberately interrupt and estrange this phantasmatic of Heimat. Unlike the traditional Heimatfilm, which casts out the stranger who threatens secure regional and national boundaries, Reitz's film affirms Adorno's post-Second World War lesson in *Minima Moralia*, that "it is part of morality not to be at home in one's house" (Gabriel, this volume). Gabriel's reading of the film's complex image-track on a figural axis of purity and contamination uncovers an attentive reading of history that not only looks back to the German national catastrophe but that also looks forward to a contemporary postcolonial moment of global and transnational encounters.

In Chapter 9,"Devastation of the Hapless Structure: Architecture and Ethics," Phyllis Lambert, founder and Director of The Canadian Centre for Architecture, introduces us to Melvin Charney's *Un Dictionnaire*. Charney's *Un Dictionnaire* was presented in 2000 as Canada's entry to the 7th Venice Biennale International Exhibition of Architecture within the larger exhibition theme of "Cities: Less Aesthetics, More Ethics." The Montreal architect-artist's work repositions images drawn from press clippings of wire-service photographs, impelling us to look again at architecture from outside its traditional status as "isolated monument." Charney orders these news images into a new kind of dictionary that frames them as "events" – as, among other categories, decompositions, ruins, frames, streets, grids, and fragments of bulldozed cities. In the end, these reconfigured images replace a static model of architecture with a dynamic one. Yet in their attention to "structures caught in an instance of celebration or, more likely, in a disaster" (Lambert, this volume), this assemblage uncannily anticipated 9/11 at the same time as it provided a retrospective look at a ruined twentieth century.

In Chapter 10, "Beyond the Frame: Ethical Encounters and Morality in Deleuze's Cinematic Theory," Daniel O'Connor deals with aspects of the technic of cinema as constitutive of ethical positioning. His analysis highlights the fractured or dislocated nature of totalities and the open space that such breaks produce for change, movement, and creativity. In analyzing moral and ethical forms of the movement of bodies within cinematography, the author moves away from the semiotic domain where images and signs are identical. Following Deleuze, he argues that cinematic perception is constituted "beyond the frame" and in the relations of visual and sound images. The chapter equates images with the movements and encounters of bodies (force relations) and, from a Foucauldian perspective on discipline, shows how moral narratives merely code the habituated flows orchestrated by montage, or the act of selecting and assembling shots. As a way of exploring the potential for a postmodern ethic in the cinema, the author illustrates the immanent strength involved in breaking the normal flows occupying the interstice and, thereby, opening up a space for competing narratives and their polysemic effect. What Chapter 10 brings to the fore is not only a critique of moralities as encodings of the dominant affects but also a renewed understanding of the ethical encounters of bodies in space and their expanding capacities, their becomings. This orientation in turn belies a commitment to the flow of social and political life as it is animated by the intermingling of bodies.

The chapters that constitute Part 5, "Relations with the Other," speak both to each other and to earlier essays in the volume in ways that confirm the interdisciplinary space of the postmodern. Chapter 11, Suzan Ilcan's "The Marginal Other: Modern Figures and Ethical Dialogues," examines the social phenomenon and construction of the marginal "other" in northwestern Turkey. Drawing on Julia Kristeva's notion of the "stranger" in the context of a perspective formulated from the work of Zygmunt Bauman on forms of "togetherness," Ilcan analyzes three forms of encounters with the stranger: monological, analogical, and dialogical. She shows how each occurs in aesthetic, cognitive, and ethical spaces, respectively. In comparison to modern authoritative encounters, which highlight a kind of individuality intolerant to difference, diversity, and creativity – a cleansing of the life-world of strangers – Ilcan depicts postmodern dialogical encounters as a form of "togetherness" that challenges rigid cultural boundaries, fosters voices from the margins, and permits the establishment of ethical relations. This ethical encounter is unbound by the practicalities and moral "orders" of everyday life and hegemonic discourse. It acknowledges the potential relevance of another's interests and allows for the creation of two speaking and active subjects. As in the chapters by Deborah Burrett, Daniel O'Connor, and Lynne Phillips, spatialized contexts in Chapter 11 disclose complex social, political and cultural cleavages that, in turn, affect the relations between ethics and the social imagination.

In Chapter 12, "Changing Health Moralities in the Tropics: Ethics and the Other," Lynne Phillips examines how a key representation of the "other" in discourses of development and health involves the created geography of the "tropics," an exotic geography that is a product of the colonial imagination. From a reflexive ethical standpoint (i.e., an awareness of the positionality of analysts and the colonizing potential of their models when writing within and across cultures), Phillips critically details and examines the political schemes aimed at healing and depicting tropical bodies in the Latin American context of rural Ecuador. By exploring the ties between competing neoliberal and biomedical discourses on health and illness in the framework of newly created forms of knowledge and power, she shows how local residents attempt to challenge existing health moralities, offer an implicit critique of colonial ventures, and displace strategies that aim to decontaminate the Other of contradictions. This political process not only raises concerns about the opening of different possibilities for one's temporalized body and for one's embodiment in a "tropical" milieu but also highlights modernity's link to an imperialism that is subtended by a discourse of the "purity" of its project. Especially significant at this juncture, and in the postmodern/postcolonial nexus, is that metanarratives and claims of progress inevitably encounter contestations to scientific practices, especially those mediated by the social body. In this chapter, and in the detailed accounts of Ruth Phillips and Deborah Burrett, we are made aware of the role that critical history performs in revealing relations between the imperial past and its legacies in the present and in signalling the politics of locations, especially their varied narratives, temporalities, and representations.

In Part 6, "Styles and Genres of the Ethical Subject," we look at how postmodernism's increased attention to the contingent narratives of those left out of authorized histories has resulted in new styles of writing as well as in intensified pressure on, in particular, the genres of life-writing and autobiography. In ways that mirror shifts within the formal discipline of historiography, this writing–back both reinstates new subject categories and identities and pays close attention to other ways of inscribing memory and history. Chapter 13, Bina Freiwald's "'Covering Their Familiar Ways with Another Culture': Minnie Aodla Freeman's *Life among the Qallunaat* and the Ethics of Subjectivity," like Loriggio's discussion of the ethics of recognition underscoring autobiographical writing (which follows), analyzes the ethical implications of the autobiographical subject in Minnie Aodla Freeman's *Life among the Qallunaat*. Freiwald begins by conceptualizing autobiographical narratives as identity discourses, which inform both the concrete practices of individual identity and the struggles of the collectivity. As such, she presents Freeman's identity-based, plurilingual text as one that tells the history and ways of "her" Inuit people through her own experience of private loss and collective displacement. Of critical significance here is Freeman's deployment of a collective memorial discourse (of remembering how things are or were in her culture), which permits her to evoke ancestral knowledge in order to understand an unfamiliar present. According to Freiwald, this discourse is a dynamic force responsible not only for creating a complex autobiographical persona but also for supporting an Inuk perspective and presenting a critique of colonial practices and history. This strategy of remembering allows for a different understanding of colonial inscription and an ethical perception of individual and collective identity. In Freiwald's words, "remembering also serves to counter one of the greatest threats faced by a colonized people, the danger that their self-knowledge ... will dissipate and disappear." By avoiding the hazards of essentializing and othering, Freeman's work produces a "postcontact (Inuk) subjectivity" that enacts the contingency of culture and identity and a "postcontact reality" that positions the subject as a stranger among strangers in ways that echo earlier chapters in this volume.

Chapter 14, Brenda Carr's "'A Network of Relations': Interdependence in Bronwen Wallace's Talking Lyric," analyzes Bronwen Wallace's conversational poems in the context of a feminist and dialogic process of openness. She examines how Wallace's lyrical language is rooted in experience and practice and is placed within the ideological horizons and webbed communities of gender, class, and ecology. She draws upon a selection of Wallace's recent poems, illustrating how their porous weave of media (literary, visual, musical, documentary) and discourses not only breaks down hierarchical categories of elite and popular culture but also opens the lyric to "self-reflective engagement with its status as a form subject to historical process and, consequently, to new articulations of ethical subjectivity." As a posthumanist humanist, Bronwen Wallace raises questions about subjectivity, agency, and voice and submits them to self-reflexive thinking by recreating women's voices, their views, and their social experiences in conversational form. Through a close reading of Wallace's lyric testimony as a social worker at Kingston's Interval House for survivors of domestic abuse, Carr identifies the ethical potentiality of her "relationally constructed and embodied poetics," which evokes other voices, speaks to the wounded place in all of us, and opens out to an expanded ethical community. Through Carr's use of Benhabib's alternative model of the self, MacIntyre's narrative selfhood, and Ricoeur's reciprocal self-esteem for the other, Wallace's talking lyric is analyzed as a democratized and ethical form. As such, Wallace's ethical poetics implies a responsibility to and engagement with others, a dialogical relationship she argues we cannot live without. Like the other chapters in Part 6, which situate the ethics of textuality within a social context of change and transformation, Carr's feminist perspective alerts us to the idea that conversational poetry can be potentially revolutionary, capable of creating new categories of knowledge and subverting the monological discourses of authority.

In Chapter 15, "Memory, Identity and Redemption: Notes on the Culture of Autobiography," Francesco Loriggio raises philosophical and ethical queries about the current popularity and fascination with life stories and the autobiography within critical writing. Loriggio's chapter offers a critique of postmodernism in literary criticism and, in so doing, permits a return to issues of subjectivity, identity, and agency that "theory," in isolation, sometimes forecloses. He begins with an assessment of Christopher Lasch's psychohistorical work on the culture of self-improvement, with its critique of the American penchant for confession and autobiography. In examining how Lasch's ideas differ from and impinge upon the current culture and performance of autobiography, Loriggio argues that, in recent contemporary debates about autobiography, there is a point where theories of self-interpretation, the emotions, and action converge. In his words, "written autobiography registers emplotted recollections ... it is remembrance twice over, memory *of* the past and memory *for* the future." In order to make room for the dialogical recognition of personal or group identity in autobiographies, Loriggio calls for a reappraisal of their purpose. In his use of Bakhtin's work on literature and culture and Taylor's ideas of agency and language, Loriggio argues that autobiographies are sources of and guides to history – sources and guides that have been written within a pluralized polytechnic horizon. Within this framework, the author decentres forms of knowledge, identity, and the subject and celebrates the reclamation of identities that are at once individual and communal in order to constitute a new horizon of historical memory.

Works Cited

Appadurai, Arjun. 1996. *Modernity at Large: Cultural Dimensions of Globalization*. Minneapolis and London: University of Minnesota Press.

Arrighi, Giovanni. 1994. *The Long Twentieth Century*. London: Verso.

Bauman, Zygmunt. 1993. *Postmodern Ethics*. Oxford and Cambridge: Blackwell.

– 1998. *Globalization: The Human Consequences*. New York: Columbia University Press.

– 2002. *Society under Siege*. Cambridge: Polity.

Bauman, Zygmunt, and Keith Tester. 2001. *Conversations with Zygmunt Bauman*. Cambridge: Polity.

Braidotti, Rosi. 1994. *Nomadic Subjects*. New York: Columbia University Press.

– 2002. *Metamorphoses: Towards a Materialist Theory of Becoming*. Cambridge: Polity Press.

Butler, Judith. 1990. *Gender Trouble: Feminism and the Subversion of Identity*. New York: Routledge.

Escobar, Arturo. 1995. *Encountering Development: The Making and the Unmaking of the Third World*. Princeton: Princeton University Press.

Fachinger, Petra. 2001. *Rewriting Germany from the Margins: "Other" German Literature of the 1980s and 1990s*. Montreal: McGill-Queen's University Press.

hooks, bell. 1990. *Yearning: Race, Gender, and Cultural Politics*. Toronto: Between the Lines.

Kristeva, Julia. 1990. *Strangers to Ourselves*. New York: Columbia University Press.

Lyotard, Jean-François. 1986. *The Postmodern Condition: A Report on Knowledge*. Manchester: Manchester University Press.

Rose, Nikolas. 1999. *Powers of Freedom: Reframing Political Thought*. Cambridge: Cambridge University Press.

Shields, Rob. 1991. *Places on the Margin: Alternative Geographies of Modernity*. London and New York: Routledge.

Smart, Barry. 1993. *Postmodernity*. London and New York: Routledge.

Spivak, Gayatri Chakravorty. 1990. *The Post-Colonial Critic: Interviews, Strategies, Dialogues*. Ed. S. Harasym. New York and London: Routledge.

– 1995. "Afterword." In *Imaginary Maps*, ed. Mahasweta Devi, 197–205. New York and London: Routledge.

Valverde, Mariana. 1991. *"The Age of Light, Soap, and Water": Moral Reform in English Canada, 1880s–1920s*. Toronto: McClelland and Stewart.

PART TWO

SPECTRES OF THE MODERN: PHILOSOPHICAL REFLECTIONS

On Being "the Last Kantian in Nazi Germany": Dwelling with Animals after Levinas[1]

DAVID L. CLARK

for Tilottama Rajan

Apes too have organs that can grasp, but they do not have hands. The hand is infinitely different from all grasping organs – paws, claws, or fangs – *different by an abyss of essence.* Only a being that can speak, that is, think, can have hands.

Martin Heidegger, *What Is Called Thinking*

I saw well why the gods do not speak to us openly, nor let us answer. Till that word can be dug out of us, why should they hear the babble that we think we mean? How can they meet us face to face till we have faces?

C.S. Lewis, *Till We Have Faces*

The Butchery of Everyday Life

"The last Kantian in Nazi Germany": this is how Emmanuel Levinas (1990b, 153) describes "Bobby," the dog who befriends him during his "long captivity" in a slave-labour camp. Thirty years after the fact, Levinas briefly tells the story of his terrible days in Camp 1492, days whose numbing inhumanity is momentarily relieved by the arrival of an animal that offers a semblance of respect. I say "semblance" because Levinas's experience of Bobby is informed by conventional assumptions about animality that make it impossible for him straightforwardly to attribute dutifulness to a creature that is not human. *Mon semblable, mon frère*: Bobby doubles for the human, yet he is not human, and this indeterminacy about his ontological and moral status at once triggers Levinas's most dogmatic claims about non-human life and tests the limits of their coherence. The enigma of the animal evokes contradictory thoughts and feelings in Levinas: it is these sentiments, and the axioms by which they are articulated, that form the focus of my remarks in this chapter. What is clear is that the dog provides welcome succour to the prisoners, but the fact that he is the last of his kind reminds us that he performs this duty – if duty is what it is – in an ashen world on the brink of extinction. Yet Levinas's essay does not begin with such searing recollections. The first half of it is taken up with a sprightly reflection upon Talmudic readings of Exodus 22:31, in which God grants certain eating rights to dogs. How can creatures of "pure nature" be said to possess "rights" (Levinas 1990b, 151)? What supreme act of faithfulness to "man" prompted God to consecrate them in this unusual way? Levinas dallies with the "talmudic Doctors" who attempt to resolve these questions, but their "high hermeneutics" and "subtle exegesis" (152) are, finally, not to his liking. As he says, he is always "thinking of Bobby" (151), and that thought unerringly returns him to the singularity and the solitude of the true task at hand, the work that his essay is destined to do; namely, bearing witness. No "allegories," no animal fables of any kind, after Camp 1492.

Levinas sets the scene with the barest of details: "There were seventy of us in a forestry commando unit for Jewish prisoners of war," he recalls; "the French uniform still protected us from Hitlerian violence" (152). As "soldiers" rather than as "civilians" – the difference, we are reminded, lies in the sheer contingency of a piece of cloth – the prisoners are spared extermination in a death camp. But of course there is nothing to shelter them from other acts of brutality – acts whose informing prejudice, Levinas suggests, is as old as Judaism itself. An "archetypal" ruthlessness characterizes his captors, for whom the Jews have never been more than "animals" and for whom bestialization therefore remains the chief means by which to render the Jews humanly unthinkable. Laden with animalistic rhetoric, Levinas's account painfully reproduces the biologism that naturalizes his incarceration. "We were beings entrapped in their species" (153), he recalls, in effect turning the "paradox" that had quickened the minds of the "talmudic Doctors" inside out: once reduced to a creature of "pure nature," the Jew obliges no one, bears no rights. His sentences weighty with the burden of the memory of this humiliation, Levinas glimpses himself through the voracious eyes of his captors – eyes that "stripped us of our human skin": "We were subhuman, a gang of apes. A small inner murmur, the strength and wretchedness of persecuted people, reminded us of our essence as thinking creatures, but we were no longer part of the world ... We were ... beings without language" (153). Robbing the prisoners of the power to speak, the Nazis cause them to question their ability to reason – language and thinking being the exemplary characteristics by which the human has always been decisively distinguished from the animal. What breaks the binding force of this animalization is an animal, "Bobby." Wandering into the camp, the dog "unwittingly" bears witness to the humanity of Levinas and the other prisoners, remembering what the Nazis, in their unremitting savagery, have forgotten. Like some strange, reversed *pharmakos*, Bobby is cast *into* (not out of) the mock-polis of the camp, restoring it – albeit momentarily – to a semblance of ethical "health." Levinas asks: Are we not *men*? In his own way, Bobby answers: yes, and again, yes! "He would appear at morning assembly and was waiting for us as we returned, jumping up and down and barking in delight. For him, there was no doubt that we were men … This dog was the last Kantian in Nazi Germany" (153).

The animal act described in this passage, the focal point of the essay's concluding paragraph, gives us much to think about. Suffice it to say I will be able here to touch upon only some of its complexities. If humans are capable of treating others like animals, then it may also be true that animals are capable of treating others *like humans*. Or like humans *should* be treated, "Kant" here operating as a kind of prosopopoeia for dutifulness and for the "oughtness" that is ordinarily said uniquely to tug on the conscience of human beings. Is Levinas's figure merely a sentimentalizing anthropomorphism, improperly attributing human qualities to an animal who in turn finds those qualities in the prisoners (i.e., grasps that they are "men," not animals)? The spectre of falling into such pathos haunts Levinas's text; midway through the essay, he stops himself: "But enough of allegories! We have read too many fables and we are still taking the name of a dog in the figurative sense" (152). It could be said that it is Levinas's allergy to animal fables that propels his narrative towards the concluding account of the slave camp, where, he hopes, a dog is just a dog. Even here, though, he must work against the allegorizing resonances of his own story, for Bobby's apparently dutiful behaviour unavoidably recalls the scene in Homer's *Odyssey* where Ulysses is greeted by his faithful hound, the last true Greek in Ithaca. Unable *not* to anthropomorphize Bobby, Levinas nevertheless preemptively attempts to distinguish his account from its epic pretext: "No, no!" he exclaims, Bobby and I are *not* like that dog and his master, for "they were in Ithaca and the Fatherland," but "here," in Nazi Germany, "we were nowhere." "Nowhere" means a historical moment – the Holocaust – where mawkishness is utterly irrelevant, "beyond pathos," as Levinas says elsewhere.[2] But it also means the dystopia of Camp 1492, where neither human nor animal is at home, the placeless place where the animalization of the Jews makes it *imperative* to (re)think the uses to which the ontotheological distinction between the two realms can be put.[3] "We," who? Who is my neighbour? To whom (or what) are obligations owed? With whom (or what) do I dwell? Levinas's work insistently raises these fundamental questions, the protoethical openings for thought that come before every ontology. What matters above all is thinking rather than dissolving the distinction between the *ethos* of the human and the animal. The "Nazi Germany" that has brought the Kantians to the threshold of extinction is all the evidence that one would ever need to grasp the foolishness and the mortal danger that comes of blurring the boundaries between human and non-human life. As Richard Klein (1995, 23) points out, the "Nazi *Lebensphilosophie* ... explicitly assimilated human striving to the impulses of animal instinct." We see at least one reason why Levinas is so nervous about the prospect of anthropomorphizing Bobby: the sentimental humanization of animals and the brutal animalization of humans are two sides of the same assimilating gesture. In humanizing the animal, these fictions risk the tropological reversal by which persons are in turn bestialized, which is to say the biologisms and racisms that naturalize ethnic cleansings and the creation of concentration camps, whether in Nazi Germany or present-day Bosnia.[4]

Those who object to the impropriety of anthropomorphic projections, Heidegger (1985, 124) once pointed out, presuppose a punctual knowledge of what it is to be properly human. But the propriety of "humanity" is what is least certain and most vulnerable for Levinas, exposed as it is to the infinite heteronomy of others. Do these others include animal others? Are we not responsible for those non-human others as they sometimes appear to be for us? But who is "*us*"? If the thought of "the animal" is in question, so be too, inevitably, is the thought of "the human" with which it has always been inextricably bound. Bobby's delightful greetings compel Levinas to consider how it is that a "mere" animal could treat him with more dignity than his human captors, captors who could be said to behave like animals[5] and to incarcerate their prisoners like animals – tellingly, fantastically, the "animal" is available as a figure for both master and slave – were it not for the fact that the question of what constitutes the animal is precisely what Bobby's dutiful behaviour raises and complicates. We might also say that, unlike the Nazis, Bobby meets and engages Levinas *face-to-face*, were it not for the fact that what constitutes a face, and whether animals can be said to possess a face (a question to which I will return) is also implicitly in question here, as it is elsewhere in his work.

What is apparent is that sentimentalizing anthropomorphisms make genuinely ethical thought, whether we understand this in Kantian or Levinasian terms, impossible because, under the guise of a certain pathos, they peremptorily annihilate differences in the name of the (human) same. We must therefore, Levinas (1990b, 152) insists, stop "taking the name of a dog in the figurative sense": that is the denunciation of rhetoric that acts as the engine of his essay. Figuring animals, we *con*figure the human. But at what cost to the animals? What is more violently exclusionary: that the Jews are animal-

ized by the Nazis or that the "animal" has for so long been used as a marker by which ferociously to abject the other? Right away, Levinas's essay
invites us to think counterintuitively for how, as is said in good conscience,
can we even consider the obligations that are due animals, "the debt," as he
says, "that is always open" (152) to them, when it is the obligations to the
human other that are most cruelly at risk, that most palpably deserve consideration in a Holocaust testimony?

Levinas's essay is remarkable for bringing these two questions into such
close proximity, almost suggesting that the two forms of prejudice – one
against the Jews, the other against animals – are in some way comparable.
The animalization of human beings leads directly to the most horrific consequences, to be sure; but before we hear of this, before Levinas tells us
about what it feels like to be incarcerated as a beast by the Nazis, he reminds
us that the animalization of animals is, in its own way, also deadly and, thus,
worthy of our concern. How are animals animalized by humans? Levinas's
answer is at once complex and brutally simple: *we eat meat*. Cloaked in a certain mocking humour, Levinas's opening paragraph circles warily around the
"carnivorous virility" of human beings. Like the dogs described in the biblical pretext for his essay, we too consume "flesh that is torn by beasts in the
field." We *are* those beasts, devouring each other in "the horrors of war,"
sublimating our carnivorous desires into "hunting games," and, finally, eating meat. This, from his opening paragraph:

> There is enough, there, to make you a vegetarian again. If we are to
> believe Genesis, Adam, the father of us all, was one! There is, at least,
> enough there, to make us want to limit, through various interdictions,
> the butchery that every day claims our "consecrated" mouths! (151)

Remember this, Levinas advises, "as you plunge your fork into your roast."
We are killing animals, even if the murderousness of that sacrifice is effaced
at the dinner table, while our mouths water and our eyes grow big. The con-
secration of flesh-sharing *is* its erasure, the spiritualization and *denegation* of
its gory reality. Derrida (1995, 283): "The putting to death of the animal, says
this denegation, is not a murder." But this other scene, the everyday "butchery" behind the veneer of civilization, competes with yet another. Levinas
makes a point of telling us that, all along, he has had something else firmly
in mind. While he speaks to us about our carnivorous appetite for the animal other, the memory of another animal intrudes. He has always already
intruded: "I am thinking of Bobby," he writes, in the present progressive
tense. These two thoughts, then, are *contiguous*, thought together, even if, in

the narrative of the essay, they are necessarily unpacked one after the other. It is Levinas's way of narrowing the distance between them without actually saying that they are the same thing. The implications of this contiguity are obvious and troublesome: the "non-criminal" putting to death of the animal is put alongside the "non-criminal" putting to death of the European Jews. About what the two thoughts say to each other, Levinas is pointedly silent: it is enough, for now, in the aftermath of "Hitler's exterminations" (Levinas 1990a, xiii), that they are considered jointly. For a scandalous instant, Levinas acts the part that Bobby will more or less play at the end of the essay; that is, as the one who, in the absence of others and in the absence of a respect for the other, *testifies* to the worthiness of the imprisoned and the murdered. Indeed, he reminds us that these others *are* murdered, butchered so that we may eat well. Here, it is *he*, not Bobby, who witnesses the biologistic, naturalized, and consecrated degradation of the other. The testimonial logic of his essay's narrative could then be expressed in this way: first, human (Levinas) on behalf of animal, then, animal (Bobby) on behalf of human. The momentous implications of this chiasmic ethical exchange are irresistible. As John Llewelyn (1991a, 235) argues, Levinas here "all but proposes an analogy between the unspeakable human holocaust and the unspoken animal one."

For all his perspicuity about Levinas's essay, however, Llewelyn may slightly understate what he sees there. By characterizing the essay as doing everything *but* making such a proposition, we must be careful not to shrink from its double scene of sacrifice. For is this not *exactly* the proposition that Levinas is making, even and especially if he does not literally write it out for us to read? Levinas proposes this analogy between sacrifices by *not* proposing it, in a whispering gesture that is strategically affirmative *and* negative: "yes," because there is no denying the implications of Levinas's opening meditation on what it means, what it really means, to be an eater of flesh; "no," because Levinas does not simply equate the two events, much less call them by the same name, *l'Holocauste*. Perhaps the point is not so much that Levinas makes the analogy between animal sacrifice and human murder but, rather, that this analogy, once made, is so difficult to read. Perhaps it is not that the "unspeakable human holocaust" is so distant from the "unspoken animal one" that it can only be denigrated by the comparison but, rather, that the notion that animals are murdered is elevated, if only provisionally, to the highest thought. In other words, the fact that the question of our obligations to animals is raised in such a maximally important context (indeed, as the opening move in the evocation of that context) puts to us that the thought of the human, no matter how profound – the incarceration and extermination of the Jews standing as the figure par excellence for what

Jean-Luc Nancy calls "an absolute responsibility"[7] – can never be wholly divorced from the thought of the animal.

To be sure, the lightness of Levinas's touch reminds us that, for him, non-human animals cannot make the same morally relevant claims upon us as can human ones. Levinas will never be confused with the animal liberationist, for whom allowing "the interests of his own species to override the greater interests of members of other species" is unacceptable (Singer 1976, 9). I would argue, in fact, that Levinas's contiguous thoughts about the "butchery" of animals and the murder of Jews resonate strangely *with*, and constitute a subtle renunciation *of*, Heidegger, who, in a series of lectures given in Bremen on technology in 1949, infamously claimed that the "motorized food industry" was "in essence the same as the manufacturing of corpses in gas chambers and extermination camps."[8] Heidegger's claim will always need to be read very slowly, since its extreme callousness makes it impossible definitively to distinguish between, on the one hand, his long-standing critique of the West's technological logic, for which the industrialization of agriculture and the bureaucratization of genocide are identical expressions of the "complete Europeanization of the earth and man" (Heidegger 1971, 15–16) and, on the other hand, a certain dehumanizing absolutism in his own thinking and politics. In this instance, as perhaps in many others, Heidegger may have become what he beheld. For Levinas, however, there is no question about the cruel basis of Heidegger's remarks, nor about their origins far back in Heidegger's work.

Levinas (1989, 488) readily concedes the critical power of Heidegger's "extraordinary book of 1927" but asks rhetorically if "there was never any echo of Evil in it." It cannot be accidental that evidence of such reverberations are to be found amid Heidegger's most violently dogmatic claims about animality. For example, in the name of more rigorously determining how the being-towards-death of *Dasein* makes it into something that surpasses living creatures (a determination that is not without its Levinasian equivalent, as I shall argue), *Being and Time* distinguishes between the dying (*Sterben*) of *Dasein* and the perishing (*Verenden*) of beings that are merely alive: the human properly dies, whereas the animal simply ceases to live (Heidegger 1972, 240). With this distinction in mind, Heidegger's Bremen assertion takes on utterly chilling consequences: in so far as the Jews perish with and *like* the animals who die in meat-processing plants – that is, as essentially similar "fabrications" of the military-industrial-agricultural complex – *they cannot be human*, which is to say, *because* the military-industrial-agricultural complex fails to distinguish between animals and certain animalized humans, it slaughters them both with impunity.

It goes without saying that none of this annihilating logic informs Levinas's comparison. Responding to Heidegger's claim, Levinas (1989, 487) says simply: "This stylistic turn of phrase, this analogy, this progression, are beyond commentary." Where Heidegger levels differences in the name of "essence," Levinas bids us, for a moment, to think two distinct thoughts together and, in doing so, safely preserves the incalculable differences between feeding people in the industrialized West and murdering them. Levinas's comparison is as unmistakable as it is delicate, dwelling within the interior, apposite spaces of his essay. In this gesture, important as much for *what* it might mean to us as it is for its being made at all, he points to the danger of making pronouncements from the relatively secure vantage point of a fundamental ontology; instead, he offers an opening and a lure for thought. He risks a question about the (animal) other, where Heidegger carelessly pronounces the death of the difference between their demise and the murder of the European Jews. Levinas quietly, almost inadvertently, allows us to think that there are other horrors capable of making a claim upon our conscience, other forms of "butchery" – Levinas's terrible, savage word so pointedly puts this to us – without for a moment suggesting that they are the *same* horror as the Holocaust. For both thinkers, the blindness of the West culminates in its arrogant faith in an instrumental reason that transforms the planet into so much raw material awaiting assimilation. But in Heidegger's desire to grasp the basis of this inherently rapacious manner of being in the world, and, more important, in his overweening confidence as a *thinker* that he can stand neutrally apart from its actual destructiveness, Heidegger threatens to *overlook* the names and the faces of the others for whom this neutrality means nothing less than annihilation. In Levinas's memorable phrase about Heidegger's failure to remember, the German philosopher proceeds "*as if consenting to horror.*" And so he embodies everything Levinas has fought against; namely, the murderous indifference to difference by which alterities are compelled to be *im Wesen dasselbe* ("in essence the same").

In this, as in so many other ways, Levinas anticipates Derrida, for whom Heidegger's extraordinary statement represents an object lesson in what he calls "the ideology of difference." In attempting to deconstruct this ideology, with its insistence upon "a single limit between white and black, Jewish and non-Jewish," animal and human, Derrida (1987, 183) is *not* arguing that difference is irrelevant, especially when we are speaking about "the difference between people and animals ... between Auschwitz and battery farms":

> No, no I am not advocating the *blurring* of differences. On the contrary, I am trying to explain how drawing an oppositional limit *itself* blurs the difference, the differance and the differences, not only between man and

animal, but among animal societies – there are an infinite number of animal societies, and within animal societies and within human society itself, so many differences.

Ideologies of difference are, in the end, ideologies of "homogeneity" (184), strategies and discourses that suppress uncontainable and irreducible variation in the name of an impossibly pure distinction between the same and the other. Criticizing Heidegger's philosophical and political investment in such purity, his high-minded distaste for mixing it up with more earthly others, Levinas (1969, 134) will say that "*Dasein* ... is never hungry." From this utterly anorexic perspective, Heidegger risks collapsing the difference between a meal and a corpse, while at the same moment and in the same gesture ferociously reinscribing the oppositional limit between those who are in a position to practise a fundamental ontology and those who are not. Speaking not from the relative safety of Bremen but from behind the barbed wire of Camp 1492, Levinas cannot afford to make such sacrifices, dissolving as they do the difference between life and death for people and animals alike.

"But enough of this theology!" (Levinas 1990b, 151). With that mock exclamation, Levinas attempts to bring sudden closure to his thoughts on animal sacrifice, making it seem as if it had all been a false start and a strange detour. But a detour from what true path? When, two paragraphs later, he interjects "But enough of allegories!" (152), we see that he is yet again working the conceit that he is writing in the "wrong" mode. Much of the essay unfolds in this self-consciously dilatory manner, one effect of which is to throw into sharper relief the purposiveness that comes only with the concluding memories of Bobby and the slave camp. And even there, as I have suggested, Levinas continues to feel as if his account could, at any moment, fall into mere fabulation, or worse, sentimentality. Throughout, the thought of the animal is always somehow too anthropomorphic, always vanishing beneath the surface of its humanistic interpretations. In his opening sentence, Levinas acknowledges the problem "of attaching too much importance to what 'goes into a man's mouth,' and not enough to what comes out" (151), but his pretense at embarrassment over succumbing precisely to this hazard puts to us that his flirtation with what he ironically dismisses as mere "theology" was worth the effort. In the apparent absence of an overarching design to the essay, the ensuing analogy between the "butchery that every day claims our 'consecrated' mouths" and the *other* butchery that haunts all of *Difficult Freedom* in effect operates as a kind of ghost narrative, linking the essay's oddly disparate thoughts and tones into a delicate whole. For a moment at least, before his allergy to making too much of animals overtakes his competing concern that we have made too little of them (especially when we sit down at the dinner table), the philosopher almost sounds as though he will abstain from animal flesh, as if he were the last vegetarian in the meat-eating West. Almost. Significantly, he does not in fact call for the end to animal sacrifice but, rather, for its thoughtful restriction. But in the name of what? On what grounds would animals oblige us to treat them in this fashion? Levinas does not say, content instead with evoking images of the feeding frenzy that lies just beyond our sight as creatures of culture. "There is, at least, enough there to make us want to limit, through various inter-dictions, the butchery" of everyday life. The careful self-distancing of Lev-inas's syntax is worth remarking upon. It tells us that he is not so much concerned with the letter of dietary laws as he is with the more general – but no less pressing – question of what it means to consume animal flesh in the first place, what it says about *us*. Who are *we* for whom the murderous violence of killing the animal other and sharing its flesh "at the family table" is so effortlessly "sublimated by intelligence" (151)?

This is not the first time that Levinas has asked his readers to consider what John Caputo (1993, 197) calls "a repressed discourse on eating in phi-losophy." A decade earlier, in *Totality and Infinity*, eating figures forth the irreducibly excessive relationship that the subject shares with the world:

> Eating … is to be sure not reducible to the chemistry of alimentation, [nor] … to the set of gustative, olfactory, kinesthetic, and other sensa-tions that would constitute the consciousness of eating. This sinking one's teeth into the *things* which the act of eating involves above all measures the surplus of the reality of the aliment over every represented reality, a surplus that is not quantitative, but is the way the I, the absolute commencement, is suspended on the non-I. (Levinas 1969, 128–9, emphasis mine)

For Levinas, our fleshliness and our utter dependence upon consuming flesh voluptuously exposes and commits the "I" to the other in ways that are "ulti-mately prior to his ontological relation to himself (egology) or to the totali-ty of things that we call the world" (Levinas 1986, 21). Always before the "I" and the "non-I," and, as the condition of the possibility of their mutual imbrication, there is "nourishment." As Seán Hand (1989, 37) remarks, "this conception of earthly enjoyment, whose forgetfulness of self is the first morality, marks a decisive break with *Dasein*." Enjoyment, nourishment, eating – all are corporeal figures with which Levinas evokes the fundamental responsibility that the self has for the frailty of the other, the other's desires, hungers, thirsts, hurts, and pleasures. In Heidegger, *Dasein* is the virile and resolute entity that ostensibly does without food so as better to fix its sights on the alterity of its own death; in Levinas, *Dasein* suffers the pangs of hunger, and in that suffering it is always already turned towards the face of the others who are also hungry and who will also die. In the slightly later essay on Bobby, however, nourishment and enjoyment suddenly take on darker meanings, for they are phenomena that consistently occur *at the expense of the animal other* whose flesh we consume. To eat, we must eat an other; one creature's nourishment means another gets stripped of its skin: that is the cold logic of us warm-blooded animals that *Totality and Infinity* represses and that Levinas's reflections upon the butchery of everyday life recover for thought. Inasmuch as the earlier text generalizes the consumed others into "things" and "aliment," figuring them as foodstuffs whose craving makes the "I" possible, it remains wholly centred on the needs of "man" and thus caught within the egology that it critiques. Where in *Totality and Infinity* the animal's sacrifice at the hands (and teeth) of the human goes unnoticed, in "The Name of a Dog" it summons us to an obligation that Levinas almost always reserves for human beings: you *ought* not kill me.

Refusing the Animal Face; or, We Are What We Eat

> There is no such thing as Animality, but only a regime of differences without opposition. The concept of animality, along with the "world poverty" of the animal, are human artifacts, indeed, artifacts that are difficult to wield; and their effect is to *efface* differences, to homogenize.
>
> Jacques Derrida, "On Reading Heidegger"

> The animal is the *dreamed* object.
>
> Luc Ferry, *The New Ecological Order*

Levinas's disturbing image of a domestic space – the dinner table – forming an alibi for murder recalls questions raised by Derrida (1995, 280) in his recent work on what he calls "the carnivorous virility" of Western cultures. Why do these cultures leave "a place ... open ... for a noncriminal putting to death" (276) of living creatures? How is responsibility to the human other also a tacit form of permission to act irresponsibly towards the animal other? How does indifference to the animal configure the human? Significantly, Derrida almost always raises these questions by rereading the philosophemes and critical positions that are central to Levinas's critique of "traditional humanism" (279). In quite different contexts (which itself attests to the fundamental nature of the problem at hand), Derrida characterizes animal sacrifice as symptomatic of a generalized carnivorous violence, a "carno-phallogocentrism" modelled upon the "virile strength of the adult male" (280; Derrida 1990, 953). According to this "schema," "the subject does not want just to master and possess nature actively. In our cultures, he accepts sacrifice and eats flesh" (Derrida 1995, 281). The killing of animals, and the concomitant construction of the "animal" *as that which may be freely put to death for the purposes of consumption*, is profoundly related to the constitution of human *Dasein*. For that reason, he argues, "If we wish to speak of injustice, of violence or of a lack of respect toward what we still so confusedly call animals, we must reconsider in its totality the metaphysico-anthropocentric axiomatic that dominates, in the West, the thought of just and unjust" (Derrida 1990, 953).

Needless to say, this reconsideration extends well beyond the question of what or whether meat should be eaten:

> The question is no longer one of knowing if it is "good" to eat the other or if the other is "good" to eat, nor of knowing which other. One eats him regardless and lets oneself be eaten by him ... The moral question is thus not, nor has it ever been: should one eat or not eat, eat this and not that ... man or animal, but since *one must* eat in any case and since it is and tastes good to eat, and since there is no definition of the good [*du bien*], *how* for goodness' sake should one *eat well* [*bien manger*]? And what does this imply? What is eating? How is this metonymy of introjection to be regulated? (Derrida 1995, 282)

Alluding to this passage, Caputo (1993, 198) observes: "We have to eat and we have to eat something living. That is the law of the flesh." As if cognizant of this imperative, Levinas does not call for an outright abstention from carnivorousness but, rather, for grasping the significance of the *law of the flesh* that articulates us, or, in his words, "that every day *claims* our 'consecrated' mouths." If we cannot *not* assimilate the other, and if what "we" *are* is irreducible to a complex spectrum of incorporation and interiorization (of which animal sacrifice is but one example), then the need to examine the axioms by which these forms of "eating" are conducted, far from becoming irrelevant, becomes all the more pressing. (On this point, Derrida differs most profoundly with Heidegger, or at least the Heidegger for whom the myriad differences between the industrial consumption of human and animal corpses had ceased to matter.) Briefly, for Derrida the point is not that we must stop eating meat – as he says, the distinction between animal and plant "flesh" is itself suspect – but to think critically about how carno-phallogocentric discourses and regimes (1) "install the virile figure at the determinative center of the subject" (Derrida 1995, 280); (2) abject those (others) who are deemed not to have the same brawny "appetites" as "men": women, homosexuals, celibates, and vegetarians (281); and (3) sacrifice animals in such a way that their being put to death is not considered killing (283).

As an example of the most profound "ideology of homogeneity," Derrida argues, carno-phallogocentrism requires that strict distinctions be maintained between "symbolic" and "real" objects of sacrifice. This is no more apparent than in the interdiction, "Thou shalt not kill," which Derrida reads after Levinas as:

> Thou shalt not kill thy neighbour. Consequences follow upon one another, and must do so continuously: thou shalt not make him suffer, which is sometimes worse than death, thou shalt not do him harm, thou shalt not eat him, not even a little bit, and so forth. (279)

On the other hand, "The putting to death of the animal is not a murder," a "denegation" or repression that Derrida links "to the violent institution of the 'who' as subject" (283). The neighbour, the neighbourhood of the human, with its attendant determinations of just and unjust action towards the other, is in this way constructed over and against the realm of the non-human, generalized and simplified as the "animal," for which the sixth commandment is inapplicable. According to the exclusionary principles of this "sacrificial" logic, humans may consume and be consumed in any number of symbolic ways but are forbidden to be carnivores of each other, "real" cannibalism figuring forth the animalizing behaviour par excellence, the very mark distinguishing "advanced" from "primitive" societies. Here, the extraordinary exceptions to the law against anthropagy prove the rule of culture. Animals and other living creatures, on the other hand, may be put to death at will. "Such are the executions of ingestion, incorporation, or introjection of the corpse," Derrida argues; "An operation as real as it is symbolic when the corpse is 'animal' (and who can be made to believe that our cultures are carnivorous because animal proteins are irreplaceable?)" (278). Only animals, *as* animals, "naturally" form real sacrifices to each other (or what Levinas [1990b, 151] calls "this devouring within species").

Yet the separation of "symbolic" from "real" operations and objects of ingestion is extremely problematical since "eating" is at best a metonym for "infinitely different modes of the conception-appropriation-assimilation of the other" (Derrida 1995, 281). Moreover, how is one to distinguish decisively between symbolic and non-symbolic forms of carnivorous violence when that distinction, in addition to "all symbolic or linguistic appropriations" that involve the capture and consumption of the other, is irreducible to a generalized "eating" that precedes and exceeds the constitution of the "human." As Derrida observes, determining a purely *symbolic* form of sacrifice that would decisively define the "human" "is very difficult, truly impossible to delimit in this case, hence the enormity of the task, its essential excessiveness, a certain unclassifiability or the monstrosity of that *for which* we have to answer here, or *before* which (whom? what?) we have to answer" (278). At what point *is* an (animal) corpse "just" a corpse or eating "simply" eating? What perspective, short of the loftily panoptic one that Heidegger adopts in his 1949 lectures, would enable us to make such absolute determinations? A radical surplus of differences and *différance* will always unsettle the oppositional limit between the human and the animal, and the man-centred determinations of "the just and the unjust" upon which the rigorous purity of this limit rests. To the extent that this excess displaces the thought of the "human" (and thus the "animal"), it is rightly felt to be "monstrous" and "unclassifiable" – and for that reason, entirely useful to the "task" of gaining a point of critical leverage on the humanisms that have always presupposed and policed an essential difference and oppositional limit between human and non-human life.

Can we say that Levinas disrupts "the boundaries that institute the human subject (preferably and paradigmatically the adult male, rather than the woman, child, or animal) as the measure of the just and the unjust" (Derrida 1990, 953)? In the opening paragraph of his essay, as I have argued, Levinas's disconcerting analogy strikes twice at the heart of a human-centred cosmos: "we" live in a culture that failed catastrophically to grasp the injustice of killing Jews; but "we" also live in a culture for which the justness of putting animals to death is simply not an intelligible consideration. The fact that Levinas is willing to raise the second question alongside the first, which is to say, in such close proximity to "'the' question and 'the' figure of responsibility" (Derrida 1995, 285) characterizing our modernity, suggests the maximal nature of what is at stake here, the radical possibilities that can be opened up when the reach of the ethical question *who is my neighbour?* is widened to include non-human acquaintances. If animals are also murdered, if their deaths are no longer denegated as merely being put to death, then to whom or what am I answerable? The unstated analogy between the murder of Jews and the killing of animals in effect creates a *rhetorical* neighbourhood in which animals and humans dwell and summon each other into responsibility.

Elsewhere in Levinas's work, including elsewhere in the essay on Bobby, this call goes mostly unheard. For example, Levinas has been asked if animals have faces and, thus, if they command the respect that the human face commands. His response is telling:

> One cannot entirely refuse the face of an animal ... Yet the priority here is not found in the animal, but in the human face. We understand the animal, the face of an animal, in accordance with *Dasein*. The phenomenon of the face is not in its purest form in the dog. In the dog, in the animal, there are other phenomena. For example, the force of nature is pure vitality. It is more this which characterizes the dog. But it also has a face ... The human face is completely different and only afterwards do we discover the face of an animal. (Levinas 1988, 169)

Much could be said about the rich interview of which this response forms a small part, and I can focus on only a few details here. We should note that, from the start, Levinas never questions whether there are "'animals' and 'humans' as such." Like Heidegger before him, the insistence upon the oppositional limit dividing the two entities presupposes that they exist as such. Even when Levinas disrupts the boundaries constituting the human, as he certainly does when he characterizes the subject as always already being held "hostage" to an absolute Other, he reinscribes the boundaries defining the animal, as if his critique of humanism remained more or less within a certain anthropological space. Levinas's somewhat evasive syntax qualifies any openness to the animal other by casting that muted act of affirmation in the form of a (double) negative: that one cannot *entirely* say "no" to the animal face means that saying "yes" is the exceptional rather than the categorically imperative act, supplemental in nature, rather than constitutive. The problem lies not with the human, who cannot or will not see this face, but decisively with the animal, whose face lacks the "purest form" that we are presumed to see with absolute clarity when the *visage* is human. What it is about the animal face that lingers once the human has finished with its refusals remains quite unclear since it is difficult to conceive of an absolute demand and responsibility – which is what the "face" usually connotes in Levinas's work – that is also somehow partial. Levinas concedes, positively, that there is something about the animal that compels us to face it; but he focuses negatively on the something else, which spoils and reduces that duty. All faces *as* faces are irrefutable, but some are less irrefutable than others. The notion that the animal face is not in its "purest form" implies that there is a continuum joining the faceless to the faced when everything else about Levinas's rhetoric points assertively towards an abyss of essence dividing the two phenomena. The animal face is "completely" other than the human face, yet the human remains the implacable standard against which the "purity" of the animal face is measured. Thus the animal both has and does not have a face; it is characterized in its essence by having (face) without having. In this redoubled and contradictory gesture, strongly reminiscent of the illogicality characterizing Heidegger's description of living creatures as *weltarm* (poor-in-the-world)[9], Levinas insists upon an absolute separation of human and animal while at the same moment reinscribing the animal face in what Derrida (1989, 55) would call "a certain anthropocentric or even humanist teleology."

The animal's face cannot be entirely ignored; yet Levinas is scrupulously careful to assert that even this fractional connection vis-à-vis the human must *not* be misinterpreted as placing animals on a developmental path that might lead to the human: "The widespread thesis that the ethical is biological amounts to saying that, ultimately, the human is only the last stage of the evolution of the animal. I would say, on the contrary, that in relation to the animal, *the human is a new phenomenon*" (Levinas 1988, 172, emphasis mine). Levinas's experience with and reflection upon Nazism makes it imperative that the "ethical" *not* be contaminated by the "biological" lest the destinal thinking of the latter become the means by which to exterminate the obligations of the former. The frankly anthropocentric insistence that the human cannot be reduced to an essence has remained, as Derrida suggests in another context, "*up until now* ... the price to be paid in the ethico-political denunciation of biologism, racism, naturalism" (Derrida 1989, 56). But this does not preclude us from tracing the axiomatic decisions, not to say the contradictions and elisions, underwriting Levinas's discourse of animality, a discourse whose very attempt to think beyond the ontological reinscribes ancient ontotheological distinctions between the human and animal. For example, one sign that Levinas resorts to the profoundest metaphysical humanism is that he proceeds as if the distinction between the "ethical" and the "biological" was *itself* not consequentially ethical in nature, a sealing off of one neighbourhood from another, and a ghettoizing of the animal in the abiding space of the "biological" – for which we may take Levinas to mean something like *Nur-noch-leben*, "just-plain-life."[10]

Levinas's move against the "biological" almost exactly reproduces Heidegger's long-standing objection to *Lebensphilosophie*, both old and new. Original thinking – that is, thinking that presupposes the originality, or "newness," of the human phenomenon – only suffers at the hands of the zoologists. For that reason, Heidegger (1993, 234) was offended by Aristotle, who had failed to set "the *humanitas* of man high enough" by calling the human an animal equipped with language. For both thinkers, the being-human of the human wholly exceeds the thought of the biological in which animality is immured; the heteronomic relation to the other, the being-ethical of the human, is unrelated to the life of the (other) living creatures, whose infinite differences from humans, but also from each other, are erased, and that erasure in turn is *fixed* by the name par excellence for natural "rule": the "biological." For Levinas, the animal face is always compromised by competing phenomena, all of them unnamed except for the most pressing, indeed, the very figure of *irrepressibility* – namely, the "pure vitality" of "the force of nature." "The being of animals," Levinas (1988, 172) will subsequently say, "is a struggle for life." The animal is imagined to be the creature for which being-alive takes precedence over all other essential characteristics: without remainder, the being-animal of the animal *is* its "vitality." Notwithstanding the radical critique of traditional humanisms that Levinas mobilizes around the notion of the "face," he resorts to the most conventional conceptual schemes when he tries to account for the animal other. According to this configuration, "Man" is exemplarily free from the blind force of nature, whereas animals are immersed in the liveliness that constitutes their animated existence to the precise extent that it deprives them of their liberty, their ability to "question," to anticipate both their "own" death and the death of another, as well as to reason, to speak, to mourn, to have a history, or to possess a soul. Levinas frankly puts to us that he "understand[s] the animal in accordance with *Dasein*"; that is, he measures the animal against the "purity" of *Dasein*, "purity" here signifying *Dasein's* prior, bare, and asymmetrical relation to the Other. The animal enjoys an excess of life over face, even if the means by which one could make, much less weigh, these relative distinctions remains completely mysterious. *Dasein*, on the other hand, is something more and better than merely being-alive. And if Levinas is also to insist, *contra* Heidegger, that his version of *Dasein* feels the pangs of hunger, then that only proves that he is forced to separate it from the being-alive of animals without making that vitality entirely inaccessible to it.[11]

When Levinas turns his mind to an animal other than a dog, he falters, as if he were at the point of exceeding the conceptual tolerances of his own argument, the place where the "ethical," already overextended into the animal kingdom and thus compromising the putative "newness" of the human "phenomenon," must finally break with the "biological": "I don't know if a snake has a face. I can't answer that question. A more specific analysis is needed" (1988, 172). Without a clear or consistent sense of what the proper trait of the animal *is*, Levinas finds himself – squeamishly? – unable either to say "yes" or "no" to the snake. Summarily to deny the snake what was equivocally given to the dog would perhaps betray too clearly how *Dasein*'s point of view is not neutrally indifferent to the "biological" but, rather, is anthropocentric and even sentimental in its hierarchization of living creatures. The earlier claim that the dog's face could not be entirely disavowed was positively predicated on the possibility, however partial, of there being something like an animal *Dasein*; but Levinas makes it clear at this point that the same claim also negatively opens the way, in theory, for a continuous gradation of refusals that increases the farther "down" the evolutionary scale one looks.

To be fair to Levinas, he does call for additional "analysis" of the question. When considered in the context of his rather dogmatic assertions about human *Dasein*, however, his hesitancy about the snake's face points to the following logic: if the dog's face is mostly denied, and if the snake's face remains unclear, then the notion of the face of, say, the insect, will be more questionable still. Perhaps that visage will be incomprehensible or irrelevant; nothing about Levinas's rhetoric of animality precludes that conclusion and exclusion. Discriminating between animal genera, Levinas never doubts that there is a uniform region – but not quite a neighbourhood – called *animality*, for which any particular creature should stand as an example. But how can one animal genus be "more" animalistic than another at the same time that "animality" as an essentializing concept is expected to maintain any kind of meaningful force? Levinas falls into an anthropological discourse that Derrida (1989, 11) would say "is all the more peremptory and authoritarian for having to hide a discomfiture" – in this case, the tacit concession that "animality" does not describe the nature of living things but is a variably meaningful figure in service of configuring and consolidating the exemplarity of the human.

Working with two different standards of animal exemplarity, Levinas reproduces the oppositional limit between human and animal *within* the realm of the biological. To do so, he relies upon at least two traditional and teleological schema. First, in evoking a biological hierarchy of relative "complexity" that ranks warm-blooded mammals "over" cold-blooded reptiles, Levinas naturalizes the superiority of the dog vis-à-vis the snake. In other words, he makes the putative "biological" proximity of the dog to the human substitute for a nearness in ethical essence – this notwithstanding his explicit insistence that thinking *Dasein* is a function of the founding difference between the "ethical" and the "biological." Second, Levinas is perhaps never more firmly within the grasp of an anthropology than in his choice of exemplary animals. For the "dog" and the "snake" are of course not two living creatures among many but (at least for Jews, Greeks, and Christians, all of whom Levinas invokes in his essay) the very emblems of, on the one hand, dutifulness and unqualified friendship and, on the other hand, irresponsibility, lowliness, and evil bestiality.

"With the appearance of the human – and this is my entire philosophy – there is something more important than my life, and that is the life of the other" (Levinas 1988, 172). By this point we need hardly say that the "other" to which Levinas refers is paradigmatically the other human, whose importance is marked by its ability to stand outside "nature" and the "biological." As Derrida (1995, 284) observes, "What is still to come or what remains buried in an almost inaccessible memory is the thinking of a responsibility that does not stop at *this* determination of the neighbour, at the dominant scheme of this determination." For Levinas, only the human is truly subjected to and by the injunction, "Thou shalt not kill." The sixth commandment is the basis for all ethics; it is the "primordial expression," "the first word" that configures the human, summoning it to an asymmetrical locution before it has said or done anything: "to see a face is already to hear: 'thou shalt not kill'" (Levinas, 8). But Levinas leaves unexplained how the human grasps the importance of "the *life* of the other" and thus comprehends the possibility of its *death*, while at the same time being something completely different from the "vitality" of living things. We might ask Levinas the same question that Derrida (1989, 120) asks Heidegger: "What is death for a *Dasein* that it is never defined *essentially* as a living thing?" What can "life" and "death" mean in the discourse of the "ethical" once it is decisively divided from the realm of the merely "biological"? (We might also reverse the terms of the question and ask what an "animal" is if it attaches "importance" to its own life but remains constitutively incapable, which is to say, *in all cases*, unable either to intimate "the life of the other" or to bear responsibility for it? But what then is "life" for the mortal animal that it should be said not to mourn the death of the other life?) If the face of the animal does not confront us, then the "asymmetrical relation with the other" (Levinas, 1969, 225) is rendered impossible, and the interdiction that is the basis of ethics has no binding effect.

Of course, within the human neighbourhood the sixth commandment can hardly be said to have been scrupulously obeyed; it is, as Levinas (1988, 169) says, an "authority … without force." The face is a "demand" that remains as the possibility of ethics whether we accept or deny that "demand." But even its refusal is reappropriated to the anthropocentric axioms governing Levinas's discourse. We see this perhaps most clearly in *Totality and Infinity*, where Levinas (1969, 222) argues that "violence" and "war … presuppose the face and the transcendence of the being appearing in the face."

If "Thou shalt not kill" means "Thou shalt not kill – except in certain cases, for example, in battle," then the privilege of this murderous exception also lies entirely with the human. Humans "hunt" animals and "labour" with nature, to be sure, but because the objects of these confrontations lack a face, Levinas claims, it cannot accurately be said that "warfare" or "violence" is carried out against them. To some extent, this curious and somewhat worrisome claim is informed by the distinction – which we have already encountered – Heidegger makes when he distinguishes between the dying (*Sterben*) of *Dasein* and the perishing (*Verenden*) of beings that are merely alive. In the case of Levinas, the entitlement of pursuing war, and thus of suffering its fatal violence, lies properly with "Man" and is an element of the propriety of "Man." According to this logic, animals are not bona fide casualties; they are hunted down and they perish, but they do not die in battle with human beings. (Interestingly, by the time he writes his essay on Bobby, Levinas will recognize this denegation of murder for what it is – making killing into a kind of sport.)

By extension, it could be argued, it *is* argued, that the agricultural-industrial-technological complex does not carry out warfare against the natural world; rather, it "develops" and "cultivates"[12] the "wilderness," the myriad regions that lie outside of the neighbourhood of "civilized" "Man." This is not merely a question of semantics but of the ways in which philosophemes like "warfare" and "violence" are put into the service of configuring the human, and of policing a series of mutually reinforcing boundaries that divide realms, each of which is imagined to be separately homogeneous – "human" and "non-human," "Man" and "nature." But if it is not warfare that has been conducted against the buffalo, the Brazilian rainforest, and the animalized human (the terrible epithets "savage" and "Gook," or, more recently, the Serbo-Croation slur, *zuti mrav* ["yellow ant" or "pest"] come to mind), to cite only a few examples, then what is it? What is effaced or ignored by restricting "warfare" to mean the systematic violence of humans against humans as something peculiar to *Dasein*, the sole creature capable of apprehending "the importance of the life of the other"? In as much as Levinas designates the human neighbourhood as the "totality" that is exemplarily capable of suffering the violence of war, he saves the global village by destroying it, or at least by exposing it to the possibility of its destruction. But, as always, the perimeter marking the human from the non-human, the faced from those without faces, is unstable, disrupted, subjected to differences that cannot be contained by the separating out the "ethical" from the "biological" (but *not* thereby collapsing one region into the other). If these complications were not always already in place, then why would there be any need for the kinds of imperious, insistent moves characterizing Levinas's discourse (and not only his, as we have seen in the case of Heidegger) with respect to the enigma of the animal?

At the risk of being too literal-minded, I might quickly recall – and then only interrogatively – the horrific case of the Vietnam War in order to throw into relief both the limitations of Levinas's claim and the need to think of a responsibility that does not stop at his determination of the neighbour. Could one meaningfully describe what the American military – among other armies – did to the human population of Vietnam as *warfare* and not extend that term to describe what it also did, and with equally systematic ferocity, to the Vietnamese countryside using Agent Orange (a herbicide whose chemical components were partly produced in Canada)? At what point could one distinguish between the destruction of an agricultural way of life and the people living that life? Perhaps only a so-called First World culture, which is to say a culture that knows nothing of the realities of subsistence farming, could afford to call one form of violence "warfare" and the other, using the jargon of the motorized food industry, the work of "defoliation." What ideology of homogeneity would need to be in place, what oppositional limits would need to be inscribed in the name of the exemplarity of human *Dasein*, in order for one to say that the American military did not *murder* Vietnam, the land, its ways of life, its peoples, its animals? Or that the peoples and the animals and the place in which they all dwelled did not *differently* command a form of absolute respect from the United States, that they did not *differently* summon the army of occupation to the originary obligation, *Thou shalt not kill*?

Although Levinas does not say it this way, only by projecting a face upon non-human others, and thus subjecting them to the rhetorical violence of a prosopopoeia, can they be said to be murdered. But who is to say that one manner of speaking about killing is rhetorically aberrant and the other proper, or that some creatures die and others cease living? *Totality and Infinity* suggests that we can say that we conduct "warfare" against animals only by anthropomorphically confusing that ferocity with what is actually happening – namely, "hunting". Similarly, "violence" bears only upon human *Dasein*, whereas bringing force to bear upon the faceless elements "reduce[s] itself to a labour" (Levinas 1969, 142). But he can make this claim only by ignoring how "warfare" and "violence" are themselves figures – figures that carry out the work of *anthropomorphizing* "Man" by differentially positing those qualities that make human living and dying *human*, over and against the non-violence that is imagined to happen to the faceless animals and elements. In this anthropocentric universe, animals and the elements of the "natural" world are the objects of human action – hunting, labour – rather than entities that oblige us fundamentally.

The being-war of war and the being-human of humanity are here openly, deeply complicit with each other, a complicity we might consider when we think of the denegations of murder once the non-human is decreed not to have a face, the alibis that always put the human somewhere else, doing something else when it comes to killing animals and dehumanized or animalized humans: the "culling" and "management" of herds, the "euthanization" of laboratory animals, but also the "cleansing" and "pacification" of human populations, the "saving" of villages by their incineration, and the "manufacturing" (*die Fabrikation*) of corpses. Above all, Levinas teaches us *not* to analogize incomparably different deaths, with too little to say or care about their differences, in the manner of Heidegger. In the essay on Bobby, as I have argued, he even obliges us to think of human and animal deaths as capable of illuminating each other in their separate darknesses. For the most part, however, Levinas's neighbourhood remains resolutely human. As Derrida (1995, 279) argues, "The 'Thou shalt not kill' – with all its consequences, which are limitless – has never been understood within the Judeo-Christian tradition, nor apparently by Levinas, as a 'Thou shalt not put to death the living in general.'" The sixth commandment has a double force in culture: not only, as Levinas contends, as the interdiction that commands obligation to the human other but also as tacit *permission* to think the animal others, and all the living things for which the "animal" comes zoomorphically to stand, as lying "outside" of the neighbourhood of call and response. To this extent, Derrida sees a striking similarity between Heidegger and Levinas: "In spite of the differences separating them, they nonetheless remain profound humanisms *to the extent that they do not sacrifice sacrifice.*" For both, the human subject lives "in a world where sacrifice is possible and where it is not forbidden to make an attempt on life in general, but only on human life, on the neighbour's life" (279).

The Cyborg Kantian

> Animals; difficulty of explaining these.
>
> F.W.J. Schelling, *On the History of Modern Philosophy*

> Beneficence toward those in need is a universal duty of men, just because they are to be considered fellow men, that is, as rational beings with needs, united by nature in one dwelling place so that they can help each other.
>
> Immanuel Kant, *The Metaphysics of Morals*

To the extent that Levinas asks us to reconsider the consecrated butchery of everyday life, Derrida's assessment cannot be entirely correct. For a moment, Levinas in fact *does* appear willing to sacrifice sacrifice, or at least to put into question the humanism that is rightly appalled at the murder of Jews but less worried about the killing of animals. But if he is willing to extend the neighbourhood encompassed by the sixth commandment to the animals at the beginning of his essay, by its conclusion he decisively returns to the anthropocentric universe in which Derrida finds him dwelling. That return and reinscription of the privilege of the human is most complexly evident in the account of Bobby with which my remarks began, especially in his characterization as the "last Kantian in Nazi Germany." Let us return to the story that is on Levinas's mind from the beginning of his essay, but whose details are relayed only in its closing sentences. For a few weeks, "about halfway through our long captivity," Levinas writes, the Nazi guards allowed "a wandering dog to enter into our lives." The prisoners call him "Bobby, an exotic name, as one does with a cherished dog." "He would appear at morning assembly and was waiting for us as we returned, jumping up and down and barking in delight. For him, there was no doubt that we were men" (Levinas 1990b, 153).

For recognizing the faces of the prisoners as *human* faces, rather than as mere instruments, the *technē* of the Nazi regime, Bobby is called a "Kantian," the last of his kind. What can Levinas's striking anthropomorphism mean in this context? The answer to that question is necessarily difficult since Levinas's conception of human obligations to the animal other is here mediated both by his complex relationship with Kant[13] and by Kant's own conception of animals. Most obviously, however, it is Bobby's seemingly dutiful behaviour towards the prisoners that attracts Levinas's ostensibly well-meaning attribution. We might recall that, according to Kant, human beings elicit respect for each other out of a compelling sense that the other person is a rational agent; that is, an agent who is capable of operating freely and thus in a disinterested fashion under the aegis of the moral law. Bobby behaves in a manner that appears to meet Kant's expectations of an unconditioned goodness, a goodness that refers neither to personal qualities or strengths (such as temperament or character) nor to obedience to the particular customs or laws of a society. Moreover, he grasps this founding quality in the prisoners, which, according to the fundamentally anthropocentric axioms of Kant's discourse, is indistinguishable from perceiving them as "men." As Kant (1997b, 14) argues, in observing the comportment of the (human) other, we apprehend the sentiment of profound respect – which he describes as something like "inclination" and "analogous to 'inclination' and 'fear'" – that subjects our "animalistic," non-rational interests in maximizing pleasure and minimizing pain to the force of rational rule. Grasping the freedom in the other to act in a manner that can be universally willed or followed, we necessarily confirm and enact the same freedom in and for ourselves. Until the guards expel him from the slave camp, Bobby is, for Levinas, a living testament to the survival of this moral life, the life that accedes categorically to the imperative: "So act that you use humanity, whether in your own person or in the person of any other, always at the same time as end, never merely as a means" (Kant 1997b, 38).

Levinas pays Bobby this high compliment but instantly qualifies it to the point of retraction. For all of the respect that the dog outwardly embodies in his delighted barking, "friendly growling," and wagging tail, and, notwithstanding the palpable way in which Levinas is moved by this show of affection and understanding, Bobby remains inwardly deficient, "without the brains needed to universalize maxims and drives" (Levinas 1990b, 153). He is too stupid, "*trop bête*," the French condensing idiocy and animality into one crassly anthropocentric expression. Bobby makes up for the absence of unconditional goodness in the human neighbourhood; indeed, he embodies the last stand of that goodness. But because he lacks the know-how and the liberty truly to stop himself from acting in a way that cannot be universalized, he is only a kind of simulation. In a land that is all but devoid of freedom and rationality, Levinas puts to us, Bobby is as good as goodness gets. But his actions are at best a moral addendum to and substitute for true dutifulness. Although he looks like a Kantian and sounds like a Kantian, and has a humanizing effect on the prisoners that is explicitly called Kantian, he is *not* Kantian. How could he be? "The dog is a dog. Literally a dog!" (152). Levinas is adamant that we not misinterpret Bobby, lest we fall into fanciful stories about the faithfulness of animals: this is not Ithaca, and I am not Ulysses, he flatly reminds us. By characterizing the ethical and ontological question that Bobby vividly poses as a hermeneutical problem, however, Levinas deflects attention from the discomfiture that prompts his austere claim that Bobby is a kind of depthless surface, the experience of which should not be confused with the apprehension of the moral law that Kant reserves for humans and humans alone.

Because he is immured in his creatureliness, Bobby is putatively not at liberty to behave otherwise than according to his more or less craven interests. As such, he embodies Levinas's (1988, 172) conviction that "the being of animals ... is a struggle for life without ethics." Seen in this light, his reiterated desire to speak as literally and as unsentimentally as possible about animals takes on somewhat less flattering connotations: "the dog is a dog" is not a benignly neutral description, still less a deanthropomorphizing attempt to let the dog be what it is, free from its human configurations but, quite to the contrary, a disciplinary action whose tautological form captures Levinas's desire to seal Bobby up in the prison of his species lest he say more or do more than what is anthropocentrically allotted him.

The most telling irony is that, in qualifying his claim that Bobby is the "last Kantian in Nazi Germany" on the grounds that he lacks "the brains needed to universalize maxims and drives," Levinas almost exactly reproduces Kant's estimation of animals.[14] As Kant (1991, 237) argues, animals are not morally relevant creatures as such since they lack reason:

As far as reason alone can judge, man has duties only to men (himself and other men), since his duty to any subject is moral constraint by that subject's will. Hence, the constraining (binding) subject must, *first*, be a person; and this person must, *second*, be given as an object of experience, since man is to strive for the end of this person's will and this can happen only in a relation to each other of two beings that exist.

Without the *logos*, animals cannot directly oblige us, and, without obliging us, we are not bound to respect them in return. "But from all our experience we know of no being other than man that would be capable of obligation," Kant contends: "Man can therefore have no duty to any beings other than men" (1991, 237). Knowing full well how animals evoke warm sentiments in us and clearly concerned that we not purchase this pathos too cheaply, too uncritically, while we gaze into the eyes of our favourite horse or dog, Kant insists that we reflect more carefully on what it is we are actually doing when we show kindness to animals. If it appears that I have responsibilities to animals, he suggests, this is because I have failed to distinguish between two distinct kinds of duties: direct duties *towards* (*gegen*) an entity regarded as an end in itself, and indirect duties *with regard to* or *on behalf of* (*in Ansehung*) an entity regarded as a means to an end (237).[15] According to this schema, Bobby cannot be "Kantian" except by a conceptual and rhetorical confusion that transposes what is properly due to the human *onto* the non-human. Kant calls this impropriety "amphiboly," but we might recognize it as the trope of prosopopoeia – the giving of a face to that which is faceless. As creatures of nature, Kant argues, animals are not ends in themselves and, as such, are closer to the category of things than to persons. This does not mean that we are free to be unkind towards them, but the argument for abstaining from cruelty is that it debases human beings, who remain the rule against which to measure all forms of respect. (Kant [1997a] thus applauds the English for excluding butchers from jury duty; it was thought that their profession would induce a bloody-mindedness towards their human peers!) In so far as animals are thing-like, they do not oblige us directly; but insofar as they are *alive*, and in that quickness capable of mimicking the freedom that is the essential trait of humanity, animals do oblige us in an *in*direct fashion:

> Animal nature has analogies to human nature, and by doing our duties to animals in respect of manifestations which correspond to manifestations of human nature, we indirectly do our duty towards humanity. Thus, if a dog has served his master long and faithfully, his service, on the analogy of human service, deserves reward. (Kant 1997a)

Like Kant, Levinas readily concedes that we have duties not to treat animals cruelly. But he is just as resolute in keeping these obligations from unsettling either a certain hierarchical order of life or the boundaries that institute the human subject. This, from the same interview in which he questions the face of the dog: "It is clear that, without considering animals as human beings, the ethical extends to all living beings. We do not want to make an animal suffer needlessly and so on. But the prototype of this is human ethics" (Levinas 1988, 172). It is unclear whether animals – without ethics and, for the most part, without a face – can be entities for which humans can have any sort of underived responsibilities, which is to say, responsibilities that would throw into question the primacy of the human neighbourhood. Bobby may be too preoccupied with his "struggle for life" to warrant the sort of obligations that are reserved for those creatures who think and have a "face" that one could turn *towards* rather than merely *regard*. As Llewelyn has brilliantly demonstrated, "in the metaphysical ethics of Levinas I can have direct responsibilities only toward beings that can speak, and this means beings that have a rationality that is presupposed by the universalizing reason that is fundamental in the metaphysics of ethics of Kant" (1991b, 57).

Like the biblical exemplar to which Levinas compares him, Bobby has "neither ethics nor *logos*" (152), and these absences have the curious effect of rendering him lifeless while still somehow remaining "alive." Signalling dutifulness without actually knowing or speaking this obligation, without phenomenologically experiencing respect in the manner that Kant describes it, as "something" like "fear," "something" like "inclination" (1997b, 14), Bobby is thus closer to a cyborg than to a sentient creature; he is not unlike an empty machine of the sort Descartes hallucinated when he looked at animals. But he is such a strangely attractive machine, fond thoughts of which haunt Levinas's darkest recollections. "I am thinking of Bobby" means, after all, "Witless creature though he is, I cannot forget him." The dog's declared moral status as a kind of animal-robot is strikingly at odds with the richly evocative details of his encounter with the prisoners, details that invite us – albeit against the grain of Levinas's anthropocentrism – to think *otherwise* about the nature of responding and responsibility, and thus to unsettle the oppositional limit that would confine what are confusedly called "language," "rationality," and "ethics" solely to the human sphere.

Perhaps in dismissing the dog as *trop bête,* Levinas denies intellectually what he is compelled to acknowledge at an affective level. He may well disqualify Bobby as an authentic Kantian on "technical" grounds, but the brusqueness of his name-calling comes across as a defensive gesture made in the face of a danger it inadvertently reveals. For what *is* Bobby doing when, by Levinas's own moving account, he so gaily greets the prisoners and recognizes them as "other" – that is, as "men"? More: what is "language" if it is not the wagging of a tail, and "ethics" if it is not the ability to greet one another and to dwell together *as* others? Levinas says Bobby is brainless, as if he were absent from his own actions, yet this claim only throws into relief the forceful and articulate enigma of the dog's *presence* in the camp, the ways in which he obliges us to reconsider what we think we mean by *logos,* "animal," and, of course, "we." Notwithstanding Levinas's desire to say "no" to the animal, Bobby's face cannot be entirely refused, not because there is something residually "human" or "prehuman" about it but precisely because of its non-human excess, because that face, screened though it is through Levinas's axiomatic discourse, constitutes a "yes" that is not a "yes," a "yes" belonging uniquely to the animal, to *this* animal, and given freely to the human prisoners. It goes without saying that "gift" and "freedom," like "animal" and "human," are all figures put in question by the call of this enigmatic communication, always before us and beyond us. What then is the *logos* that it cannot account for Bobby's languages, and for the multiplication of languages and the differences between languages across the oppositional limit dividing human from animal? Language is the implacable human standard against which the animal is measured and always found wanting; but what if the "animal" were to become the site of an excess against which one might measure the prescriptive, exclusionary force of the *logos,* the ways in which the truth of the rational word muffles, strangles, and finally silences the animal?

These questions are worth asking, it seems to me, because of the "audible" gap between what Bobby says and what Levinas hears him say. To his ears, the dog's language sounds like silence, albeit a silence with an illustrious pedigree. As the essay's concluding sentence confidently informs us, Bobby's "friendly growling, his animal faith, was born from the silence of his forefathers on the banks of the Nile" (Levinas 1990b, 153). In Exodus 11:7, to which Levinas is here referring, the dogs fall silent as mute witnesses to the righteousness of those who belong to the living God of Israel. While death moves across Egypt to claim all of its firstborn and an unprecedented out-pouring of grief is heard across the land, Israel remains tranquil and safe. Even the witless dogs are compelled to recognize that fact:

> A rabble of slaves will celebrate this high mystery of man, and "not a dog shall growl." At the supreme hour of his institution, with neither ethics nor *logos*, the dog will attest to the dignity of its person. *This* is what the friend of man means. There is a transcendence in the animal! (152, emphasis mine)

Levinas's exclamation has several connotations here. It recalls the Tal-mudic scholars who are wondrously struck by the phenomenon of a crea-ture who finds itself out of its place in the order of things: "the paradox of a pure nature leading to rights" (152). "Transcendence" also reminds us of Bobby's function as a silent and surrogate witness. As Shoshana Felman (1992, 3) argues, for Levinas the "witness's speech is one which, by its very definition, transcends the witness who is but its medium, the medium of the realization of the testimony." This transcendence would seem literally and even parodically to be the case with the dog, who involuntarily attests to the dignity of "man" without grasping the significance of what it has done. But where the lacuna between the witness and the witness's speech (or, we could say, between the performative and constative functions of the testimonial act) exposes the human to "the absolutely other," to whom it is held "hostage," in the animal this transcendent convocation serves the sole function of confirming the exemplarity of the human: it is the animal's privilege not only unwittingly to be held hostage by the human other but also never to be *autrui* for "man." According to an authoritarian logic that informs almost all of Levinas's essay, by which the animal has in the mode of not-having, the dog is granted the power to be more than itself only insofar as it rigorously remains itself – *dans l'animal* – vis-á-vis "Man." The terms of this paradoxical, and, as it were, one-sided responsibility are cor-roborated by Levinas's uncertain pronoun reference – "This" – which makes it impossible to determine whether the dog is "the friend of man" in spite of or *because* it lacks "ethics" and "*logos*." It may well be that, as long as animals are quiet, as long as they remain speechless and stupid, they will be allowed into the neighbourhood of the human – but always under the threat of deportation – to perform a certain supplemental witnessing work.

If the animal speaks, it will speak only silence, in deference to those who truly possess language and ethics.

What is important here, however, is the way in which the muteness of the animal resonates with Levinas's account of his treatment by his captors. In this silence, which is decidedly *not* a silence at all but, rather, articulate gestures and sounds peremptorily *figured* and denegated as silence, it is impossible not to hear an echo of the muteness to which Levinas is reduced by the Nazis. For Levinas, nothing captures the violence of anti-Semitism more powerfully than the Nazis' unwillingness to hear the suffering voices of their prisoners. The unspeakable Holocaust begins with an assault on the language of its victims, and, for that reason, Levinas's account of life in Camp 1492 is rich with semiotic metaphors and turns upon a series of thwarted, interned, and strangled speech acts. "The strength and wretchedness of persecuted people" resounds through the camp yet is reduced to "a small inner murmur" (Levinas 1990b, 153), heard only in the heart of the prisoners. Their richly diverse languages – written, gestural, affective – go perversely unnoticed, held in a kind of suspended animation: "our sorrow and laughter, illnesses and distractions, the work of our hands and the anguish of our eyes, the letters we received from France and those accepted for our families – all passed in parenthesis" (153). So important is the connection between language and responsibility that Levinas can only describe the heartless abrogation of the latter in semiotic terms as the sundering of significance itself. For him, Nazi racism "shuts people away in a class, deprives them of expression and condemns them to being 'signifiers without a signified'" (153). Summing up the experience of these silencings, Levinas asks: "How can we deliver a message about our humanity which, from behind the bars of quotation marks, will come across as anything other than monkey talk?" (153). Monkey talk? For the Nazis a languageless human is nothing more than an animal; but what is "animality" that it not only names the incoherence to which the Nazis reduce the Jews but also represents the figure that comes most readily to hand to describe what it feels like to live and survive that degradation?

Reading this bestializing figure, I am thinking of Bobby's barking and of the ancient assumption, against all intuitive evidence, that animal sounds are merely *phonē asēmos*, "signifiers without a signified." When we are told that Levinas and his fellow prisoners "were beings entrapped in their species … beings without language" (153), we might be forgiven for recalling what this essay so matter-of-factly says about Bobby in almost exactly the same words. For a disconcerting moment, the prisoners and the dog threaten to exchange their differently silenced spaces – a crossing made all the more troublesome in an essay that begins, as I have argued, by asking us to consider the butchery of animals against the backdrop of the extermination of the Jews. Can we find the words to answer for the contiguity of these silences? How *not* to speak of it? How to read the Nazi subjection of the Jews and Levinas's subjection of the animal *slowly enough*?

Levinas naturalizes his anthropocentric projections on Bobby by seeing them from the reverse angle: the prisoner watches the dog watching the prisoners and, in watching, ostensibly witnessing the truth of their humanity. Simultaneously welcomed, regulated, and expelled, Bobby traces and retraces the oppositional limits that configure the human and the animal. Surviving "in some wild patch in the region of the camp" (Levinas 1990b, 153), he is the subaltern who, for a time, moves freely from the untamed margins of Camp 1492 into its closely surveilled and policed interior. He is the outsider who accidentally befalls Levinas's world, yet the very fact that he instantly recognizes the men *as* men reminds us that he is a domesticated creature and, thus, already a dweller *inside*, with and among humans. As befits the savagely dystopic conditions of the slave camp, the dog reverses the function of the scapegoat and is received *into* the polis to perform a certain purifying work, only to be cast out by the guards after "a few short weeks," thereby returning the camp to its savage "integrity." The introjection of Bobby's (simulated) goodness restores a minimal health to the camp, yet his inclusion is also inseparable from his summary exclusion from the neighbourhood of human freedom and rationality. *Mon semblable, – mon frère*: at once beneficial, inasmuch as he augurs the last remnants of a Kantian dutifulness (and, for that is named and cherished), *and* risky, insofar as he provisionally substitutes for the human, speaking out of turn when no one else speaks (and, for that, carefully treated with unsentimental caution). He is the good medicine whose salutary effects are powerful enough to reach far forward into Levinas's future; but his impact is finally only a placebo effect, or perhaps a form of animal triage in a time of terrible need. Bobby performs a limited testimonial function, speaking for the other without the *logos*; but this role is a temporary measure, in earnest of the true human witness whose account – in the form of Levinas's essay – has always already usurped Bobby's place in our reading of it.

Notes

1 Versions and portions of this chapter were presented at the meetings of the Modern Language Association (San Diego 1994), the North American Society for the Study of Romanticism (Durham 1995), and the Kentucky Foreign Language Association (1996). For listening to and commenting upon this chapter, I am very grateful to Peter Babiak, Stephen Barber, Rebecca Gagan, Jennifer Ham, Alice Kuzniar, Matthew Senior, Patricia Simmons, and Tracy Wynne. This chapter was prepared for republication with the able assistance of Naureen Hamidani and Lisa Devries. Research for this project was partially funded by the Social Sciences and Humanities Research Council of Canada and by the Arts Research Board of McMaster University.

2 "Beyond Pathos" is the title of the opening section of *Difficult Freedom*.

3 The homelessness of this "home" is brought out by Levinas (1990b, 152), who remarks upon the "extraordinary coincidence" of the "fact that the camp bore the number 1492, the year of the expulsion of the Jews from Spain under the Catholic Ferdinand V."

4 And yet one way of instantly complicating this point would be to consider more carefully the telling ambiguities and strange torsions characterizing conceptions of animality in Nazi Germany. "Virtually nothing has been written about the Nazis' bizarre attitudes towards animals," Goldhagen (1996, 566) points out (but see Arluke and Sax 1992). By way of initiating the important task of that history, Goldhagen documents the dutiful attention that Germans paid to animals. Police battalions were regularly issued orders compelling Germans to provide dogs with good veterinary care - this, of course, while Jews were barred from medical attention or were summarily executed for being sick or being characterized as sick. Goldhagen rightly asks, "Did the killers ... not reflect on the difference in treatment they were meting out to dogs and Jews?" (268).

> The orders concerning dogs might have provoked the Germans to think about their vocation if their sensibilities had remotely approximated our own; the comparison in their expected treatment of dogs and their actual treatment of Jews might have fostered in the Germans self-examination and knowledge. Yet, however much the reading of these orders about dogs would have evoked disturbing comparisons in non-Nazified people, the effect of the series of orders sent out regarding "cruelty to animals" (*Tierquälerie*) would have likely been to the non-Nazified psychologically gripping, even devastating. (269)

Does Levinas's essay spring from such devastating knowledge? That is, does his reflection upon "Bobby" and upon animals emerge in part from the realization that it is the Nazified Germans who are being urged to be "Kantians," according to animals the fundamental respect that is denied to the Jews?

A history of the Nazis and animals would undoubtedly need to include a discussion of the phenomenon of keeping animals for viewing and for pleasurable entertainment *within* the death camps. What, we might ask, is the mirroring status of a "camp" devoted to the incarcerated preservation of (animal) life *inside* a camp whose function it is to annihilate (human) life? See, for example, the extraordinary photographs of the zoo cached within the confines of Treblinka in Klee, Dressen, and

Reiss (1988, 226–7). Others who have written tellingly about the Nazis and animals include Ferry (1995) (see especially the chapter entitled "Nazi Ecology: The November 1933, July 1934, and June 1935 Legislations" [91-107]). Examining the legislation regarding the treatment and protection of animals drafted out at the behest of the National Socialist party, Ferry makes the fascinating point that the Nazis were radically original in "that, for the first time in history, the animal, as a natural being, is protected *in its own right, and not with respect to men.* A long humanist, even humanitarian, tradition defended the idea that it was indeed necessary to prohibit cruelty toward animals, but more because it translated a bad disposition of human nature, or even risked inciting humans to perform violent acts, than because it was prejudicial to the interests of the animals themselves" (99). In other words, the Nazis urged Germans to accord animals the respect that they categorically demanded by virtue of being *alive.* From the point of view of the *Tierschutzgesetz* (laws providing for the protection of animals), the Kantian notion of respect is lacking because it confines dutiful obligation only to other human beings. And as Ferry points out, the argument for the sanctity of animal life is made at the same time as "Jewish barbarity" involving "ritual slaughter" of animals is condemned, and while pages are devoted to ensuring the safe passage of animals "by train" across Germany and German territories (101).

5 Matthew Senior has reminded me that Eugène Ionesco "animalizes" the Nazis in *Rhinoceros.*

6 The phrase is from Jacques Derrida and is discussed at length later in this chapter. See Derrida (1995, 280).

7 Nancy uses this phrase in one of his questions to Derrida. See Derrida (1995, 285).

8 I follow the translation of Sheehan (1988). Part of the German text is found in Schirmacher (1983, 25).

9 Derrida discusses the "contradictory and impossible" logic underwriting Heidegger's claim (in *Sein und Zeit*) that "the animal has a world in the mode of not-having" (Derrida 1989, 47-57).

10 I am thinking here of Heidegger's use of this phrase in *Being and Time.* See Heidegger (1972, 50).

11 I borrow and modify David Farrell Krell's (1992, 8) insight into Heidegger's vexed view of animal life: "Unfortunately, the clear division of ontic from ontological, and biological from existential, depends upon a scission in being that ostensibly would divide Dasein from just-plain-life without making such life absolutely inaccessible to it."

12 William Spanos (1993, 196), whose work on Heidegger and on the technological perspective of the West *after* Heidegger powerfully informs this section of my chapter, points out that "to cultivate and bring to fruition" means "'to colonize' in the Roman sense of the word."

13 Space prevents me from addressing the important question of how Levinas's critique of Kant colours the argument of "The Name of a Dog, or Natural Rights." We should recall that, for Levinas, Kant's understanding of "obligation" is insufficiently scandalous. As Jean-François Lyotard (1988, 112) argues: "If I am obligated by the other, it is not because the other has some right to obligate me which I would have directly or mediately granted him or her. My freedom is not the source of his or her authority: one is not obligated because one is free, and because your law is my law, but because your request is not my law, because we are liable for the other. Oblig-

ation through freedom or consent is secondary." Perhaps one way in which Levinas signals the "secondariness" of Kantian obligation is by ambivalently attributing it to an *animal*, indeed, an animal whose kind is on the verge of extinction. The fact that respect has, as it were, gone to the dogs, may say as much about the inherent limitations of Kant's conception of obligation as it does about the exterminating violence of "Nazi Germany."

14 For a useful summary of Kant's position with respect to animals, see Broadie and Pybus (1974) and Naragon (1990).

15 For the German, see Kant (1912–23, vol. 7, 256).

16 Levinas (1981, 125): "The responsibility for another, an unlimited responsibility which the strict book-keeping of the free and non-free does not measure, requires subjectivity as an irreplaceable hostage."

Works Cited

Arluke, Arnold, and Boria Sax. 1992. "Understanding Nazi Animal Protection and The Holocaust." *Anthrozoos* 1 (Spring): 6–31.

Broadie, Alexander, and Elizabeth M. Pybus. 1974. "Kant's Treatment of Animals." *Philosophy* 49: 375–83.

Caputo, John D. 1993. *Against Ethics: Contributions to a Poetics of Obligation with Constant Reference to Deconstruction*. Bloomington and Indianapolis: Indiana University Press.

Derrida, Jacques. 1987. "On Reading Heidegger: An Outline of Remarks to the Essex Colloquium." *Research in Phenomenology* 17: 171–88.

– 1989. *Of Spirit: Heidegger and the Question*. Trans. Geoffrey Bennington and Rachel Bowlby. Chicago: University of Chicago Press.

– 1990. "Force of Law: The Mystical Foundation of Authority.'" Trans. Mary Quaintance. *Cardoza Law Review* 11 (5–6): 919–1039.

– 1995. "'Eating Well,' or the Calculation of the Subject." Trans. Avital Ronell. In *Points: Interviews, 1974–1994*, ed. Elisabeth Weber, 155–87. Stanford: Stanford University Press.

Felman, Shoshana. 1992. "Education and Crisis, or the Vicissitudes of Teaching." In *Testimony: Crises of Witnessing in Literature, Psychoanalysis, and History*, by Shoshana Felman and Dori Laub, 1–56. London: Routledge.

Ferry, Luc. 1995. *The New Ecological Order*. Trans. Carol Volk. Chicago: University of Chicago Press.

Goldhagen, Daniel Jonah. 1996. *Hitler's Willing Executioners: Ordinary Germans and the Holocaust*. New York: Vintage.

Hand, Seán. 1989. "Time and the Other." In *The Levinas Reader*, ed. Seán Hand, 37–8. Oxford: Basil Blackwell.

Heidegger, Martin. 1968. *What Is Called Thinking*. Trans. J. Glenn Gray. New York: Harper and Row.

– 1971. *On the Way to Language*. Trans. Peter D. Hertz: New York: Harper and Row.

– 1972. *Sein und Zeit*. Tübingen: M. Niemeyer.

– 1985. *Schelling's Treatise on the Essence of Human Freedom*. Trans. Joan Stambaugh. Athens, Ohio: Ohio University Press.

– 1993. "Letter on Humanism." In *Basic Writings*, ed. and trans. David Farrell Krell, 213–65. San Francisco: Harper Collins.

Kant, Immanuel. 1912–23. *Immanuel Kants Werke.* Gen. Ed. Ernst Cassirer. Vol. 7. Berlin: Cassirer.

– 1963. *Lectures on Ethics.* Trans. L. Infield. New York: Harper Torchbooks.

– 1991. *The Metaphysics of Morals.* Intro. and Trans. Mary Gregor. Cambridge: Cambridge University Press.

– 1997a. *Lectures on Ethics.* Ed. Peter Heath and J.B. Schneewind. Trans. Peter Heath. Cambridge: Cambridge University Press.

– 1997b. *Groundwork of the Metaphysics of Morals.* Ed. and trans. Mary Gregory. Cambridge: Cambridge University Press.

Klee, Ernst, Willi Dressen, and Volker Reiss, eds. 1988. *"The Good Old Days": The Holocaust as Seen by Its Perpetrators and Bystanders.* New York: Free Press.

Klein, Richard. 1995. "The Power of Pets." *The New Republic,* 10 July. 18–23.

Krell, David Farrell. 1992. *Daimon Life: Heidegger and Life-Philosophy.* Bloomington and Indianapolis: Indiana University Press.

Levinas, Emmanuel. 1969. *Totality and Infinity: An Essay on Exteriority.* Trans. Alphonso Lingis. Pittsburgh: Duquesne University Press.

– 1981. *Otherwise than Being; or Beyond Essence.* Trans. Alphonso Lingis. Pittsburgh, PA: Duquesne University Press.

– 1986. "Dialogue with Emmanuel Levinas." In *Face to Face with Levinas,* trans. Richard Kearney, ed. Richard A. Cohen, 13–33. Albany, New York: State University of New York Press.

– 1988. "The Paradox of Morality." In *The Provocation of Levinas: Rethinking the Other,* trans. Andrew Benjamin and Tamra Wright, ed. Robert Bernasconi and David Wood, 168–80. London and New York: Routledge

– 1989. "As if Consenting to Horror." Trans. Paula Wissing. *Critical Inquiry* 15 (Winter): 485–8.

– 1990a. "Foreword." In *Difficult Freedom: Essays on Judaism.* Trans. Seán Hand, xiii–xiv. London: Atholone Press.

– 1990b. "The Name of a Dog, or Natural Rights." In *Difficult Freedom: Essays on Judaism,* trans. Seán Hand, 151–3. London: The Athlone Press. (Published originally in *Celui qui ne peut pas se servir des mots,* Montpellier: Fata Morgana, 1976.)

Lewis, C.S. 1956. *Till We Have Faces: A Myth Retold.* Glasgow: William Collins Sons.

Llewelyn, John. 1991a. "Am I Obsessed by Bobby? (Humanism of the Other Animal)." In *Re-Reading Levinas,* ed. Robert Bernasconi and Simon Critchley, 234–45. Bloomington and Indianapolis: Indiana University Press.

– 1991b. *The Middle Voice of Ecological Conscience: A Chiasmic Reading of Responsibility in the Neighbourhood of Levinas, Heidegger and Others.* London: Macmillan.

Lyotard, Jean-François. 1988. *The Differend: Phrases in Dispute.* Trans. Georges Van Den Abbeele. Minneapolis: University of Minnesota Press.

Naragon, Steve. 1990. "Kant on Descartes and the Brutes." *Kant-Studien* 81, 1: 1–23.

Schirmacher, Wolfgang. 1983. *Technik und Gelassenheit.* Freiburg: Alber.

Sheehan, Thomas. 1988. "Heidegger and the Nazis." *New York Review of Books,* 16 June, 38–47.

Singer, Peter. 1976. *Animal Liberation: Towards an End to Man's Inhumanity to Animals.* London: Jonathan Cape.

Spanos, William V. 1993. *Heidegger and Criticism: Retrieving the Cultural Politics of Destruction.* Minneapolis: University of Minnesota Press.

The Transject: The Ethical Subject of Postmodernity

BARRY RUTLAND

Is there a subject that is not an ethical subject?[1] To what is any subject sub-jected if not ethical exigency – by which I mean, not the necessity to choose to follow this or that ethical prescription but, rather, the unrefusable given-ness of being-in-the-world-with-other-subjects, the state of affairs summa-rized negatively in Sartre's (1962, 91) *Huis clos*, "L'enfer, c'est les Autres"? The positivities of this situation are explored in the writings of Emmanuel Lev-inas (1969, 1981): here ethical exigency reduces, in the Husserlian sense of leads back, to the Face – the demand from the other as a physical body for acknowledgment, recognition, response – before all choosing, before dis-course. Cognitive research indicates that human neonates respond instinc-tively to faces through a precultural genetic engram excited by two dots and a slit within an oval – the maternal face. Indeed, animal ethology suggests that we are not the only species so equipped. Those we live with most inti-mately are precisely the ones that can look us in the eye – as do dogs and cats, who gaze us into attention; wild animals tend to avert their faces from the human gaze. Response to the face – that is, to its labile orifices from which power emanates, the gaze from the eyes and the voice from the mouth – is the ur-semiosis and the ghost of presence that haunts all discourse (see Derrida 1978). Thus the moment of the face-to-face encounter is the moment of relationship, the ethical moment – the inescapable moment of response-ability, answer-ability: Levinas's "Categorical Imperative" of unlan-guaged bodies.

In the following pages I outline a theory of the ethical subject in terms of an understanding of the postmodern moment as a suspension of all imper-atives save that of the Face. I do so by weaving strands of thought drawn from a variety of writers who do not constitute a coherent school but whose ideas resonate dialogically around this issue. The method is allusive rather than rigorous – an eye-glance survey of twentieth-century reflections on lan-guage, discourse, and subjectivity that remarks a state of being under con-ditions of radical incertitude.

Analyses of the ethical, both synchronic and diachronic, could be carried out on the basis of responses to the Face and the historically varying structures of relationship that have evolved to cope with the Face. Who has the right to look who in the face? Whose gaze commands attention, exacts obedience? The (political) subject may approach the sovereign only with eyes downcast or averted (may be obliged to crawl on all fours, face in the dust); only with the acknowledging regard or voice of the sovereign (the sovereign's face may be screened, as at the imperial court of China) can the subject speak: the other bestows identity, being. The face of the sovereign is that which comes before the subject, that posits the subject in its subjectivity; but the sovereign is posited equally by the face of the subject, even in the effacement of abjection, the face in the dust, the no-face. Response to the face – relationship – multiplies it from one to two.

Relationships are gradients of power. Lovers exchange glances, kisses, from face to face, reciprocating power; the racist executioner denies the humanity of the other's face in a one-way channel of abjectification and death. The Face, in the singularity of its bodily materiality, inaugurates relationship; but relationships are realized through genres of discourse and ritual that define and govern their particularity and difference in the name of transcendent law. While posited as a priori and universal, ethical law is the contingent product of particular exigencies, each precisely located historically and culturally. Prescriptive ethics arises from the necessity to transpose the encounter of face to face from bodies to discourse, to make bodies signatory. In Levinasian terms, this is the distinction between the Saying (Dire) and the Said (Dit) – between bodily singularity and discursive iterability (Levinas 1981). With Levinas, it is the ethical moment of the Face that is transcendent, that forever surpasses all the prescriptivisms that arise from encounters with it and that seek to mask and control it. The Face, we might then say, is an immanent transcendence, like the Derridean trace that both is and is not, the process of *différance* whereby communicable meaning arises from the eternal play of undecidability (Derrida 1973). The Face is like the pharmakon of Plato's *Phaedrus* in Derrida's (1981, 63–171) deconstructive reading, at once both cure and poison; it is the Stranger, whose radical otherness challenges one's identity, one's Oneness, with friendship/hostility.

How does One encounter the challenge of the Other of the Face? Generally by countering its immanent transcendence with a ready-made prescriptive transcendence, an ethical rule grounded in the logic of identity. Levinas's (post-Heideggerian) project critiques the metaphysical tradition whereby the Otherness of the Other is subjugated to the Same or the One as its defining binary as, for example, in feminine/masculine, orient/occident (1969, 33–52). Such discursive ready-mades are available in ideology or, more precisely, the Ideological, the rich stew of heterogeneous beliefs, values, representations, images, and rituals in which we all live and move like fish in the sea. Language is generally at hand to name the Face in terms of a limiting identity, honorific or derogatory – to elude its challenge, to reduce it to one's Oneness, assimilate it to one's Sameness. It was Levinas's mission to assert the otherness of alterity – alterity as irreducible to the One or the Same and, thus, a source of knowledge and energy.

Language is generally available in the heterogeneous richness of the Ideological – as long as the Ideological is unconscious of the incommensurabilities and contradictions of that heterogeneity. What, then, of the Face in the Ideological of postmodernity?[2] As a first approximation, we can follow Jean-François Lyotard (1984) and define postmodernity as the condition of culture without ideological centre and boundaries, without the program of what he calls the *grands récits* of progress and emancipation that informed (and justified) the historical conduct of the dominant West from eighteenth-century Enlightenment to twentieth-century Modernism. "Postmodern" signifies a culture that cannot claim to be governed by any hegemonic ideology. Lyotard argues for the end of ideology and the beginning of a culture of narrative pluralism. But the ideological is coextensive with humanness and could end only with the end of language and textuality. At any moment, including that of postmodernity, in any complex culture numerous ideologies, both formal disciplined discourses and informal doxa and mores, are in play; however, generally one, or, what is in fact the usual case, an amalgam of several, is dominant. Thus the bourgeois Enlightenment produced a general ideology that narrativized history as an epic of universal material progress and politico-juridical emancipation compounded of the theory of the social contract, classical political economy, a world system as a concert of autonomous nation-states, the mapping of nature by human reason, the conquest of nature by technology, and the secular perfectability of the species. That these ideological formations are incommensurable (e.g., the artificial state/the natural economy, rationalist universalism/nationalist particularism) is neither here nor there: the Ideological has no more regard for formal consistency than does the unconscious, it being the true collective unconscious of humanity, a vast reservoir of beliefs and practices, both historically realized and *in potentia*, an unbounded ocean of infinite alterity, as the current resurgence of atavistic ideologies demonstrates.

This compound-complex construct hegemonized history from its Euro-American centres for 200 years, marginalizing or co-opting other ideologies, residual or emergent; thus religions, nationalisms, and populisms were harnessed to the bourgeois project, in spite of contradictions and resistances. With the failure of confidence in the bourgeois narrative – at least among those who promoted it in their own interests (i.e., the Europatriarchy) – hitherto residual formations have returned as default ideologies: the fundamentalisms – religious (Islamic, evangelical Protestant, conservative Roman Catholic), political (nationalism, ethnicity), economic (neo-Manchester School, the default ideology of the Anglo-American world) – that are so conspicuous in the postmodern landscape. Simultaneously with the default status of hitherto residual ideologies, new radical ideologies have emerged out of the dissolution – or more accurately, the dissemination – of the Enlightenment project, notably (in the West) those of gender-based movements (feminism, gay/lesbian liberation) and the complex phenomenon known as postcolonialism, grounded in the claims of marginal and subaltern groups, historically excluded from the Enlightenment project, to the desiderata of the *grands récits*. We have not been emancipated into a state of freedom from ideology – the last delusion of the liberal bourgeois narrative – but into ideological flux and ontological incertitude.

Postmodernity foregrounds process over product. Awareness of process, of itself as an effect of process, is central to the postmodern subject and its ethicality. It is not so much a loss of the *grands récits* as the dissolution of those narratives back into the process that generated them in the first place. Poststructuralist theory of subject and text (a distinctive feature of postmodernity as a historical moment) locates subjectivity in process and defines process as discursive: the poststructuralist subject, constituted in and through language – the Ideological – and aware of being so constituted, is the postmodern subject. This process is grounded in alterity. The category of alterity threads through major bodies of poststructuralist theory: the Levinasian, the Bakhtinian,[3] the Derridean, the Lacanian, the Lyotardian inter alia. These alterities differ from one another in terms of the way that each functions within its respective conceptual ensemble: thus the Face of the Other is the ground of a dialogistic ethics with Levinas; the relation of soliciting self to responsive other is the basis of Bakhtin's dialogism; Derrida deconstructs texts precisely to elicit an occluded but constitutive alterity of meaning; the Lacanian subject is precipitated through an encounter with the specular other; Lyotard celebrates the reign of the *petits récits* that assert one's alterity among the alterities of others. These various deployments of the category, differing in provenance and trajectory, nevertheless intersect in terms of the subject and its agency, with implications for a postmodern ethics. Indeed, all are *au fond* ethical in motive and purport: contrary to the view of its detractors, poststructuralism and postmodernism are not dismissive of, but, if anything, preoccupied with the ethical.

Jacques Lacan proposes a subject constituted in and by culture, or the Symbolic Order – the big-O Other of the Ideological, grand and blind like the king of Poe's story, whose non-knowledge nevertheless governs the circulation of the purloined letter (Muller and Richardson 1988). A subject is precipitated at the "second birth" into language and the social order. The process is initiated with the misrecognition of the body of the self in that of the representative other at the Mirror Stage and is brought to operational status through entry into language, which constrains the subject to acknowledge that s/he is (1) a variable term in a kinship system and (2) a shifting pronominal position in discourse – the root experience of othering and being othered. This inaugural event is subsequently reiterated throughout the life of the subject-in-culture. Actual others are read in terms of the symbolic big-O Other of the Ideological that, in Althusser's (1971) phrase, "hails" or interpellates the subject to a vertiginous state of contingent being. The Ideological imbricates the Oedipal Law-of-the-Father with the belief and value systems that, at the level of greatest generality, constitute the governing information of any culture. The subject ex-sists,[4] outside of itself in the desired Other, for desire is always of the Other, in both senses – the Other's desire (the model of the subject's desiring) and desire for the Other's desire, for the Other's constitutive gaze and reassuring voice – desire for/of the Face.

Lyotard's Big Narratives were of the very essence of the big-O Other as hegemonic ideology and universal interpellator in that they provided the guiding and justifying information for the world culture of industrial modernism, capitalist and socialist alike. The discrediting of the *grands récits* by events of the twentieth century, from the First World War to the Holocaust and the Bomb, brought about the shift from modernity – and the heroic culture of modernism – to postmodernity and self-ironizing postmodernism. For the postmodern subject, all the variables have slipped from their traditional hierarchical configurations, and the ensembles are thrown into relations of turbulence, marked by the emergence of new *alter*native discourses that challenge the old and the hegemonic (see above). Postmodern subjectivity manifests itself differentially, according to positioning relative to ideological interpellation: thus men experience feminism as a challenge to patriarchal privilege, women as a challenge to self-assertion; migrants from the Third World experience postcoloniality as pressure to demand recognition from the First World "other," First World citizens as pressure upon their Enlightenment good faith. Indeed, the unfixing of ideological ligatures has brought to the surface of postmodern discourse the presence of the other as a defining category: natives of the First World undergo the dissociating experience of being "othered" by those who historically have constituted the defining margin of their privileged identity. The deconstruction of defining margins entails the reciprocation of "othering" as hitherto abjected faces gaze and speak back. This is the event that conditions postmodern subjectivity and any postmodern ethics.

The socialist versions of the *grands récits* are in eclipse. The capitalist version appears to have triumphed and is without rival as Universal Information. However, it is drained of teleological content: few seriously any longer believe that the capitalist system is the ground and matrix of progress and emancipation. In spite of the fundamentalist revival of "classical" market metaphysics, particularly in the English-speaking world, no one apart from a noisy minority of fanatics really believes, as Enlightenment political economists believed, that private profit-seeking in an unfettered market by rational individuals is the basis of political and moral order and the engine of species progress. What we now have is Social Darwinism without Enlightenment teleology, a thermodynamic process without a goal beyond the reproduction of capital itself. Capitalism is just a way – the only viable way? – of effecting (highly selective) economic growth; otherwise, it is a mindless machine devoid of transcendental purpose. It is pure process. The Father whose rigorous but beneficent discipline informed his children's lives is no more. There is no longer an Interpellator. The postmodern subject is a nonpellated or underpellated or overpellated subject – any of these exclusively or in any combination at any moment: the subject who asks of the noisy surrounding void the Lacanian (1977, 312) question *Che vuoi?* and receives no response.

Is Being possible for such a subject? As far as the discursive field of poststructuralism is concerned, Being is a fiction, posited in relation to the Other. In Lacanian terms, being is a gap, a *béance*. More appropriate than the word "subject," the "thrown under," would be "transject," the "thrown across" – thrown across the gap of non-being that constitutes the site of posited beingness, like the space between the terminals of a spark plug where the spark occurs, an energic leap produced by a gap in the flow (Lacan 1977, 157). The notion of agency is unavoidable in a discussion of the ethical subject, but with a transjective subject it is problematized. Availing oneself of the curious "swivel" character of "agent" in legal discourse, the subject can be defined as simultaneously the actor and the acted upon: an agent is s/he who acts on behalf of another, the principal. "Agent" and "agency," then, combine the conditions of delegation and responsibility. That which the agent does is assigned by the other, the principal, who may remain utterly concealed – indeed, who, as the big-O Other, does not even exist, merely exsists, according to Lacan. Who is responsible? The individual actor responds to the sociocultural Other as the agent of the Other, which cannot manifest itself except through the action of the agent, who cannot act except as constituted and in-formed by the Other. The individual as subject is s/he who at one and the same time is both the passively predicated and actively predicating in terms of agency. A "settled" culture organized in terms of relatively fixed value parameters permits a relatively "steady state" of ethical subjectivity: the agent knows who its principal is and how to conduct its agency. It knows how to respond to which faces. Such a settled culture involves reiterated interpellation and sustained, uniform repression. The conditions of subjectivity itself are concealed in apparent ineluctability. An "unsettled" culture throws the process into relief, reveals the critical condition of subjectivity, subjectivity as transjectivity, agency as predicated predicating – no longer "thrown under" the conquering wheels of triumphant Truth but "thrown across" the now palpable ideological emptiness. The subject becomes uneasily aware of the process that produces it.

What modalities of agency are available to the postmodern transject exposed to awareness of constitutive processes hitherto concealed by cultural integuments? How is an ethics possible for a subject who encounters the face of the other without mediation, so that the Face is always, so to speak, in one's face? Before addressing this question, let us dwell a moment on what appears to be no more than a fortuitous concurrence between a feature of the Levinasian Face and the Lacanian Real. Each is prediscursive: the face in the immanent transcendence of mute (ethical) Saying challenges all that is confidently (ontologically) Said; the Real confronts the Symbolic order as unspeakable Thing (see Benevuto and Kennedy 1986, 166). Reflection on this coincidence suggests a homology of Face and Thing: Levinas's positive "take" on the moment of the Face is the benign other of Lacan's irruption of the Real into the Symbolic, into the self-sealing illusory plenitude of an ethical subjectivity constituted in terms of ethical normativity. Thus response to the Face through resort to ready-made valuations is a compulsive swerve to plug the sudden puncture in subjectivity that opens a vertiginous window on to both menace and promise. To problematize Levinas by way of Lacan: the Face is trauma – hence its ethical force.

Ethics is a matter of mediations (behavioural and discursive), acts performed and words spoken, that constitute the imperative and perilous step from the challenge of the singular event of the Face to palliating response – hitherto in terms of resort to an iterable principle that claims transcendent status and thus enables neutralization of the transcendence of the Face. For the transjective agent of postmodernity, transcendent princi*ple* lacks precisely the guarantee of a transcendent princi*pal*. Pre-scripted agency is impossible where response in every encounter has to be improvised without rehearsal, on the spot. Hence the attraction of a fundamentalism such as ethnicity, with its ready-made ethic for the encounter with the Face of the Other: shoot thy neighbour on sight.

Let us return to the fundamental postulate of postmodern (poststructuralist) theory of the subject: that the subject is constructed and sustained in language, in discourse, in culture – language as semantic displacement along the interminable chain of ever-proliferating signifiers; discourse as the complex weave of semantic states configured and reconfigured within language; culture as the shifting ensemble of discourses and their cognate institutionalities and practices – and that this subject (transject) has no essence prior to its precipitation through entry into language and all that language entails. Perhaps the ethical practice of the postmodern subject can be located within contributions to the theory of the postmodern subject. Levinas, Lyotard, and Lacan have been cited already; we turn now to three other writers, Jacques Derrida, Mikhail Bakhtin, and Maurice Blanchot.

To begin with Derrida: Derridean deconstruction offers a theory of language and text, homologous with the Lacanian subject, as perpetual deferral of meaning in an open system of difference summed up in the neologism "différance": différance is (textual) otherness. A deconstructive reading seeks to destabilize a particular text, generated within a particular order of discourse and realized through implementation of genre protocols, in order to elicit its occluded but constitutive other meaning(s), the very repression or marginalization of which makes possible the asserted meaning. As Simon Critchley (1992, 26) puts it, "The goal of deconstruction ... is to locate the point of otherness within philosophic or logocentric conceptuality and thus to deconstruct this conceptuality from the position of alterity." Deconstructive practice remains rigorously within the text, working the fabric of rhetoricity to undo logocentric knots. It seeks to "exceed the orbit of [logocentrism's] conceptual totality" (26), not in a greater totality but by displacing texts from limited and limiting contexts into the limitless context of textual process, the "general text" of semantic "free play."

Bakhtin's work constitutes a general theory of language, discourse, and culture grounded in the assymetrical relationship of the monological to the dialogical: monologic closed semantic states exist within the open semiosis of dialogy and its potential for meaning. The relationship to Derrida's practice of deconstruction is that of complementarity: logocentrism implies the closure of discourse in a central, centring canonical "truth" that occludes semantic alterity. Deconstruction, by putting the text into free play, performs Bakhtinian dialogy: it dismantles logocentric monology by opening discourse to semantic alterity. The Derridean general text is the Bakhtinian field of dialogic potentiality, realizable out of what Derrida terms the alterity of particular texts. Bakhtinian dialogy refers to a molar process of general ongoing de-monologization of discourse; deconstructive reading is a deliberate practice at the molecular level to de-monologize – de-logocentrize – actually existing texts, to set in motion the dialogic process in a principled exploitation of semantic interminability.

The filiations between Bakhtin and Levinas are readily apparent: Bakhtinian theory of language, text, and culture is grounded in the subject-other relationship, as Bakhtin's early work, *Towards a Philosophy of the Act* (1993) and the texts published in English as *Art and Answerability* (1990), makes clear. As such, it offers a specifically ethical dimension to the post-structuralist/postmodernist theory of language and thus to that of subjectivity. In contrast, it is perhaps initially surprising that Derrida should evince an affinity with Levinas in that the Face would seem to constitute, in Derridean terms, yet another version, and a very strong version, of Presence; it is not surprising, however, when one takes into consideration the importance of alterity in deconstructive practice. Levinas addresses what he sees as a problem in Western thought, a tendency to assume difference in the subjective Same, to deny the agency of the Other – the Other's status as a subject in his or her own right – by reducing the Other in acts of ontological finalization to the defining margin of the authoring, authoritative, authenticating One or Same. Like Levinas a post-Heideggerian, Derrida developed his deconstructive practice precisely to counter the ontological finalization that suborns alterity to the exigencies of power, a subornation that Heidegger's egology, like Husserl's, sustains. The horizon of Derrida's work is "ethical unconditionality," concomitant with Levinas's moment of ethical alterity (Critchley 1992, 31). Derrida's deconstructive ethical moment occurs at the point of the Levinasian body-discourse articulation, before rhetoric and logic have moulded "truth" in canonical terms.

Dialogism and deconstruction accord with the ethics of the Face in that they bear upon the subject's principled response to the other in the ethical encounter: to deconstruct prescriptivist closure, to open speech and behaviour to dialogic potentiality. Deconstructive dialogization acknowledges that ethical discourse partakes of the general condition of language and meaning: as spuriously transcendental law it is always deferred along the chain of ethical practice; that is, concrete ethical situations always modify any existing codification of ethical rules, just as every utterance alters (i.e., others) the context within which any utterance achieves meaning. "There is no ethics without the presence of the other, and consequently without absence, dissemination, detour, difference, writing," Derrida (1974, 139–40) states in *Of Grammatology*: "the eye of the other calls out the proper name." The Face precedes, underwrites, and undoes all ethical discourse.

The Bakhtinian concept that is homologous with the implications of Derridean textual practice as read within Levinasian ethical theory is transgredience. The term occurs only in the book-length essay "Author and Hero in Aesthetic Activity" (Bakhtin 1990); however, just as the foundations of the overarching ethical project of Bakhtin's oeuvre is laid down in that and other early works, so the idea of transgredience colours the Russian thinker's mature writing on language and cultural evolution. Transgredience – which may also be rendered as transgradience, a stepping across – specifies Bakhtin's notion of the ratio of self to other, which is not that of the collapse of the self into the other (which would be no more than the obverse of the reduction of the Same to the One) – but a dialogic process of working through the exigencies of relationship (in effect, of the Face) by sustaining productive difference. The Face instantiates the elusive trace of différance that grounds the closure of meaning even while ungrounding it in open potentiality. Every strange Face is a traumatic moment of dialogic overture to a beyond of the monologic closure of identity and familiarity. It challenges with the danger and possibility of the transgredient moment.

We come then to a dialogics of the face and an ethics of transgredience. I turn to another thinker of the postmodern, a precursor to Derrida, Maurice Blanchot – to his remarkable book, *The Infinite Conversation* (1993), particularly to the first section, "Plural Speech," where he engages in dialogue with the Levinas of *Totality and Infinity*. What is pertinent here is Blanchot's location of subjectivity in language: infinite deferral along ongoing multivocal channels of formulation and dissemination. Blanchot's notion of conversation, or *entretien*, to cite his French term with its connotation of "keeping it up," keeping the conversation going without definitive closure, accords with Bahktin's notion of the dialogic chain of utterance in relation to the function of transgredience. Blanchot poses his inquiry in the following question:

> How can one speak of speech that is essentially plural? How can the search for plural speech be affirmed, a speech no longer founded upon equality and inequality, no longer upon predominance and subordination, not upon reciprocal mutuality, but upon dissymmetry and irreversiblity so that, between two instances of speech, a relation of infinity would always be involved as the movement of signification itself? (8)

In other words, how can communication be deconstructive, dialogic, maintaining openness to alterity. This is stressed in a later passage, cast in dialogue form:

The unique dignity of the relation philosophy proposes I entertain with what would be the unknown … consists in its being a relation such that neither myself nor the other ceases to be, in this very relation, preserved from everything that would identify the other with myself, that would confuse me with the other, or alter both of us through a middle term: it being an absolute relation in the sense that the distance separating us will not be diminished but, on the contrary, produced and maintained in this relation … That therefore consists in preserving the terms that are in relation from what would alter them in it; a relation that excludes, therefore, ecstatic confusion … mystical participation, but also appropriation, every form of conquest, and even, when all is taken into account, the seizing that comprehension always is. (51)

What Blanchot calls for, in Bakhtinian terms, is principled transgredience, avoidance of the slide into closure by way of the One and the Same. This is an invitation to an ethics for postmodernity, and it is grounded in a response to the Face in its immanent transcendence of unconditional difference and otherness – an otherness to be neither assimilated nor surrendered to but, rather, worked with freely in concert with one's own irreducible otherness, scrupulously maintained as otherness. Thus the ethical relation serves as the basis for the political and all other relations in our postmodernity of decentred flux and unstable hierarchies, where "othering" is everyone's business and everyone is always being othered.

The ethic that emerges from the discourse of postmodernity as situated in the writings of poststructuralism is a rigorous discipline – but a necessary one. The postmodern subject, as ethical, has the choice of either being sucked into one of the black holes of fundamentalist totalization and absolutism or accepting the condition of ideological non-givenness and negotiating from deconstructive positions the terms of its relations to others. Alterity means both otherness and changedness, or transformability. The postmodern subject is a subject conscious of its status as an other and as an otherer – a condition of radical ethical egalitarianism; it is conscious of itself as a transject precipitated in the gap of transgredience. It is obliged to accept its transjective condition and cease to hope for a big-O Other, a clear and certain interpellator, to reappear over the horizon of history. In place of grand narratives of illusory totalization, it must be content with Lyotard's little narratives, which preserve and put into play one's alterity in the ethical game, the game of justice. The choice – and it has no more, but no less, to go on than terms congruent with those of the Pascalian wager – the choice made, the postmodern subject accepts incertitude, openness, risk as the condition of its being-in-the-world, and it works to keep up the infinite, dialogizing conversation of sociality. The payoff is ethical performance that does not seek to evade, but draws energy from, the precipitous trauma of the Face.

Notes

1 "Subject" is obviously a contested term in postmodernity. The death of the subject has been confidently proclaimed by major thinkers such as Heidegger and Foucault, but a "subject function" remains indispensable. Lacan offers a theory of the subject that escapes the limitations of the subject of Western thought that evolved from Descartes to Kant, the subject as a non-extended substance prior to experience (for an illuminating discussion of the provenance of the term see Balibar 1994). The Lacanian subject is posited: for Lacan, "'the subject is never more than supposed' ... The subject is not anything that can, in any sense, be directly observed; it is rather as assumption or supposition on our part (albeit a necessary one), and one must always check to see whether anything really corresponds to this supposed subject" (Fink 1995, 204, n.5). Moreover, "subject" in the singular refers to a category that covers a multitude of actual posited subjectivities conditioned by variables of class, race, gender, ethnicity, and ideology, constituting specific historically sited sociocultural ensembles.

2 A distinction must be made between "postmodernism" and "postmodernity": the former can be defined as a complex of stylistic constructs on the part of contemporary artists, architects, composers, writers, and other primary cultural producers as well as the theoretical constructs elaborated by scholars and critics to account for them; the latter refers to the historical condition that these artifacts and concepts enunciate.

3 See Rutland (1991) where I argue that the writings of Bakhtin and his circle anticipated and contributed to poststructuralism, that they are "inaugural and constitutive" in spite of temporal distance and Bakhtin's near isolation from Western intellectual trends.

4 "Ex-ists" is a Lacanian term that points to a virtuality rather than an actuality, but a virtuality that is necessary to sustain the effect of actuality, like a term "under erasure" in discourse. See Fink (1995, 25).

Works Cited

Althusser, Louis. 1971. "Ideology and Ideological State Apparatuses." *Lenin and Philosophy*. Trans. Ben Brewster. London: New left Books.

Bakhtin, Mikhail. 1990. "Author and Hero in Aesthetic Activity." In *Art and Answerability: Early Philosophical Essays by M.M. Bakhtin*, trans. Vadim Liapunov, ed. Vadim Liapunov and Michael Holquist, 4-256. Austin: University of Texas Press.

– 1993. *Toward a Philosophy of the Act*. Trans. Vadim Liapunov. Ed. Vadim Liapunov and Michael Holquist. Austin: University of Texas Press 1993.

Balibar, Etienne. 1994. "Subjection and Subjectivation." In *Supposing the Subject*, ed. Joan Copjec, 1–15. London and New York: Verso.

Benevuto, Bice, and Roger Kennedy. 1986. *The Works of Jacques Lacan: An Introduction*. London: Free Association Books.

Blanchot, Maurice. 1993. *The Infinite Conversation*. Trans. Susan Hanson. Minneapolis and London: University of Minnesota Press.

Critchley, Simon. 1992. *The Ethics of Deconstruction: Derrida and Levinas*. Oxford and Cambridge, MA: Blackwell.

Derrida, Jacques. 1973. "Différance." In *Speech and Phenomena and Other Essays on Husserl*, trans. David B. Allison, 129–60. Evanston: Northwestern University Press.

– 1974. *Of Grammatology*. Trans. Gayatri Chakravorty Spivak. Baltimore and London: Johns Hopkins University Press.

– 1978. "Violence and Metaphysics: An Essay on the Thought of Emmanuel Levinas." In *Writing and Difference*, trans. Alan Bass, 79–153. London: Routledge and Kegan Paul.

– 1981. *Dissemination*, trans. Barbara Johnson. Chicago: University of Chicago Press.

Fink, Bruce. 1995. *The Lacanian Subject: Between Language and Jouissance*. Princeton: Princeton University Press.

Lacan, Jacques. 1977. *Ecrits: A Selection*. Trans. Alan Sheridan. New York and London: Norton 1977.

Levinas, Emmanuel. 1969. *Totality and Infinity*. Trans. Alphonso Lingis. Pittsburgh: Duquesne University Press.

– 1981. Otherwise Than Being, or Beyond Essence. The Hague: Martin Nijhof.

Lyotard, Jean-François. 1984. *The Postmodern Condition: A Report on Knowledge*. Trans. Geoff Bennington and Brian Massummi. Minneapolis: University of Minnesota Press.

Muller, John and William Richardson, eds. 1988. *The Purloined Poe: Lacan, Derrida and Psychoanalytic Reading*. Baltimore: Johns Hopkins University Press.

Rutland, Barry. 1991. "Bakhtinian Categories and the Discourse of Postmodernism." In *Mikhail Bakhtin and the Epistemology of Discourse*, ed. Clive Thomson, 123–36. Amsterdam: Rodopi.

Sartre, Jean-Paul. 1962. *Huis clos*. New York: Appleton-Century-Croft.

PART THREE

MUSEUMS AND MEMORY

Salvador Allende and the Construction of a Harmless Icon: Museums and Memory

JOSÉ LEANDRO URBINA

Even the dead will not be safe from the enemy if he wins.
And this enemy has not ceased to be victorious.
Walter Benjamin, *Theses on the Philosophy of History*

Are we, ourselves, the Pinochet museum?

"I know you. You're from Iquique. I knew your sisters. Good people." Former General Augusto Pinochet adopts a kindly, paternal tone in speaking to Dr. Luis Fornazzari, who, along with other experts, examines him over a four-day period at the military hospital to determine whether he is fit to undertake a judicial process for the crimes committed under his watch. Pinochet remembers. How can he remember? Fornazzari was exiled to Canada three decades ago, after the coup d'etat headed by his patient in 1973. Now in 2001, they smile. The diagnosis, following a reading of the tests, is to be "slight to moderate subcortical vascular dementia."

Sitting before the computer screen, where I click on a series of images from the past, I try in vain to recognize the doctor. The photograph is hard to read. The figures in it are standing with their backs to the camera, looking towards a building in the background. I met Fornazzari briefly in Toronto several years ago at a friend's house. I look for him in the photograph, try to imagine him in the examination room. I'd like to peer over his shoulder. I envy his eyes contemplating the general in an uncomfortable position, looking into the head of this father who murders his own children, this thief of memories who still inhabits the corners of the rooms where we sleep.

Pinochet kidnapped us, tied his name to our lives, and won't let go. There is always a point when he comes into our generational memory to contaminate what might have been a happy time. The more fortunate among us who didn't go to prison or disappear practised, even in exile, deleting our friends' names and faces, telephone numbers and addresses that might be compromising. We put our past through the sieve and what was left remained irreparably impregnated with Pinochet. That meant we had the untenable option of either opening our mouths and letting him invade the present or not saying his name and falling into a silence that marked the road to banality and evasion. And now, there he is, on the Internet. I can't help tensing up as I look at that benevolent patriarch's face that Pinochet has carefully cultivated with the help of his supporters and an often-unwary press. Once our strict father, now he's our grandpa. That affable "I know you" sends a shiver down my spine, coming, as it does, from the mouth of a man who once said that not a leaf moved in Chile without his knowing about it.

Incredible, Fornazzari! To be there in front of the general like a kid with a stick prodding an old circus lion that you still have to keep an eye on. An old lion who makes faces like a cartoon villain and cries crocodile tears to bring us close and then swats us with his huge paw. We are Pinochet's Other. Our Otherness is determined by our political desires and shaped by our relationship to that other figure omnipresent in our history, another physician: Salvador Allende.

We organize history, history organizes itself, around moments and conditions and actors and narratives that start with Cain and Abel and travel in pairs through the history of patriarchy. Someone is left standing and someone dies. The pair of protagonists, necessary if we want drama, represents a mix of desires. The rest will come along; it's that easy. Those who don't want to participate are dragged along by the storm of history. The one who is left standing holds onto the images of the others.

What does Pinochet have in his head? Does he know me? Does he have my picture in some shelf of his brain, on the walls of his neurons, along with millions of other pictures of his political adversaries? Are we, ourselves, the Pinochet Museum? All of us who have donated our passport pictures, our police photos? Maybe we're all there, hanging in a great gallery, where, on the verge of senility, he takes his afternoon walk. He must feel proud, and maybe a little nostalgic, about so many young people looking at him, looking through him. He lives on us, he lives with us, and he knows we're getting older too. We are his museum; at the four corners of the earth we breathe.

Meanwhile, where is the Salvador Allende Museum? Where is the museum that celebrates his idea, our idea of a country shaped by a dream, that idea that still beats like a tell-tale heart beneath the floor? Allende is institutionally celebrated. The place reserved for him by the country's elites, the place they need to concede to him so that nothing changes, is a museum built of the remains of a shipwreck. A museum that conserves a few relics from a time that is considered, with relief, to be gone forever. Ironically, it is the so-called "real" museum that seems most at risk in being the guardian of memory, its four walls an architecture of ruins. What kind of ideological work is being performed in the construction of such a museum? Does such a national shrine restore something of the once dangerous meaning of the man or merely tame and neuter it by making it safe, by institutionalizing it in a way it was never intended to be?

A few years ago, the cultural pages of foreign newspapers and notices on the social pages of certain Chilean newspapers celebrated the founding of the Salvador Allende Museum. Designed as a showcase for contemporary artworks, it was assembled from the remains of the former Solidarity Museum project: an initiative by a group of artists and intellectuals who had taken part in the conference "Operation Truth" in March of 1971. Among those participating were the Spanish art critic Moreno Galván and Carlo Levi, the great Italian writer and painter.

Perhaps the central reason for holding the conference was to endorse Allende's socialist government for its support of artists and freedom of creation. In the heyday of the Cold War, the democratic election of a Marxist president could not be tolerated by the United Sates. Henry Kissinger explicitly announced the Chilean people's choice as "irresponsible." Even before Allende's inauguration he warned that the Popular Unity government would be a psychological blow for the United States and would mean a triumph for Marxist ideals. Not surprisingly, the demonizing mythology of Stalinism was mobilized to inflame American and world opinion. Debates around freedom of the press and respect for artists often masked what was really at stake: whether a country had a legitimate right to opt for a socialist alternative by electoral means. Within Chile many considered this a historical right, especially given the resounding failure of local capitalism to improve well-being and to create the opportunities to which Chileans aspired. The Popular Unity and its supporters saw Chile as a country dependent upon American imperialism and dominated by sectors of the bourgeoisie with links to foreign capital – links that prevented them from addressing the country's fundamental problems as these were derived from class privileges and would never be given up voluntarily.

Instead of speaking to these fundamental structural issues at home, the discussion was about the Gulag and Solzyenitzin, and psychiatric hospitals filled with writers and poets; Russian painters were invoked, whose only wish was to flee socialist realism by living in New York. Yet, despite all information to the contrary from the CIA, the country enjoyed a democratic environment with full freedom of expression, and a group of European and Latin American artists dared to go to Chile and testify that the secret police did not stop them at the airport or accost them in the streets. The aim of that solidarity museum, then, was to provide testimony to the counter-reality, and its voice was amplified with works donated by artists from all over the world. In the end, it didn't count for much. Two years later, Augusto Pinochet orchestrated a military coup to excise the Marxist threat and to protect the freedoms that those hiding behind Allende were no doubt plotting to eliminate, once and for all.

The military claimed that it had been forced to come to the rescue of Chilean culture. If the leftist project were successful, they argued, then artists would only be able to write about Allende and socialism in the prescribed vein of socialist realism. Ironically, most of the "liberated" artists in whose name the coup was in part executed were soon either being held prisoner in stadiums and concentration camps or preparing to take the path of exile. They were voting with their feet.

Although the original concept of the museum remained under wraps in the basement of the Fine Arts Building, the idea of a museum remained alive among the committee members during the time of exile and was talked about in homes and coffee houses abroad. Mainly expatriates in Europe, these people continued to receive donations from artists now firmly united against the coup, against Pinochet, against repression and torture. The new donations were used to organize travelling exhibitions in order to draw attention to the situation in Chile and to call for a return to democracy.

On the cusp of the 1970s, as the United States was pulling its defeated troops out of Vietnam, Latin America fell to a series of military dictatorships fed by the ascendance of the now well known domino theory. According to this theory, the entire subcontinent, squeezed between Cuba and Chile, was in danger of falling into the hands of communist dictators. The lingering idea of the solidarity museum, kept alive largely abroad now, represented an attempt to counter the mythology of a "kingdom of evil" in Chile. The truth was that repression and torture continued to be the price paid for undertaking a project of alternative social justice in a largely collectivist country. It was a project to which Chile's artists continued to be wedded, even at the risk of being called utopians.

When democracy returned to Chile in the 1990s, the Santiago works of art originally destined for the solidarity museum were recovered. Carmen Waugh, a well known art dealer and gallery owner, became curator of the collection that was to form the basis of the new museum. In interviews she has spoken of the shock of uncovering, in the basement of the Museo de Bellas Artes, paintings by Miró or Frank Stella wrapped up in newspaper like abandoned objects. But the restoration of the original project had now begun in earnest. Donations from the Spanish and French governments were used to renovate the nineteenth-century former teachers college in Yungay Street that today houses the Salvador Allende Museum. This is one of the oldest neighbourhoods in Santiago, and the building's adobe walls culminate in a traditional red tile roof. High Moorish-style windows look onto Compañía Street, named after the Company of Jesus. Here colonial and republican Santiago come together. Here, the past is everything.

Today, firmly in the grip of neoliberal business groups, Chile has enthusiastically joined the global economy. Against that backdrop, another political event of interest, also born during the 1990s, took place at the same time as the museum's founding: the inauguration of a statue of Allende, sculpted in accordance with a law passed by Congress in 1994. His remains had been recovered and a proper burial had taken place, with all the appropriate honours, in the family tomb. The memorializing statue was the next step. The sculptor was Arturo Hevia, a self-declared artist of the right who said he would like to erect a statue to General Augusto Pinochet to show that "Chile belongs to all, Moors and Christians," thus reviving the enemies of an older era to allude to more recent antagonists. The Allende statue, made of Huasco stone – petrified wood – was inaugurated in June 2000 before a number of national and foreign guests, including government authorities and parliamentarians from Spain, France, Italy, and other countries. The presence of newly elected President Ricardo Lagos, a socialist and Duke University graduate who had participated in the Allende administration in an academic capacity, lent the proceedings the status of a state ceremony. The theme was "reconciliation" among all Chileans, the ideological work of this statue all but transparent in the very choice of sculptor and the claim for historical even-handedness. Yet, in spite of speeches about national unity and forgiveness and the calls to forget the past, there was still the unfinished business of the bodies of the murdered not yet returned to their families. But who could argue when Allende's own daughter, the director of the Allende Foundation that managed the museum, said she would not, herself, be opposed to a statue of General Pinochet.

In *State and Revolution*, a book by Lenin that Allende admired, the Bolshevik leader complains that, during the lifetimes of great revolutionaries, the oppressing classes constantly hound them, receiving their theories with malice and furious hatred, along with the most unscrupulous campaigns of lies and slander. After their deaths, attempts are made to convert them into harmless icons, to patronize them, and, to a certain extent, to hallow their names for the "consolation" of the oppressed classes, the object being to dupe the latter while robbing the revolutionary theory of its substance, blunting its revolutionary edge and popularizing it.

He may not be the thinker du jour, but Lenin's reflections have a particular resonance in the case of the commemoration of Allende's memory. Both the statue and the museum stand for the creation of a new image for the former president. It's not that Allende was a great revolutionary like the ones Lenin talks about; he came from a middle-class professional family with progressive ideas and intellectual links to the French Revolution – a family who believed in the power of ordinary citizens to bring about social change within the republic. Many, in fact, considered him merely a democratic reformer. Régis Debray, in a television interview on Mexico's *Zona abierta*, gave a Freudian explanation of the president's death. Allende's superego had taken on the model of Che Guevara and that, in turn, led him to suicide. Then Debray added, "as you know, he was a man who liked to live well, a man of compromise, a true collectivist." That was, of course, a vision of Allende promoted by the right: Allende the bon vivant, the hypocrite who visited the poor in their slums and then had his clothes disinfected. But all that is forgotten, lost with the political struggle of the time. True, Allende was no revolutionary in an olive-green uniform. He wore a suit and tie, was speaker of the Congress, an excellent orator. But he took on the legacy of the home-grown liberals who had waged the anticolonial war, and on the very same day of his election he declared: "We are the legitimate heirs of the founding fathers, and together we will attain Chile's second independence – economic independence." And this he sincerely believed. That is why he was respected by many leaders of the left, internationally and nationally: for his ability to carry through an electoral-based independent socialist project, for his deep knowledge of local political tradition, and for his familiarity with the international scene.

Yet Allende had foregrounded a historical battle that made him both loved and hated within his own country, one that engaged the other current of desire, no longer underground, of settling economic and political inequities. Then his relationship with the Chilean working class and the popular party militants he'd worked alongside all his life spawned a long-standing alliance of inevitable concern to both the Chilean bourgeoisie and the American government. After all, Chile might become a model for all of Latin America. Its attempt to produce social change through democratic means was seen as a dangerous and unacceptable experiment. So Nixon pounded on the table, demanding that his agencies unseat that SOB in Chile – as Richard Helms, head of the CIA, wrote in his notebook during a meeting with the president "$10,000,000 available, more if necessary, make the economy scream."

If the rest is history, then what is left of Allende's dream? Santiago in the 1990s flourished under the centrist coalition that led the transition to democracy, while preserving the neoliberal patterns introduced by Pinochet. The right showed its "new" face and won votes among the working class. Lagos's election in 2000 brought a bland, domesticated left to power. During the celebration, Allende's face was projected onto a huge screen. People called out the dead president's name. Yet which Allende do we read into that simulacrum on the screen? The audience can't agree. There's more than one Allende roaming around Santiago, a ghost of many shapes. He may be sleeping near a statue sculpted by one of his enemies, in the reopened courtyards of Government House, in some corner of the museum directed by his daughter. No doubt his picture still hangs in low-income neighbourhoods, on the wall of a house where the inhabitants paid in blood for their insolence in the 1970s.

Now comes the time to ask ourselves some hard questions. In the context of Chile today, what does it mean to memorialize Allende via a museum, a statue, speeches of reconciliation, the legitimization of leftist administrators who no longer challenge the rhetoric of neoliberalism? Who and what is being memorialized in this construction of a "harmless icon"? When discussions about the role of institutions in controlling forms of dissension or resistance begin to affect theoretical productions by intellectuals calling for a critical reflection on the forms of domination, it is especially difficult to say anything at all about the complex relationship between politics, art, and cultural initiatives. It's hard to say or write certain things, lay bare complicity, stake out a place to pontificate. But it's no easier to creep off the stage, leaving it to a motley crew who are not the least bit ashamed to reel off the same old repertoire or reinvent it in a wave of nostalgia.

It is said that the museum is vindicating Allende's memory. Which memory? There is the memory of Allende as one of the twentieth century's major political figures in Chile and Latin America as a whole. The memory of a politician who sought, through unexpected, non-violent tactics, to build a popular democracy that would capture the imagination of the Chilean people and channel all their utopian energies. The memory of women who still speak of him as a brother who rescued their dignity. The memory of artists around the world who saw the ethical and aesthetic potential of his project and donated their canvases to offset Richard Helms's ten million dollars to finance the coup. The memory of those who were able to feed their families well for the first time.

Each group has its own memories. It has to do with who we were, who we are, who we want to be. As individuals, we both remember and forget in order to preserve our very sense of self, and something of the same process takes place at the national level. But there is another memory that respects neither left nor right, whose images penetrate the present and dance to the rhythm of time in its ancestral dominion. That memory puts us on notice, warns us that if we're not careful, as Walter Benjamin says, *not even the dead will be safe.*

I'm glad Allende has his museum, but I don't want him to *become* a museum. I want to remember him as a doctor, going by his affectionate nickname of "Chicho." I like the image of him sitting at the table in a *población*, surrounded by workers, everybody smiling like kids, wearing new shoes, visiting universities and schools. Yet all of a sudden, all the homages and symbolic systems drawn upon to rehabilitate him are turning him into just another bourgeois politician, one more leader with links to universal art and the best liberal traditions. For the others, who don't go to museums or rub elbows with the international political elite, this Allende goes over their heads. To bring him back, we have the memory of walking through the streets with our heads held high, and of the social gauntlet he threw down on his election night, 4 September 1970, a gauntlet picked up by the Chilean people and adopted as a historical pact: "Revolution implies not destruction but construction, not razing but building, and the people of Chile are prepared for that great task at this transcendent time in our lives ... Tonight, as you kiss your children goodnight, as you seek your rest, think about the harsh tomorrow that awaits us" (<http://www.abacq.net/imagineria/discur2.htm>).

Commemoration/(de)celebration: Super-shows and the Decolonization of Canadian Museums, 1967–92

RUTH B. PHILLIPS

The late twentieth century has seen profound changes in relationships between Canadian museums and First Nations, changes that are transforming the professional practices that control the way museums represent Aboriginal people.[1] Today, in institutions large and small, the development of an exhibition on Aboriginal art or culture is likely to be shaped by intensive consultations with Aboriginal communities and by the active participation of Aboriginal curators. These interventions can affect everything from the initial conceptualization of an exhibition to the writing of its storyline or narrative to design, installation, and interpretive programming,

The contrast with past practice is dramatic; until recently an individual non-Aboriginal staff curator, usually trained as an ethnologist or an archaeologist, was in almost sole control of the representation. To be sure, the curator incorporated understandings gleaned through periods of field-work in Aboriginal communities, but – inevitably – these were filtered through the standard social-scientific academic paradigms in which s/he had been trained. In the process that is under way, the force of Western scientific discourse is still, of course, in evidence. A hierarchy still operates in many large museums, for example, in which those disciplines perceived to be closest to "hard" science are accorded the most prestige (e.g., natural science over archaeology, archaeology over ethnology, or ethnology over art history). But many revisionist projects are interrupting such traditions and are replacing the authority of individual curators and particular disciplines with interdisciplinary and collaborative approaches guided by a new ethics of multivocality. The resulting exhibitions often juxtapose Aboriginal ways of knowing with Western epistemologies; they acknowledge the authority of oral traditions alongside archivally based historical research; and they promote integrated forms of understanding over older typological schemes of classification.

The list of revisionist projects has been growing so rapidly that it is possible here only to suggest their nature with a few examples picked almost
at random. A 1990–91 planetarium show at the Manitoba Museum of Man
based on Anishinabe star lore omitted the most important stories out of
respect for Aboriginal customs according to which they can be narrated
only by authorized individuals at the correct season; Kwakwạkạ'wakw
masks and regalia are presented at the U'Mista Centre at Alert Bay, British
Columbia, in the context of the painful history of colonial repression of
the potlatch rather than in standard Western stylistic or functional groupings (Clifford 1991); large urban art galleries display contemporary paintings that construct equivalences between the science of Einstein and the
cosmology of Sitting Bull; and at the Canadian Museum of Civilization a
major new hall narrates the origins of the First Nations both in Aboriginal
creation stories and in archaeological stories of migration across the Bering
Straits. There can be little doubt that we are witnessing a major shift of
representational paradigms in which a system based on the presumption
that the creators and viewers of exhibitions are unitary subjects is being
replaced with one posited on the assumption of multiple and fragmented
subject positions. The new professional practices reflect the decentring and
the interruptions of metanarratives that have resulted from postmodernist
theory; they inscribe a respect for difference in accordance with postcolonial critiques.

Decolonizing the Canadian Museum

It can be argued that the practice of the new ethics of museum representation began earlier, and has achieved a broader acceptance, in Canada and
other settler colonial countries (such as Australia and New Zealand) than it
did in the United States. In countries where the intellectual establishment is
still engaged in a reflexive critique of its own colonial history it is, perhaps,
more difficult to avoid awareness of the obvious parallels with its oppression
of indigenous peoples. Of equal importance to the exhibitions discussed in
this chapter, the intellectual and political elites have regularly appropriated
the cultural heritage of indigenous peoples in their efforts to construct distinctive national identities.[2] Among the many interrelated factors that have
contributed to Canada's precocity the most important is undoubtedly, however, the acuity of Canadian Aboriginal cultural activists, who early recognized both the importance of museums as interfaces between academic and
public knowledge formations and their strategic availability as targets for

revisionist campaigns. Specifically, First Nations artists and cultural workers maximized the opportunities presented by exhibitions about Aboriginal peoples staged at three moments of national celebration or commemoration during the twenty-five years between 1967 and 1992. They used these shows not only to embarrass governments and institutions into initiating change in museums, but also to bring larger issues (such as land claims, sovereignty, and funding for social programs) before the public eye. With growing historical distance these three exhibitions and this twenty-five-year period are emerging as the crucial phase in the postcolonial reform of Canadian museology.

The first exhibition to become the focus of revisionist activism was installed in the Indians of Canada Pavilion built for the Montreal World's Fair, Expo '67, hosted by Canada to commemorate the 100th anniversary of Canadian Confederation. The second and most explosive controversy took place in 1988 around *The Spirit Sings: Artistic Traditions of Canada's First Peoples*, organized by the Glenbow Museum as the centrepiece of the cultural program for the Calgary Winter Olympics. The third episode occurred in 1992, the year of the Columbus quincentennial, during which two of Canada's national museums, the Canadian Museum of Civilization and the National Gallery of Canada, mounted landmark exhibitions of contemporary Aboriginal art, *Indigena*, and *Land, Spirit, Power*, respectively.

The politics of these four exhibitions, are, of course, interrelated. The communities of museum professionals and Aboriginal activists in Canada are relatively small, and many of the same individuals were involved as advisors, curators, or critics in more than one of the shows. Most important, the controversy surrounding *The Spirit Sings* was the immediate stimulus for the creation, in 1989, of a national Task Force on Museums and First Nations by the Assembly of First Nations and the Canadian Museums Association. The guidelines and policies developed by the Task Force influenced not only the development of the 1992 Columbus year exhibitions but also most exhibition projects dealing with Aboriginal life that were begun during and after its deliberations. As a curator of *The Spirit Sings*, a member of the Task Force, and an academic student of the museum, I write as both insider and outsider, and also as someone whose practices as scholar and curator have been profoundly influenced by the history I recount.

In the following pages I look in some detail at the four exhibitions, examining both their contents and the strategies of confrontation and revisionism adopted by Aboriginal people in relation to each. I argue that, taken together, they comprise a mini-history of a process of change that is historically significant and irreversible, though also uneven and incomplete. As we will see, in charting this exhibition history I do not trace an uninterrupted vector of progress towards decolonization but, rather, an uneven line whose dips and rises mirror swings from liberalism to reaction in Canadian politics. The analysis of this period, then, presents a field in which to explore more general patterns of relationship between exhibition histories, the political map, and the pluralist ethics of the new museology.

The Indians of Canada Pavilion at Expo '67: From "Dreamworld Forest" to "Telling It as It Is"[3]

The year 1967, which marked Canada's 100th birthday, was a year of nationalist euphoria. Expo '67, the Montreal world's fair, was the most dazzling of the many commemorative projects organized to celebrate the centennial. By a process unanticipated at the outset, the Indians of Canada Pavilion emerged as a surprise highlight of the fair. It is perhaps typical of the decade of the 1960s that the pavilion proved popular not because it acceded to the general mood of celebration but because it mounted a radical critique of the standard progressivist representations of Aboriginal history. The realization of this critical project was, in turn, the product of a campaign for self-empowerment waged by Aboriginal people working within the federal bureaucracy during the preceding years. In retrospect, the more focused political process that led to the creation of the pavilion left a legacy for the history of contemporary Aboriginal art and museology that was at least as important as was the innovative nature of the pavilion's exhibitions.

To appreciate the significance of the processes of political empowerment that were taking place during this era it is useful to look briefly at the larger historical context. In 1962, when planning for Expo '67 began, status Indians in Canada had been able to vote in federal elections for only two years. Enfranchisement had resulted from a revision of the Indian Act (a piece of Victorian legislation under which Canadian Aboriginal peoples still live) and was the culmination of a new era of opposition to official assimilationist policies that had begun in the years following the Second World War.[4] During the late 1950s and early 1960s, too, Aboriginal self-empowerment was strengthened by models provided by the American civil rights movement and global movements of national liberation.

The decision to establish a separate Indian Pavilion at Expo can be seen as one result of this climate of growing political activism. Initial plans for the 1967 World's Fair had assumed that, as at previous fairs, the stories of Aboriginal peoples and other "ethnic groups" within Canada would be folded into the master narrative of a single Canada Pavilion.[5] The initial concept thus conformed to the conventional, totalizing vision of Canadian history in which distinct groups within the population were subsumed as "contributors" within a unified and linear historical trajectory.[6] Early plans, dating from 1963, also indicate that, within the Canada Pavilion, the contributions of Aboriginal peoples would be temporally distanced by locating them in the pre-Confederation period. Indians were thus to be effectively excluded from the main story – the century since Confederation – that was the focus of the celebration. Inside the building, as one bureaucrat envisioned it, "some Indian artifacts [would] be dimly spotlighted amidst a dreamworld forest."[7]

Federal officials recognized a need to involve Indians in the development of the pavilion fairly early in the planning process, though in carefully delimited ways. Among the Aboriginal people brought in to serve on various committees, however, the desire for a separate representation at the fair grew steadily. At the end of 1965 the decision was taken to create a separate Indians of Canada Pavilion to be organized under the auspices of the federal Department of Indian and Northern Affairs (DIAND).[8] Members of the Indian Advisory Committee set up by DIAND became increasingly frustrated, however, by the interventions and occasional acts of censorship of federal bureaucrats, and, in particular, by their control over the advisory committee's membership and the agendas of its meetings. A showdown came in 1966, when members threatened to walk out and take their complaints to the press (Manuel and Poslins 1974, 172). Confronted in this way, DIAND officials surrendered control over the design and the storyline of the pavilion's exhibits to the Indian Advisory Committee, despite their worry that their own department's sorry history as the agent of repression and racism would occasion "negative" statements.[9]

The in-house DIAND architect for the pavilion, J.W. Francis, had already come up with a design for a tall conical building intended to echo a Plains tepee, "an Indian dwelling that would be uppermost in the public's mind," as Francis wrote at the time.[10] Although the tepee form of the Indians of Canada Pavilion seems to have been well accepted by Aboriginal peoples, it also played to the dominant popular-culture and touristic stereotypes of Indianness. The tepee, juxtaposed with a fine totem pole commissioned of noted Kwakwaka'wakw carvers Tony and Henry Hunt, conjured up the two signs of Indianness most widely disseminated in popular culture.[11]

The outside of the pavilion also featured an ambitious program of commissioned murals, paintings, and sculptures made by artists from across the country (e.g., Norval Morrisseau, Alex Janvier, Tom Hill, Gerald Tailfeathers, George Clutesi, and the Hunts), many of whom had gained public recognition only within the previous five or ten years (Brydon 1997). Since in 1967 the average Expo visitor's expectation of "Indian art" was still conditioned largely by tourist arts, the vitality of the contemporary art displayed at the pavilion must have come as a revelation. The use of modernist abstract styles by many of the artists demonstrated their facility with the formal vocabulary of mainstream fine art and, therefore, communicated the contemporaneity of Aboriginal cultures. In a complementary fashion, the works newly created in traditional idioms countered the still widespread impression that traditional Indian art – and culture – had disappeared. In their cultural diversity the contemporary art works also deconstructed to some extent the fiction of homogeneous Indianness invoked by the pavilion's architecture.

The art project of the Indians of Canada Pavilion brought together, for the first time, Aboriginal artists of different generations and from different parts of the country. No collaboration of Indian artists on this scale had occurred prior to Expo. Tom Hill, one of the participating artists who is today a museum director and a prominent figure in the Canadian art world, believes that the Pavilion project "brought a sense of the power of the artists, people all of a sudden realized what they could do, as artists, to communicate ideas" (personal communication to Sherry Brydon, Ottawa, 18 March 1991).

On a number of occasions, however, the desire of government officials to monitor the content of the pavilion generated considerable tension. Alex Janvier told a journalist that, when the government asked the artists to paint a positive, cheery picture, he and the other Aboriginal artists bristled. "How come our people are dying in the jails and rotting in the mental hospitals and here we're going to tell the world we're doing great?" they asked. "Let's tell it as it is."[12] The coming together of artists at Expo '67 established a powerful precedent for future national Aboriginal artists' organizations (such as the Society of Canadian Artists of Native Ancestry [SCANA]), which have, among other things, lobbied effectively to loosen the exclusive hold of ethnographic museums on contemporary Aboriginal art and to insert it into Canada's art galleries. The more recent exhibitions of contemporary art I discuss later in this chapter are, in a very real sense, a direct result of this initial coming together of Aboriginal artists from across Canada.

If the overall effect of the exterior visual ensemble of the pavilion was to attract visitors through references to the familiar, the interior presented them with something they had not seen before. As the exhibition brochure told the visitor, the installations presented the answers given by Aboriginal people across Canada to the question: "What do you want to tell the people of Canada and the world when they come to Expo in 1967?" In March and April of 1966 members of the Indian Advisory Committee, together with a hired public relations agent, had travelled across Canada to test their draft storyline at meetings with Aboriginal people.[13] This tour, though hurried and informal, represents one of the first attempts at a broadly conceived national sampling of Aboriginal opinion. The organizers were careful to make clear in the exhibition text and publication that their authority to speak was grounded in the consultative process.[14] As with so many of the features of the pavilion project, community consultation – modelled on time-honoured Aboriginal methods of consensual decision making as well as on the Canadian tradition of the travelling Royal Commission – prefigured initiatives that are only now becoming general practice.[15]

The critique of historical and contemporary relations between Aboriginals and non-Aboriginals in Canada contained in the pavilion was by far the most comprehensive that had ever been presented in so public a forum. Mid-twentieth-century museum representations of Aboriginal culture had changed little from those of the late Victorian period, continuing to locate a "pure" and "authentic" era of Aboriginal culture in the remote past and to accept both the inevitability and the benefits of assimilation. In contrast, the Indians of Canada Pavilion stressed the negative aspects of contact on the one hand, and the currency and value of traditional practices, on the other. The guiding principle was, as an internal report to the Indian Advisory Council noted, that "the Past should not dominate the Present and the Future; the Present is the crucial part which should be projected."[16]

This shift in emphasis was highly significant; it overturned a century of museum representations of Aboriginal life in which exhibits focused almost exclusively on the pre-contact and early contact periods as the locus of authenticity. The new approach was evidenced first of all by the allocation of space within the pavilion. The representation of the pre-contact period was contained in two anterooms, while the focus in the main exhibition area was squarely on the present and the recent past. The first of the introductory anterooms, devoted to "The Land," affirmed the theme of pervasive spiritual presence and of a primordial harmony between humans and the natural world at the time of creation. The second area, "The Awakening of the People," contained displays of artifacts that illustrated the pre-contact period adaptations of Indian nations to their different environments.

The main area, inside the tepee proper, was a large circular space called "The Drum." Six bays opened out of it, each of which examined a different aspect of European contact from an Aboriginal point of view. The first bay introduced the arrival of the Europeans, illustrated by early trade objects and by objects representing the gifts of Indian food, tools, and canoes that had been essential to European exploration. The second bay addressed the changing political, economic, and military roles of Aboriginal peoples in the early nineteenth century and the rapid disintegration of their traditional ways of life once Euro-North Americans no longer required their support as military allies. In the third bay the impact of missionaries was presented. The objects displayed included Iroquoian False Face masks and a sculpture of a celestial bear. The bear, carved by Nathan Montour, interpreted a traditional Delaware image, although it had a broader general reference since beliefs in the bear as an extremely important spirit being are held by many Algonkian peoples.

The installation constructed around this image was the most politically charged in the pavilion. A shaft of light in the form of a Christian cross was projected onto the bear to express the imposition of foreign belief systems onto indigenous religious expressions. This visual juxtaposition subverted the supremacy of Christianity by identifying Aboriginal religion as the victim of the violent repression and torture associated with the crucifixion. The text panel behind the bear read: "The early missionaries thought us pagans. They imposed upon us their own stories of God, of heaven and hell, of sin and salvation." Across from this panel another affirmed the validity of Aboriginal spirituality. It displayed historic pictographs and read, "but we spoke with God the Great Spirit in our own way. We lived with each other in love, and honoured the holy spirit in all living things." DIAND officials were initially concerned that this section would offend Roman Catholic French Canadians, but no concerted protest materialized.

Following this display the visitor came to a bay entitled "The Government and the Indians," illustrated by a large geopolitical map of Canada upon which reserves were marked. A journalist noted the diversity that was represented, "ranging from the very small to the very large, the most remote to the almost urban, the virtual slums, to the well-ordered communities."[17] The intention of this section was to make clear the importance to Aboriginal peoples of the reserve, one of the strongest messages that had emerged from the 1966 national consultations.[18] As a text panel read, "the reserve is our last grip on the land, many of our people fear that, if the reserve should disappear, the Indian would disappear with it."[19] The brochure further emphasized the special historic responsibility of government to Indians and listed the current Aboriginal concerns as, "the retention of an Indian identity, a sense of independence, the right to manage their own affairs, and to determine their own destiny."[20]

The next bay, representing "Work Life," was constructed in the form of a barrel vault on which photo panels were mounted portraying Indians engaged in a wide range of occupations, from trapping to nursing and teaching. But the brochure pointed out that, even though Aboriginal people engaged in the same range of activities as did non-Aboriginals, there were an "abnormally high number living on government relief." It also pointed out the particular problems of non-status Indians. The last image the visitor saw on leaving this bay was a large photograph of an unsmiling and poorly dressed woman standing with her four small children at the door of their log cabin.

The final bay addressed the problem of education, focusing on the challenge facing the Aboriginal child in "the White man's school, an alien land for an Indian child." This alienness was spelled out in one of the text panels:

Dick and Jane in the storybook are strangers to an Indian boy. An Indian child begins school by learning a foreign tongue. The sun and the moon mark passing time in the Indian home. At school, minutes are important and we jump to the bell. Many precious hours are spent in a bus going to a distant school and coming home again.[21]

Adjacent to these texts the public was confronted with "large blown-up photographs of tattered, unhappy-looking Indian children placed beside pictures of white Canadian children playing in the comfort of suburbia."[22]

From the drum a staircase led visitors down into the final exhibition space, "The Future." Phones were arranged around the fire; when visitors picked them up they heard a message, spoken in an archaic poetic diction, that summarized the themes that had been presented and articulated a vision of the future:

Some of my people see in the dark coals a world where the Indian is a half-remembered thing and the ways of the old men are forgotten.

But I see another vision, I see an Indian, tall and strong in the pride of his heritage. He stands with your sons, a man among men.

He is different, as you and I are different, and perhaps it will always be so. But, in the Indian way, we have many gifts to share.

The message urged the importance of mutual respect and sharing but also stressed the necessity of separation and distinctness. Finally, the rejection of paternalism was clear: "The trail we walk is our own, and we bear our own burdens. That is our right."

The Indians of Canada Pavilion constituted a moment of dramatic rupture with many key conventions of colonialist representation. This break was not, and could not have been, total, and in several important ways the pavilion's installations continued to employ the discourse of the dominant society. Throughout the pavilion, for example, the masculine voice was used exclusively: the "Indian" was always "he," despite the use of female images in the photographic visuals. The privileging of the masculine in the pavilion seems particularly relentless even in relation to the general English usage of the 1960s.[23] All the commissioned artists were men, and there were no women on the Indian Advisory Committee despite the fact that women, such as the Odawa painter Daphne Odjig, were available to fill these positions. The privileging of the male voice evidences the success with which patriarchal norms had, during the centuries of colonial rule, come to overlay Aboriginal practices based on very different notions of gender and power. In retrospect the exclusion of the female voice seems an omen of the degree to which gender would become a site of increasing difficulty in Aboriginal politics in the years to come.

The doubleness and divided subjectivity imposed on Aboriginal people by a still colonial bureaucracy was also revealed by the alternation of first- and third-person narration in the texts associated with the pavilion. While the text panels addressed the visitors in the first person, speaking directly as "we" to "you," the brochure spoke in the third person – of how "the Indian" had fared in the past and of "his" goals for the future. Although, as we have seen, the substance of the brochure seems to have been a remarkably faithful summary of the community consultations and advisory committee discussions, its messages are distanced by the reportorial, ethnographic voice of the public relations consultant hired to compose it. It thus continued to mediate the Aboriginal voice according to a paternalistic ethos that had not yet entirely given way to a fully empowered Aboriginal community.

The critique of historical and anthropological discourse initiated by the Indians of Canada Pavilion would become more profound in the years that followed, but in 1967 there was still an acceptance of the dominant society's categories. Although the use of quotation marks in the text panels and brochure ironized and distanced words like "Indian," the terms continued to be employed. Similarly, the use of the standard anthropological culture-area concept as an organizing principle limited the degree to which totalizing representations could be deconstructed. Perhaps the most enduring of the Western literary and anthropological conventions invoked in the pavilion was the romanticized construction of the pre-contact past as an Edenic paradise free of conflict or want – a convention that remains intact today in the rhetoric of many environmentalists, adherents of new age religions, and in the new wave of Hollywood Indians. The opening lines of "The Beginning" in the Pavilion brochure – "All the creatures of the world lived, one with another, in harmony and order. All owed each other respect and reverence" – read very much like an animist version of Genesis. At other moments the use of a Longfellowian English to evoke an ideal future – "Sit now by the fire and rest, my brother. We will talk of the time to come" – seem to reference a related millenarian tradition. As with the question of gender discourse, the evocation by Aboriginal people of a Judeo-Christian trope of original harmony is problematic. Many Aboriginal creation stories (with their great trickster figures and careful dualities of good and evil) structure chaos, order, and morality differently, and against these narratives the overlay of doctrines of the noble savage and the lost Eden seem alien.

Yet these tropes were deployed at Expo '67 in a carefully calculated manner to invert progressivist and evolutionist doctrines associated with assimilationist policies. Their rhetorical power derives from their resonance both for non-Aboriginals and for Christianized Aboriginal people. As Homi Bhabha (1991, 82) has observed:

Colonized countries have had to construct their cultural forms by hybridizing the indigenous culture with the colonizer's culture ... Strategies of resistance, of identification and of mimicry all came into play. But mimicry can be subversive; you use the language of the master in an alloyed form, in order to deflect the dominating ideologies being imposed on you.

The combination of mimicry and subversion inside the pavilion was analogous to that found on the outside; the installations, like the architecture, exploited popular and touristic images of Indianness while simultaneously resisting them.

Museums and other institutions were slow to pick up the challenges raised by the Indians of Canada Pavilion: it would take two more decades and the crisis provoked by the Aboriginal boycott of *The Spirit Sings* exhibition mounted for the Calgary Winter Olympics in 1988 for the issue of museum representation to be addressed seriously on a national scale. By and large, between 1967 and 1988 the representation of Aboriginal culture in major expositions and cultural events retreated to pre-Expo conventions, and there was a parallel stalemate in active governmental attempts to address the problem of Aboriginal rights. The representation of Aboriginal history in the Canadian pavilion at Vancouver's Expo '86, for example, was, in comparison to Expo '67, reactionary. Like the initial ideas for the Canada Pavilion that were ultimately rejected for Montreal, Expo '86 positioned the contributions of the First Nations as little more than an opening chapter in the national history (Ames 1992, 117–24).[24]

The Spirit Sings

The staging of the Winter Olympics in Calgary, Alberta, in 1988 was the next international event to be held in Canada that was on a scale comparable to that of the Montreal World's Fair. The rules of the International Olympics Committee require every host country to mount a cultural program that is both reflective of its own culture and international in scope. The decision to focus the major art exhibition of the Calgary cultural festival on Aboriginal art was in part the result of circumstance; Calgary's largest and most active museum, the Glenbow Museum, happens to specialize in western history and ethnography. The decision, however, also conforms to the pattern of borrowed identity (Graburn 1976, 27–30) that characterizes constructs of national identity not only in Canada but also in the United States. Both countries have historically appropriated the images of their Aboriginal peoples not only to express their difference in relation to Europe but also to assert Euro-North American claims to ownership of the land.

The decision to focus the exhibition on the early contact period resulted from a desire to make use of the special opportunity afforded by the Olympics.[25] In 1983, when planning for the exhibition began, virtually all non-Aboriginal museum curators, anthropologists, and art historians regarded early-contact period objects as the most authentic and valuable because of their relative lack of European influence. A large proportion of early-contact period objects is held by widely scattered European museums, taken there by missionaries, government officials, soldiers, and curiosity collectors. While the project of gathering them together in order to further historical and aesthetic understandings of Aboriginal culture had always been dear to the hearts of scholars, only the kind of super-budget available for a show connected to an event like the Olympics could support such a project. The rarity of the objects also appealed to the popular "treasures" model that often lay behind the super shows of the 1970s and 1980s. Like the other curators, I began the project enthusiastically, confident of its usefulness for scholars and the general public, both Aboriginal and non-Aboriginal.

The Spirit Sings, at a budget of 2.6 million dollars, was one of not only the most expensive exhibitions in Canadian museum history but also the most controversial. The corporate sponsor of the exhibition, announced more than mid-way through its five-year incubation period, was Shell Oil. Soon after the sponsor's name was made known a boycott of the exhibition was announced by the Lubicon Cree, a band of Alberta Aboriginals, in support of their land claim. Forty years earlier the Lubicon had been quite literally "overlooked" by a government agent sent to assign reserve lands, and their efforts to obtain justice in the intervening years had been fruitless. In the early 1980s, when oil was found on their land, leases were issued to Shell and other companies. The Lubicon were evicted, resulting in myriad forms of suffering, ranging from severe economic loss, to social breakdown, psychic trauma, and epidemic disease. The announcement that Shell was to sponsor an exhibition celebrating the past glories of Aboriginal art and culture at the same time as it was to be a partner in a development project that was destroying a contemporary Aboriginal community appeared the ultimate hypocrisy. Lubicon strategists began an energetic campaign to persuade the approximately 100 museums of whom loans had been requested to observe the boycott. Although an earlier Lubicon call for a general boycott of the games had not been heeded, the boycott of the exhibition met with more success, attracting a great deal of publicity and widespread support in the academic world. It also generated fierce debates within many of the museums that were contacted, particularly in Europe. Some felt that it was wrong to try to stop an exhibition that addressed all the Aboriginal peoples of Canada on behalf of one group, especially when the show promised to be a valuable educational experience for the wider public. Others felt bound to observe the boycott, especially after it gained the support of the Assembly of First Nations, Canada's largest Aboriginal political organization. In the end, most museums did lend to the exhibition, in some cases because of pressure exerted by the Canadian government through diplomatic channels. However, one of the largest potential lenders, the Museum of the American Indian in New York, and most of the German and Scandinavian museums, refused to participate.

The Spirit Sings was seen both in Calgary and at the National Museum of Man in Ottawa.[26] It displayed approximately 600 objects, a great many of which were unpublished and almost totally unknown, and had never before been returned to North America or even been on public exhibition in the museums that owned them. Although nearly all came from ethnographic museums, the Glenbow (a general museum containing ethnographic, historical, and art departments) sought, in keeping with other museums during the 1980s, to blend the two dominant twentieth-century display paradigms for non-Western objects – "art" and "artifact" (Feest 1984; Price 1989; Phillips 1994). I would argue that some of the problems the exhibition eventually encountered arose from the confusion that resulted from this mixture of display styles. There was, on the one hand, a great deal of exhibition text – too much to read comfortably, according to many people – whose aim was to contextualize the objects historically and culturally by providing extensive ethnographic information, numerous maps, historical photographs, and other paintings. In certain areas of the exhibition groups of objects were aestheticized through dramatic lighting effects and a spare, modernist, "primitive art" installation style. This was most pronounced in those sections dealing with regional traditions (notably Inuit and Northwest Coast) that had found the readiest acceptance as "art" and that conformed most closely in scale and medium to the Western fine art genres of sculpture and painting.[27] In other sections, however (Woodlands, Plains, and Western Subarctic), the design of the cases intentionally evoked the specimen cabinets used in early ethnographic and natural history museums, a form of postmodern quotation fashionable in the 1980s. The historicizing and ironic content of this case design was lost on most viewers, and audiences tended to read them, rather, as affirming the validity of the earlier, objectifying scientific mode of display.[28] The installations, then, sent mixed messages both about the status of the objects as curio, specimen, and/or art, and, consequently, about the position the museum was advocating for the representation of Aboriginal cultures.

The boycott of *The Spirit Sings* had begun as a strategic manoeuvre, but it soon stimulated a much more wide-ranging critique of museum practice. Corporate sponsorship proved to be only one of several problematic areas highlighted by reaction to the show. The decision to focus exclusively on the early-contact period was, for example, also criticized. While many Aboriginal viewers welcomed the opportunity to see early pieces, objections were raised to the exhibition's failure to address more fully the negative effects of colonialism or to include a section on contemporary problems and lifestyles. As we have seen, these were precisely the issues Aboriginal activists had fought hard to foreground in the 1967 Indians of Canada Pavilion. For many Aboriginal viewers, furthermore, the sight of the beautiful old objects, many made with techniques and skills long forgotten and ordinarily hidden away in distant museums, was not a cause for celebration but, rather, a painful reminder of loss.

Further debates developed regarding repatriation, the question of authority in the museological interpretation of Aboriginal cultures and the display of sacred objects. A lawsuit was brought to remove from display an Iroquois False Face mask I had included in the Northern Woodlands section. (Although the suit was not upheld by the courts, the National Museum of Canada sought to honour the spirit of the protest by replacing the mask with a copy during the Ottawa venue.) For me, as for the other curators and museum staff involved, the conflicts that developed around the boycott were extremely painful. To a person, the members of the curatorial committee had embarked on the project with a desire to enhance the general public's respect for the depth and complexity of Aboriginal belief systems and artistic achievements as well as to make available for further study (by both Aboriginals and non-Aboriginals) a large but little known corpus of great Aboriginal art. The controversies that erupted, however, forced all parties to reassess their most basic premises about scholarly research and to accept the inherently political nature of all processes of representation. Ultimately, it forced most museum practitioners to accept that exhibitions are never pure or "disinterested" scientific inquiries but, rather, complex events that give voice to the interests of particular communities. The logical conclusion that the interests of First Nations should be taken into account when their communities are being represented began to acquire a normative force.

As the boycott gained momentum and as the debates heated up during the winter and spring of 1988, the country was preparing for a federal election scheduled to take place in November, just after the closing of the exhibition. Aboriginal leaders were quick to exploit the connections between the issues the exhibition had raised and the larger questions of sovereignty that were, as usual, on their broader political agenda. It was in this context that the director of the Canadian Museum of Civilization, George MacDonald, committed his institution to help organize a national forum that would provide the opportunity for a full airing of the concerns of the Aboriginal community.[29]

This conference, held at Carleton University in early November of 1988, led directly to the commissioning of the Task Force on Museums and First Nations, which was to study the problems and to develop mutually acceptable guidelines that would prevent them from recurring. Its 1992 report, "Turning the Page: Forging New Partnerships between Museums and First Peoples," articulates the new ethics of museum practice stated at the opening of this chapter. It seeks to create new relationships of partnership and collaboration between museum professionals and Aboriginal communities based on principles of sharing and mutual respect, and to ensure that these principles inform all future projects of research and representation (Nicks 1992). More specifically, the report acknowledges the rights of Aboriginal peoples to have access to all objects of Aboriginal heritage and to repossess human remains and all objects held illegally. Just as *The Spirit Sings* was a pivotal moment in twentieth-century Canadian museum history, so the Task Force report that followed it was a characteristically Canadian document, whose unique aspects are revealed in a comparison with the American response to similar issues and problems (Wilson, Erasmus, and Penney 1992). The Native American Graves and Repatriation Act, passed in 1990 by the United States Congress, legislates that all public museums must disclose to Aboriginal communities their holdings of Aboriginal material and must return to them upon demand all human remains, sacred objects, and objects of cultural patrimony. The Task Force report, in contrast, enjoins voluntary compliance and negotiated solutions to disputed claims. These claims are to be worked out on a case by case basis, guided by an ethics of mutual respect and a recognition of shared interests in Aboriginal heritage. A greater historical distance will be required to assess the failures and successes of these two strategies.[30]

Indigena and Land, Spirit, Power

At the same time that the Task Force on Museums and First Nations was carrying out its work, two major exhibitions of contemporary Aboriginal art were being developed.[31] Each had the prestige of a national museum behind it and put into practice a slightly different model of power sharing. Each, finally, responded in its own way to the issues of voice and representation raised by the Indians of Canada Pavilion and *The Spirit Sings*.

Indigena: Contemporary Native Perspectives, was organized for the Canadian Museum of Civilization by its curator of contemporary Indian art, Gerald McMaster, and his associate, Lee-Ann Martin. It brought together paintings, sculptures, and installations, many of them specially commissioned, that presented Aboriginal artists' perspectives on the impact that the 500 years since Columbus's arrival has had on the indigenous peoples of the Americas. The exhibition was the first show to be mounted by a large Canadian museum in which all the key participants – curators, artists, and the writers who contributed essays and poems to the catalogue – were members of the Aboriginal community.[32] *Land, Spirit, Power: First Nations at the National Gallery of Canada* was organized by a team of three curators: Diana Nemiroff (the gallery's curator of contemporary Canadian art), Charlotte Townshend-Gault (an anthropologist and art critic), and Robert Houle (a prominent Saulteaux artist and curator). In a narrow sense the exhibition was the gallery's celebratory response to the sustained lobbying of the Society of Canadian Artists of Native Ancestry for inclusion in its permanent collections and exhibition spaces. But in a larger sense *Land, Spirit, Power* was simply a show whose time had come. Through its presentation of a broad range of work by American and Canadian Aboriginal artists it acknowledged the maturing of a continent-wide contemporary Aboriginal art movement.

Despite the commonalities of styles and conceptual approaches among the artists represented in these shows, the two exhibition projects complemented rather than paralleled each other.[33] The works of art in *Indigena* mounted a powerful lesson about history and cultural survival, while those in *Land, Spirit, Power*, while not eschewing the political, were presented first of all as aesthetic expressions. *Indigena* was, by intent, a profoundly didactic exhibition. The paintings, sculptures, and installations all confronted the visitor with the retelling of history from an Aboriginal point of view. It was a "de-celebration" of 500 years of European intervention in Aboriginal life, chronicling and mourning a tragic history of repression and death yet also affirming the strengths that had allowed Aboriginal peoples to resist annihilation and survive. So comprehensive and revisionist a critique had not been mounted in a major Canadian museum since the Expo '67 exhibition. In *Land, Spirit, Power*, the National Gallery also took up the challenge of accommodating pluralism, and in this sense its project was no less radical. The exhibition relied, however, not on a rhetoric of confrontation but, rather, on one of seduction through the positive and life-affirming power of art and beauty. Many of the works were lightened by humour and wit, which contrasted with the darker and more sombre emotional tone of the works in *Indigena*.

Space does not permit a detailed examination of all the works in these two exhibitions, so I focus on two works that illustrate the contrasting intentions and atmospheres of the two shows. Both are large, complex installations, and each occupied a central position within its exhibition, both in concrete spatial terms and, I would argue, in conceptual terms as well. They are Joane Cardinal-Schubert's "Preservation of the Species: DECONSTRUCTIVISTS (This Is the House that Joe built)" in *Indigena*, and Rebecca Belmore's "Mawu-che-hitoowin: A Gathering of People for Any Purpose." "Preservation of the Species" was a summary work that brought together themes Cardinal-Schubert had been pursuing for many years. Haunting landscapes remembered from childhood, the suicide of an Aboriginal boy, the petroglyphs that mark the Prairies with ancient histories, family photographs, an altar to lost souls – all were brought together with a Duchampian peep-show and a fenced-in reserve peopled by stick figures in babushkas that recalled both sacred offerings and rural poverty. On the claustrophobic black-painted walls of this room Cardinal-Schubert wrote out a whole history book, lessons for strangers constructed as cultural other.

Belmore's work was very different. It was spare, quiet, and minimalist. On a plywood platform painted with flowers that suggested both old linoleum and the flitting shadows on a forest floor, Belmore arranged a circle of chairs taken from her own kitchen and the living spaces of the women who are closest to her. The work issued a tacit invitation to sit down, to put on the earphones dangling over each chair back, and to listen to the voices of Belmore's female community talking about the lives they have lived as Aboriginal women in Canada, of their struggles and their joys and the sources of their strength. On many days at the gallery people waited patiently for a free chair so that they could join this circle, glancing at each other, smiling briefly.

Both of these works were at once broadly conceived and intensely personal. Both spoke of stereotyping, racism, and the toll paid by the victims of these evils. Both were, furthermore, interactive installations, relying on words as much as on visual images: but here lay the difference. Cardinal-Schubert wanted to destroy the equilibrium of her viewers, to make them uncomfortable. She addressed viewers in their own medium, the written word, and appropriated Dadaist strategies to subvert the avant garde of the Western art world together with everyone else (a similar strategy was adopted by Loretta Todd in her essay from the *Indigena* publication). There is no ambiguity in Cardinal-Schubert's intention. Near her Duchampian peepshow she wrote: "It is uncomfortable to peek through the little holes of this site. You miss some of the picture. What's more, it is an uncomfortable and unsettling experience. Good! Now you know how I have felt for most of my life."

Belmore, in contrast, made use of the testimony of the human voice, of the oral tradition, of common discourse. She welcomed visitors into the circle of the Aboriginal community and used traditional Aboriginal tactics for reaching understanding – talking in council, listening to elders. Traditionalism characterized the art in *Land, Spirit, Power* in other ways as well. Works built around pre-contact Aboriginal iconographic and stylistic traditions (especially in the contributions of artists from the Northwest Coast) were more prominent at the gallery than at the museum. A tricksterish reversal of the conventions occurred. Make space for Aboriginal artists and what do you get? Deconstruction in the museum and ethnography in the art gallery. In the context of the preceding exhibitions, then, the 1992 exhibitions witnessed – at least temporarily – a reversal of the usual division of gallery and museum into spaces for fine art and ethnology, and they erased the difference between art and artifact installation paradigms that the Expo '67 pavilion had purposely juxtaposed and that *The Spirit Sings* had unsuccessfully attempted to finesse.

In *Indigena* and *Land, Spirit, Power* text and image – history, politics and art – were inextricably melded. This mixing, I would suggest, is not just postmodern pastiche but, rather, a postcolonial reaction to the objectification of the other through hierarchical classifications of objects into realms of art and science. Both exhibitions stimulated mixed responses. The explicit expressions of anger in *Indigena* upset many people, including some strong supporters of Aboriginal empowerment in the museum community. The political messages and stylistic eclecticism of *Land, Spirit, Power*, on the other hand, led the art critic of Canada's major newspaper to condemn it as opportunistic.[34] Despite these reactions, however, and despite their internal contrasts, both shows were important therapeutic moments for the artists and their audiences. The public expression of anger is a necessary stage in a process of reconciliation; the public acknowledgment of injury implicit in the staging of these exhibitions in Canada's national museums was in important step in a healing process that is necessary before real change can occur. Taken together, these two shows illustrated that art can be both sword and balm. As Jimmie Durham wrote in one of his works in *Land, Spirit, Power*, "If we do not let our memories fail us / The dead can sing and be with us. / They want us to remember them, / And they can make festivals in our struggles." In *Land, Spirit, Power* the dead were feasted at the same time as their pain was remembered. In *Indigena* they were mourned with an angry grief too long pent up and denied the dignity of public commemoration.

Conclusion

It has become a commonplace, in the rapidly growing analytical literature on the museum, to recognize "the idea that a museum is a discourse, and an exhibition an utterance within that discourse," to quote Mieke Bal (1996, 214). Foucauldian notions of the disciplinary nature of museums and their installations, and the construction of power relations through the museological manipulation of the viewer's gaze have also been successfully argued by writers such as Eilean Hooper-Greenhill (1992), Donald Preziozi (1989), and Tony Bennett (1996). And Carol Duncan has demonstrated the way in which the behaviour of visitors to museums and galleries should be understood as a specialized and important form of public ritual behaviour.

Such analyses of the politics of representation make clear why any exhibition might become the focus of a protest. How much more so, then, large or "definitive" exhibitions such as those I have discussed. As John Miller (1996, 269) has recently pointed out, the super- or mega-show, because it is the most ambitious product of the twentieth-century museum establishment, invites protest and controversy in a particular way: "Blockbuster exhibitions ... by engendering surplus frustration as a ritual in its own right, tend to recuperate dissent as part of the totality of the overall event." As Miller argues, the inherent impossibility of the process of the decontextualization, or "reification," of individual art works upon which the mega-show is posited invites contestation in and of itself.

There are also practical reasons that render the mega-show an unstable mix. Museums welcome major anniversaries and events as opportunities to mount projects that would normally be beyond their scope. A simple equation usually applies: the bigger the event, the more ambitious the exhibition and the bigger the budget. Because these shows are conceived from the start on a scale far beyond normal levels of institutional and governmental funding they must seek corporate sponsorship and/or special allocations of public money. In consequence, the museum's ties to the business and political establishments are unusually tight and transparent. The super-show that is linked to a historical anniversary, the Olympics, or the "year" of some group or country, is, then, the ultimate (con)test case. Like a raking light, the glare of publicity picks out the sponsors' logos on posters, advertising, and exhibition signage, laying open to the public gaze a relationship of dependency that is normally at least partly masked.

Unlike a normal super-show (such as a retrospective devoted to the work of a single artist), the large commemorative exhibition combines pretensions to authoritative representation with moments of self-conscious historical commemoration or communal stock-taking *and* the patronage of a national institution, a government, or a large corporation. When the subject of the show is the heritages of internally colonized peoples specific tensions are produced through the settler nations' appropriation of the iconic values of these heritages. When presented to international audiences these tensions are further intensified, and the exhibitions become ideal sites of protest. Skilled cultural critics (such as contemporary indigenous artists) make use of such "show times" to reveal dominant discourses and relations of power, and to generate public scrutiny of the West's imperial past and present.[35] In these moments the dominant discourses and relations of power can be revealed with exceptional clarity. At the end of the twentieth century, such an event is virtually predestined to become the site of protest.

Finally, the ritual dramas of exhibition and protest can have a "real" and significant impact on the political process. In March of 1994 – in the aftermath, one could argue, of the Columbus quincentennial – the Canadian government announced plans to dismantle the federal Department of Indian and Northern Affairs (DIAND), a paternalistic agency set up to oversee Aboriginal peoples, who were regarded as incapable of running their own affairs. This decision, taken even as *Indigena* and *Land, Spirit, Power* were continuing their national tours, repeated, with a precision that is almost uncanny, the time interval between the Indians of Canada Pavilion in 1967 and the issuance two years later of a government White Paper proposing the repeal of the Indian Act. At that time, however, protest from Aboriginal people fearful of losing the vital financial subsidies guaranteed them by treaties forced the minister of Indian affairs (Jean Chrétien, who became prime minister in 1994) to retract the proposal. The parallels between these two pairings of radically revisionist exhibitions and dramatic shifts in government policy are striking.

I do not want to suggest a direct cause and effect relationship between museum exhibition and political response; rather, a combination of liberalized public opinion and Aboriginal activism lay behind *both* the museum representations *and* the realpolitik in Parliament. In both cases the confrontational exhibitions that preceded momentous acts of state seem to have been rehearsals for the actions that followed. As the new millennium opens, both national politics and Aboriginal activism in the museum have moved into a new register, one that has shifted from the rhetoric and the reality of decolonization to that of sovereignty. The continuing constitutional and cultural struggles over Quebec separation again find their echoes in the stepped-up pace of comprehensive Aboriginal land claims negotiations. A number of First Nations have been seeking not only recognition of their claims to territory and resources but also the segregation and return of museum collections of their objects and information.

Throughout the long history of Canada's internal colonization of its Aboriginal peoples, the power to determine what shall be remembered and how has been vested in a narrow stratum of the population. What the twenty-five-year history that has been recounted in this chapter illustrates is a process by which a new cultural intelligensia, this time comprised of Aboriginal artists and intellectuals, has been reappropriating the right publicly to remember the past and to represent the present according to other measures of value and importance. This history reveals the important steps taken by the Canadian museum community towards the institutionalization of multivocality, and it argues that these participate in a new ethical stance associated with postmodernism and postcolonialism. Perhaps more interestingly still, these exhibition histories illustrate the value of studying museum exhibitions not only as discrete physical installations and assemblages of objects and works of art but also as existing within broad social and political contexts.

Notes

1 This paper was first delivered at the Harn Museum of the University of Florida in March 1994 and revised for publication in 1996. Since then the published literature and theses on museums and on the specific exhibitions discussed here have multiplied greatly. I regret that I have not been able to incorporate these valuable contributions; rather, I offer this essay as a record of the evolving relationship between First Nations and museums in Canada as I understood it in the mid-1990s. See Phillips 2001, 2003, and forthcoming for an updated discussion of collaborative models of contemporary museum practice and for other versions of this paper.

2 For some examples of the contestation of comparable museum exhibitions about Aboriginal peoples in Australia and New Zealand, see Bennett (1989) and Ames (1991). For the United States, see Rushing (1994).

3 The following account of the Indians of Canada Pavilion is based on a longer exploration of the subject being prepared for publication under the title "'Arrow of Truth': The Indians of Canada Pavilion at Expo '67." I am greatly indebted to Sherry Brydon's (1991) undergraduate honours thesis.

4 The return of the disproportionately large numbers of newly politicized Aboriginal soldiers who fought in the Second World War and the heightened consciousness of the dangers of racism resulting from that conflict were both important factors in rupturing the status quo that had endured for nearly a century (Miller 1989, 220-3).

5 One bureaucrat envisioned, for example, that, "Indian paintings should be a part of the general Art Exhibit ... [and] the contribution of the Indian, of maize, potatoes, and tobacco might be part of a general display of agricultural achievements, as his use and design of sleds, birch-bark canoes, toboggans and snowshoes might be part of a general story of the development of transportation." Letter of June 1963, from H.M. Jones, Acting Deputy Minister, Indian Affairs, to J.A. Roberts, Deputy Minister, Department of Trade and Commerce. Department of Indian Affairs and Northern Development Archives (hereafter DIAND) 1/43-3, v. 1.

6 The use of an inclusive historical narrative has been typical of other former European colonies in the Americas and elsewhere. Official Australian celebrations of the bicentennial in 1988, for example, also considered aborigines as an earlier wave of "immigrants." Aboriginal reaction paralleled the Expo '67 story: "this inclusive invitation was tellingly resisted, and its double-dealing rhetoric just as tellingly exposed, by the slogan governing the Aboriginal protest against the First Fleet re-enactment: 40,000 years don't make a Bicentennial" (Bennett 1989, 160).

7 "Storyline, Government of Canada Pavilion, Montreal 1967," December 1963, DIAND 1/43-3, v. 1.

8 The Department of Indian and Northern Affairs is now referred to as Indian and Northern Affairs Canada (INAC).

9 Memos of the period show that officials knew that "the traditional image of the federal Indian Affairs Branch is not a good one among Indians," that the branch had been guilty "until very recently" of "a blind attitude of cultural superiority from which Indians were viewed by other Canadian groups." "Participation in Canada's Centennial by People of Indian Ancestry – Some Policy Considerations, (unsigned), 24 September 1964, NAC, RG 10/8575 1/1-2-2-18, pt. 2, p. 2.

10 NAC, RG 71. v. 447, J.W. Francis, "Indians of Canada Pavilion – Expo '67, Press Conference – Ottawa, July 1966: Presentation of Theme and Design Concept," p. 3.

11 The juxtaposition of totem pole and tepee recalls touristic images of Indians, evident in a still widely distributed type of tourist souvenir – the miniature wigwam with a totem pole next to it. For a discussion of the totem pole as a popular icon of Indianness, see Jonaitis (1999).

12 David Staples, "Artist Alex Janvier," *Edmonton Journal,* 31 January 1988.

13 Meetings were held with "groups of Indian leaders, craftsmen, artists and others" in Vancouver, Edmonton, Montreal, and Amherst, Nova Scotia.

14 Canada, Controller of Stationery, *Indians of Canada Pavilion – Expo '67,* 1967. The brochure was ten pages in length and contained an expanded version of the text mounted in the installations.

15 A number of path-breaking exhibition projects in the United States have also followed this pattern of consultation. See, for example, a special issue of *Museum* on "Museums and Native Americans: Renegotiating the Contract," January/February 1991.

16 This is the first point noted in the discussion of the pavilion's content – a discussion that followed the presentation of the architectural plans to the Indian Advisory Committee (IAC). Its importance is reinforced by the sentence that follows: "The Past may appear more evident than the others in the present stage of design only because this is the section initiated in the design work ... the theme on the Present actually has been assigned a greater physical area than the Past." KRCC, "Minutes of the Second Meeting of the Indian Advisory Council," held at Montreal, 20-2 April 1966, p. 6.

17 "Presentation of Theme and Design Concept," NAC, RG 71, v. 447, J.W. Francis, "Indians of Canada Pavilion – Expo '67, Press Conference – Ottawa, July 1966, Presentation of Theme and Design Concept, p. 6.

18 Andrew Delisle, former chief of the Mohawk reserve of Kahnawake, was appointed commissioner-general of the Pavilion and noted in connection with this aspect of the installation that, in the 1960s, the major political concern of Aboriginal peoples was with the protection of treaty rights rather than the recognition of Aboriginal rights or sovereignty, which are the goals of current politics (personal communication, Kahnawake, Quebec, 6 May 1992).

19 Quoted in "Canadian Indians at EXPO '67," *Sanity,* July-August 1967.

20 *Indians of Canada Pavilion,* Canada, Controller of Stationery, Indians of Canada Pavilion – Expo '67, 1967, p. 9.

21 Documented by a photograph in the Public Archives of Canada. The exhibition pamphlet was even more explicit: "School curricula and text books are usually designed for children of a European background and have very little relationship to the Indian child's home experience."

22 Rosemary Speirs, "Indian Pavilion Shocks Complacent Non-Indians," *Leader-Post* (Regina and syndicated to newspapers in Ottawa, Toronto, and Montreal), 1 May 1967, 6.

23 The official theme of Expo '67 was "Man and his World," and the subthemes, realized by several official pavilions, were: "Man the Creator," "Man the Explorer," "Man the Producer," "Man the Provider," and "Man and the Community."

24 At the closing ceremonies of the Montreal Olympics of 1976 white performers paraded in stereotypical Indian costumes despite protests from local Mohawk and Seneca. Although initial plans for the opening ceremonies at the Calgary Olympics in 1988, which called for the staging of Indian parties attacking a stagecoach, were cancelled after protests from members of the organizing committee, the official logo

retained a stereotypical war-bonneted chief's head juxtaposed with the emblems of Olympic winter sports.

25 From the start the exhibition project was intended to include an important research component. The six curators were asked to assemble as comprehensive as possible a record of the location and histories of early contact-period Aboriginal objects that would serve not only as a basis for the selection of objects in the show but also as a permanent information bank. The curatorial files have been deposited and are available to the public at the Glenbow Museum and at the Canadian Museum of Civilization.

26 Because its new building was not yet ready, the National Museum of Man (now the Canadian Museum of Civilization) used the recently vacated office building on Elgin Street in Ottawa (formerly occupied by the National Gallery of Canada). See Harrison (1993) and Stainforth (1990) for further discussions of the exhibition.

27 For discussions of twentieth-century redefinitions of Aboriginal objects as "primitive art," see Feest (1984) and Rushing (1995).

28 For a later, much discussed but equally unsuccessful, attempt to use irony as a form of critique in the installation of the equally controversial exhibition *Into the Heart of Africa*, see Schildkrout (1991), Hutcheon (1992), and Burrett (this volume).

29 The announcement was made at the press conference held prior to the Ottawa opening of the exhibition, in part, one can reasonably conclude, to deflect potential criticism of the National Museum's continued support of what had become an extremely controversial exhibition.

30 American museums were given until 1996 to complete and make public their inventories – the necessary step that precedes the majority of expected claims from Aboriginal communities. In Canada some Aboriginal nations have been using strategies not foreseen by the Task Force (e.g., treaty negotiations) as a means of reclaiming objects from museums. The agreement signed by the Nisg'aa Nation, for example, provides for the repatriation of objects from the Royal British Columbia Museum and the Canadian Museum of Civilization as part of their land claims settlement.

31 Catalogues were published for both exhibitions (McMaster and Martin 1992; Nemiroff, Houle, and Townshend-Gault 1992). For a longer version of the discussion of these exhibitions, see Phillips (1993) and Rushing (1993).

32 Important precedents existed for indigenous curatorship and control in exhibitions mounted by smaller institutions, such as the University of British Columbia's Museum of Anthropology's *Robes of Power*, which was curated by Doreen Jensen, in 1986. First Nations cultural centres, such as the Woodlands Indian Cultural Centre at Brantford, Ontario, and the Ojibwa Cultural Foundation in West Bay, Ontario, has also been organizing exhibitions throughout the 1980s.

33 Both exhibitions included painting, sculpture, and installation pieces; *Indigena* also included a video work, and *Land, Spirit, Power* included a piece of virtual reality computer art. Except for three artists – Carl Beam, Domingo Cisneros, and Lawrence Paul Yuxweluptun – the artists selected for the two shows were different.

34 John Bentley Mays, "Breaking Traditions," *Globe and Mail*, 10 October 1992.

35 Exhibitions displaying indigenous objects organized in connection with the Australian bicentennial, the Seville Olympics, the Columbus quincentennial, and other such recent events have all been targeted by indigenous peoples as occasions on which to contextualize colonial representations of their cultures.

Works Cited

Ames, Michael. 1991. "Biculturalism in Exhibitions." *Museum Anthropology* 15 (2): 7–15.

– 1992. *Cannibal Tours and Glass Boxes: The Anthropology of Museums* Vancouver: UBC Press.

Bhabha, Homi, 1991. "Art and National Identity: A Critics' Symposium," Art in America, 9 September, 80–4.

Bennett, Tony. 1989. "1988: History and the Bicentenary." *Australian-Canadian Studies* 7 (1-2): 154–62.

Brydon, Sherry. 1991. "The Indians of Canada Pavilion at Expo '67: The First National and International Forum for Native Nations." Honours thesis, Department of Art History, Carleton University, Ottawa.

Clifford, James. 1991. "Four Northwest Coast Museums: Travel Reflections." In *Exhibiting Cultures: The Poetics and Politics of Museum Displays*, ed. Ivan Karp and James C. Lavine, 212–54. Washington, DC: Smithsonian Institution Press.

Feest, Christian F. 1984. "From North America." In *Primitivism in 20th Century Art*. Vol. 1: *Affinity of the Tribal and the Modern*, ed. William Rubin, 85–97. New York: Museum of Modern Art.

Graburn, Nelson H.H. 1976. *Ethnic and Tourist Arts: Cultural Expressions from the Fourth World*. Berkeley: University of California Press.

Harrison, Julia. 1993. "Completing a Circle: 'The Spirit Sings.'" In *Anthropology, Public Policy and Native Peoples in Canada*, ed. Noel Dyck and James B. Waldram, 334–57. Montreal: McGill-Queen's University Press.

Hooper-Greenhil, Eilean. 1992. *Museums and the Shaping of Knowledge*. New York: Routledge.

Hutcheon, Linda. 1994. "The Post Always Rings Twice: The Postmodern and the Postcolonial." *Textual Practice* 8 (2): 205-38.

Jonaitis, Aldona. 1999. "Northwest Coast Totem Poles: The Commodification of an Image." In *Arts and Commodities: The Authenticity of the Object in Colonial and Postcolonial Worlds*, ed. Ruth B. Phillips and Christopher B. Steiner, 104–21. Berkeley: University of California Press.

McMaster, Gerald and Lee-Ann Martin. 1992. *Indigena: Contemporary Native Perspectives*. Vancouver: Douglas and McIntyre.

Manuel, George, and Michael Posluns. 1974. *The Fourth World: An Indian Reality*. New York: The Free Press.

Miller, John, 1996. "Shows You Love to Hate: A Psychology of the Mega-Exhibition." In *Thinking about Exhibitions*, ed. Reesa Greenberg, Bruce W. Ferguson, and Sandy Nairne, 269–74. New York: Routledge.

Miller, J.R. 1989. *Skyscrapers Hide the Heavens: A History of Indian-White Relations in Canada*. Toronto: University of Toronto Press.

Nemiroff, Diana, Robert Houle, and Charlotte Townshend-Gault. 1992. *Land Spirit Power: First Nations at the National Gallery of Canada*. Ottawa: National Gallery of Canada.

Nicks, Trudy. 1992. "Partnerships in Developing Cultural Resources: Lessons From the Task Force on Museums and First Peoples." *Culture* 12 (1): 87–94.

Phillips, Ruth B. 1993. "Making Space." *Canadian Forum* 71 (816): 18–22.

– 2003. "Community Collaboration in Exhibitions: Toward a Dialogic Paradigm – Introduction." In *Museums and Source Communities: A Routledge Reader*, ed. Laura Peers and Alison K. Brown, 155–70. New York: Routledge.

—Forthcoming. "Show Times: De-Celebrating the Canadian Nation, De-Colonizing the Canadian Museum, 1967–1992." In *Making History Memorable: Past and Present in Settler Colonialism*, ed. Annie E. Coombes. Manchester: Manchester University Press.

Rushing, W. Jackson. 1993. "Contingent Histories, Aesthetic Politics." *New Art Examiner* 20: 14–20.

—1994. "Contrary Iconography: The Submuloc Show's Quincentenary De-Celebration." *New Art Examiner* 21 (10): 30–5

—1995. *Native American Art and the New York Avant Garde*. Austin, TX: University of Texas Press.

Schildkrout, Enid. 1991. "Ambiguous Messages and Ironic Twists: 'Into the Heart of Africa' and 'The Other Museum.'" *Visual Anthropology* 15 (2): 153–60.

Stainforth, Lis Smidt. 1990. "Did the Spirit Sing? An Historical Perspective on Canadian Exhibitions of the Other." MA thesis, Department of Canadian Studies, Carleton University.

Wilson, Thomas, George Erasmus, and David W. Penney. 1992. "Museums and First Peoples in Canada." *Museum Anthropology* 16 (2): 6–11.

"Into the Heart of Africa": Curatorship, Controversy, and Situated Knowledges

DEBORAH BURRETT

> If the exhibition was a reading of the material according to certain historical assumptions, the negative response to it was a reading of the exhibition according to a different set of assumptions. And the space between these two readings was so huge that it appalled everyone who caught a glimpse of it.
>
> Robert Fulford

> It is difficult to remain detached from depictions of racism "in history" when racism itself is not history.
>
> Brenda Austin Smith

Into the Heart of Africa, an exhibition that ran from November 1989 to August 1990 at the Royal Ontario Museum (ROM) in Toronto, began as a scholarly and somewhat provocative inquiry into the historical sources of the ROM's African collection and ended up the centre of a prolonged and bitter controversy in which the museum and the curator were accused of racism. The exhibition and the resulting controversy brought to the fore issues that are central to the consideration of the role of the museum in a contemporary multi-ethnic, multi-racial society. Museums, whatever approaches they choose to take, are sites of ideological production where the links between knowledge and power are forged.[1] And the question of *whose* knowledge will be represented, whose understanding of the past and its shaping of the present will be recognized within these institutions, is becoming increasingly urgent.

While this is true in all multicultural, postcolonial societies, the city of Toronto's specific local conditions played a critical role. As has been frequently observed, changing immigration patterns since the Second World War have transformed the make-up of Canadian society outside Quebec to the extent that Canadians of British descent no longer form the majority in the largest urban centres.[2] Toronto has become home to large immigrant populations from southern Europe, South Asia, East Asia, the Middle East, Central and South America, Africa, and the Caribbean – a situation that has generated undeniable tensions and conflicts.

The city's growing African-Canadian community has been struggling with, among other things, the issue of low economic and employment levels in some sectors, questions of whether the education system is meeting its needs, perceptions of damaging stereotypes in media representations, and strained relations with the police.[3] At the time of this exhibition, anger within the black community was particularly strong because of several controversial police shootings of black youths – a situation made all the more troubling by the insistent majority perception that Toronto is a tolerant, egalitarian city free of any systemic forms of racism. Within this situation the politics of identity and representation had become crucial.

The issue of representation poses a profound challenge to contemporary ethnographic museums. The growth of ethnography as a discipline and the emergence of the modern museum as a repository and conveyor of scientific knowledge were both grounded in the Enlightenment view of science as objective, value-neutral, and universal. Ethnography's authority to represent other cultures derived from its status as a science. But in recent years feminist, poststructuralist, and postcolonialist critics have mounted a concerted attack on the modernist belief in scientific objectivity and have called, instead, from their various perspectives, for a recognition of knowledge as partial, provisional, and positioned. The totalizing concept of universal knowledge has been countered by that of local or situated knowledges.[4] The knowledge generated within scientific disciplines is understood as radically contingent, historical, and bound up with the political and the ethical. At the same time, groups defined on the basis of ethnicity, class, and/or gender who feel that their histories and identities have been either misrepresented or excluded have begun to demand access to the power of representation embodied in the museum. Within this context of challenges to the authority of science and the museum, and growing demands for access, the role of the curator has become increasingly exposed to critical examination.

Into the Heart of Africa was curated by Jeanne Cannizzo, who was on contract as a guest curator with the ROM.[5] Her task – and the purpose of the exhibition – was to interpret and display the ethnology department's collection of objects from Africa. The ROM's ethnology department had never had a systematic program of collecting African objects, its primary mandate having been the study of the Aboriginal peoples of Canada. The African collection was the product of individual donations rather than the result of sustained curatorial direction. As a result, it lacked "chronological depth, geographical concentration [and] ethnographic focus" (Cannizzo 1991, 150). Therefore, there was no "possibility of a major exhibition focused on a single cultural group, a single topical theme, or any overview of the immensely complex history of the continent" (150).

What the collection did have were old catalogues containing an unusually rich amount of information about the donors of the objects and how they had originally collected them. According to Cannizzo (1991, 150):

it became clear that the majority of the early donors were either Canadian missionaries, inspired by the exploits of David Livingstone, or Canadian soldiers who joined the British Army and campaigned against Africans resisting the imperial advance, or occasionally against competing European armies during what historians have described as "the scramble" for African colonies. These people returned home bearing souvenirs and trophies of their victories on spiritual and temporal battlefields. Those objects eventually ended up in the museum.[6]

As a result, Cannizzo proposed to examine the colonial history of the objects – when, how, why, and in what context they were acquired; how they were viewed and used by the original collectors; how they became part of a museum collection in southern Ontario; and what they can tell us, therefore, about that museum (Cannizzo 1991, 151; see also Ottenberg 1991, 79). In other words, the exhibition was intended as a critical examination of the relationship between late nineteenth- and early twentieth-century Ontario and Africa, an exploration of the interweaving of British imperialism, popular culture, and the growth of the museum's African collection. This emphasis was not simply dictated by the nature of the ROM's collections: it resulted as much from Cannizzo's own ongoing interest in "museums and their collections as forms of visual ideology" (Fulford 1991, 27). The exhibition catalogue suggested:

A museum collection may be thought of as a kind of cultural text, one that may be read to understand the underlying cultural or ideological assumptions that have informed its creation, selection, and display. Within such a collection, objects act as an expression not only of the worldview of those who chose to make and use them, but also of those who chose to collect and exhibit them. (Cannizzo 1989b, 62; see also Cannizzo 1989a, 156–7)

Cannizzo (1989b, 62) argued that the nature of one of the most enduring public institutions might be understood more fully "when the museum itself is analyzed as an artifact, existing in a particular social milieu and historical period." She also noted her interest in exploring the "life histories" of objects as they move from one context to another – in this case, for example, from ritual object to missionary souvenir to museum specimen –

and in examining the ways in which the significance of the object changes according to context (Cannizzo 1991, 151). The transformational power of context, she argued, "is particularly evident in museums, which, like anthropology, are also essentially 'fictional' in their nature. That is, the meaning of their collections is generated in the interaction between the curator, the object, and the visitor. As such negotiated realities, museums are crucial to understanding one's cultural self as well as the ethnographic other" (151).

Furthermore, she also wanted to acknowledge the complaint that museums and art galleries had not fully recognized the consequences of the colonial period: she noted that anthropology as a discipline has been dealing with issues of appropriation and representation as well as problems of colonialism in field work. The ROM's African collection, while not the direct product of ethnographic practices, presented an opportunity to explore related issues of colonialism within the institution of the museum (151).

Clearly, Cannizzo's intention was to create a critical, self-reflexive exhibition – one that opened the role of the museum in society to questioning and that was sensitive to the history of colonial violence and exploitation normally masked in museum collections. Her approach to these issues was at the forefront of critical thinking on the part of progressive museum professionals in the 1980s. Indeed, Cannizzo had begun to explore these problems in a public forum as early as 1982 in a series for the CBC Radio program *Ideas*.[7] Her work on *Into the Heart of Africa* was well underway when the Smithsonian Institution hosted its influential conference, "The Poetics and Politics of Representation," in 1988. In their introduction to *Exhibiting Cultures: the Poetics and Politics of Museum Display*, the first of two volumes of papers from the conference, editors Ivan Karp and Steven Lavine wrote of the need for "experiments in exhibition design that try to present multiple perspectives or admit the highly contingent nature of the interpretations offered" (Karp and Lavine 1991).[8] Cannizzo's attempt to create an exhibition that revealed the ideological basis of the museum collection was clearly in keeping with this goal. Indeed, it could be understood as a necessary step towards the larger goal of making the museum responsive to postmodern, postcolonial society. Given the importance of the issues that informed Cannizzo's approach, how, then, did this exhibition elicit such controversy?

There have been many analyses of this show written by members of the African-Canadian community as well as by other cultural critics, literary theorists, anthropologists, and curators. Yet what is missing from this contentious debate is a close examination of the material form and content of the installation itself. Is there something we can learn from choices made in this model case of exhibition crisis that can help us in the future? Museum displays communicate through their spatial organization. It is worthwhile, therefore, at the start, taking the time to "walk through" the exhibition before posing critical questions around what went wrong.

Into the Heart of Africa included some 375 objects, plus several maps and over twenty blowups of photographs taken by Canadian missionaries and military men.[9] The exhibition space was divided into a linear series of rooms, each with a separate emphasis and distinctive appearance.[10] The entrance of the exhibit was marked by large maroon-coloured blocks between which the visitor had to pass. The intention was to emphasize movement from one realm to another. This was also meant to underline the idea of the title, *Into the Heart of Africa*, which was chosen for its associations with the nineteenth-century (e.g., with a popular travel book, *The Heart of Africa*). It was also meant to evoke Conrad's novella, *Heart of Darkness*, with its own implied critique of the "darkness" of the colonialist enterprise (Cannizzo 1991, 151). According to Cannizzo: "The title signalled that the exhibition was dealing with the past, with journeys, interaction and the disjunction between Canadian images and African realities"(151–2). Yet it should be noted from the start that there were no explanatory texts presenting these ideas to viewers of the exhibition; in short, there was nothing explicit at this point to direct the association of "darkness" away from Africa and Africans and towards the history of colonialism.

After passing through a small vestibule, the visitor entered the first major space – the introductory room. This room made use of a combination of illustrations, text, and objects in order to establish the purpose of the exhibition. The room opened with two large graphic panels. On the right wall was a scene from the *Illustrated London News* in 1874 of a British military scouting party approaching an Asante priest; on the left wall was a scene from a missionary travel account of travellers using a fallen log as a bridge. Both images conveyed exoticism and adventure, and, whether intentionally or not, established Africa as "a place where Europeans did things" (Harold Wright, qtd. in Fulford 1991, 23).

The wall panel accompanying these images set out the central themes of the exhibition: the history of the collection, the imperial context, the African cultural context, and the ensuing problem of cultural misunderstanding. It read:

Africa in the 19th century was still "the unknown continent" to most Canadians. Ignorance promoted powerful images of a mysterious land full of "barbarous" people. But Canadian soldiers and missionaries became full participants in the New Imperialism of Queen Victoria's later reign. They ventured through savannah and rainforest, encountering unfamiliar cultures with worldviews radically different from their own. Their experience of Africa, as seen in this exhibition, was very different from the way Africans perceived themselves, their own cultures, and these events. Those who returned brought home many souvenirs of their journey into the heart of Africa, objects that today remind us of a little-remembered era in Canada's past. (Cannizzo 1991, 152)[11]

This panel also introduced a strategy that was practised throughout the exhibit – the use of quotation marks to signal that certain terms, such as "barbarous" and "unknown continent," were part of the complex of nineteenth-century European attitudes and beliefs rather than those of the curator of the museum. This citational practice was meant simultaneously to convey the colonialist ideology and to call it into question. Despite its critical intention, the strategy became one of the most contentious elements of the exhibit. Many viewers read the use of quotation marks as a form of ironic distancing from the attitudes expressed; however, many others read them as a reinscription of racist attitudes.[12]

Four objects were displayed with the intention of further refuting the nineteenth-century notion of "barbarism": two collected by missionaries (a carved staff from Angola and an anthropomorphic pot from Zaire) and two that came on the market as a result of military conquest (a leaded bronze plaque from Benin and a gold Asante necklace) (Cannizzo 1991, 152).

The second part of the introductory room focused on the history of Canadians in Africa during this period. A wall panel quoting a popular history published in the Jubilee year (1897) revealed British Canadians' identification with, and participation in, Britain's imperialist endeavours.[13] Among other evidence was a blow–up of a Canadian postage stamp showing the extent of the British Empire, further emphasizing this identification. A map showing products of Africa and competing European interests spoke to economic motivation. Also displayed were examples of Canadian missionary Rev. A.W. Banfield's translations of religious texts into Nupe (a Nigerian tongue) and the dress helmet of Canadian soldier, Captain J.F. Crean. All the objects in this room were displayed in locked case, thus, according to Cannizzo (1991, 153), "ethnographizing" the European artifacts. This is one possible reading, but it is a rather subtle one, only likely to occur to viewers already oriented towards issues of museum display. Given that the walls were painted dark blue and the ceiling was covered with a Union Jack, it is not surprising that many viewers interpreted this use of display cases as implying that these relics of the Imperial past were the treasured objects of Empire.[14]

The next room was devoted to the display of objects collected by Canadian soldiers in Africa. The room was painted khaki, the colour of their uniforms, and objects were displayed in turn-of-the-century walnut cases (i.e., the type of case in which they might have been displayed at the time they were acquired) – again, a subtle reference to the history of collection and display. Three kinds of information were given about the objects:

> Something about the objects themselves including material, function or significance in the originating African culture, something about the donor or the war during which the objects were collected, and finally a museological subtext conveying to the visitor a way to think about how and why museums collect certain objects. (Cannizzo 1991, 154)

To give one example, a large introductory graphic panel, again taken from the *Illustrated London News* (1879), showed a mounted British officer stabbing a Zulu warrior through the breast. It was captioned simply, "Lord Beresford's Encounter with a Zulu." Next to this were mounted on the wall a number of Zulu spears, shields, and other weapons. The accompanying text discusses how, due to stereotypes common to that period, museum collections came to have disproportionate numbers of some kinds of objects – the image of the Zulu as warriors, for example, obscured other elements of their culture (Cannizzo 1991, 154). This emphasis was in part explained by the fact that British troops were defeated by the Zulu in 1879 (at the Battle of Isandhlawana), which led to soldiers bringing home Zulu weapons to celebrate their survival and the Empire's eventual victory. These weapons then often became part of trophy displays in British and Canadian homes – the next stage in their transformation from weapon to eventual museum specimen (154). This type of display was recreated in a period room at the end of the hall.[15] Thus the newspaper image and the objects were intended to illustrate the collecting practices of the past.

The depiction of the killing of an African man, however, became one of the most controversial elements of the exhibit. Faced with the violence of this image, many viewers were simply not interested in the issue of collecting practices. As African-Canadian poet Ayanna Black says: "I watched when they came upon that picture of the Zulu warrior. It was such a shock, some just froze and couldn't go on" (qtd. in Crean 1991, 27). Lawyer and community activist Charles Roach attempted to convey to the ROM the black community's dismay at this image, pointing out that "the photograph of the soldier plunging his sword into the African's heart is pretty chilling in light of the police shootings of [Lester] Donaldson and [Sophia] Cook in Toronto" (qtd. in Nazareth 1990, 11). In this example it becomes clear that the wider social context within which the exhibition was mounted played an inevitable role in generating the meaning of its displays.

For those who did continue beyond the military hall, next came the missionary room, cruciform in shape, with white walls signifying the "light" the missionaries believed they were bringing to the "dark continent" (Cannizzo 1991, 155). The objects displayed here were collected by Protestant missionaries who felt their mission was to "replace 'paganism' with Christianity, the slave trade with legitimate commerce, and 'barbarous' customs with their own form of civilization" (155). Again, quotation marks were used to ironize key terms. Numerous photographs documented the missionaries' efforts to inculcate such Victorian values as industriousness, modesty, and so on. Other displays showed themes that could be located within the ROM collection: for example, there were numerous so-called fetishes surrendered by converts and therefore prized as spiritual "trophies" by missionaries. The combination of objects, historical photos, and period quotations pointed, as in the military hall, both to the process of collecting and to the individuals who did the collecting.

At the end of the missionary room was a theatre where a seven-minute fictional, narrated lantern show – based on the museum's collection of period lantern slides – recreated the type of illustrated lecture missionaries gave in Toronto in the early part of this century (ca. 1919). A warning as to the offensiveness of the attitudes expressed was posted on a wall panel outside the theatre and repeated at the beginning and end of the lantern show; however, viewers were free to drift in and out at any point (Cannizzo 1991, 156; see also Ottenberg 1991, 80; and Schildkrout 1991, 19).[16] Immediately following the missionary room was a life-sized recreation of part of the Ovimbundu compound at Chisamba, Angola, where one Canadian missionary worked.[17] Wattle and daub huts were built by museum staff, while objects from the collection surrounded by foliage and accompanied by a sound track of birds and insects, represented yet another form of traditional museum display – one that, in this instance, repeated the trope of the African as "nature" against European "civilization."[18]

The rooms described thus far made up roughly half of the exhibition, and at this point the interpretive emphasis changed. In the African room, where African objects were displayed in their own right, "the theme is no longer the history of the collection. Rather, as far as possible within a museum, the objects begin to speak of the varied economies, political or cosmological complexities, and artistry of their African creators" (Cannizzo 1991, 156; see also Ottenberg 1991, 79). In this larger room, painted maroon and yellow sand tones, there was no longer any restriction on the visitor's path: he or she was free to wander from display to display in a less linear, regimented way.[19] Headsets were available for listening to music made from instruments similar to those on display.[20] Objects were grouped according to form or function; different aspects of culture were demonstrated through groups of related objects such as textiles, instruments, funerary sculpture, and so on. Furthermore, there was greater emphasis on the skill exhibited in the works (Cannizzo 1991, 156). Also, the labelling in this room was significantly different from that in the other rooms: the emphasis was on the name of the cultural group from which the object came and on the function and significance of the object rather than on the history of the donor (156). An introductory panel explained that this standard museological approach was one with which museum goers at the turn of the century would have been familiar; that is, this room was also about the nature of the displays in which these objects might have been seen at the time of their collection.

The final room of the exhibition contained photographs of present-day Africa; they were meant to emphasize the realities of industrialization and urbanization and to address the complaint that museums only display cultures as "dead." A program of lectures, symposia, films, and dance and music performances, developed by an African historian and a community arts organizer, was also intended to provide a view of contemporary African culture to balance the weight of the past.[21] Thus, *Into the Heart of Africa* made use of a range of different approaches to the display and contextualization of objects in order to enable a reading of the collection as the product of imperialist activities and attitudes. Yet, these meanings were contingent upon already existing cultural critiques and ironies that were far from explicit. What is more to the point, settings and modes of display often unintentionally repeated existing traditional colonial practices.

There is considerable evidence that the ROM took a number of steps to avoid potential problems: in the months before the opening of the exhibition an African-Canadian publicist was hired; four months before the opening, black leaders were invited to a presentation of the exhibition's purpose; advertising and promotional material were tested on African-Canadian focus groups. As a result, the title was changed from *Into the Heart of Darkness*, and $25,000 worth of promotional material was thrown out because of potentially offensive wording. At the end of this process, the overall response seemed positive, and the museum was confident enough to move back the closing date of the exhibition so that it could be seen by visitors to Caribana –Toronto's annual Caribbean festival – that summer (Fulford 1991, 22).

Into the Heart of Africa opened uneventfully to moderately good reviews in November 1989. However, four months later, on 10 March 1990, a group called the Coalition for the Truth about Africa began to picket the museum, claiming that the exhibit was racist and that it failed to tell the real history of Africa (Cannizzo 1991, 157).[22] Their initial demands, conveyed to the museum through the Ontario Ministry of Citizenship, were relatively modest, concerning changes to several labels and getting rid of the large image of the mounted British soldier stabbing a Zulu warrior. The museum was prepared to meet a number of the demands and suggested enlarging the offending image to show the full page of the *Illustrated London News*, thereby putting it more clearly in its historical context. However, by that time the coalition's position had hardened and it was insisting on both an apology and the closing down of the exhibition.[23]

By 5 May the demonstrators attempted to enter the museum, leading to a confrontation with police, who by that time were regularly stationed at the entrance (Young 1993, 178). The museum sought and won an injunction restricting the demonstrators from getting within fifty metres of the entrance. Brenda Austin-Smith (1990, 52) has pointed out the irony of a situation in which "police are called in to protect [the museum] from the people it was apparently expressing some solidarity with." More ominous yet was Paula Todd's (1990, 52) description: "Outside the Royal Ontario Museum, four uniformed police officers are in a huddle on the sun-warmed steps. Another officer eyes visitors who swing through the museum's massive doors. Black patrons are given special scrutiny."

The picketing continued every Saturday until the end of the exhibit in August, and the coalition's charges of racism intensified. Attempts continued to be made to bring the two sides together, including the creation of an African-Canadian mediating group, but negotiations were never able to be resumed and each side became increasingly frustrated with the other (Fulford 1991, 80; Young 1993, 178–80). Cannizzo has argued that the demands of the coalition were ultimately irreconcilable with the aims of the exhibit. The coalition was insisting on an exhibit that would celebrate the contributions of Africans to such fields as medicine, science, mathematics, astronomy, architecture, and art. In other words, it was demanding a radically different exhibition advancing what has been described as an emancipatory view of African history and essential black identity, to be curated by someone of African descent and vetted by the coalition (Hutcheon 1995, 16; see also Cannizzo 1991, 159; Ottenberg 1991, 81).

Although the museum kept the exhibition open for its planned run, four other North American museums – the Canadian Museum of Civilization, the Vancouver Museum, the Natural History Museum of Los Angeles County, and the Albuquerque Museum – cancelled their plans to mount the exhibit. Furthermore, Cannizzo herself became a target: her house was spray-painted with graffiti, she received abusive telephone calls, and in the fall of 1990 she took an extended sick leave from her teaching position at the University of Toronto, finding it impossible to teach in the face of continuing harassment in her class (Fulford 1991, 26–7; Young 1993, 174).

The museum responded to this controversy as though it were primarily an issue of academic freedom (Cannizzo 1991, 157, 159; Ottenberg 1991, 80; Young 1993, 174, 181, 184). Along with a number of commentators, it questioned the legitimacy of the Coalition for the Truth about Africa, characterizing its members as radical extremists who did not speak for the black community as a whole, and who were exploiting the high level of racial tension in Toronto at the time (Cannizzo 1991, 157; Fulford 1991, 24).[24] However, while many members of the African-Canadian community did dissociate themselves from the coalitions' actions, the fact remains that many visitors to this exhibition, both black and white, felt that it was inherently racist (Fulford 1991, 24). Given that Cannizzo's intention was to create an exhibit that exposed the racism in the colonialist attitudes of the late nineteenth- and early twentieth-century, what went wrong?

To begin with, although Cannizzo wrote of the importance of understanding the museum within its social context, she neglected to take that very context into account in her approach; that is to say, she failed to understand the audience for the exhibit in a number of important ways. For one thing, she did not take into account the general expectation that a museum exhibition speaks with an authoritative voice. Cannizzo deliberately avoided the imposition of a strong narrative in this exhibition; instead, she relied on viewers to recognize more subtle tensions and ironies that she had attempted to establish between objects, images, and texts and so to arrive on their own at the specific critical reading she hoped to stimulate (Ottenberg 1991, 80; Schildkrout 1991, 19).[25] However, a number of critics have argued that the museum-going public tends to look for a clear message delivered by the museum as authoritative and, therefore, tends to read an exhibit as a transparent text (Fulford 1991, 28; Hutcheon 1995, 5; Schildkrout 1991, 22). Moreover, the public usually assumes that what is presented in a museum is for admiration and edification; the last thing they expect to find there, in short, is a self-critical statement of historical museum practice. Thus, for most viewers, the reading that Cannizzo hoped to foster would have required a more explicit statement of curatorial intent (Ottenberg 1991, 80; Schildkrout 1991, 20).

This brings us to a contradiction at the heart of the exhibition. By creating an exhibition that foregrounded the idea that the meaning of objects within a museum display is a construction – and only one of many possible meaning frameworks – Cannizzo was radically challenging the perception of the museum as authority. In short, she was critiquing the claims of objectivity and universality embedded in traditional museum displays. In presenting the ROM's collection as a cultural text that required to be "read" self-consciously, she failed to anticipate that, given their own situatedness within contemporary Canadian culture, different groups would arrive at radically different framings (Crean 1991, 27; Philip 1992, 105). As journalist Robert Fulford (1991, 21) put it:

> If the exhibition was a reading of the material according to certain historical assumptions, the negative response to it was a *reading of the exhibition* according to a different set of assumptions. And the space between these two readings was so huge that it appalled everyone who caught a glimpse of it. That space, apparently, was just as great as the space between [Canadian missionary] A.W. Banfield's intentions in 1905 and our reading of him in 1991. (see also Schildkrout 1991, 53)

African-Canadian writer and critic Marlene Nourbese Philip (1992, 105) offered a more situated account of this yawning gap: "The same text resulted in contradictory readings determined by the different life histories and experiences. One reading saw these artifacts as being frozen in time and telling a story about white Canadian exploration of Africa; the other inserted the reader – the African Canadian reader – actively into the text, who then read those artifacts as the painful detritus of savage exploration and attempted genocide of their own people."

The failure to anticipate that many African Canadians would respond with pain and anger to the representation of Africans as seen through the eyes of English-Canadian colonialists suggests that the exhibition was conceived with a limited view of its potential audience. One rationale given for its focus was that Canadians were largely unaware of this aspect of their own history. The exhibition thus could be seen as a form of "consciousness-raising."[26] But this, of course, raises the question of *whose* consciousness, or, as Nourbese Philip put it, "which Canadians the ROM had in mind. European or African Canadians? Or was the ROM perhaps defining 'Canadian' as someone of European heritage"(105). What was at stake for African Canadians, she argued, was a visceral, lived history: "African Canadians know the history of colonialism in a painfully intimate way; they often live its implications and repercussions every day of their lives in this country. It is, of course, a not-so-astonishing *and* racist oversight that the ROM would assume that the only meaningful audience of this exhibit would be white Canadians" (ibid.).

It is clear that the museum failed to take into account the profound cultural differences existing within the Canadian audience.[27] A number of critics have suggested that this could have been avoided if the museum had consulted with the African-Canadian community from the outset rather than limiting consultation to marketing focus groups. Betty Julian, former director of the artist-run gallery A Space, commented: "It's important that in the development of any type of exhibition, it is the responsibility of the curator to involve people from that specific culture in terms of how that work is going to be contextualized and how the audience will receive it" (qtd. in Nazareth 1990, 11). As anthropologist Simon Ottenberg (1991, 82), reviewing the exhibition for *African Arts*, suggested, "it becomes a question of contacts, negotiations, and bargaining undertaken from the outset of the planning, not after the ideas are fully conceived." Ottenberg concluded: "This all takes time, money, and energy, but our society is increasingly one where minorities are more and more vocal and politically significant. This may mean establishing regular relationships for the long term (not just before preparing for an exhibit), incorporating minorities into museum staffs and boards, and reaching for representatives of different interests within any particular minority group" (82). The question of community consultation raises, in its turn, a number of complex and difficult issues regarding the role of expert knowledge and the scholarly independence, authority, and responsibility of the curator – issues that arise, on the one hand, from the challenge to the authority claims of scientific knowledge and, on the other, from the existence of different discursive communities claiming access to the power represented by the museum (81).[28]

Another problem frequently cited by critics was that, in the first half of the display (the introduction, military hall, and missionary room), the colonialists were personalized (mueseum-goers were given their names, their stories, and their connection to history) while the Africans were, for the most part, nameless. We didn't learn their individual stories, nor did we hear any response to colonialist activity from the African cultures directly affected (Crean 1991, 24; Schildkrout 1991, 20). The only voice that clearly emerged was that of the colonialists, which, once more, confirms the absence of an unambiguous curatorial voice to counter the explicit imperialist viewpoint (Crean 24–5; Schildkrout 20).

It was also argued that the African objects that were intended as counterevidence to European perceptions simply didn't present a direct enough challenge (Schildkrout 1991, 18). To cite one example, after passing under the Union Jack and viewing Captain Crean's helmet encased as a treasure object, the viewer entered the military hall to be confronted by the enlarged image of the killing of a Zulu warrior. The viewer then came upon a case of Asante gold objects and brass weights used for measuring gold, presented as the African "answer" to colonialist perceptions; that is, they were meant to engender an appreciation of the complexity and sophistication of the cultures being disrupted (Cannizzo 1991, 154). But, as curator Enid Schildkrout (1991, 18) pointed out, the approach was too oblique. "It was at this point in the exhibition ... that the visitor needed to hear the African response to colonialism. In a dialogue about colonialism and the history of collections a showcase celebrating the artistry of goldweights was irrelevant and confusing." And, again, the African voice was lost.[29]

In the end, it was the very focus of the exhibition that was seen as fundamentally flawed. *Into the Heart of Africa* was publicized as the first major African exhibition in Toronto, creating the expectation that this would be an extensive presentation of African culture: it was not and was never intended to be that (Ottenberg 1991, 81). The ensuing disappointment was expressed by one protester, who said, "All my life I've been looking for my roots, I come here looking for them – and you've shown me nothing"(Fulford 1991, 23). On one level, this might be seen simply as a failure in marketing and advertising. But on another level, this response registers a widely felt frustration over the fact that a significant occasion had been squandered: the ROM's first extensive exhibition of its African collection told the story not of Africans but of white colonialists. As critic Errol Nazareth (1990, 10) pointed out: "The victors ... have always got to tell the tale, and they [the black community] see no reason why a public institution should once again give voice to those who destroyed Africa's ancestral culture."

Closely related to the issue of voice is the problem of the use of irony as a form of critique in this exhibition. Literary theorist Linda Hutcheon (1995, 15) analyzed this use of irony in terms of its attempt to be "postmodernly deconstructive" on the one hand and "postcolonially oppositional" on the other. The use of irony, she argued, is an effective strategy for undermining assumptions of "apolitical, detached objectivity and a positivist commitment to science" (5) – the assumptions upon which the modernist project was founded. Clearly, both the growth of museums as institutions and of ethnography as a discipline were part of that project. But as Hutcheon further pointed out, the history of ethnographic collections cannot be separated from the history of imperialism, although the ideological view of knowledge as neutral and value-free has tended to either mask or legitimate that connection (5).

It was precisely this relationship between the growth of the ROM's collection and Canadian participation in the imperialist past that Cannizzo had set out to deconstruct. Ironic cues such as quotation marks around words like "savage," "barbarous," "cannibals," and "Dark Continent" were expected to be adequate indications of the distance between the colonialist viewpoint and that of the exhibit itself (Crean 1991, 21; Schildkrout 1991, 25). In short, irony was intended to be sufficient to cast the colonialist into the role of the other (Philip 1992, 106). Though the strategy worked for some viewers, for many others it clearly did not. The difficulty, in Hutcheon's view, was that, while irony may be useful in effecting a postmodern critique of the modernist institution, it is much less reliable as a weapon for challenging the legacy of colonialism itself. In order to be effective in that arena, irony must be used "oppositionally from within" (Hutcheon 1995, 12). But, as Hutcheon goes on to say, the irony in *Into the Heart of Africa* "was perceived as coming from a colonial source, even if a self-deconstructing one, and even if the irony was largely at the expense of imperialists not Africans" (12).

Brenda Austin-Smith (1990, 52) articulated this problem from the African-Canadian community's perspective:

Perhaps the organizers of the show ... relied too much on an assumption of its audience's emotional and political detachment from the pain of the distortions being re-presented in the exhibit itself. Irony requires a degree of coolness, a measure of distance on the part of the perceiver in order to succeed. That distance comes easily to those whose history has not been one of brutal oppression. It is difficult to remain detached from depictions of racism "in history" when racism itself is not history.

As Austin-Smith argued, "Asking black audiences to put aside their lived experience in order to participate as ironic perceivers of themselves seems to pit the ROM's expressed intention of using irony as a way of questioning historical perceptions of blacks, against blacks themselves" (52). The division between those who "got the joke" and those who did not was further reinforced by commentators (art critics, columnists) who suggested that "getting it" was a matter simply of sophistication, of literacy – or the lack of it.[30]

Finally, linked to the problematic use of irony is the question of how appropriate it is to continue the circulation of visual imagery containing profoundly racist messages. There were many examples of this in *Into the Heart of Africa*. The infamous engraving form the *London Illustrated News* showing the British soldier stabbing the Zulu warrior was one such image. Another enlarged engraving from the same source showed Africans fleeing in terror or crouching in submission as British soldiers entered their village. A 1904 map displayed in the "Missionary Room" showed the unevangelized areas of the continent as "Darkest Africa" (Ottenberg 1991, 80). But perhaps the most problematic images were several of the photographs taken by missionaries showing Africans submitting to white instruction and/or supervision. In one example, African women were shown carrying water to be used in the construction of a church, while a white man stands to the side, clearly overseeing their labour. In another example, a white woman stands over a group of African women washing laundry in a tin tub.

While labels accompanying these images were often meant to undercut the racism portrayed, it is questionable how effective they were. For example, the label accompanying the laundry photo read, "Taken in Nigeria about 1910, this photograph shows missionary Mrs. Thomas Titcombe giving African women 'a lesson in how to wash clothes.' African labour was the mainstay of mission economies" (in Hutcheon 1995, 12). Here again, quotation marks were used to suggest an ironic reading of the label and, by extension, of the situation depicted. Yet labels are only effective if people read them; many do not and, therefore, receive *only* the messages conveyed by the more powerful visual images. For this reason Schildkrout (1991, 21) argued that "it may be a requirement of the exhibition format that visual messages and verbal texts convey the same idea," even if this limits the use of irony. Similarly, Fulford quoted a ROM security guard, Tom Hanik, who had observed people's responses over the length of the exhibit and pointed out that many people did not read the labels and panels, or read them only in part, and therefore reacted primarily to the visual imagery:

> What if the visitors acquired only a visual impression? They would go away, Hanik claimed, with a powerful image of white racial superiority. "Walk through the exhibit and pretend you can't read. You will find image after image of superiority: the mounted swordsman over the spear carrier; the military leader over his troops, the missionary over the convert ... Wherever whites and blacks were pictured together, whites were superior. It was, Hanik suggested, "a bombardment of superiority." The liberal view of the texts was simply overwhelmed by the much more powerful imagery. (qtd. in Fulford 1991, 25. See also Crean 1991, 25; Schildkrout 1991, 21)

Mieke Bal (1991) has argued that the reproduction of racist, colonialist imagery leads to reinscribing the very attitudes and assumptions that the critic is attempting to expose and analyze. Great care must be taken to frame this imagery in such a way that the critique – and *not* the racist content – is predominant. It is fair to ask whether *Into the Heart of Africa* did this. Many of the images were troubling for viewers who felt assaulted by the racist perspectives embodied.[31] The museum's stated purpose of revealing an aspect of Canada's colonial past and of making the African collection understandable as a product of that past was lost for many viewers – cancelled by other, more vivid, issues. Indeed, as the reactions of many viewers to the use of irony and the inclusion of racist images revealed, one of the basic problems with *Into the Heart of Africa* was its failure to frame objects and images in such a way that the critical intent of the show would have been unambiguous. A more fundamental problem, however, was its lack of foresight in recognizing the profound differences in the assumptions and expectations of the multiple audiences this exhibition would attract. In her worthwhile attempt to make the colonialist past embedded in the ROM's African collection available for reflection, Cannizzo unwittingly failed to anticipate the fact that, for many viewers, that history was experienced as still alive in the present. Furthermore, for many members of Toronto's African-Canadian community an exhibition that once again told the tale of white imperialism within the framework of an establishment institutional context ignored their felt need to explore their own cultural heritage.

It is certainly possible that no African exhibition mounted by the ROM in 1989 could have avoided controversy, given the racial tension of the moment, and a fuller understanding of the historical place of this museum controversy would return it to an even wider national, and transnational, history. What remains clear is that the museum ought to have been more aware of and responsive to the African-Canadian community's needs when it undertook to mount its first major African show. The disappointment expressed by one protester bears repeating: "All my life I've been looking for my roots, I come here looking for them – and you've shown me nothing." Time and time again, criticism of *Into the Heart of Africa* comes back to the issue of recognizing the heterogeneity of the audience – recognizing that individuals attending the show would come from different communities and knowledge frameworks. Curators cannot assume that they have accounted for such differences in advance. If, as Cannizzo rightly argues, museums present negotiated realities, then the challenge remains one of opening the museum structure to allow wider mediations to take place on the ground.[32]

Notes

1 For an extended discussion of the ideological role of museums, see Hooper-Greenhill (1992). See also Bennett (1995); Clifford (1988); Carol Duncan, "Art Museums
   and the Ritual of Citizenship," in Karp and Lavine (1991, 88–103); and Hutcheon
   (1995).

2 See Hutcheon (1995, 7). Note that this is not meant to imply that there has not
   been significant immigration to Quebec but simply that my focus is the shrinking
   majority position of Canadians of British descent.

3 For a discussion of the political implications of this situation, see Ottenberg
   (1991). It should be noted that the term "African-Canadian community" is not
   being used to imply the existence of a single, homogenous group. Within the black
   population of Toronto there are those whose families have lived in Canada for generations, while other groups have arrived more recently from a range of Caribbean
   and African nations. And of course differences of religion, class, gender, sexual orientation, and so on combine to make that population as heterogenous as is that of
   the "white community."

4 To cite only a few examples particularly relevant to this chapter, see Clifford (1988);
   Geertz (1983); Haraway (1988); and West (1990).

5 Cannizzo's training was in social and cultural anthropology, and she had fieldwork
   experience in Sierra Leone.

6 It should be noted that, like the ROM's African collection, many museum collections
   have grown without systematic programs of collecting. One interesting result of this
   has been that, despite their haphazard appearance, these collections are often
   proving to be rich sources of information about the preferences and priorities, the
   worldviews and self-understandings, of those who collected the objects. Also, the
   information accompanying these objects – formerly dismissed as "unscientific" –
   is now being reconsidered for the new insights it might provide into the cultures
   that produced the objects and the nature of the cultural exchanges that took place.
   (I would like to thank Ruth Phillips for pointing this out.)

7 "Old Images/New Metaphors," a three-part series for *Ideas*, CBC Radio, 1982.

8 See also I. Karp, C. Mullen Kreamer, and S. Lavine, eds., *Museums and Communities: The Politics of Public Culture* (Washington: Smithsonian Institution, 1992).

9 Cannizzo worked as a member of a six-person team to create this exhibition. The others included an architect, a graphics designer, a coordinator, an artist, and an interpretive planner. There were accommodations made to conservation and security
   requirements, public programming, and so on. Cannizzo (1991, 151) also refers to
   difficult negotiations "that revolved around the institutional subculture, the decades
   long praxis determined by 'custom' and 'tradition' at this particular museum"; however, she does not explain what these "negotiations" involved or in what they resulted.

10 The description of the exhibition is taken largely from Cannizzo's own description
   and therefore contains references to the intentions of the exhibit as well as to its
   physical appearance. See Cannizzo (1991, 151); Ottenberg (1991, 79–80); and E.
   Schildkrout (1991, 18).

11 It should be noted that the length of the panel text was determined in part by conventional museum wisdom as to how much a visitor will read. Also, the typeface,
   "Berkeley," was chosen for its nineteenth-century look.

12 See Crean (1991, 25); Fulford (1991, 26); and Schildkrout (1991, 20-1). For an extended analysis of the use of irony in this exhibition, see Hutcheon (1995). See also Linda Hutcheon, *Irony's Edge* (London and New York: 1994).

13 The text of the panel read: "There was no exact dividing line between a Canadian Briton and a British Briton. Their accents were diverging it is true, but they carried the same passport and usually honored the same ideals ... Hundreds of thousands of British Canadians regarded the imperial saga as part of their own national heritage. The excitement of the New Imperialism was almost as intense in Toronto as it was in London (James Morris, qtd. in Cannizzo 1991, 152)."

14 For example, see Crean (1991, 24).

15 This period room was based on a 1911 photograph of the hallway in the Toronto home of an officer in the imperial army. See Cannizzo (1991, 154).

16 Susan Crean (1991, 25) points out that the voice-over of the lantern show could be heard throughout the room so that the racist ideas of the missionaries were heard by everyone passing through.

17 The recreation was based on 1895 photographs taken by missionaries. See Cannizzo (1991, 154).

18 For a discussion of the complex contemporary associations with the idea of the "primitive" (the "not-civilized"), see Torgovnick (1990).

19 Cannizzo (1991, 153) has noted that it was her intention that the military hall and the missionary room both "should in some way reflect the regimentation and order which Europeans often sought to impose on what they perceived as the 'chaos' of African cultural practices and social life."

20 Cannizzo notes (in response to criticism) that, for practical reasons, it had been impossible to have the music playing in the room rather than only through headsets (156; see also Crean 1991, 26).

21 Cannizzo (1991, 157) notes that two consultants – an African historian from Uganda and a Toronto community arts organizer – had been involved in planning the public programming.

22 Others have noted that negative responses to the exhibit began to be heard gradually during the four-month period before the picketing started. See Fulford (1991, 22); Schildkrout (1991, 16).

23 T. Cuyler Young (1993, 175–80) gives a "blow-by-blow" account of the breakdown of negotiation as seen from the museum's perspective.

24 Schildkrout (1991, 16–17) argues that, while there were unusually high levels of tension in Toronto, the situation was hardly unique and, therefore, not a sufficient explanation: "There is no question that the appropriate bridges had not been built, that the public relations organized for the exhibition were poor, and that racial tensions in Toronto were high and could easily be galvanized by an exhibition at a major cultural institution. On the other hand, most North American cities have equally serious racial tensions, and many major museums ... have monumental entrances which can serve as platforms for publicity-seeking protesters." However, it should be stressed that the history of blacks in Toronto is different from that of the black urban populations in the United States, and the situations may not be directly comparable.

25 For a discussion of the relationship between objects, labels, and viewers, see M. Baxandall, "Exhibiting Intention: Some Preconditions of the Visual Display of Culturally Purposeful Objects," in Karp and Lavine (1991, 33–41).

26 Ruth Phillips, in discussion.

27 It should be noted that African Canadians were not the only ones offended by this exhibiton: some contemporary missionaries and descendants of earlier missionaries and soldiers objected to the criticism of their, or their forebears', actions. See Fulford (1991, 25-6); Schildkrout (1991, 17).

28 For a discussion of the changing role of the "majority museum," see James Clifford, "Four Northwest Coast Museums," in Karp and Lavine (1991, 212–54).

29 As Schildkrout (1991, 19) writes: "Where we should have had an African voice answering the imperialist collector, we had instead a dense filter of anthropology, ethnography, and art history shrouding the African side of the objects' life histories."

30 One example of this type of commentary (from the *Globe and Mail*, 29 December 1990, p. D1) is quoted by Cannizzo (1991, 158): "A show full of content and thought-provoking ironies for educated white Torontonians was being 'read' in a completely different way by some black visitors (by no means all), who saw in it only shame, humiliation, and racism. One had to be very literate and sophisticated to appreciate the show as the curator intended." See also Ottenberg (1991, 82); Schildkrout (1991, 21).

31 Ayanna Black described the situation as follows: "They used the propaganda of the period without proper explanation or preamble. [The curator] did not want to manipulate the material, but she ended up implanting racist images because the critique of 'intellectual arrogance' did not come through. People missed it" (qtd. in Crean 1991, 27).

32 Th exhibition *Into the Heart of Africa* continues to be discussed in terms of the politics of identity and representation and their implications for museum practice. See, for example, Jean Cannizzo, "Gathering Souls and Objects," in *Colonialism and the Object: Empire, Material Culture and the Museum*, ed. Tim Barringer and Tom Flynn (London and New York: Routledge, 1998); Shelley Butler, *Contested Representations: Revisiting* Into the Heart of Africa (Australia: Gordon and Breach, 1999); Eve Mackey, "Postmodernism and Cultural Politics in a Multicultural Nation: Contests over Truth in the Into the Heart of Africa Controversy," *Public Culture* (Winter, 1995); H. Riegel, "Into the Heart of Irony: Ethnographic Exibitions and the Politics of Difference," in *Theorizing Museums: Representing Identity and Diversity in a Changing World*, ed. S. Macdonald and G. Fyfe (Oxford: Blackwell/The Sociological Review, 1996); and Carol Tator, Frances Henry, and Winston Mattis, *Challenging Racism in the Arts: Case Studies of Controversy and Conflict* (Toronto: Univeristy of Toronto Press, 1998).

Works Cited

Austin-Smith, Brenda. 1990. "Into the Heart of Irony." *Canadian Dimension*, 24: 51-2.

Bal, Mieke. 1991. "The Politics of Citation." *diacritics* 21 (1): 25–45.

Bennett, Tony. 1995. *The Birth of the Museum: History, Theory, Politics*. London and New York: Routledge.

Cannizzo, Jeanne. 1989a. "Reading the National Collections: Museums as Cultural Texts." In *Toward the 21st Century: New Directions for Canada's National Museums*, ed. Leslie H. Tupper,Ottawa: Canadian Museum of Civilization.

– 1989b. *Into the Heart of Africa*. Toronto: Royal Ontario Museum.

–1991. "Exhibiting Cultures: 'Into the Heart of Africa.'" *Visual Anthropology Review* 7 (Spring): 150–60.

Clifford, James. 1988. *The Predicament of Culture: Twentieth-Century Ethnography, Literature, and Art.* Cambridge and London: Harvard University Press.

Crean, Susan. 1991. "Taking the Missionary Position." *This Magazine* 24 (February): 23–8.

Fulford, R. 1991. "Into the Heart of the Matter." *Rotunda* 24 (Summer): 19–28.

Geertz, Clifford. 1983. *Local Knowledge: Further Essays in Interpretive Anthropology.* New York: Basic.

Haraway, Donna. 1988. "Situated Knowledges: The Science Question in Feminism and the Privilege of Partial Perspective." *Feminist Studies* 14 (Fall): 575–99.

Hooper-Greenhill, Eilean. 1992. *Museums and the Shaping of Knowledge.* London and New York: Routledge.

Hutcheon, Linda. 1995. "The Post Always Rings Twice: The Postmodern and the Postcolonial." *Material History Review* 41 (Spring): 4–23.

Karp, Ivan and Steven D. Lavine, eds. 1991. *Exhibiting Cultures: The Poetics and Politics of Museum Display.* Washington and London: Smithsonian Institution.

Nazareth, Errol. 1990. "Showcase Showdown." NOW (29 March–4 April): 10–12.

Ottenberg, Simon. 1991. "Into the Heart of Africa." *African Arts* 24 (July): 79–82.

Philip, M. Nourbese. 1992. "Museum Could Have Avoided Culture Clash." In *Frontiers: Selected Essays and Writings on Racism and Culture, 1984–1992.* 103-8. Toronto: Mercury Press.

Robertson, Heather. 1990. "Out of Africa, Into the Soup." *Canadian Forum* 69 (September): 4.

Royal Ontario Museum. 1990. "News Release: Planned Stops of the Royal Ontario Museum Exhibition 'Into the Heart of Africa' cancelled by other Canadian Museum Venues." 20 September.

Schildkrout, Enid. 1991. "Ambiguous Messages and Ironic Twists: Into the Heart of Africa and the Other Museum," *Museum Anthropology* 15 (2): 16–22.

Todd, Paula. 1990. "African Exhibits Inspire Awe and Anger." *Toronto Star*, 7 May, A6.

Torgovnik, Marianna. 1990. *Gone Primitive: Savage Intellects, Modern Lives.* Chicago: University of Chicago Press.

Valpy, Michael. 1990. "ROM Show Portrays a Bygone Canada," *Globe and Mail*, 6 June, A8.

Vincent, Isabel. 1990. "Two Museums Cancel ROM's Controversial Show on Africa." *Globe and Mail*, 21 September, C9.

West, Cornel. 1990. "The New Cultural Politics of Difference. In *Out There: Marginalization and Contemporary Cultures.* Cambridge: Harvard University Press.

Young, Jr., T. Cuyler. 1993. "Into the Heart of Africa: The Director's Perspective." *Curator* 36: 174–88.

PART FOUR

VISUAL CULTURE

The Unbearable Strangeness of Being: Edgar Reitz's *Heimat* and the Ethics of the *Unheimlich*

BARBARA GABRIEL

How do we confront that which we have excluded in order to be,
whether it is the return of the repressed or the return of strangers?

Julia Kristeva

It is part of morality not to be at home in one's house.

Theodor Adorno

The appearance of Edgar Reitz's film chronicle *Heimat* on West German television in an eleven-part film-length series in the autumn of 1984, after a premiere at the Munich film festival earlier in the summer, marked an important foray into cultural debates around the nation's place in twentieth-century history. Though both a film and an "event" that would eventually spiral into an ongoing project, it was initially designed to take back the history that had been "stolen" from Germany in the American television series *Holocaust.*[1] Its wider context, however, was the ongoing labour of national memory-work taking place around what Adorno had called an "unmasterable past," one that spanned the wider cultural as well as political sphere (Maier 1988). Its discourses were those of Bitburg and the historians' debate, its cultural practices as broad as a New German Cinema now widely disseminated abroad, the paintings of Anselm Kiefer and Gerhard Richter, and the shuttle movement back and forth between an East and West German literary scene whose divided histories would erupt into a contest of memories in the ensuing decade.

Reitz's own intervention in this national labour against forgetting is explicit in the very title of his article, "Let's Work on Our Memories," sparked by the controversy that followed the widely viewed American melodrama series in Germany (Elsaesser 1989, 272). Yet, even on the face of it, his own response to this appropriated national history staged a confrontation with the past inevitably shaped by its focus on the rural Simon family in the village of Schabbach in the Hunsruck region of Germany in the years between 1919 and 1982, a story of the "little people" caught up in the vortex of events at a certain remove. Not only were these villagers often conveniently off-stage from a terrible history, but their very ordinariness invited audience identification in a structure of spectatorship heightened by the episodic structure of the event.[2] Viewers could tune into successive installments with growing familiarity with characters whose fortunes followed through a generational saga not unlike that of their own family histories. Yet, despite widespread success when it was screened in Munich and at film festivals in Vienna and London, it was not long before a number of critics at home and abroad challenged *Heimat*'s history writing. Considerable scholars, like Miriam Hansen (in *Dossier* 1985, 5) echoed concerns about "the ambiguous marginalization of the Holocaust" in Reitz's film text. It was an issue raised even more forcefully by Gertrud Koch's argument that "Whenever real horror would have to be thematized, the film resorts to these fade-out strategies which are analogous to the defensive mechanisms of experience" (qtd. in *Dossier* 1985, 17). In order to tell the myth of *Heimat*, she concludes, "the trauma of Auschwitz has to be bracketed from German history" (13).

Yet what is this "myth" of Heimat, which nearly all critics agree is integral to assessing the film's responsibility to history? In giving the name of "Heimat" to his film chronicle, Reitz was explicitly situating it within the established national genre of the Heimatfilm. Countering the notion that German film after 1962 created itself ex nihilo out of the rubble of a spent and morally compromised national tradition, Eric Rentschler (1982, 104) argues for a recognition of several points of continuity in German cinema, not least of which is the Heimatfilm genre itself: "As powerful a force in the popular imagination as the Western in America, the Samurai film in Japan and the partisan epic in Yugoslavia, the Heimat film by dint of its persistence throughout the entire span of German film history, acts as a seismograph, one that allows us to gauge enduring presences as they have evolved over the last eighty years." Anticipating the recent work of historians around German discourses of Heimat, Rentschler suggests that it is only after Heimat can no longer be taken for granted that it begins to emerge as a concept.[3] In other words, it is precisely with the loss of a traditional rural peasant life, through the mobility and increased urbanization that flowed from the Industrial Revolution, that Heimat surfaces as an ideal. Even at its inception, then, we are already face to face with a phenomenon that has the psycho-ontology of a fantasy.

Though a number of characteristics typically define the genre, none is more central than its narrative axis of the *Heimat* (homeland), on the one hand, and the *Fremde* (foreigner), on the other hand, who threatens to invade and disrupt it.⁴ Any incursion on the part of this stranger into this closed domain must be repelled in order to restore the order before the mythic Fall. Not only can such an idyll be seen to be complicit in the blood and soil discourses of Nazi Germany, but any framing of twentieth-century German history in such a space of pastoral longing can already be charged with an escape from ethical responsibility: not memory work but, rather, *forgetting* in a way that directly repeats the silences and evasions of the immediate postwar period. To what extent, then, is Reitz's history-chronicle complicit either with the traditional Heimatfilm's presiding assumptions or the longer story of Heimat, itself, which is governed by the same geographies of desire? This is the question that shapes my argument here, one that simultaneously revisits the concept of Heimat and moves the Freudian category of the *unheimlich*, in its beginnings an aesthetic category, onto a field increasingly charged with ethical implications – in a historical moment when unhomely-home stands at the centre of our global and transnational concerns.⁵

In what follows, I propose to unravel a strange 1984 *Heimat*, one that, among other things, not only stages Freud's "The Uncanny" as a self-conscious intertext but that also puts into play central elements of E.T.A. Hoffman's "The Sandman," the German Romantic tale that is Freud's own model for the *unheimlich*.⁶ While, on the face of it, all that connects the words "Heimat" and "unheimlich" is a tenuous link of origins, it is worth remembering that Freud begins his own now classic essay in an extended performance of the term's etymological connections. This stubborn and overdetermined concept of the *unheimlich*, so elusive and hard to pin down in its earliest investigations, has had an important afterlife in recent cultural theory in ways that extend its explanatory potential for a revisioning of both the subject and the nation-state in postmodernity: categories central to plumbing Germany's National Socialist past as well as its emerging place in the new multicultural Europe, whose changing realities were the immediate social and historical context of the production and reception of *Heimat*.⁷ Within Germany itself in the 1980s debates around foreigners that echoed uncannily with the period of National Socialism were beginning to surface in both local politics and the media, while the tensions they reflected would erupt into full-scale violence in the early 1990s. At the same time, the predicament of minorities with their own hybrid memories and identities troubled older definitions of Heimat. These new realities could not help but situate Reitz's historical chronicle as operating in doubled-time from the start, a Benjaminian history of a present apprehending the past as it flashes up at a moment of danger (Benjamin 1969, 255).

Yet if *Heimat* continues to have ongoing relevance to an unfolding and sometimes agonistic European drama of nation and belonging, then that is also because of the kind of history-writing that is at stake here. Far from effacing the darkest corners of twentieth-century German history, Reitz's epic film is engaged in both their representation and a radical analysis of the structures of the subject that enabled them, explicitly figured in the foundational metanarratives of National Socialism. Part of the discomfort he felt at the response to the American series *Holocaust* was that it registered "the horrible crocodile tears of our nation" in response to a film that had reduced truth to an abstraction – one that, in his own words, in an interview with Gideon Bachmann, had "destroyed for me, the moral impetus of the real, historical and proven events" (Reitz 1985b, 18). Far from being innocent about the historical complicity of a discourse of Heimat in the National Socialist project, Reitz has acknowledged that in German culture there is scarcely a more ambivalent feeling than the experience which stands behind the dream of Heimat. Yet, the ambitious double task he set for himself in his film chronicle was to stage the longing for that dream at the same time as he exposed its murderous potential, born of a logic of disavowal.[8]

Heimat's over-arching thematics, I want to suggest, is a critique of purity and homogeneity that directly engages history in its challenge to those operations of the subject engaged in the making of the stranger. Reitz's film continues a long line of cultural work since the Frankfurt School, which reads the National Socialist catastrophe on an axis that is both social and psychoanalytic, formations of culture and nation inseparable from those that produce a historical subject. The understanding of the nation itself as a "state of fantasy," in Jacqueline Rose's (1996) turn of phrase, serves to remind us that a diverse range of cultural sites needs to be mobilized to uncover national fantasies at particular times and places. In turn, these imaginary formations span a range of heterogeneities both within and beyond the borders of the nation-state. Yet this national unconscious is not merely an expanded historical archive to be read: it is also a charged index of ongoing moments of crisis that generate new meanings and continue to have material consequences for lived bodies.

Reitz's complex film text both stages and undoes this fantasy of home across a range of sites that extend from region and nation to the primordial landscape of belonging, which spirals back to childhood and the Mother. Many of the themes that drive this epic chronicle are intensely personal (Reitz himself is returning to the Hunsruck he left as a young man of nineteen), caught up in a landscape of memory and longing that, at times, operates as thinly veiled autobiography. Yet, in the end, this journey of sometimes uncompromising self-analysis (which includes coming to terms with nostalgia for a place that never really was) also enables some of the most radical connections in the film text around the ideals of Heimat and the stranger, masculine and feminine, the self and the other, in that violent logic of boundary making that returns us to the dark excesses of national history.

In representing this longing for Heimat, along with the ways in which it is always already sundered from within, the 1984 *Heimat* closely follows Freud's (1964, 224) own refusal to read the *"heimlich"* and the *"unheimlich"* as opposites: "What interests us most ... is to find that among its different shades of meaning the word *'heimlich'* exhibits one which is identical with its opposite – *'unheimlich.'"* Reitz's film repeats Freud's argument that these two seeming antinomies are really doubles, which readily slip and slide into one another. Yet this is only one of the ways in which *Heimat* echoes "The Uncanny." By the end of the film-chronicle we will have explored virtually all of the secret spaces of Freud's overdetermined notion of the *unheimlich* in a catalogue of Recurrence and Return, the Haunted House, the Double, Death and the Death Drive, Enucleation as Castration, the Prostitute, and, finally, the primordial Uncanny as Maternal Womb.

The narrative surface of *Heimat*, with its long takes and real time, has sometimes obscured its own formal and thematic undoing across a lengthy film text whose reception history is further complicated by the mass medium of television (Geisler 1985). Yet there are other reasons for the underreading of what is widely regarded as one of Germany's major cultural texts of the 1980s. Many of the sequences cited as providing an idealized and consolatory vision of home or belonging (typically heightened by the soundtrack and lighting) are, in fact, a self-conscious setup in a complex dialectical structure – one that instates a range of spectatorial identifications before the rug is pulled out from under the viewer. This play of oppositions operates across both single-shot montage sequences and scenic juxtapositions of longer duration in the text. Reitz has spoken explicitly of this double movement, one that travels across the whole of the film text only to be provoked to a crisis in the final episode, "The Feast of the Living and the Dead," which gradually unmoors the spectator in its intensified dislodging of the *unheimlich* from its narrative props.

It's my hope that in the relationship spectator-film something like an icy surface will form on which one loses one's footing; where for a time one has the feeling that the film is speaking my language- that it's me up there on the screen – and suddenly one slips and falls and thinks, that's not me anymore, or now I've lost my bearings. (Reitz qtd. in Santner 1990, 96)[9]

While the film invokes a Brechtian estrangement at a number of points (the ironic titles of a number of key episodes are in this spirit), more typically *Heimat* needs to be read as producing another order of ontological making-strange, one in which the spectator's positioning is always precarious. Destabilizing movements in the film spiral back to Surrealist figures and themes in key sequences, but more typically they draw on the grammar of Weimar cinema. Thomas Elsaessser (2000, 92–5) has argued that the "uncanny moments" of Weimar cinema served the important function of keeping the spectator in a position of knowing and not-knowing, the body of the perceiver in control at the same time as he experiences being out-of-control. In *Heimat*, these moments typically serve to undermine earlier ones which hold out the false promise of secure spectatorship and subjectivity, typically associated with the dream of Heimat. Yet, if in the final episode, even this utopian promise comes crashing down as the body becomes a sensorium in disarray, the identification/disidentification tension that prevails throughout echoes the way in which the *heimlich* and the *unheimlich* are theorized as a one-within-the-other in Freud's own essay. Cumulatively, these formal strategies produce a making-strange that performs the structuring thematics of the film, itself, refusing the place of *Heim*, with its ground in an ontology of pure and homogeneous Being.[10]

Neither this complex dialectical movement nor the tight formal organization of the image track should come as a surprise to readers of the text written and compiled concurrently with the work on *Heimat*. While the second half of *Liebe Zum Kino* is an informal diary of the two-year period Reitz spent with fellow screenwriter Peter Steinbach in the Hunsruck region researching and writing the film script, the first part is a theoretical discussion of cinema, whose concerns with lighting, editing, and montage are marked with the attention to detail that is characteristic of Reitz's cinema throughout. It is also worth keeping in mind that Alexander Kluge has called Reitz "a cameraman of genius" (qtd. in Elsaesser 1989, 101). Although Reitz introduces his discussion in *Liebe Zum Kino* with something of a disclaimer for its "academicism," situated as it is in some of the theoretical work done with Kluge at their film school under the roof of the Ulm School of Advanced Design, viewers of *Heimat* would do well to anticipate a film whose formal structure is both complex *and* remarkably attentive to detail. More specifically, they will need to be on the lookout for the extra-diegetic organization of the film text through recurring figures and concepts that serve to organize and bind its meanings. While the film builds in satisfactions and narrative pleasure in ways that are widespread in the New German Cinema, the destabilizing counter-text both shapes the film's central argument and refuses to be restored to a consolatory fiction.

The opening episode establishes all of the elements that recur in discrete episodes and scenes throughout the film: the representational problems introduced by traumatic national histories; the anthropological and psycho-analytic reading of National Socialist hygienic discourses; and, finally, the figure of vision as both uncanny eye and cinematic apparatus, which refuses a model of purity and operates in a projective mode that, once more, returns us to the dark excesses of German history. In the end, many of the most ambivalent impulses of the film are focused in the composer figure Hermann, Reitz's own alter-ego in the chronicle, who will become the central protagonist of *Heimat Two*. In the person of this Schönbergian artist-musician whose own dissident and estranged Oratorio gathers up some of the central themes I have been tracing, the autobiographical intensities of the film are joined up with a reading of a wounded national history.

Germany's Haunted House

The opening sequence of "Call of Far Away Places" (*Fernweh*) shows us Paul Simon returning home to his village in the Hunsruck after wartime captivity in France. The year is 1919, the very date of first publication of Freud's (1964, 241) "The Uncanny," an essay that tells us, matter-of-factly: "some languages in use today can only render the German expression 'an *unheimlich* house' by 'a *haunted* house.'" It is an observation worth keeping in mind as we consider the kind of history writing at stake in *Heimat*, a chronicle that moves from the national devastation of the First World War through the darkest days of the Reich and forward to the mid 1980s.

When Paul enters the village after a gradual descent from the hill, which affords a panoramic view, what he sees is caught in a slow pan of the farm animals and a bucolic world untouched by the experience of the trenches. What follows is another sequence in which he silently, wordlessly, takes up where he left off in his father's forge. On the face of it, it is a scene that enacts the re-establishment of male bonds in the rhythms of unbroken seasonal time, rendering the idyll of Heimat in the most traditional terms. Yet this world of timeless pastoral is about to be challenged by the new technologies of modernity, which are introduced in the opening episode: wireless radios, photography and film, the automobile and the airplane. Seen in close-up, they are fetish objects that will not only transform the cultural landscape and challenge all the old categories of space and time but will also be mobilized actively in the construction of a spectacular Fascism. Even more ominously, the telegraph poles that dominate the skyline as Paul leaves the village key in a motif that returns in the third episode to register the

1

2

3

4

twinning of technology and the concentration camps. It is an implicit evo-cation of the Frankfurt School critique of the relationship between technol-ogy and instrumental reason.

Yet this uncanny of modern technology will soon enough be caught up in another kind of history that ruptures traditional space-time. Paul's hallu-cinations in the family kitchen conjure up his dead friend Helmut in the apparitional guise of an angel, a recurring image that has its place among a range of figures drawn from dream and phantasmagoria in the film. After departing the village abruptly one day without explanation, leaving behind his wife and two children, he encounters a fellow German émigré in a near-by bunk at Ellis Island. This soldier, half-mad from shell shock due to his experiences in the Great War and closeted out of sight in Germany, tells Paul that he was "buried alive" at Verdun. It is one more image drawn from Freud's Cabinet of the Uncanny.

Traumatic histories are always, in a sense, ghost histories: they present a hard case of the problems of the historical archive generally. Following the classic Freudian structure of trauma as *nachträglich*, marked by temporal deferral and delay, in which a later event retroactively instates an earlier unassimilated one, they trouble the primary historical category of time

(Gabriel 2003). In *Heimat*, the German national catastrophe of 1945 is written over the earlier wounding of the First World War in a doubled-time that becomes explicit in Hitler's radio speech announcing the invasion of Poland and assuring the nation that they are prepared now as they were not before. This haunting history is figured in tragi-comic terms in the awkward contraption Eduard proposes to patent for the thousands of war memorials being raised throughout Germany. The sheet that flies up in the unveiling of the Schabbach War Memorial to showcase this invention resembles a child's storybook version of a ghost (Figures 1 and 2), yet it returns in two separate guises in the final episode of *Heimat*, "The Feast of the Living and the Dead," first in the fluttering curtains in the aging Paul's window (Figure 3) and then in the uncanny image produced by the towel draped over his head as he takes an inhalation from his English nurse (Figure 4).

From the very beginning, then, we see a history writing that foregrounds the relationship of national fantasies to both the unfolding of material events in history and their representation. In recent years a sense of the need to understand the hauntings of a culture has taken hold in ways that productively fuse concerns previously thought through under the proper names of Marx and Freud. What has resulted is a greatly expanded sense of what belongs to the historical archive. Though the reading of history as spectral inevitably troubles any transparent model of history writing, it is a framework that belongs as much to Marx's material history as to Freudian discourses. In *The Eighteenth Brumaire of Louis Bonaparte*, Marx (1978, 603) famously suggested the ways in which the figure of Napoleon stalks the 1851 coup d'etat of his nephew, "haunts the subsequent acts of the drama like a ghost." This is history as doubled-time: "the old dates again arise, the old chronology." (596) Shadow doubles and hauntings are integral figures for recovering the trajectory of national history in *Heimat*. The most important image for the national drama of wounding and loss is the anti-heroic bent and stooped soldier of the Great War Memorial that dominates the central square of the village of Schabbach throughout the chronicle and appears in every subsequent episode, its meaning-clusters interrupting events as diverse as Hitler's birthday celebration and Eduard Simon's approach to the meeting with farmers to discuss the new Nazi Farm Laws designed to promote the peasantry as the blood source of the nation. Yet, although this memorial dominates the central square of the village for fifty years (until it is taken down in the penultimate episode of the film) and appears in frame and partial frame throughout, the map of Schabbach announced by Glasisch at the start of the closing episode makes no mention of its existence, past or present.

In a close-up as held in the form of a miniature replica of the memorial made by the baker, who has lost three sons, this figure that graphically renders a detumescent phallus is an explicit image of national wounding, the scene of brokenness that will not go away.[11] Yet it is also a harbinger of the Germany in ruins yet to come, and in this double figuration of trauma and prolepsis it stages the historical arc inaugurated by this opening episode. At this point the ruined nation is traced over the morphology of the soldier's body in ways that recall the stagings of Fassbinder's ruined masculine (Rentschler 1985a ; Silverman 1992, 214–96). In place of Alois Riegl's historic ideal of the monument as an "agent of memory," in terms that supplied the basis for the cultural and political constitution of the city from antiquity to the Renaissance, this memorial is a bearer of unconscious memory, staging repressed material (Vidler 1992, 177). Even more to the point, it destabilizes this classical ideal at the very site of the male body hypostacized within the National Socialist imaginary, refusing to shore up a wounded masculine. This graphic figure of castration operates as a disruptive history in the text, not the shared communal memory that constructs the fantasy of nation but, rather, one that stages its fissures.

Already in this first episode, then, we have radical supplements to official history: traumatic history interrupting temporal flow and doubled; and history traced over the body that serves as dissident archive and countermemory. Yet, just as the later event is inscribed over the earlier one, this opening episode anticipates all of the dark events to come. The figural clusters and themes that organize the film are all put into play in this opening episode. The nation is moving along an inexorable moral path for which the fourth episode, "The Highway," provides the allegorical title, and Kat's repeated Cassandra-like warnings of the price to be exacted in the future present a solitary Greek chorus throughout the chronicle. When the orator at the War Memorial invokes the humiliation at Versailles and presages the coming of a charismatic leader, a before and after is traced that moves beyond a history of cause and effect. *Heimat* restages the compensatory fantasy of the Thousand Year Reich implicit in this promise of deliverance in key allusions to Wagner's Ring Cycle. The Frenchwoman in "The Middle of the World," who rides into Schabbach on a white steed that echoes images from Fritz Lang's *Parsival,* is looking for the ruined castle of Baldeneau of a thousand years ago, yet as a fantasy constellation she is also exemplary of the dream-logic of a text that draws conspicuously on a grammar of doubling, condensation, and displacement. The dream of the Reich merges with the figure of the Arc de Triomphe (Hitler's own fantasy of entering Paris) to remind us of the ways in which private and national phantasmatics intervene in material history. In a logic of projection that will become central to the film's analysis of National Socialism, the Frenchwoman is both the object of desire and fear. In a later episode, Maria's lover, Otto, the father of Hermann, will wear a Death's Head ring at the front, the fetish object in vogue everywhere, which "means something different to each person." In the end, the heroic Ring of the Nibelung will turn into an emblem of Hitler's Death's Head phalanx.

These overdetermined figures serve to remind us that history is out of place here as well as out of time, literally dis-placed and moved over onto new sites that require careful reading. In fact, many of the film's meanings are produced through structures of metonymy that are dispersed along both the diegesis and the image-track. A number of critics have commented on the way in which the shattering of the Jew's window above the watchmaker's shop operates as a passing allusion to *Kristallnacht*. Yet, far from being an isolated episode, this sequence has both an immediate afterlife, which extends its meaning, and a recurrence and return in a resonant poetic image. Paulina is cut by the shards of broken glass from this broken window, the bacteria from her wound a literal source of purity and contamination, according to her mother's atavistic superstitions. Later, seeking to profit by the fate of Jewish victims caught up in the spiralling towards the death camps, Marina and her husband, the watchmaker Robert, reason that they will soon enough be able to buy the upstairs flat cheaply. What follows is the apparent silence that critics of *Heimat* have read as an effacement of the Holocaust and a moral abdication of history. But here, as throughout the chronicle, the National Socialist metanarratives that enabled the death camps motivate both individual sequences and the central logic of the film text. In a subsequent episode, two shots of this upstairs window repeat the low-angle shots of the *Kristallnacht* episode to make new connections; in both instances the window has become the scene of children crying. Martina explains that she, too, used to be afraid when her parents went away: "Make sure the gas oven was turned off properly," she reminds them. Then, following Hitler's historic radio address announcing the invasion of Poland, there is another rhyming shot of the children crying at the Jew's window. Given the preoccupations of both the young Hermann sequences and much of *Heimat Two*, with the generation of 1968 and the burden of "Hitler's Children," this almost allegorical evocation of the sins of the fathers moves history over onto a new site.

In a review article of Derrida's *Specters of Marx*, entitled "Marx's Purloined Letter," Fredric Jameson (1995, 86) begins by reprising Derrida's argument: "Spectrality does not involve the conviction that ghosts exist or that the past (and maybe even the future they offer to prophesy) is still very much alive and at work , within the living present: all that it says, if it can be thought to speak, is that living present is scarcely as self-sufficient as it claims to be; that we would do well not to count on its density and solidity, which might under exceptional circumstances betray us." Derrida's own refiguring of the lessons of Marx's *Eighteenth Brumaire* for our own moment resonates closely with the kind of history writing at stake in Reitz's chronicle of twentieth-century Germany – one that repeatedly conjures up, as we have seen, ghosts and shadow worlds. Yet it is not only national history that is at issue in this refusal to grant our ability to rid ourselves of spooks with any finality, to valorize the historian or writer or filmmaker as ghost-buster. It is also the history of the subject that is at stake. When Derrida asks what it is that can replace Ontology, or Being, the answer comes easily enough to a Frenchman: "hauntology." The two words become uncanny doubles of each other in an undoing of the myth of pure presence.

It is this second version of haunting that is also critically in play in *Heimat*, refusing the rigid oppositions of inside and outside that structure the Fascist state and subject. Characters and events are doubled throughout the film chronicle. Anton's post-Second World War trauma in the kitchen deliberately echoes his father's hallucinations at the pillar in the same room at the close of the First World War. Hermann leaves the village in ways that repeat the self-exile of Paul. Klärchen is cast out from Schabbach in a direct echo of the scapegoating of Appolonia as gypsy-stranger. Yet the way in which these characters operate to make textual meanings, rather than as characters in a naturalistic mode, becomes even more complex when we fold in their function as phantasies, imaginary formations of the subject that operate across both conscious and unconscious registers (Laplanche and Pontalis 1973, 317ff.). Paul (as the larger-than-life postwar American) and Maria (as the Mother-Madonna) move over into the register of screen images whose ontological reality is contingent upon the projection of the subject. In the end, the dream of *Heimat* is shown to proceed from the same fetishizing structure, a lost object of yearning that can never be reclaimed or found, its plenitude based on an operation of disavowal. *Heimat*, in this sense, is more a phantom limb than a place on a map, yet it is also born of a structure of desire that has radical implications for the making of material histories.

To an American interviewer, Reitz has acknowledged the historical situatedness of the term within the German Romantic tradition, defined, almost always, in an affective structure of memory and *longing:*

"the word is always linked to strong feeling, mostly remembrances and longing. 'Heimat' always evokes in me the feeling of something lost or very far away, something which one cannot easily find again. In this respect, it is also a German romantic word ... 'Heimat' is such that if one would go closer and closer to it, one would discover that at the moment of arrival it is gone, it has dissolved into nothingness" (qtd. in Kaes 1989, 163).

There are a number of important sequences in the film where a deliberately comforting and even heightened idyll of pastoral or home is first established and then abruptly broken up by its opposite. In operating rhythmically in this way, Reitz's film performs a mimesis of Freud's reading of the *unheimlich* as always already inside the *heimlich*, a one-within-the-other structure that is integral to Reitz's doubled and ghosted vision throughout *Heimat*. Two examples can serve to show how this structure of idyll disrupted operates in the film text. Near the end of the opening episode, Maria awakens Paul, safely asleep in their bed, to what threatens to be an intruder in the house: a literal enactment of the stranger who threatens the borders of home. As in the uncanny tales of both Hoffman and Poe, there are promises of a rational explanation. The intruder turns out to be Paul's own father, Matthias, who is chasing a marten that escaped into their attic. Yet what is stabilized at the diegetic level is destabilized once more in terms of lighting codes that paint his face in a monstrous chiaroscuro mask, constructing an Expressionist bogeyman.

The same structure of broken idyll characterizes the opening of the second episode. The women of Schabbach move through the forest berry-picking and singing in a bucolic scene that appears to operate entirely within the idealizing cycle of seasonal time, which typifies the genre of the pastoral. Yet it is soon radically disrupted by its generic opposite of horror - with a return to the *unheimlich* in the form of the body of the murdered female nude, which shatters the harmony of the masculine bonds in the earlier forest sequence. When several women bring Maria the torn remnants of the clothes that they have found, she responds hysterically in explicit terror and disavowal of this incursion of death and the uncanny: "*They have nothing to do with me.*"

Yet, if both of these scenes elicit the experience that Heimat is already ruptured from within, the final episode, "The Feast of the Living and the Dead," stages the phantasmagoric play of doubleness to come in its very title. At the same time, it also brings together all of the chronicle's persistent play of meanings around Heim and Heimat. When the priest intones his consolatory words at Maria's funeral, he cautions: "Maria finds her final dwelling" as well as "yet we know we have no permanent home." Soon enough, the Simon

5   6

family house itself becomes the central site of contested meaning. Relatives from Brazil (now visibly hybrid in their identities), who are attending the funeral, stop to examine its slate exterior. Ernst, whose commercial stock-in-trade is the dismantling of old homes and the construction of fake history in kitsch new ones, is charged by Anton with authorizing the removal of its contents even before his mother is buried. Yet when Anton boards up the house to prevent Ernst's access, the cruciform barrier he erects extends his preoccupation with boundary-maintenance throughout the film. Paul, in turn, preserves the historical status of the family home in his role as American philanthropist, but the plaque affixed to it also thereby turns it into reified memory. Hermann, who has chosen the path of the artist but who is also a wanderer across the globe, can only recall a family "who used to be in one house" but is now scattered throughout the world. Yet there is a side of him that still longs for *heim* in ways that deliberately expose *Heimat* as gendered idyll. This final episode confirms the central connection between the Simon home and the figure of the Mother/Madonna in the film's masculine imaginary. With Maria dead, Paul and Hermann lament, "Now the two of us no longer have a home anywhere." It is against the repeated verbal echoes of *heim* throughout the film that the *unheimlich* of the final episode unfolds, staging the deaths of both Maria and, then, Glasisch, who has been our narrator and guide throughout, his dying reveries crossed with the menacing shadows of the Oktoberfest sequence (Figures 5 and 6). In the end, the characters are dogged by ghostly doubles, and the Simon residence itself turns out to be a haunted house.

Far from narrating an idyll of the *heimlich*, the film is shadowed by the primordial uncanny of Death throughout. It is already there in the memorial of the First World War that hovers over the centre of the village, literally marking its geography from the opening episode through to the penultimate sequence fifty years later. It invades the Berlin brothel where

Eduard and Lucy first meet and where the prostitute Martina recalls her first sight of a corpse at the age of six, eros and thanatos colliding in a sequence that returns as stray dialogue in the last episode. In this final gathering up, which begins with a funeral and a deluge, Paul and his son Anton are also stalked by death, and Hermann learns the lost Hunsruck dialect of his childhood from an old man in a cemetery. Lucy herself, in a flashback to Maria's seventieth birthday party, sums up the central paradox: "Ach, what a life this is, with all this dying." In the central fairground sequence, the quick and the dead trade places, in a formal register whose canted frames, distortions, and expressionist lighting codes, move the film over to the haunted screen of 1920s Weimar cinema.

Yet, if Reitz's film chronicle figures the *unheimlich* in all its overdeterminations as the repressed of the *heimlich*, then this structure is nowhere more present than in the choice of Karl Glasisch as narrator. This bumbling character, who opens every episode with a reshuffling of the photographs Eduard is seen taking throughout the film and who serves to bind the episodes in narrative form, is also an unreliable narrator whose cues to the viewer are both partial and incomplete. Yet his meaning in the film goes beyond the epistemological questions raised by those still images which, like the embedded film texts in the chronicle, raise conspicuous questions about historical truth and lies, documentary and feature film, the active role of the spectator in constructing pockets of identification and disidentification.

Glasisch calls Maria, the matriarch of the Simon family, "our living calendar." What is left out of this description is that he is Maria's uncanny double and another living archive in ways that, throughout the film, connect him to central structures of disavowal and projection. This character who is born and dies in the same year as the matriarch of the Simon family is her im/pure Other, and he operates, like the First World War Memorial, as the repressed of history. With his hands scarred by mustard gas during the war, he is a figure of abhorrence, above all to Maria's father, the Nazi Wiegand, who repeatedly registers his disgust at his "scabby hands." Wiegand refuses to eat out of the same pickle jar into which Glasisch has put his scarred fingers; he tries to push him out of the posed photograph of the villagers and to efface him from the official record. Glasisch tells Paul that if he had been killed in the war he would have been honoured by having his name appear on the memorial; as it is, however, his disability disqualifies him for active service in the Second World War and he is merely left behind as the "village idiot." Yet, although the revulsion over his scars is prompted by that operation of censorship that belongs to the traumatic archive, national history will have its uncanny return. In the end, it is Glasisch's own death reverie that

7   8

closes the chronicle – a jarring and dissonant taking up of all the themes of
the film in a staging of the *unheimlich* whose formal grammar of the unconscious can no longer be covered over or contained.

Tropes of Purity and Danger

Reitz has commented on the musical structure of his history chronicle, an
observation that is worth taking seriously. In fact, the opening and closing
episodes repay reviewing for any careful reading of *Heimat*. Virtually all of
the major themes to follow are introduced in the "Fernweh" episode, which
begins in 1919, and are then woven through the whole of the cinematic text;
in the end, they are gathered up in the final episode, which is both a retrospective and an intensified scene of haunting. Yet no other motif in the
opening episode more clearly beckons towards the national catastrophe of
the Hitler era or provides an anatomy of its foundational narratives more
unambiguously than does the extended drama of Kat's spilling of the bacteria from her daughter Paulina's hand: a wound that directly flows from her
daughter's cutting of her hand on shards of glass from the broken Jew's window in the prefiguring of *Kristallnacht*. "These are the bacteria from Paulina's hand," she tells Paul, in a gestural demonstration of their polluting
presence (Figure 7). Immediately afterwards, she sends the pregnant Maria
away ("Not in the house ..."), re-drawing the boundaries of home that mark
inside and outside, pure and impure, throughout the film chronicle. As she
contemplates the range of ills that can flow from spilling this liquid bowl of
bacteria, her face contorts into a silent scream that recalls the classic frame
from the Odessa steps sequence in *Potemkin* (Figure 8). Yet, this time round,
her atavistic fear forecasts the horror of another kind of history, one that will
be born of a ritual scene of purity and contamination, one that Mary Douglas

(1995) reminds us works cross-culturally to police boundaries. In her influential anthropological account, Douglas defines dirt as "matter out of place," a relational logic that confirms its epistemic place within a wider symbolic system. More telling yet for its application to the hygienic metanarratives of National Socialism is her understanding that purity ritual is typically called into play in times of category-crisis.[12]

Within a National Socialist narrative of degeneration, the Jew and the Gypsy, along with the homosexual and the infirm, came to stand in for the occluded Other in a structure of abjection that was compelled to produce its object: an operation performed in almost paradigmatic terms in the 1937 National Socialist Exhibition of Degenerate Art. Though the story of this production, in a range of discourses and representations whose outcome was mass murder, remains an integral part of the history of the Hitler era, *Heimat* is concerned to stage their conditions of possibility in terms of the tropologies of purity ritual. In this sense, the two years of fieldwork that Reitz and his fellow screen-writer, Peter Steinbach, spent in the Hunsruck was a prelude to an analysis that was anthropological in a more theoretical sense. Reitz himself has said that the Jews were treated as "refuse" within National Socialism. A closer look at *Heimat* uncovers a film text that turns on a radical understanding of the tropics at work in this making of the abject stranger.

What we quickly come to understand in this opening episode is that the *heimlich* of Schabbach is subtended by a model of homogeneity made possible only by a constituent "outside."[13] The figural logic of this dream of purity is first established in the bacteria episode. Panicked by the danger posed by the germs of Paulina's wound from the glass splinter that has fallen from the Jew's broken windows, Kat first bathes Paulina's finger in a bowl of water and then frantically contemplates where she might safely throw the now-polluted water so it will bring no harm to the family. When the bowl of water falls on the ground before the pregnant Maria, Kat fears she will now miscarry. The whole sequence enacts the full force of the mythos of contamination: a dramatization of the self-same boundary making at stake in the construction of both the subject and the nation-state, in which an inside is projected onto an outside that then becomes constitutive of its borders. As with Maria's refusal of the tattered clothes of the dead female nude ("they have nothing to do with me"), what this scene performs is a reading of the operations at stake in the dream of Heimat itself.

Towards the close of this inaugural episode, the villagers who come upon the dead body of the woman will speculate on her identity. She is variously "not from this district" or a "Jewess." I want to return to this episode at a later point, but, for the time being, it is sufficient to remark on her naming as the "stranger" in an exercise of boundary-making that is integral to the construction of Heimat. Though the casting out of first Appolonia and then Klärchen has been accurately read within a typology of the "scapegoat," this motif is by no means discrete or incidental in the film text. On the contrary, it operates within a pervasive mapping of purity ritual that enacts the very logic of the death camps. The work of constructing refuse or dirt as boundary is present as early as "Fernweh" in the Simon kitchen, where Eduard reads from the newspaper about new postwar laws which call for French and American manure to be placed "outside village boundaries." The fantasy that Appolonia has murdered her baby (a condensation of her role as "gypsy" and the proto-medieval fantasy of the infanticide of the Jews) leads to rumours that she has buried it in the "midden": the place of garbage and refuse. In at least two episodes, this pervasive tropics of National Socialism moves over to the soundtrack. When Paul meets up with Appolonia pushing her baby carriage, singers in the background intone about the way in which the French "pollute" the "*pure* Rhine." Later, in "The Best Christmas Ever," the only episode that directly represents a concentration camp, the singers on the radio intone that "as *pure* stock we German people stand." Finally, in response to the love affair between Klärchen and a younger Hermann, Anton blackmails his half-brother's older lover on the basis of her "filthy" morals, reflecting his own obsession with purity.

In reclaiming the story of the "gypsy" Appolonia in the opening episode (it is part of the point that this naming is myth-history, as much rumour and projection as something founded in evidence), Reitz is narrating what, as recently as 2000, has been described as "one of the most neglected chapters" in the history of the Nazi era (Lewy 2000, vii). In 1933 the German Ministry of the Interior began drafting laws that excluded Jews from full citizenship. On 15 September 1935, at the conclusion of the annual part congress in Nuremberg, Hitler announced two anti-Jewish laws, which were soon understood to cover Gypsies as well. A ban on interracial marriages extended to all cases in which "one had to expect progeny that would endanger the purity of the German blood" (42). This was followed by a decree issued by ministry of the interior Frick in November, which identified others besides Jews who "polluted" the German blood: gypsies, negroes and their bastards. This racial policy involved both decisions as to who constituted a gypsy, along with a proto-scientific classifying of the whole gypsy population in 1939. Public health officials would maintain that gypsies, like Jews, represented "a biologically foreign body" (51). Though the final numbers are unclear, in the end, there were some 23,000 gypsies at the special gypsy camp; of those who ended up in Auschwitz, some 85 per cent died. This largely untold story surfaces in numerous small ways in Reitz's film chronicle. At the end of the 1984 *Heimat*, Hermann listens to his oratorio to the Hunsruck from a gypsy caravan-like trailer, a pointed image for the artist-hero of *Heimat*, who has chosen homelessness. Later, gypsy music returns to haunt the soundtrack of the opening episode of *Heimat Two*.

Appolonia embodies the figure of abjection in complex and multivalent ways. She is a figure of both projected disgust and desire. Glasisch will accost her sexually, asking if gypsy women "shave below," while the villagers, as a whole, construct her as an object of dark racial anxiety. Yet if she is drawn as a phantasmatic born of the mythos of purity, *Heimat* is even more explicit about the lies and distortions of this dream of pure "race." In the episode "Herbst," which begins in 1938, we see Maria's lover, Otto, losing his job because his mother is Jewish. The more important consequence of this connection is that it makes Hermann, the artist-musician, who is Reitz's alter-ego in the text, both a "bastard" and part-Jewish. Even more to the point, the whole Simon family at the centre of Reitz's history chronicle has a highly ambiguous ancestry. The drama of Paul's failed re-entry into Germany during the war years is that he is suspect under Nazi Germany's racial laws. The Simon name itself has a suspiciously Jewish "ring," and the genealogy books (pored over by Wilfried and Eduard in an extended episode) inconveniently turn up family ancestors with the names of Abraham and Daniel. In commenting on their finds, even Wilfried, the only Simon family member drawn as an ss officer, unwittingly exposes the whole fiction of racial purity: "Europe is a melting pot of races." By the ninth episode, the young Hermann will have become exemplary of a whole postwar generation who would turn upside-down the hygienic myths of National Socialism: "Healthy minds make me sick."

The Uncanny Eye

Heimat's critique of the ontology of purity complicit in the making of the abject other turns up in one of the central figures of the film text – one that has gone completely unread, though it, too, returns us to Freud's 1919 essay. What becomes increasingly clear is that the *unheimlich* is more than an arbitrary framework for describing the film's ethics as well as aesthetics of ontological estrangement. The film deliberately circles back to almost all the topoi of Freud's 1919 text: in recurring figures of spectres and shadow-doubles; history as a return of the repressed; home as haunted house; the phenomenon of the strange as what is also most familiar; the *unheimlich* as death and the death drive; and the uncanny as the sight of woman's body, spiralling back to the mother as primordial home. Yet if the centrality of these motifs confirm that Reitz is deliberately revisiting "The Uncanny" for his destabilizing of the notion of Heimat and the traditional Heimatfilm, at least one recurring figure in the film provides compelling evidence that he has also returned to Freud's own literary model for his history chronicle.

The figure of the uncanny eye resonates throughout *Heimat* as both the natural and the prosthetic eye, extending a reading of both the subject and the cinematic apparatus in psychoanalytic discourses of loss and projection. In the end, these themes summon up a historical field that is also ethical, caught up not only in the national memory work in a more obvious sense but also repudiating that structure of forgetting that belongs to the ontology of the homogeneous subject (Lyotard 1990). What results is a narrative that rewrites history and the making of the stranger around categories of castration, desire, and phantasmatic projection. In the beginning, this eye operates in an intertextual relationship with the literary model of the uncanny evoked by Freud – E.T.A. Hoffman's (1969) "The Sandman" – in ways that echo the motif in Werner Schroeter's *The Death of Maria Malibran* (1971). Reitz, himself, had earlier adapted a Hoffman tale, "Das Fraulein von Scuderi," for his 1969 film *Cardillac* (Elsaesser 1989, 86–7). In turn, a poster from the film turns up in *Heimat Two*. For his 1984 film Reitz takes up, instead, Hoffman's most famous tale in order to elaborate figures and themes that weave throughout the chronicle, once again in a register that, like the earlier Hoffman project, veers repeatedly in the direction of the allegorical.

Freud argues that the uncanny aspect of "The Sandman" rests in the dread of losing one's eyes, an anxiety that he reads as standing in for the fear of castration. This anxiety is connected to something originally familiar that has been repressed, though in his 1926 paper entitled "Inhibition, Symptom, and Anxiety" he would reverse these terms to suggest that it was anxiety that produced repression. At this time, as Samuel Weber (1973) reminds us, castration is no longer one fear among others but the very heart of the Freudian theory of the uncanny. Yet even in the 1919 essay he has already drawn the lesson to be learned from the child's frequent fear of losing his eyes: ocular anxiety becomes a displacement for castration anxiety. Its locus classicus in film is the scene in *Un Chien Andalou*, by Salvador Dali and Luis Buñuel, where the slitting of the woman's eye with a razor (Buñuel substituted the eye of a dead cow for the shock-effect) produces the image repeated in the jelly-like object that throbs on the table at the banquet in *Heimat*'s final episode – only to disappear in a puff of smoke. Like Buñuel's image, this uncanny object invokes the Surrealist fascination with the *informe*" In his

"Dictionary" entry for the term in the journal *Documents*, Bataille (in Krauss 1985, 55) does not so much define this viscosity that troubles habitual frameworks as proclaim its function: one of undoing formal categories. What Rosalind Krauss (1985, 55) describes as the "crumbling of boundaries" in the *informe* is in play in the very associative logic of Bataille's *Histoire de l'oeil*, where it explicitly stages Freud's linking of the eye with castration. It is a reading that resonates with *Heimat*'s own persistent suspicion of boundaries.

As we have seen, the figure of castration is first introduced in the Great War Memorial, where it is graphically figured as a detumescent phallus; it remains as the repressed history of national loss and shame that shadows the village for most of the chronicle. In the eighth episode, "The American," set in 1945 (after the prologue scene of Martina in a Berlin reduced to rubble), the young Hermann retrieves the severed finger of a dead German soldier from a tank, brandishing it in front of the adults. Yet it is Freud's own figure for castration, the enucleated eye, that carries the burden of this thematics for much of the film text. As we have seen, "Fernweh" stages Paul's 1919 shell-shock in a scene that will later be ghosted by the rhyming sequence of his son Anton's war trauma in the same kitchen at the close of the Second World War. It is worth remembering that the First World War was the inaugural scene of trauma theory within an emerging institutional psychoanalysis as the European nation-states tried to come to terms with the phenomenon of shell shock consequent upon the slaughter in the trenches. Paul Virilio would later remark that "1914 was not only the physical deportation of millions of men to the field of battle; it was also … a diaspora of another kind, the moment of panic in which the American and European masses no longer believed their eyes" (qtd. in Jay 1994, 211).

Almost immediately, this scene of death and the uncanny finds its referent in the little boy at the window. Paul stares at this boy with one eye, who presses against the windowpane and makes an appearance in two subsequent frames (Figures 9 and 10). When Paul asks about the identity of this apparitional figure, he is told he is the basket-maker's boy, Hänschen, "whose brother took his eye out with a fork" at his confirmation party. Hänschen turns up once more at the window immediately after Paul's hallucination of his dead friend Helmut as a beckoning angel (a tableau that spirals forward to the fantasy of Maria as angel in the closing episode). Yet it is at the unveiling of the War Memorial in the opening episode, that primal scene of national trauma and loss, that the dialogue track accompanying the figure's uncanny presence confirms his central allegorical meaning in the film: "*He's here, too.*"

In the scene of the picnic among the ruins in the opening episode (the nude woman's body in the woods), we see the little boy with the enucleated eye once more. He also turns up in a single shot, hovering near the scene of the dead child stricken in an epidemic of diphtheria and, once again, following the funeral of Lucie's parents, who were killed in an automobile accident. Immediately after we are told that Lucie was injured in one eye, the camera cuts to the one-eyed Hänschen. Given the centrality of the character's spectral gaze, it is not surprising that it is through his single eye that we see the only representation of a concentration camp in the film – in a pivotal sequence to which I will return. Yet Hänschen's meaning is also extended in the chiaroscuro lighting of Paul Simon in the image that closes the first episode and that, thereafter, serves to evoke Paul in the memory-photographs that Glasisch produces throughout the film. This study in black and white effectively darkens one side of Paul's face to produce the image of doubleness and shadow worlds that haunts the film, but it also graphically refigures the film's protagonist in the representational idiom of the enucleated eye (Figure 11).

Yet is there more to this little one-eyed Hänschen who turns up, first through the window, and then recurs repeatedly in frames (often in close-up) at uncanny moments? What is the meaning of enucleation in Freud's own "The Uncanny," and how does my reading spiral back, in turn, to "The Sandman"? Finally, who is "Little Hans" in Freud's own case histories? Given the ubiquitous presence of Reitz's own little Hans in key scenes already coded in terms of death and the uncanny, these are questions that need to be pursued. Even a preliminary attempt at answers foregrounds the film's deliberate destabilizing of the idyll of Heimat. In Freud's (1959, 147–289) own case history "Hänschen," known in English translation as "Little Hans" ("Analysis of a Phobia in a Five Year Old Boy"), the child, like Reitz's own character, is a figure plagued with fear of castration in a drama of sibling rivalry. "We know from psychoanalytic experience," Freud (1964, 231) remarks in "The Uncanny," before going on to provide the exemplary model of "The Sandman," "that the fear of damaging or losing one's eyes is a terrible one in children." In the fifth episode, "Herbst," there is an easily overlooked small drama in which Ernst observes the fractured arm of Otto in a cast, which functions as a visual marker of castration. He immediately asks his mother's lover and his own Oedipal rival how he can urinate, turning then to his mother to ask her to help him do the same, only to hear her respond laughingly that he no longer needs her help. It is an almost exact replication of an incident in Freud's own case history of Little Hans.

Freud's own association of ocular anxiety with castration may have been sparked by a remarkable dream he had the night before his own father's

9   10

11   12

funeral. In *The Interpretation of Dreams* he writes: "I had a dream of a print-ed notice, placard or poster – rather like the notices forbidding one to smoke in railways waiting rooms – in which appeared either '*You are requested to close the eyes,*' or '*You are requested to close an eye*'" (Freud 1965,352; emphasis added). Many of the major characters in *Heimat* experience trouble with their eyes following scenes of trauma in a thematics which inaugurates a topos of traumatic witnessing. In his interview with Gideon Bachmann, Reitz (1985b, 19) recalls the single scene in the film

where there is mention of concentration camps and a woman asks for details, but is given only the reply: "I cannot say any more in front of the children." This is a true situation. When I was ten years old and listened to the conversation of adults, I couldn't understand their meaning. All these things were actually lived and hidden. Anybody making a film or writing a book which takes place in that period is faced with the major problem … It is almost impossible to show how some ss officers could do what they did and be as sympathetic with their own families as they were. *It is really too much for our eyes.* (emphasis added)

While Hitler is characterized as "a man of vision" by the Nazi Wiegand, on the occasion of the Führer's birthday in "The Middle of the World" (*Die Mitte Der Welt*), trauma is signalled throughout the film by a troubling of vision. Maria notices that there is something in Otto's eye as he contemplates the dilemma of his love for two women, one of whom he will have to betray. Lucie's eyes are temporarily damaged after the death in an automobile accident of her parents, who will now "never see Schabbach with their eyes". In "Herbst," after Paul's letter comes from America, we are told that his father, Matthias, "goes round and round the forge" (the scene of the exploding eyes in "The Sandman"): "Now he can't see so well, since the letter came, he's blind in one eye." The episode "The Home Front" opens with photographs that include the chiaroscuro portrait of the one-eyed Paul and Glasisch's commentary on the previous episode, in which the family receive a letter from Paul in America for the first time in eight years. Glasisch recalls that "from the time the letter came, Matthias was almost blind." Later in the episode, Matthias himself will remark: "It's just the one eye that won't work." The centre of this episode is the proxy marriage of Martina at home and Anton at the front, as filmed by the army's propaganda unit. But the event, itself, is preceded by Eduard's receipt of the news that Little Hans is dead. What follows the news of the death of this one-eyed spectral figure is a close-up of the camera eye. The scene cross-cuts between the war front and the home front, where Eduard is seen "rubbing his eye" against the sentimental strains of the violin. Eduard continues the gesture while Wilfried Wiegand makes the only explicit reference to the death camps in the entire chronicle: "The final solution is being executed mercilessly, up the chimney, I mean the Jews." When Robert and Paulina's daughter ask: "Who goes up the chimney?" there is no answer. But this time Lucie asks Eduard pointedly: "Why do you keep blinking one eye?" Eduard replies with the news of the death of Hänschen and his own guilt in teaching him how to shoot. Yet the more insistent connections are those made at the extra-diegetic level, in the montage juxtapositions of three scenes of staging: the enucleated eye, the distortions of the cinematic apparatus, and the moral catastrophe of the death camps.

The human eye and the prosthetic eye are interwoven figures throughout the film. The close-ups of Eduard's camera as he takes the photographs, which will subsequently frame and set up each episode, register the apparatus as the fetish-object of modernity (Figure 12). In the important episode of the picnic among the ruins at Baldeneau, the single camera lens rhymes directly with Hänschen's own enucleated eye so that both become a kind of one-eyed Cyclops. And when the young boy turns upside down, what the spectator sees is the upside-down that is the photographic image itself

(Figure 13). The uncanny eye of Hans will both come to a climax and gain a retrospective meaning in the young boy's accidental sighting of the concentration camp for politicals in the Hunsruck, an episode extended by his encounter with the soldier who, remarking the peculiarity of his single eye, tells him he is a "born sharpshooter" (Figure 14). Yet, the figure of the uncanny eye embodied allegorically in the personage of this character until his death is also displaced in the film text. It interrupts even the promised stability of the sequence in episode ten, "The Proud Years," when Willy Brandt announces, "I'm now firing the starting pistol for colour television" in an association of eye and gun that returns us to Hänschen's sharp-shooting but is also a twinning of television and death. This conflation anticipates Maria's refusal of Anton's gift of a colour television in the next episode, on the basis that she does not want to be like the others, "dying in front of the TV." In an even more dramatic incarnation in the final episode, this figure returns to graphically resonate with the image of the uncanny eye from *Un Chien Andalou*, a disembodied object on the banquet table, which first appears, as in a horror tableau, and then, just as quickly, disappears, in a mysterious puff of smoke (Figures 15 and 16). With Hänschen's death, then, the figure of the enucleated eye becomes the anxious object that can no longer be recuperated to normalizing frames: it throbs viscerally as a scene of wounding.

I want to consider some of the implications around this rhetoric of the eye within recent visual theory to show how it is both a marker of the scene of trauma and a participant in the pervasive critique of purity that is at the heart of the thematics of *Heimat*. In a rhetoric of making-strange that belongs to an aesthetics of the uncanny, Reitz's deliberate turn to the generic codes of Surrealism here to interrupt the Heimatfilm genre confirms the self-consciousness of this deployment of the figure of the eye in this dissident *Heimat*. Yet how can this formal strategy also be read as an ethics, which is to say as a responsibility to history and memory in the face of the German national catastrophe?

In what follows, I suggest some of the ways in which this overdetermined figure of the eye participates in what I am arguing is a pervasive critique of ontological purity and wholeness in Reitz's film text. In addition to serving as a register of trauma and opening out to a historical representation of the new visual technologies in the making of a spectacular Fascism, this extended figure of the uncanny eye registers another complex operation: the double movement of castration and fetishism born of disavowal.

As we have seen, it is Freud himself who reads the child's fear of castration into the motif of the enucleated eye in Hoffman's gothic tale. Reitz's film draws on Freud's rendering of this figure in a central way, staging it in

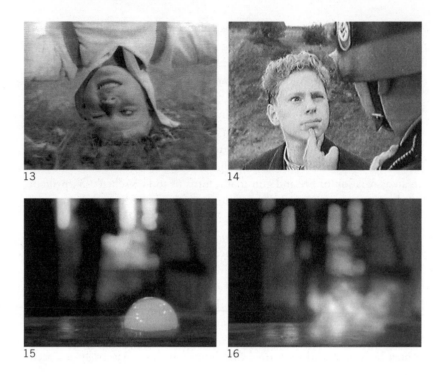

13
14
15
16

the character of Hänschen as well as distributing it across the text in a range of dispersed meanings. Yet there is also one important sense in which *Heimat* returns to central emphases that belong to "The Sandman" rather than to Freud's own interested and truncated reading. What Reitz's chronicle captures from Hoffman's tale is yet another constellation of concerns. For while we need go no further than Freud's essay to map a rhetoric of castration onto "The Sandman," by returning directly to Freud's model tale we uncover yet another thematics central to the 1984 Heimat: the concept of projection bound up with the making of the Other.

"The Sandman" is framed as an epistolary tale in which the student Nathaniel recounts his meeting with the optician Coppola, who recalls for him a figure of dread from his childhood – the enigmatic Sandman who visited his father regularly. The mysterious figure turns out to be the lawyer Coppelius, whom Nathaniel catches engaging, with his father, in alchemical experiments upon the stove. Nathaniel sees a vision in which "all about human faces were becoming visible, but without eyes – horrible deep black holes instead." When Nathaniel cries out in horror, the Sandman reaches to tear out his eyes, which are saved only by the intercession of his father, who, one year later, will be found dead after a terrible explosion in front of the stove. The exchange is intended for Lothar, the brother of Nathaniel's fiancee, Klara, but in a curious Freudian slip *avant la lettre* is addressed to Klara instead. As a result, it is Klara who answers him, folding her discussion with her brother into her advice to her beloved: "If there is a dark power which treacherously attaches a thread to our heart to drag us along a perilous and ruinous path ... it must form inside us, from part of us, must be identical with ourselves (146). But it is the authoritative male voice of her brother that is invoked to dash Nathaniel's fears. Those strange shapes we summon forth in the external world are engendered by inner delusions: "It is the phantom of our own ego" that "flings us into hell or transports us to heaven" (146). As in Reitz's film, the phantasmatic projection of the subject constructs both the idealized love-object and the paranoid enemy. The core of the narrative of "The Sandman" is bound up with Nathaniel's mistaken identification of the automaton doll Olympia with a flesh-and-blood woman in ways taken up in Fritz Lang's *Metropolis*. Yet, shorn of the earlier film's extended narrative frame, what is foregrounded here is even more conspicuously what Joan Copjec (1989, 68) calls "a field of vision ... neither clear nor easily traversable. It is instead ambiguous and treacherous, full of traps."

The atavistic superstition surrounding the eye is already present in Kat's fear of the "Evil Eye" of the French woman in the opening episode. Yet the projective gaze is double in *Heimat*. Appolonia, another figure from the Greek pantheon, like Hoffman's Olympia (Klärchen echoes the second female protagonist, Klara), exemplifies both the idealizing and abjecting power of this gaze. To Paul she is the dream object of desire, bound up with the figure of the Mother. In an extended sequence that takes place three years after she has left Schabbach, he insists on landing a plane when he "sees" her on the ground below. In fact, his vision turns out to be another woman with a baby carriage, an implausible frozen frame of his last meeting with Appolonia walking her own infant in a carriage. Yet, to others in Schabbach, she is the "dirty" and unruly figure of the Gypsy, already a harbinger of a Nazi rhetoric of degeneracy. This same split structure of disgust and desire informs the figure of Klärchen Sisse, who is both driven from Schabbach as the enemy and idealized by her younger lover, Hermann, who, before she goes away, tells her, "I will *see* you everywhere."

This reading of the projective gaze is extended in the film's central concern with structures of screen identification. As we have seen, spectator identifications are an important first step in Reitz's own film aesthetics in *Heimat*, which proceed from the sense that "it's me up there" to a making-strange that constitutes an almost bodily vertigo ("suddenly one slips and falls") in a deliberate bumping up of the *unheimlich* against the *heimlich*. No such estrangement is advanced by the director of the propaganda unit in episode five, "The Home Front," who explains that "the idea is to get something on film that moves the heart." He insists that the camera is to be used as a gun: "Did Dante really enter his inferno? Did Bosch really enter his garden?" Citing the directive of Goebbels, he criticizes the director for showing too much "reality": "We can imprint better than their own eyes. We achieve that with the camera." Yet the lie of this propaganda work is exposed in the cross-cutting between the filming and the violent scene of murder on the Eastern Front, which Anton watches in horror. In a similar way, the filming of the proxy marriage of Anton and his wife takes place in a framework of a faked reality that foregrounds the staged nature of National Socialist propaganda film generally. What becomes clear from these sequences is that the camera does not provide unmediated access to the "real" – and in the hands of the Fascist dictatorship it is actively mobilized in the making of a National Socialist subject. Central to *Heimat*, then, is the refusal of any notion of disinterested vision. What we have, instead, is a persistent motif of the projective gaze that is soon enough implicated in the cinematic apparatus itself.[14]

In a number of important respects, *Heimat*'s reading of the eye and the apparatus participates in what Martin Jay (1994) has called the critique of Western ocularcentrism, repudiating the Enlightenment faith in unmediated vision as the guarantor of universal truth. To refuse the lesson of the eye and the apparatus as already castrated, in Lacanian terms sundered in desire and division, is to succumb to the model of purity repudiated throughout the film text. Let me conclude this section with a reading of an enigmatic episode that, I want to argue, stages this refusal of optical purity in no uncertain terms.

On the face of it, Anton Simon is the exemplar of the traditional values of the discourses of *Heimat*. Unlike his father or his step-brother, the musician Hermann, he does not abandon his regional homeland but sets up a lens factory in the pure air of the countryside, dedicated to revitalizing the Hunsruck for the modern era. What happens, then, when representatives of a multinational corporation based in Brussels visit to buy out his factory in the tenth episode, "The Proud Years," which takes place between 1967 and 1969? On the one hand this sequence appears to operate within a critique of American-led commodity capitalism. Yet it would be a mistake to read Anton as an ideal. In what appears to be an entirely unmotivated, even puzzling, scene, Anton leaves his Brussels visitors to engage in conversation with one of his employees. He tells him that, for personal reasons, he intends not to sell and casually rehearses his history: "I took up photography as a boy of 14 with a box camera and a tripod for my work. We photographed houses

and buildings. No distortion. Wide Angle. A modern camera can't do that."
His goal, he continues, is to develop an "objective" lens that has some focal
adjustment. "We'd have to separate the lens from the barrel and then connect them with a variable adjustment." What is the function of this exchange,
the most "technical" in the film and one that seems entirely unmotivated by
the drama of the offer to buy out his lens factory?

Anton's desire for a lens that would satisfy a classical model of vision
("objective," "without distortion") is at odds with the eye of *Heimat*
developed throughout: the enucleated eye of traumatic wounding, the eye
mediated by desire, the evil eye that constructs an abject other, the eye of
uncanny death. His disavowal of both the natural and the prosthetic eye as
already mediated by language and desire can be seen to connect up with his
own obsessive work of boundary making, in a logic that spirals back to an
earlier moment in the text, the trauma of his witnessing of the most explicitly violent scene in the entire film: the execution of a group of captured
partisans on the Russian front. At the time, he is working for a propaganda film company for which he is both a projectionist and an assistant documentary cameraman – war-time experiences that simultaneously motivate
and give the lie to his postwar faith in the unmediated image.

Anton's opposition to the Nazi Wiegand's polluting the Hunsruck air,
which was the very reason for his setting up of *Optische Werke Simon Ltd.* in
Schabbach, has been read as reflecting the film's own Left-Green environ-
mentalism (Geisler 1985). But, as we have seen, purity is far from a positive
value in *Heimat*. In fact, the film chronicle seems to anticipate Uli Linke's
(1999, 122) recent work in analyzing the continuities between a Fascist discourse of purity and that of the Green party and the Left, testimony to an
ongoing obsession with blood and racial purity in the only European nation
where citizenship, until recently, continued to be defined through the idiom
of descent as articulated in the Latin *jus sanguinis*. Even today, Linke argues,
"members of the German Left and the militant Right draw on a surprisingly common repertoire of images, symbols, and metaphors in their representation of body and difference" (25). Such readings confirm the ongoing
relevance of Reitz's dismantling of the foundational tropes of National
Socialism to a contemporary National Imaginary once more undergoing category crisis in the exchange of borders and bodies.

Just as Appolonia is driven away from Schabbach as the dark gypsy-
foreigner in the first episode, it is Klärchen Sisse who is cast out when her
affair with the younger Hermann is uncovered. It is Hermann's half-brother Anton, in the ninth episode, who writes her a blackmailing letter, threat-
ening her with the full force of the law and branding her a "criminal." He

tells Hermann that she can go to prison and adds, in a by now familiar trope: "We'll make sure you never *see* her again." In terms that directly connect up with the purity/contamination discourse of the chronicle (and repeat the paranoid-fantasy associations of Appolonia with the midden), he accuses her of having a "filthy" mind. Doubly mothered by two women – his wife and his secretary Lotti – Anton is intent on bourgeois respectability. Yet, in the end, his preoccupation with purity spirals into a transgressive as well as a comic return of the repressed in the carnivalesque Octoberfest final sequence of the film, where he is first made ill and then cavorts drunkenly with a prostitute on each arm.

Projection and National History

There is a surplus to this story of the eye and the projective gaze that returns us not only to central riddles in the text but also to the nightmare of history. While the central thematics of purity at the centre of the film provides a critique of the enabling mythos of the death camps, is this enough to counter the widespread criticism that *Heimat* effaces the historical fate of the Jews? To put it another way, is it really the case that, in this long film chronicle of twentieth-century Germany, there is only one passing reference to the Nazi Holocaust, the brief exchange in which the family ss officer, Maria's younger brother, Wilfried Wiegand, tells of the Jews going "up the chimney" before being silenced by the presence of the children? We have already seen how sequences like the *Kristallnacht* tableau in the first episode open out directly into the more extended staging of purity ritual and the rhyming scenes of children crying at the former Jew's window to create a much more significant staging of historical connections. There is also a considerable point in making this exemplary Hunsruck family, whose lives provide a twentieth-century chronicle of Germany, racially suspect themselves in the 1930s. Then there is the inescapable fact that the stand-in for Reitz himself, and the ongoing musician-artist protagonist of *Heimat Two* (1993), is himself both partly Jewish and a figure who has chosen the life of uprootedness and exile. But is there even more analysis as well as representation of the historical uncanny of the Jew in the 1984 *Heimat* in ways that would confirm this film chronicle's responsibility to the burden of German history?

The third episode, "The Best Christmas Ever," provides the only sequence in which we actually see a direct representation of a concentration camp – a camp that is a holding ground for political prisoners. I want to argue that, together with the fourth episode, "The Highway," this constitutes a pivotal drama threaded through the character of Eduard Simon – one that is developed together with another picture-puzzle in the text. The third episode opens in 1934, the year in which Nazi supporters thronged in Nuremberg in September, forming parades and raising enthusiastic banners that were staged as spectacle in Leni Riefenstahl's *Triumph of the Will*. In a sense, then, this episode allows us to read another history writing of the same year to see the way in which the ripples of this mood, as well as concrete National Socialist policies, were filtering down even to the rural Hunsruck. Agriculture was a cornerstone of Nazi policy, central to its idealization of the peasantry in a mythos of blood and soil as well as economic frameworks. As the mayor of a Hunsruck village, then, Eduard Simon is not merely on the fringe of history but presides over one of the important building blocks of National Socialism in its early years of political consolidation. Yet what we see in the establishing, deep-focus shot is a figure dwarfed by his desk who seems to be curiously troubled by something. Even his employee looks around and shakes his head at this superior who seems conspicuously un-at-home in his office. Eduard rocks back and forth in his chair and then leans back to look upside down at the room, to construct one more image of the uncanny eye (see Figure 17).

In the next sequence he is more robust in his public persona as both mayor and party member, explaining new official Nazi farm laws as a "healthy thing for our entire policy." He reassures the farmers that, with regard to entailed estates, a distinction will be made between farmers and landed proprietors: "The farmer with his own farm is sacrosanct and protected. What Jews and speculators sowed during the Weimar Republic we now refuse to harvest." It is the historic moment of the Farm Entailment Laws of 1933, but the association of "Jews" with "speculators" will come to have a fuller meaning in these two linked episodes. The sequence that follows begins with a shot of telegraph poles and a close-up of Hänschen looking up; he takes up his bicycle and appears to be following something as he passes row after row of poles, drawing the viewer ever deeper into the mystery. Over two full minutes into this extended sequence, in which the wind whistles eerily on the soundtrack, he is passed by Eduard and Lucie in an open car, who call out, " Hänschen, what are you doing?" Shortly after, we get the most extended and erratic tracking shot in the entire film, as what seems to be a hand-held camera moves through the sky and grass like a nervous animal.

It is only then, in a witnessing of history that foregrounds the quasi-allegorical meaning of this character, that we see what the one-eyed Hänschen sees. As he looks down on the scene of the camp below, a guard confronts him, initiating an exchange on the subject of the "look." "What are you doing?", he asks. "I'm just looking." "Then look around." Then, taking a better look at the one-eyed Hänschen himself, the guard insists, "If you want a proper look, open the other eye." It is only when Hans explains that he cannot open his other eye that the guard tells him he is a born sharpshooter. What is conspicuously missing from this dialogue is any information about the meaning of the scene below: the prisoners in striped uniforms, the guard dogs, and the high lookout. What can they be doing in the Hunsruck? In lieu of narrative explanation, what we get is a set of directions about sharpshooting, which, in a Brechtian ironic mode, unravels the spectacle as a future scene of murder. "This is the rearsight and that is the foresight. Anyone else has to close one's eye. See that man with the pick? If he tries to run, I shoot him in the back. I align rearsight and foresight. I squeeze the trigger and he falls down." Neither here nor in the future does Hans ever register a conscious understanding of the scene of violence that has just been explained to him. Yet the actions that follow on his part two sequences later create another order of logic in the text.

What follows is a scene in which the ambitious Lucie is seen leaving the Gauleiter's house with her husband, Eduard, in tow. For the first time there is talk of the Jew Blaustein, whose name is not yet revealed. Eduard pleads with his wife not to deal with the Jewish bank and insists he'll be happy when the loan is all paid. What follows is a remarkable sequence at the building site of their new mansion, which is shot through a blue haze on a site that looks like a crater on the moon. Lucie asks her husband to lay a foundation stone in an ironic *liebestod* in which she addresses him: "*Du und Ich.*" Yet what is at issue here, it will soon become clear, is not high romantic love but love of gold. The souvenir to be buried in the cavity of the foundation stone so that future generations will know "why we did it" is a piece of that Hunsruck gold that spirals back to the opening episodes of the film. Lucy unravels her stocking in a pose that mimes Lola-Lola in *The Blue Angel* and answers Eduard's fear that it may only be "fool's gold" by assuring him that "at a quick glance everything is gold".

The film cross-cuts once more to Hänschen, who is on his bicycle, shouting "yahoo" as he shoots at the glass insulators on the telegraph poles. The officer who brings him into the mayor's office immediately afterwards announces that it is "sabotage" and makes clear that Hänschen is destroying "all the important official lines from Simmern to Kirchber." Instead of scolding the boy, Eduard refuses to take the charge seriously; yet, he is soon interrupted by Wilfried, who tells him of the Führer's march into the Rhine and his own responsibility for the Bundenbach-Stipshausen section. What becomes clear from this growing constellation of information is that the concentration camp being set up in the Hunsruck, the ss officer Wilfried Wiegand's being sent to the district from Berlin, and Eduard's growing responsibilities are all part of the emerging larger historical drama. It is in this context that, when the mayor asks his subordinate to "laugh off" Hänschen's seeming pranks, the officer refuses: "Sabotage, I say." In the sequence that follows, the boy continues to shoot more insulators, and just after Eduard praises him once more for being a "crack shot," we see the close-up of an insulator in freeze-frame. By this time the ubiquitous telegraph poles of the opening episodes, which recur in the repeated shot of Paul leaving the Hunsruck, open out to a twinning of technology and the death camps.

The sequence that follows is, on the face of it, a sentimental scene of Christmas, 1935, capped by Mass in a Roman Catholic church. A number of other concerns run through it: seemingly idle gossip about the source of the money that has financed the villa of Lucie and Eduard, the ticking of the clock that interrupts the music on the soundtrack, the ironic juxtapositions of the scene of Christ in the manger and the concentration camp world unfolding in the parishioners' midst. At the same time we are told that the Christmas tree that Wilfried brings home was purchased next to Dr. Goebbels in Berlin; Ernst is in uniform as a member of the Hitler youth; and the Horst Wessel song are being played on the radio, with lyrics that once more invoke the National Socialist master trope of purity: "For we must, we want to free our land / So as pure German stock we stand." Only Kat's by now mournful dirge warns that "It's all on tick," while the metonym of the children crying is repeated in Lucie's description of their "tear-filled" eyes in the church. But it is Paulina who supplies the ironic title of the episode as the worshippers gather after Mass: "This is the best Christmas ever," she tells Lucie, "when I think of our turnover in the last three weeks, my God! ... even after closing time we sold three gold watches."

Hänschen's uncanny eye has already delivered up to us a glimpse of the dark historical drama unfolding. It is against this certain knowledge that the full meaning of Lucie's opera-bouffe is exposed as the top Nazi brass depart her house prematurely without eating their banquet lunch. Soaking her feet in a tub, she plots further means of Eduard's advancement, invoking the figures of fire and burning, and concluding: "We must have a catastrophe ... But in the Hunsruck nothing every happens." Yet, we already know that something *is* happening in the Hunsruck; we also know that Eduard, the mayor, and Lucie know, too, having passed Hänschen in their car as he neared the enigmatic site of the mystery he was pursuing. Soon enough, in the next episode, we will understand more about this bumbling mayor who, having laid the foundation stone (with its cache of Hunsruck gold) for a mansion of fifty-two rooms, huddles with his mother in her farmhouse kitchen and wistfully remarks that "home is best."

The title of the fourth episode, "The Highway," is less ironical than allegorical, though in its fatal arc it, too, carries a moral: history as Kantian *prognostikon* and warning (Geyer 1997). The highway that the "Todt Engineering Corporation" is building is both a road that will no longer move from "village to village but bunker to bunker" and a national trajectory that marks impending death and catastrophe. One more piece of the picture puzzle from the previous episode falls into place as Glasisch tells us that Lucie and Eduard "borrowed the money from a Jewish banker in Mainz, so the rumour went." When Paulina and Maria come home from the cinema, Paulina tries on her new coat, paid for by money she has secreted away from her husband, exulting in the customers who cannot buy enough of their "gold and silver" articles. In turn, when Robert returns from his trip to buy new stock later that evening, motifs already established in these two episodes are intensified. He shows his sister-in-law the hallmarked rings he buys for three marks thirty and sells for the nine marks fifty. Even the detail of this excessive profit, which he cautions Maria to keep secret, is not incidental in the film, although there is more meaning yet in this death's head jewellery being snapped up by the road workers, engineers, and the *Todt* corporation building the highway. Maria is frightened by the red rubies that stare back at her with their "eyes"; however, although unnamed in the film, this is not just any icon. Since 1934, the death's head, in fashion everywhere, was the insignia of the ss Guard units of the concentration camps, and their name, *Totenkopfverbande (Death's Head Units)*, is deliberately invoked in the name of the highway being built as well as the jewellery being snapped up even in the Hunsruck. Already, then, the elements of gold, speculation, death, and the concentration camps are starting to weave an uncanny pattern. Yet, when Maria asks why Otto wears the death's head ring, he replies: "They're alike, but they mean something different to every one." What is at issue here is the twinning of Fascism and death, but Reitz persistently returns us to radical questions of the subject and desire in national history.

It is only at the end of this episode that the riddle of that establishing shot of Eduard in his mayoral office in episode three begins to unravel, and seemingly unrelated information coalesces into another order of narrative and analysis. Why does Eduard rock distractedly to and fro in his office chair and what, really, is the significance of the Jew Blaustein? In an arc of deliberate mystery, the information is withheld until near the end of the fourth episode. Lucie explains to her houseguest, Martina, that the Jewish banker has been arrested for foreign exchange improprieties: "Now Eduard is afraid the party will find out about our loan." But the party has said nothing, "and we've heard nothing from the Jew either. Nobody wants the money." Lucie's framework for viewing the crisis is viewed through a simple lens of profit and loss as she quotes the National Socialist law for the cancellation of such debts. By contrast, Eduard's anxiety is bound up with a range of ethical issues: "If anything happens to Blaustein, I don't want to be guilty of his death. Besides, debts are debts, no matter to whom you owe the money."

Once again, his unsettled state is registered as a crisis of *heim*: "Those were marvellous times in Berlin, " he tells his wife, "I thought I could bring it home with me." What follows is a central sequence in the film, one that is punctuated by its performance in the register of a theatrical soliloquy, with Eduard standing still in a medium shot and the clock ticking behind him. It is a speech that calls out for the inexorable movement towards cataclysm to be halted. It is not separable from the certain knowledge of the establishment of concentration camps, harbinger of worse to come, confirmed in his brief presence with Lucie in the Hänschen sequence, the return of the family ss officer Wilfried Wiegand from Berlin to the Hunsruck, or his own position as mayor enacting a range of new laws within the tightening circle of National Socialist control of all levels of government: "This is the present moment that time ought to stand still / Everything we've achieved should remain still / The new highway. The whole life / And we shouldn't want anymore / And everyone should remain healthy, everyone we know / Including Blaustein, with his bank in Mainz."

There is nothing noble in this *crise de conscience*, which does little more than establish Eduard's weakness and passivity in a national spiralling towards evil. Yet it stands in contrast to Lucie's grand designs for both money and power, and Martina's single-minded ledger of cash flow. The Berlin prostitute responds to Eduard's high-flown speech in ways that make clear she has understood her former Madame's explanation of the gain to be had by the fate of the banker-Jew: "Then you'd have all your old debts." I have suggested that the remarkable sequence in which Eduard and Lucie lay the foundation stone for their house brings together a number of important figural clusters, which once more tilt towards the allegorical. The absurdly large fifty-two-room house built with the money lent by the Jewish banker Blaustein reflects their own greed. Embedded for luck in its foundation stone is a piece of the Hunsruck gold. All this takes place in a scene shot through with brilliant blue light, which recalls another dream-world, Leni Riefenstahl's famous *Bergfilme*, *The Blue Light*, based on the symbolist image that beckons young men to their doom as they fall from the height of the mountain to which they have been lured.[15]

Yet more is at stake in their burying a piece of that Hunsruck gold as the foundation stone for their house, in Lucie and Martina's wish for the death of Blaustein so that their debt will be cancelled, in the greed and profit-gouging that characterize Robert and Paulina, as well as in the persistent references to gold throughout both of these episodes. I have suggested that all of the central thematizations of Reitz's film chronicle are put into play in the opening episode. What that seemingly idle piece of Hunsruck gold from Eduard's pocket spirals back to are the sequences in both the opening episode, "Fernweh," and the second episode, "The Middle of the World," in which Eduard leads the search for gold in the Hunsruck. These literal speculators after gold stare into shop windows in Simmern, dreaming of the goods ("I'll buy six pairs of shoes. Fur coats...") they will buy in an explicit staging of commodity fetishism. Like the sequences dealing with purity ritual, violence, and the casting out of strangers, this speculation for gold provides both a foreshadowing and an analysis of the dark historical event that is the structuring absence of the text. Almost certainly, what is being woven through the mystery of the Jew Blaustein and the Hunsruckers' greed for gold is the same structure of disavowal and projection that we have seen operating throughout the film. The phantasmatic of the crooked Jew-speculator is their own disavowed screen image.

It is an analysis almost certainly drawn from the final chapter of *The Dialectic of Enlightenment*, in which Horkheimer and Adorno (1973) analyze the historical spectre of anti-semitism in the immediate aftermath of the Holocaust.[16] Horkheimer and Adorno argue that "paranoia is the dark side of cognition" within a more fully elaborated philosophical engagement with the problems of the subject and projection, which theorizes this paranoia as arising from the absence of reflection. (195) Yet their analysis also draws explicitly on Freud's "The Uncanny" for a reading of the Jew as the *unheimlich* of modernity: "What seems repellantly alien is in fact all too familiar." In ways that resonate explicitly with *Heimat's* own preoccupation with the logic of screen projection, the essay argues that anti-semitism is based on false projection. In fact, Adorno and Horkheimer's "illusory conspiracy of corrupt Jewish bankers" sounds remarkably like Reitz's Blaustein, who has been charged with stock-exchange fiddling. There are even more aspects of this essay that resonate with Reitz's 1984 *Heimat*: the bloody death's head figure, the accusations of infanticide, the fetishism of commodities. "Bourgeois anti-semitism," they conclude, "has a specific economic reason: the concealment of domination in production" (173). This operation proceeds from the forgotten of economic and social relations: "And so people shout: Stop thief! But point at the Jews. They are the scapegoats not only for individual maneuvers and machinations but in a broader sense, inasmuch as the economic injustice of the whole class is attributed to them" (174).

Given the importance of Adorno to Reitz's own theoretical work as well as to *Heimat*, in particular, it is not surprising that he would draw on the reading of the Frankfurt theorist for his analysis. But there is additional evidence that Adorno and Horkheimer's post-Holocaust reading of anti-semitism had not been forgotten in the period immediately preceding Reitz's making of the 1984 *Heimat*. Responding to the controversy and charges of anti-semitism levelled at his own unperformed but printed 1976 play, *Garbage, the City, and Death*, Fassbinder argued: "The bourgeoisie therefore needed the Jews so that it would not despise its own motivations, so that it could feel proud and large and strong. The final consequence of such subconscious self-despising was the mass extermination of Jews in the Third Reich: *in reality one wanted to eliminate that which one did not want to acknowledge in one's own person*" (qtd. in Rentschler 1984, 149; emphasis added).[17]

As we have seen, Reitz not only develops this analysis across two central episodes but also sets it up as an integral part of the arc of his history writing from the opening episodes of his film, establishing the central motif of greed for gold as well as introducing themes of the projective gaze and the uncanny eye that will only gradually come to join up with each other. In the end, this uncanny figure of the eye provides not merely a staging and an analysis but also an intensely imagined moral framework for Hänschen's traumatic scene of witnessing – one that provides a retrospective logic to this central character's ocular wounding: *it really is too much for our eyes.*[18]

Woman and Mother

Freud's spiralling back to the Mother as the scene of origins for the experience of the uncanny leads us, by a route almost as vertiginous as Freud's own, to the primordial structure of abjection bound up with the making of the stranger. The Uncanny argues that, "In this case too, then, the *unheimlich* is what was once *heimisch*, familiar; the prefix '*un*' is the token of repression" (Freud 1964, 245). Kristeva (1982) extends this reading by arguing that the separation from the mother, which constitutes the pre-Oedipal bond, is experienced by the infant literally as an abjecting of the body of the mother. This turning of the mother into an Other, an object separate from the self, is the foundational act of autonomous being, one that brings in its wake an irretrievable experience of loss. It is the disavowal of this primordial splitting, she argues, with its ensuing fiction of the pure and homogeneous subject, that provides the template for all other structures of abjection.[19] In the end, then, this is not only a story of the subject but also a narrative of

17   18

19   20

ethical crisis. How are we to negotiate the perilous journey towards auto-nomous selfhood without violence and murder?

Kristeva's account joins up with a widespread postmodern critique of ontology that reads into the Western philosophical tradition of Being a repudiation of the difference and division at the heart of the subject, and it can be traced in Levinasian themes that inform both Derrida and Lyotard, among others (Gabriel 2004). One of the more remarkable accomplish-ments of *Heimat* is that it fuses Freud's association of the uncanny and the Mother as Woman's body with a pervasive critique of the dream of purity – a knitting together of themes that bears comparison at key points with Kris-teva's (1982) own reading of Fascism in *The Power of Horror*. Yet it should be stressed here that *Heimat*'s critique of a National Socialist mythos of purity is mapped onto all of the figural and discursive clusters examined so far: in the haunted histories of the nation and the subject; in discourses of purity and contamination that are connected with boundary maintenance; in the figure of the uncanny eye of castration and desire that refuses any model of pure, unmediated vision. These sedimented critiques of both ontological and epistemological purity return us to the idyll of Heimat itself, a dream of homogeneity made possible only by the violent exclusion of what Bataille terms the *heterogeneous*.

Reitz's history chronicle acknowledges the perpetual longing for this irrecoverable site of Heimat at the same time as it insists on its character as phantasmatic – as much a screen object as the projected figures of Woman and Mother within a masculine imaginary. His staging of the *unheimlich* resonates with the Adornian dictum in *Minima Moralia* (1991) – "it is part of morality not to be at home in one's house" – in ways that move it forward into an emergent moment of crisis in postmodernity. Reitz's revisioning of this ethic within a complex reading of the figures of Woman and Mother marks an unexpected and radical supplement to this argument. Yet it is already there in Freud's (1964, 245) own account of the *unheimlich* as the return of the repressed of the Mother's body, "the place where each one of us lived once upon a time and in the beginning." Freud extends his reading of this longing as the dream of Woman, an insight so overwhelming that it can only be presented as a joke of sorts: "There is a joke saying that 'Love is homesickness'; and whenever a man dreams of a place or a country and says to himself, while he is still dreaming: 'this place is familiar to me, I've been here before,' we may interpret the place as being his mother's genitals or her body" (245).

It is the return of the repressed of this memory of origins that leads to the uncanny of woman's body, a scene explicitly staged in the opening episode of *Heimat*, where the pastoral idyll of the men's work together in the forest is interrupted by the dead body of a woman found in the woods. The owner of the look in this classic shot-reverse-shot sequence of the nude is a still shell-shocked Paul, recently returned from war (Figures 18 and 19). Yet the responses that frame the discovery of this body make clear that the figure is soon enough moved over into the realm of collective masculine fantasy. The villagers who accompany Paul project onto this uncanny figure all of the tropes of the abject stranger. Not only is she "not from this district" but "she could be a Jewess or Haarmann sex murder." Like the figure of Appolonia, this eroticized body is already coded as an abject object of disgust as well as desire, the constellation of meanings projected onto her proceeding from a gendered historical subject. The Orientalism of the Jewess establishes one historical cluster, but so, as we shall see, does the reference to Haarmann. In her study entitled *Lustmord: Sexual Murder in Weimar Germany*, Maria Tatar (1995) maps the relations of crime, contagion, and containment onto sexual murder in the Weimar Republic before moving onto the representation of women in art, narrative, and film. She begins with the verse that she had heard sung by Germans, both in real life and in movies such as Fritz Lang's

M, which opens with the rhyme (the words "black man" substituted for the murderer in yet another historical scene of abjection):

Just you wait 'til it's your time,
Haarmann will come after you,
With his chopper, oh so fine,
He'll make mincemeat out of you.

Tatar's cultural study traces the mass-media discourses around serial murder in the early 1920s. Haarmann was a homosexual mass killer of young men, and he fuelled the fears of dissolving sexual boundaries that would erupt into the policing of gender and sexuality in the decade to follow. But the Haarmann sex murder was only one of a series of scandalous sex murders in the period that connect synchronically with other cultural representations of the murder of eroticized women in visual culture. They include the work of Georg Grosz, Wedekind, and Otto Dix, who also represented the wounding and slaughter of the trenches. Klaus Theweleit (1989) has provided the fullest account of the way in which this shoring up of a broken masculine is part of the story of an emergent Fascist imaginary in the German *Freikorps* literature of the interwar years. The visual coding of Reitz's own fractal female body even more clearly echoes the Surrealist woman as body-in-pieces that has been read as operating in a similar structure of disavowal and fetishism. The nude woman that Paul stumbles over in the woods and that provokes a range of fantasies is an almost direct quotation of Man Ray's *Le Primat de la matiere sur la pensee* (1931), eroticized and carefully posed to foreground body parts: breasts, pudenda, arms at angles like one of the broken dolls of Hans Bellmer. In his study of the Surrealist uncanny, Hal Foster (1995) reads these dolls of the only German associate of the French Surrealists as figurations of a Fascist imaginary responding to the crises of both the war and modernist technology. Interesting for our own purposes here is the fact that these dolls were, themselves, inspired by Bellman's encounter with Offenbach's *The Tales of Hoffman*. In ways that return us once more to Freud's essay (as well as Bunuel), this figure also explicitly quotes death: a close-up shot of the woman's face uncovers the encroaching insect world which portends the decay and dissolution of the body (Figure 20).

We have already noted how Appolonia and Klärchen are both objects of abjection and desire, their very names echoing with the split-woman of Hoffman's "The Sandman": Olympia and Klara. Yet the most conspicuous staging of the fantasy of Woman in this text is reserved for the final episode:

"The Feast of the Living and the Dead." Reitz's Roman Catholic upbringing undoubtedly alerted him both to the incorporative fantasies at play in the celebration of the Mass and the complex representations and desires enacted by the iconography of the Madonna. These are first established in *Heimat* through paintings that hang on the walls of the Simon family home. When Paul gets into bed with his wife in the first episode, the camera pans slowly up the wall over the full length of a Baroque-like painting of a reclining woman surrounded by *putti*, an association that will be restaged in the final episode where Maria appears as angel. Similarly, in the final episode when Paul is in his sickbed, cared for by the British nurse, the painting over his bed is conspicuously that of a Madonna and Child (Figure 21).

The figure of the Mother as Madonna governs masculine desire throughout the text in ways explicitly bound up with the dream of Heim and Heimat. The connection is made explicit in Hermann's lament to Paul upon the death of Maria: "Now the two of us no longer have a home anywhere." Predictably, Eduard's fate is sealed early on when he and his future wife lie nude in bed together for the first time, and Lucie cradles his head in her lap: it is a profane pieta performed by the madame of a Berlin brothel. "You need someone to look after you," she tells him. "I suppose your mother did that for you at home." In turn, Anton is mothered both by his wife at home and Lotti, his secretary, at work. Even Ernst, sexually promiscuous and obsessed with flying (the airplane being his own fetish object), finally proposes marriage when his mother dies, at last declaring himself in need of a permanent "hangar." Finally, a psychoanalytic case history is traced for Hermann's own repeated failures with women. After Otto's death, he becomes both stand-in for the husband who ran away and the lover who was killed in the war. "You're all I have left now," Maria tells him, establishing an intense private drama from which the young man will soon enough escape.

This radical reading of the relationship between the dream of Heimat and the masculine fantasy of Woman and Mother provides further evidence of the extent to which Reitz's epic chronicle refuses the mythos of the traditional Heimatfilm. In fact, *Heimat* deliberately stages the gap between the fantasy of Woman as Madonna-Prostitute (Eduard turns the one into the other while Anton can only accommodate im/pure woman in the drunk space of carnival) and the lived experience of "real" women's histories. Yet, in ways that mime the representation of Heimat throughout the film text, Reitz both performs this space of longing and exposes it as fantasy, moving from a radical self-analysis to an analysis of the processes of the Subject in history. We can unravel some of these threads in Reitz's own statements about his film's beginnings. After the failure of his film *The Tailor of Ulm*, and view-

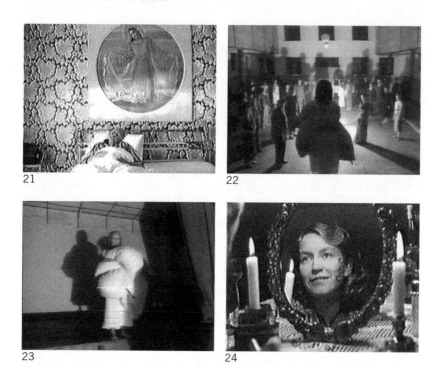

21

22

23

24

ing what he perceived as the American melodrama of his own national history on television, he went through a personal depression: "*Holocaust* put me at the lowest possible ebb," he explained to Gideon Bachmann, "in a kind of Tarkowsky-like desire to return to the womb. I felt the unfulfillable desire to return to childhood and security" (Reitz 1985b, 18). In this remarkably explicit personal confession, Reitz explicitly connects up this longing with the desire for Heimat, a fantasy that he reads as proceeding from impossible nostalgia: "people wanting to go back to a place where they were happy as children. The drama lies in the fact that one can never return. And I think *that is really the problem of our century*" (17, emphasis added).

More than one critic of *Heimat* has argued that Reitz's complicit fantasy of Heim is evidenced in the traditional representation of gender in the film, which repeats the gender ideologies of both the Heimatfilm and the National Socialist era. Exemplary of this, it has been argued, is *Heimat*'s use of the idealizing lighting codes (drawn from ufa conventions) that frame the representation of Maria in the film (See Schlupmann and Koch in *Dossier* 1985, 18–19). I want to suggest that this exaggerated lighting is designed to frame Maria in a self-conscious, oneiric register, whose status as fantasy soon enough comes unravelled, in the same alternative setting up of identificatory schemata and unmooring of the spectator that characterizes the film's strategies throughout. This time round, however, the estrangement of the fantasy of Mother operates simultaneously as a Brechtian *verfremdungseffekt* and a making-strange in the idiom of Hoffmanesque haunting. After her death, Maria is the centrepiece of a flashback scene to her seventieth birthday party, conjured up by Glasisch's hallucinatory memory of her presiding spirit at the time of her death. She descends as a winged angel in alternating high and low angle shots that establish her as the hovering figure of the family chronicle, the idealized Mother figure who presides over the whole of the film (Figure 22). Yet her own outlines are doubled in the reflection on the wall, just as all the personages below are multiplied by outsize shadows on the wall in a chiaroscuro haunting that returns us to ghosts along with angels. In one of the most radically estranging moves in the whole film, Reitz theatrically *exposes* the trick-effect of her image as an angel in a two-sided shot that delivers up her wings as nothing more than an illusionistic device: the shadows produced by the bedding that she carries (Figure 23).

This is an image that spirals back directly to the scene in which she descended the stairs with her bedding to encounter her lover Otto, temporarily returned from the front, to meet their son for the first and last time. What the spectator sees in Maria, in short, is what Otto and the others *see* in her, a fetishized projection of their own dreams and longings. Far from merely flagging the machinery of the cinematic apparatus in a self-reflexive mode, then, this is a scene of critical psychoanalytic import: a making-strange that exposes the Mother-Madonna as a fantasy. Like the gendered idyll of Heimat itself ,she is uncovered as a site of primordial loss that can never be recovered or reclaimed.

The price of this vision of Maria-Madonna as figure of purity is the bar of repression. As Freud (1964, 245) himself puts, it in ways that explicitly prefigure the logic of deconstruction: "the prefix 'un'['un-']is the token of repression." What is repressed, then, in the fantasy of the Mother as excluding the im/pure or heterogeneous body? It is Glasisch, the narrator of *Heimat* who describes Maria as the "living calendar" of Schabbach, inscribing her in a history writing and a temporality that silences a range of exclusions. But Maria and Karl Glasisch are born and die in the same year, and, as I have said, there is a critical sense in which he is her double in the film text. What he returns us to is not only that historical scene of repression opened up by the First World War Memorial in the first episode but also that more dangerous structure of forgetting, which belongs to the operations of the subject. The film persistently returns to Glasisch's scarred hands, particularly in the final episode where they are seen ungloved and in close-up in the kitchen during Maria's funeral and before his own death, developing a motif of hands that Reitz treats at length in *Liebe Zum Kino*. Repelled by his scabrous hands, the Nazi Wiegand tries to push Glasisch out of the group photographs, which provide the memory bank of Schabbach, in order to efface the memory of him altogether. Yet this Other of Maria, the abjected im-pure of a traumatic history, is also the teller of the tale of this strange *Heimat*, an unreliable narrator but one whose very framing of the film text disrupts the mythos of homogeneous *heim*.

If the dream of pure woman is, in the end, a masculine fantasy, just as *Heimat* itself may be a gendered fable, then what are the contradictions lived by "real" historical women in the film? Far from conforming to the pure ideal demanded of her, Maria is represented as actively sexual in the film text, the calculated seducer of both her future husband and then her lover, Otto, while both are still caught up in allegiances to other women. While Paul is crying over his lost Appolonia, she cradles him first in her lap, in one more staging of the iconography of Madonna and Child, and then in a more compromising position that deliberately ensnares him in a declaration of love. In the case of Otto she takes advantage of his broken arm to nurse him back to health, with clear designs of taking him on as a lover. The film also recovers an emancipated Maria during wartime, when she is engaged in mail delivery, driving a truck and pointedly wearing pants. When she picks up her future daughter-in-law at the train station, the women bond by singing a song of subversive gender: "Yes, *mein herr* ... we'll do just what we want."

Finally, as Boa and Palfreyman (2000) have shown, Reitz stages a scene of dissident spectatorship as she and Paulina read Detlef Sierck's 1937 melodrama *Habenera* against the grain. As in the embedded film text of Carl Froelich's *Heimat*, it is the film star Zarah Leander who serves as fantasy vehicle in one more rendering of the pervasive motif of screen projection that threads through the film chronicle. Yet *Habanera* extends my reading of *Heimat*'s purity-contamination discourses in still more important ways. The narrative follows a Swedish woman, played by Zarah Leander, who, ensnared by the image of an exotic Puerto Rico, falls in love with a Hispanic bullfighter.[20] The island is figured as a place of contagion and disease until a Swedish doctor comes to cure them and rescue both the Leander character and her son. Instead of taking up the position of pure Northern woman made available to them in the text, Maria and Paulina read the film subversively and identify with the racial Other. In an extended sequence, where the two women are tipsy from too much wine, Paulina styles her hair so she comes to resemble Zarah Leander as the exotic but also degenerate Other of

National Socialist discourses. Yet, in an even more radical move in the film text, when Maria retires to her room, she draws the same curls on her mirror, turning the reflection into her double and graphically re-encoding the im-pure other as a space of desire as well as disavowal (Figure 24). Like the windows and self-conscious framings in the film, which (in ways strongly suggestive of Fassbinder) persistently operate to suggest the mediation of projected desire, the mirror and the screen change places. The figures of Women and Mother, then, like the space of *Heimat* itself, operate on a grid of purity and contamination that returns us to the central conceptual axis of the film. The dream of purity is exposed not only as an operation governed by repression but also as one whose structure of inclusion and exclusion operates as a zone of danger for lived bodies in history.

Heimat takes up the risk of simultaneously staging and refusing the fantasy of plenitude and wholeness that lies behind the imaginary idyll of Heimat. This contradictory space is most fully embodied in the character of Hermann, who is the film's closest stand-in to the director himself, a Schönbergian musician-artist figure who departed the Hunsruck, like Reitz himself, at an early age. Reitz has gone so far as to call him his "alter-ego" in the film and to confirm the ways in which his vocation as musician lies close to his own. In the end, Hermann composes an Oratorio to the lost Hunsruck, in a musical finale that has been read as the film's final paean to the idyll of Heimat. In fact, the discourse of Nature which subtends the dream of Heimat is resolutely refused and overturned here. The sounds that Hermann takes from "Nature" are synthesized through electronic technologies, while the lyric "in Heaven they speak the Hunsruck dialect" has a thoroughly Brechtian irony. In fact, Reitz has learned almost all of the dialect terms woven into the Oratorio from an old man who sits among the dead in the cemetery. More to the point, the central antinomies that structure the lyrics refuse the model of homogeneity at the heart of Heimat and explicitly foreground the textual system of the film itself: "ABOVE/BELOW, INSIDE/OUTSIDE."

The music is played in a huge cavern below the ground, a womb-like space that stages *Heimat*'s own reading of the dream of Heim as primordial fantasy. Yet instead of inhabiting this intra-uterine space, Hermann listens to the performance of the Oratorio that closes the film through earphones and from the distance of his trailer: not "Home," after all, but something that more closely resembles the homelessness of a gypsy caravan. As a member of the postwar generation raised in lies and silences, Hermann was taught the poem of Goethe's beloved oak at school, without reference to the fact that this oak stood in Auschwitz. In the end, instead of the stabilizing

25   26

Figures 1–26 are from the 1986 German television series *Heimat* by Edgar Reitz.

mythos of Heimat, he has chosen the difficult road of *heimatlose*, his own music embodying Adorno's dictum that estrangement from the world is a moment of art. The outside of 1919, provoked to a historical crisis in the purity ritual of National Socialism, is now visibly inside Germany at the banquet table in 1982. The family relatives who return from Brazil look visibly indigenous to Central America, while Lotte's two adopted children (Hoa and Hou Vilsmeier) are Vietnamese in origin. In this new space of global and transnational identities , contaminated by the ethics as well as the aesthetics of strangeness, the outcast Glasich's response to Hermann's dissonant music, so alien and jarring to the ear of the composer's mother, Maria, confirms both his role as her double and the site of exclusion he embodies throughout the film text. In the final episode, where death and its shadow world break up the idyll of innocence, the camera lingers on the quiet drama of Glasisch's scarred hands which have served to figure his function as the *im*-pure Other of Schabbach throughout the film. (Figures 25 and 26). Fittingly, then, it is his own intuitive response to this estranged music that affirms and encapsulates the hierarchy of value that informs the whole of Reitz's 1984 *Heimat*: *"so beautiful, so foreign ... and yet, so different ... as if from different lands."* [21]

Notes

Thanks are due to the following friends and colleagues who generously read this chapter and offered their astute comments: Chris Faulkner, Mitchell Frank, and Zuzana Pick.

1 The series was seen by more than nine million viewers, or 26 per cent of the viewing public, while some twenty-five million, or 54 per cent, saw at least one episode (Geisler 1985). Yet, even before the 1984 *Heimat* spiralled into an ongoing series, which included *Heimat Two* and *Heimat Three* as well as a range of media tie-ins (which included a Web site), Reitz had conceived of it as both a film (rather than a television serial) and an "event" that tested questions of duration and audience participation: "I made *Heimat* as a film, not a television serial. I feel that nobody can yet know what a film is or can be ... I think the cinema now needs new forms of 'events'" (interview with Gideon Bachman 1985).

2 My reading here is intended to open up a space for a second-stage problematic around *Heimat*'s dissemination and reception. Were the textual meanings I elaborate here largely overlooked by viewers and, if so, why? The film's rather tricky two-step, one in which classical film codes are mobilized to absorb the viewer into a diegetic space that elicits identification before destabilizing this space in intervals that are highly varied (within the shot, across shots, across shorter or longer sequences) undoubtedly played some role. Yet the film's horizon of expectation also played and continues to play an important part in its under-reading; what unfolds is less a representation of the Holocaust than an analysis, one that both extends the social-psychoanalytic critique of the Frankfurt theorists and that has ongoing relevance to a contemporary social moment of ethical crisis around global and transnational identities. Important recent work on the self-reflexivity of the film (see Wickham 1991 and Boa and Palfreyman 2000,180 ff.) already alerts us to the sophistication and self-consciousness of Reitz's film text in ways that make his mobilizing of a naïve discourse of Heimat implausible.

3 Work on the German discourses of Heimat continues to grow exponentially. Among those studies that I have found most helpful are Boa and Palfreyman (2000); Blickle (1992) and Applegate (1990). Anthony Vidler's (1992) wide-ranging *The Architectural Uncanny* explores the long-standing ambivalence to the ideas of home and Heimat within modernity.

4 For discussions of the Heimatfilm genre as well as the post 1960s anti-Heimatfilm, see Elsaesser (1989, 141ff.); and Rentschler (1984, 109–12).

5 The literature on Freud's classic essay is growing in ways that suggest its emerging status as the locus classicus for the shocks and dislocations of modernity. See the special issue of *Paradoxa* for a provisional recent bibliography. More directly relevant to my own concerns here is the way in which the *unheimlich* has recently been taken up in postcolonial theory in ways that challenge the value of "home" in a late modernity characterized by exilic and transnational identities. In *DisseminNation* Homi Bhabha (1972, 315) rewrites Freud's uncanny to describe "the radical disruption presented by the outsider, or 'people of the pagus,' in which 'pagus' indicates both 'pagan' and margin. These include colonials, postcolonials, migrants, minorities, wandering people who will not be contained within the 'heim' of the national culture and its unisonant Discourse, but are themselves the marks of a shifting boundary that alienates the frontiers of the modern nation." As Edward Said (2000)

acknowledges, Adorno shadows this reading of the uncanny stranger of postmodernity. See Nico Israel's nuanced reading (2000).

6 Though Weimar cinema's interest in the uncanny is well established, I am making a case for the mobilization of its thematics and unsettling effects in the service of an ontological making-strange, one that repudiates the mythos of a pure and undivided *heim* that is grounded in an ontology of pure Being. I am bracketing a longer discussion of the Brechtian line of estrangement, which descends from Russian formalism and would appear to operate within a different set of denaturalizing imperatives. See Watney (1982) for one reading of this line of inheritance.

7 For a discussion of shifts in German broadcasting around the discourse of Home, see Frachon and Vargaftig (1995). Nothing could confirm the palimpsestic relationship between Germany's traumatic national past and the challenges of the present better than the actual title of a series broadcast daily in Germany on ARD between 1965 and 1990 (when it went weekly): *Ihre Heimat – Unsere Heimat* (Your homeland – our homeland). The program focused on each of Germany's immigrant communities in turn. On 19 November 1991 a Remembrance Sunday broadcast, which lasted from noon until midnight, was entitled *Fremde Heimat* (Foreign heimat). This time round, the three discussion groups that framed the collected documentaries, films, and features uncannily echoed the structure of Reitz's 1984 film: *Weggehen* (Leaving), *Dableiben* (Staying), and *Zuruckkehren* (Coming back). See Frachon and Vargaftig (1995, 175). The program's producer Eckart Stein described his concept as an ethical as well as historical task of memory work, one motivated by the emergence of a new kind of multicultural national (175). Reitz's 1984 *Heimat*, I am arguing, stages German history against the same moment of heightened crisis around the notion of *heim*, one in which National Socialist discourses of purity are not only no longer ethical but are also untenable.

8 Reitz suggests: "A theme for *Heimat*, which is a period film, must be noted right off: period films tend to be nostalgic, when they limit their vision to purely historical scenes. Our task will be to sublimate this compulsion (*diesen Zwang aufzuheben*) and to allow some of our present day reality to come into view so that we can thematize this compulsion" (qtd. in Santner 1990, 180). Adorno would appear to shadow this double movement of longing and dissolution, like so much else in Reitz's film. Frankfurt School Critical Theory (including Marcuse, Adorno, and Habermas) was central to the curriculum of the film school at Ulm, which Reitz and Edward Kluge directed. See Reitz (1983).

More particularly, Reitz is likely deliberately drawing on an Adornian aesthetic that refuses reconciliation in favour of preserving existing tensions (see Jay 1997) in a way that also resonates with Freud's notion of the *heimlich* and the *unheimlich* as a one-within-the-other. See Buck-Morss (1977, 63) for the "logic of disintegration" Adorno was to formulate, first as a principle of non-identity and then, later, as "negative dialectics." The aesthetics of Heimat I am arguing for is one consonant with Adorno's own musical model of Schoenberg, whose philosophy of dissonance, at the level of technique, "requires that one hand always be ready to undo the work of the other" (qtd. in Hullot-Kentor 1997, 311).

9 Eric Santner frames this statement within the rhetoric of mourning and loss that informs his essay as a whole, in a figure of memory as working-through that Reitz shares with his contemporaries. While Santner's reading provides a helpful account

of the influential work of the Mittlerisches in analysing Germany's postwar response to the loss of the ideal imago of Hitler, there is little match between this emphasis and the recurring patterns and themes that organize Reitz's film-chronicle. It is instructive that this lengthy analysis provides only one shot from *Heimat*'s highly self-conscious image-track.

10   While the key terms in play in my own reading of *Heimat* resonate with contemporary postcolonial as well as poststructuralist discourses, they have a longer line of inheritance in relation to the rethinking of identity, which challenges what Heidegger has called the "ontotheological tradition" (Taylor 1986, 14). In Levinas's (1989, 86) terms: "To be or not to be – is that the question?" In his own thoughtful essay on the question of Heidegger's fraught relationship to National Socialism, "Heidegger and "the Jews," Lyotard (1990) places "the jews" in quotation marks to mark the place of both the historical victims of the death camps and the forgotten of Western philosophy. For Lyotard, what Heidegger forgot to deconstruct, in the end, was the ideal of "Home."

11   Rentschler's (1985b) nuanced reading of "Ich hatt einen Kamaraden" (I once had a Comrade) across five films includes an account of the important sequence of the First World War memorial in which the baker Bohnke, who lost three sons in the war, slowly walks down the lane to the sound of the band playing the song. While Rentschler concludes that the film is guilty of "abandoning the critical framework of the film's initial episode," his close reading of the dissonant structure of this scene may be nearer the mark to what is taking place throughout the film: "The song is linked to the body: the past has imprinted itself on the baker, leaving him with a sorrow etched on his face and the symbolic expression of castration clutched in his hands, the miniature monument that stands for parts of him lost in the war" (81–2). Rentschler's connecting up of this section with Fassbinder is also productive. Arguably, Reitz's own stagings of a wounded masculine are naturalized more readily than are Fassbinder's dissident choreographies, which interrupt a normative grammar of gender and are not so readily recuperated to dominant frames.

12   *Heimat*'s critique of purity resonates not only with Bataille's themes of the heterogeneous and the enucleated eye but also with the more explicitly Bataillean notion of the im/pure sacred. As Maria's double/other, Karl Glasisch (his very hands marked as *stigmata*) can be read as what has been left out of certain strands of Christianity. As noted, religious iconography dominates the paintings in the Simon household, while two paintings of Madonna and Child figure conspicuously in key sequences.

Woman as fantasy projection in a more carnal mode has a longer history in the German literary and theatrical tradition that Reitz would have been aware of, not least of all in Wedekind's *Lulu* plays, where it is the other side of the Madonna/ Prostitute dyad that is uncovered as fantasy projection. The femme-fatale's whole identity in the *Lulu* plays is a construction of the desire and *gaze* (prefiguring Pabst's cinematic version) of others.

13   Recent cultural theory around abjection moves deconstructive as well as psychoanalytic readings around the relationship between insides and outsides onto the category of social subjects (see Butler [1990, 1993]). Kristeva's (1982) own analyses bring together the work of Mary Douglas and Bataille; what is new here, arguably, is the mapping of this theory onto the domain of historical subjects, shifting the synchronic work of anthropology into a diachronic register in ways ignored by Douglas's

pioneering work. I am indebted to Matti Bunzl for the insight that symbolic anthropology was long resistant to historical frameworks.

14 At times, *Heimat* reads like a staging of apparatus theory as it dominated film criticism of the 1970s and 1980s. See Joan Copjec (1994, 21ff.) for an overview of the debates developed in France and England by Jean-Louis Baudry, Christian Metz, Jean-Louis Commoli, Stephen Heath, and others, which posited that "the screen is a mirror. The representations produced by the institution of cinema, the images presented on the screen, are accepted by the subject as its own." By self-consciously staging this imaginary relationship, Reitz also exposes it as a mis-recognition. In an interview with Don Ranvaud (1985a, 126), he explicitly describes it as a structure of screen projection in the early National Socialist period: "You only have to think of the fact that people in the 1930's, for example, were *projecting* their dreams and fantasies on to black and white images of stars like Zarah Leander and Carl Frohlich" (emphasis added). It is worth noting that Kluge (1981-2) invokes the term "phantasy" to describe a mode of spectatorship which involves the active relationship of the viewer to the screen image.

15 Arguably, the figure of Appolonia in *Heimat* rewrites Riefenstahl's Junta in *The Blue Light*. Tropes of height and depth are repeated throughout the film in ways that almost certainly spiral back to the mythical figure of Icarus, who flew too high in Reitz's earlier film *The Tailor of Ulm*. Ernst's fetishization of flying comes to an impasse after the war, when his superiors tell him Germans will not be able to go up in the air for ninety-nine years. Ernst replies, "But we can't just crawl on the ground."

16 The discussion of projection in *The Dialectic of Enlightenment* takes place within a larger post-Kantian problematic of the Subject's relation to the Object, which is central to Adorno's concept of non-identity. The "speculation" for gold of the opening episode (which turns out to be "fool's gold") spirals forward to the fantasy of the speculator-Jew (Blaustein) in a logic of disavowal and fetishism that extends the thematics of paranoid projection. It is worth noting that Reitz has said that Cardillac was also a portrait of his father, who was both a clockmaker and a goldsmith.

17 Fassbinder's *The Garbage, the City, and Death* anticipates not only the figure of refuse in *Heimat* but also conspicuously stages the Jew as projective figure who haunts the contemporary German imaginary. The play is in many ways a tissue of quotations from the major plays of Genet, fusing the phenomenological mirroring of identities in *The Balcony* and the French colonial figures of abjection, the Algerians, in *The Screens*. It is interesting to note that, in spite of the earlier charges against the play which attended its planned performance in Germany, it was performed by the Yoram Lowenstein studio of Performing Arts in Tel Aviv in 1999.

18 For a study of the figure of the eye and vision in relation to the ethical act of witnessing around Hiroshima-Nagasaki, see Maclear (1999).

19 Bringing a Lacanian perspective to bear on these issues, Joan Copjec (1994, 34) describes the process of subject construction as the rejection of our "non-selves" and the subsequent "inclusion within ourselves" of whatever is rejected. Lacan calls that constitutive negation the "extimate," a term Copjec (following Jacques Alain Miller) uses to designate something that, though "in us," is "not us" (35). The relationship between the uncanny and the abject has not escaped readers of Freud's essay. See, for example, Lydenberg (1997). I want to argue that such a theory becomes more productive when crossed with historical frameworks, instances in which one or more of the categories that secure the fiction of ontological stability are provoked to a crisis.

20 Once more, the echoes of Adorno are unmistakeable. As Shierry Weber Nicholsen (1999, 84) notes, the topic of foreign words is central to Adorno's theory of language. They must be defended "precisely where they are at their worst from the point of view of purism: where they are foreign bodies assailing the body of language" (Adorno qtd. in Weber Nicholsen 1999, 87). These Adornian themes once more anticipate central postcolonial discourses of hybrid and exilic identities. Edward Said (2000) explicitly draws on Adorno in ways that suggest Reitz's Hermann, invoking both the Adornian theme of the "damaged life" and "no fixed address." While *Heimat*'s artist- musician may long for heim, his whole way of life marks him out as having chosen something closer to postmodern "nomadism" (See Peters 1999, 30ff.) We might well revise the title of Reitz's 1984 film chronicle to read *Damaged Heimat*.

Works Cited

Adorno, Theodor. 1991. *Minima Moralia: Reflections from Damaged Life*. Trans. E.F.N. Jephcott. New York: Verso.

– 2002. "On the Contemporary Relationship of Philosophy and Music." In *Theodor Adorno: Essays on Music*, ed. Richard Leppert, 135–61. Los Angeles: University of California Press.

Applegate, Celia. 1990. *A Nation of Provincials: The German Idea of Heimat*. Berkeley and Los Angeles: University of California Press.

Benjamin, Walter. 1969. *Illuminations*. Trans. Harry Zohn, ed. Hannah Arendt. NY: Schocken.

Bhabha, Homi K. 1972. "DisseminNation." In *Nation and Narration*. London, New York: Herder and Herder.

Blickle, Peter. 2002. *Heimat: A Critical Theory of the German Idea of Homeland*. Rochester and Woodbridge: Camden.

Boa, Elizabeth, and Palfreyman, Rachel. 2000. *Heimat: A German Dream – Regional Loyalties and National Identity in German Culture, 1890-1990*. Oxford: Oxford University Press.

Buck- Morss, Susan. 1977. *The Origin of Negative Dialectics: Theodor W. Adorno, Walter Benjamin, and the Frankfurt Institute*. New York: Free Press.

Butler, Judith. 1990. *Gender Trouble: Feminism and the Subversion of Identity*. New York: Routledge.

– 1993. *Bodies That Matter: On The Discursive Limits of Sex*. New York and London: Routledge.

Copjec, Joan. 1994. *Read My Desire: Lacan against the Historicists*. Cambridge and London: MIT Press.

Derrida, Jacques. 1994. *Specters of Marx: The State of the Debt, the Work of Mourning, and the New International*. Trans. Peggy Kamuf. New York: Routledge.

Dossier on Heimat, with contributions by Karen Witte, J. Hoberman, Thomas Elsaesser, Gertrud Koch, Friedrich P. Kahlenberg, Klaus Kreimeier, and Heidi Schlupmann. 1985. *New German Critique* 36 (Fall): 3–24.

Douglas, Mary. 1995. *Purity and Danger: An Analysis of Concepts of Pollution and Taboo*. London: Routledge.

Elsaesser, Thomas. 1989. *New German Cinema: A History*. New Brunswick: Rutgers University Press.

–2000. *Weimar Cinema and After. Germany's Historical Imaginary.* London and New York: Routledge.

Fassbinder, Rainer Werner. 1985. *"Garbage, the City, and Death."* In Rainer Werner Fassbinder. *Plays,* ed. Denis Calandra,161–89 ,Baltimore and London: Johns Hopkins Press.

Foster, Hal. 1995. *Compulsive Beauty.* London and Cambridge: MIT Press.

Frachon, Claire, and Vargaftig, Marion. 1995. *European Television: Immigrants and Ethnic Minorities,* London: John Libbey and Co.

Freud, Sigmund. 1959. *Analysis of a Phobia in a Five-Year-Old Boy.* In *Collected Papers.* Vol. 3 (1908–59), trans. Alix and James Strachey, 149–288. New York: Basic.

–1964 *The Interpretation of Dreams,* trans. James Strachey. New York:

–1964. *The Uncanny.* Vol 17: *The Standard Edition of the Complete Psychoanalytic Works of Sigmund Freud,* ed. and trans. James Strachey, 219–56. London: Hogarth.

Gabriel, Barbara. 2003. "The Wounds of Memory: Mavis Gallant's "Baum, Gabriel (1935–)," National Trauma, and Post-War French Cinema. *Essays on Canadian Writing* 80 (Fall): 189–216.

–2004. "Writing against the Ruins: Towards a Postmodern Ethics of Memory." In *Postmodernism and the Ethical Subject,* ed. Barbara Gabriel and Suzan Ilcan. Montreal: McGill-Queen's University Press.

Geisler, Michael E. 1985. "Heimat and the German Left: The Anamnesis of a Trauma." *New German Critique* 36 (Fall): 25-66.

Geyer, Michael. 1997. "The Place of the Second World War in German Memory and History." *New German Critique* 71 (Spring-Summer): 5–41.

Gilman, Sander. 1991. "Plague in Germany, 1939/1989: Cultural Images of Race, Space, and Disease." In *Nationalisms and Sexualities,* ed. Andrew Parker, M. Russo, D. Sommer, and P. Yaeger, 175–200. New York: Routledge.

Hoffman, E.T.A. 1969. "The Sandman." In *Selected Writings of E.T.A. Hoffmann,* ed. and trans. Leonard J. Kent and Elizabeth C. Knight, 137–67. Chicago and London: University of Chicago Press.

Horkheimer, Max, and Theodor W. Adorno. 1973. *Dialectic of Enlightenment.* Trans. John Cumming. New York: Allen Lane.

Hullot-Kentor, Robert. 1997. "The Philosophy of Dissonance: Adorno and Schoenberg." In *The Semblance of Subjectivity: Essays in Adorno's Aesthetic Theory,* ed. Tom Huhn and Lambert Zuidervaart, 309–19. Cambridge: MIT Press.

Israel, Nico. 2000. *Outlandish: Writing between Exile and Diaspora.* Stanford: Stanford University Press.

Jameson, Fredric. 1995. "Marx's Purloined Letter." *New Left Review* 209:75–109.

Jay, Martin. 1994. *Downcast Eyes: The Denigration of Vision in Twentieth-Century French Thought.* Berkeley: University of California Press.

–1997. "Mimesis and Mimetology: Adorno and Lacoue-Labarthe." In *The Semblance of Subjectivity: Essays in Adorno's Aesthetic Theory,* ed. Tom Huhn and Lambert Zuidervaart, 29–54. Cambridge, MA: MIT Press.

Laplanche, Jean, and Jean-Bertrand Pontalis, ed. 1973. "Phantasy (or Fantasy)." In *The Language of Psychoanalysis,* 314–19. London: Karmac.

Kaes, Anton. 1989. *From Hitler to* Heimat: *The Return of History as Film.* Cambridge and London: Harvard University Press.

Kluge, Alexander. 1981–2. "The Significance of Phantasy". In *New German Critique* 24/25

Krauss, Rosalind. 1985. "Corpus Delecti." *October* 33: 31–72.

Kristeva, Julia. 1982. *Powers of Horror*. New York: Columbia University Press.

– 1991. *Strangers to Ourselves*. Trans. Leon S. Roudiez. New York: Columbia University Press.

Levinas, Emmanuel. 1989. *The Levinas Reader*. Ed. Sean Hand. Oxford and Cambridge: Blackwell.

Lewy, Guenter. 2000. *The Nazi Persecution of the Gypsies*. New York and Oxford: Oxford University Press.

Linke, Uli. 1999. *German Bodies: Race and Representation after Hitler*. New York and London: Routledge.

Lydenberg, Robin. 1997. "Freud's Uncanny Narratives." PMLA II2 (4): 1072–86

Lyotard, François. 1990. *Heidegger and "the Jews."* Trans. Andreas Michel and Mark S. Roberts. Minneapolis: University of Minnesota Press.

Maclear, Kyo. 1999. *Beclouded Visions: Hiroshima-Nagasaki and the Art of Witness*. Albany: University of New York Press.

Maier, Charles S. 1988. *The Unmasterable Past: History, Holocaust, and German National Identity*. Cambridge and London: Harvard University Press.

Marx, Karl. 1978. "The Eighteenth Brumaire of Louis Bonaparte." In *The Marx-Engels Reader*, 2nd edition, ed. Robert C. Tucker, 594–617, New York and London: W.W. Norton.

Metz, Christian. 1982. *The Imaginary Signifier: Psychoanalysis and the Cinema*. Bloomington: Indiana University Press.

Nicholsen, Shierry Weber. 1997. *Exact Imagination, Late Work: On Adorno's Aesthetics*. Cambridge, MA: MIT Press.

Peters, John Durham. 1999. "The Stakes of Mobility in the Western Canon." In *Home, Exile, Homeland: Film, Media, and the Politics of Place*, ed. Hamid Naficy, 17–44. New York and London: Routledge.

Reitz, Edgar. 1983. *Liebe Zum Kino: Utopien und Gedan Ken Zum Autorenfilm, 1962–1983*. Bremen: CON.

– 1985a. (in interview with Gideon Bachman) *Film Comment* 21 (4): 16–19.

– 1985b. (in interview with Don Ranvaud) *Sight and Sound* 54 (2): I24–9.

Rentschler, Eric. 1984. *West German Film in the Course of Time: Reflections on the Twenty Years since Oberhausen*. Bedford Hills: Redgrave.

– 1985a. "The Body in/and/of Fassbinder's *Berlin Alexanderplatz*." *New German Critique* 34 (Winter): 194–08.

– 1985b. "New German Film and the Discourse of Bitburg." *New German Critique* 36 (Fall): 67–90.

Rose, Jacqueline. 1996. *States of Fantasy*. Oxford: Clarendon.

Said, Edward. 2000. *Reflections on Exile and Other Essays*. Cambridge: Harvard University Press.

Santner, Eric L. 1990. *Stranded Objects: Mourning, Melancholia and Film in Postwar Germany*. Ithaca and London: Cornell University Press.

Silverman, Kaja. 1992. *Male Subjectivity at the Margins*. New York and London: Oxford University Press.

Tatar, Maria. 1995. *Lustmord: Sexual Murder in Weimar Germany*. New Jersey: Princeton University Press.

Taylor, Mark C. 1986. "Introduction: System ... Structure ... Difference ... Other." In *Deconstruction in Context: Literature and Philosophy*, ed. Mark C. Taylor, 1–34. Chicago and London: University of Chicago Press.

Theweleit, Klaus. 1989. *Male Fantasies*. Vol. 2: *Male Bodies: Psychoanalyzing the White Terror*. Minneapolis: University of Minnesota Press.

Vidler, Anthony. 1992. *The Architectural Uncanny*. Cambridge, MA: MIT Press.

Watney, Simon. 1982. "Making Strange: The Shattered Mirror." In *Thinking Photography*, ed. Victor Burgin, 154–76. London: Macmillan.

Weber, Samuel. 1973. "The Sideshow, or Remarks on a Canny Moment." *MLN* 88: 1102–1133.

Wickham, Christopher J. 1991. "Representation and Mediation in Edgar Reitz's Heimat." *German Quarterly* 64 (1): 35–45.

Devastation of the Hapless Structure: Architecture and Ethics[1]

PHYLLIS LAMBERT

Melvin Charney's *Un Dictionnaire* ... was presented in 2000 as Canada's entry to the 7th Venice Biennale International Exhibition of Architecture. The exhibition as a whole was given the theme of "Cities: Less Aesthetics, More Ethics." The thematic of the exhibition is embodied in *Un Dictionnaire* ..., which is composed of a collection of press clippings of wire-service photographs classified into numerous series and sub-series. Charney has observed that the images of news events tend to focus our attention on particular places "and attribute an aura, a certain cachet of consequence, to hapless structures caught in an instant of celebration or, more likely, in a disaster."[2] The images are mounted as plates with a transparent brushstroke of paint over the surface, thus repositioning the initial images, removing them from their original context to the realm of an exhibitable workplace in a gallery. The assembly of the many plates in space allows numerous levels of reading of images that disclose the interaction between people and the constructed world.

Looking at a system from the outside is revelatory and provides fresh, incisive views. The unexpected events transmitted by the wire-service news photographs – selected, classified, and collated by Melvin Charney to construct his *Un Dictionnaire* ... – confront us with the shock of recognition that allows us to see architecture from outside its presentation as an isolated monument. *Un Dictionnaire* ... presents the late twentieth-century habitat as material in a constant state of change directly engaged in the flux of life. Charney chooses from the ideas enclosed in the pre-packaged "news" images and orders them into a "dictionary," categorized as events, decomposition, ruins, generic envelopes, frames, streets, grids, walls, structure of structures, fragments of buildings and cities, cities on the move. They evoke a world of exclusion and effacement, of suspension of time and space, of the formless, the conform – act in cross-reference to define and redefine each other, establishing moral and ethical positions. Fragmented, multilayered, endlessly unique, and uniquely repetitive, the news images have the same texture as does the city. Encompassing everyday life, they are accessible to the interpretation of each individual. Through Charney's critical

Detail view from *The Structure of Events*: Series 4, *Decomposition*.

Un Dictionnaire ... 1970–2001. Detail view from *The Structure of Events*: Series 7, *Ruins*. From a work comprising 402 plates arranged in forty-six series. Acrylic on gelatin silver print mounted on board, 27.8 x 35.5 cm [each plate]. Collection Centre Canadien d'Architecture/Canadian Centre for Architecture, Montreal. Acquired with the assistance of the Canada Council for the Arts and by gift of Dr D.A. Charney. © Melvin Charney.

assemblage of the ubiquitous, *Un Dictionnaire* ... reminds us that architecture is simultaneously a material environment, a set of practices, and a rush of images and ideas.

Begun in 1970, *Un Dictionnaire* ... reveals the banality with which images had become repetitive events of the late twentieth-century city – war-torn fragments of streets and buildings, a house washed off its foundations, "a tall building stripped of its envelope by a bomb exposes supports and connections." The twenty-first century has been previewed. Event-generated monuments become permeated with meaning, "singled out and widely displayed in their moment of eminence and drama." Charney's *Un Dictionnaire* ..., in its ideation, construction, and form, is more than a surrogate of events; in its ability to elucidate, make connections, and move us, it also proves the power of aesthetics in ethics.

Melvin Charney practises as an artist, architect, and teacher. He has influenced several generations of students through the Unité d'architecture urbaine of the school of architecture at the Université de Montréal. The Unité's approach was based on the understanding of architecture as a cultural practice grounded in the study of the city's form as a collective and universal entity. Working at the intersection of art and architecture, Charney manifests this approach through a diverse body of works compromising site-related installations, drawings, photo collages, and texts. He is widely known for large-scale, temporary installations such as *Les maisons de la rue Sherbrooke* in Montreal (1976) and *A Chicago Construction* (1982) as well as for his permanent works for public spaces. The latter, which include the "Canadian Tribute to Human Rights in Ottawa" (1988–90) and the "Sculpture Garden of the Canadian Centre for Architecture" in Montreal (1987–91), make manifest the layers of meaning connecting large areas of the city and its history.

Notes

1 This text is adapted from my Preface to *Tracking Images: Melvin Charney Un Dictionnaire* ... (Montreal: Canadian Centre for Architecture, 2000).

2 This and other quotations in this chapter are taken from Melvin Charney's essay in the catalogue of the 7th Venice Biennale International Exhibition of Architecture, *Tracking Images: Un Dictionnaire* ...

Beyond the Frame: Ethics and Morality in Deleuze's Cinema

DANIEL O'CONNOR

There will always be breaks and ruptures, which show clearly enough that the whole is not here, even if continuity is re-established afterwards. The whole intervenes elsewhere and in another order, as that which prevents sets from closing in on themselves or on each other – that which testifies to an opening which is irreducible to continuities as well as to their ruptures.

Gilles Deleuze

Introduction

The purpose of this chapter is to analyze morality and ethics in cinema. This analysis is based on the assumption that morality and ethics are discourses of conduct and character. Moral discourse concerns itself with the appropriateness of conduct and action relative to situations. Rather than prevent changes in conduct and character, morality (at least in its cinematic forms) aims to control their flow and regulate their transformation (see Deleuze 1992 on control). The extent and effectiveness of these efforts can be recognized in the regularities of movement they produce. Ethics also involves movement and change, but it is concerned with transformations that appear only when moral connections are held in abeyance or suspended. Ethics involves the reflexive transformation of situations and actions. Its discursive strategies depart from the norm and return to events to assess the multiple potentials contained therein. To this end, ethics imparts an aesthetic dimension to the processes of transformation. While morality works to authenticate or problematize regularities of movement and orderly flows, ethics works to disturb the flow and interrupt the normal motion of bodies, texts, and things. An analytic that aims to understand the moral and ethical dimension of cinema must be cognizant of the nature of its images and their mobility. Moreover, it must attend to the non-discursive relations established between these moving images as they act and react upon one another as well as the discursive formations that express and articulate these relations.

One of the key, often undertheorized, aspects of the cinema is that it does not require additional motion or motivation for its images to make sense.

The material of cinematography is neither textual nor narrative but, rather, mobile sections, or *shots*, that already express relations of change and transformation. These shots are not stable surfaces for reflection or interpretation. To reduce shots to stills is to eliminate what is specifically cinematic about them. An analytic of cinema must go beyond the analysis of figures (including the linguistic figures or tropes) and frames. The work of cinematography is not the work of narration but, rather, of montage, which selects and assembles mobile sections to constitute movement-images that pass through each shot and each frame. Cinema is a fluid medium of change and transformation. As such, it destabilizes the solidity and solidarity of boundaries (see Bauman 2000 on the characteristics of fluidity; Grosz 1995, 131, on porosity of borders).

Whether as architecture, art, or cinema, boundaries and frames are shot through with intervals, with the openings, thresholds, and gaps through which the inside extends and alterity enters. The interval is a space of mixture, a place of hybrids and composites, where new bodies are created and new assemblages are constituted (see O'Connor 2002). In the cinema it is montage that produces a variety of cinematic assemblages (affection-images, perception-images, and action-images). As in modern architecture, "calculated openings" (see Foucault 1979, 207) are important analytical devices in understanding modern exercises of power – where openings are designed to regulate mixtures and to control flows, to legislate and coordinate the movement of bodies, to create dissymmetry in the flows of light and information, to instil habits, to mark out the stages in the hierarchical evolution of moral subjectivity, and to produce organized bodies (see O'Connor 2002). Since power is a relation and is only exercised against agents (see Dean 1999; Rose 1999; Rose and Miller 1992) or those faced with possibilities, it is necessary to conceive of the power of cinema in relation to its openings and the mechanisms at work to control movement.

Semiotic and Cinematic Intervals

The analysis of the cinema and other audio-visual media has been largely dominated by semiology and metalinguistics (see, for example, Stam 1992; Fiske 1989a, 1989b; Kaplan 1987; Metz 1974). The dominant tendency has been to treat cinematographic images as if they were signs. On the one hand, this has resulted in attempts to show a mimetic relationship between images and reality by articulating the analogical codes that link images to everyday experience. In this sense cinematographic images are placed within a semiotic framework comprising signifiers, signifieds, and their arbitrary relations. From this point of view, cinematographic images (shots) are sign fragments linked by narrative schemes. Such "schemings of language" (Chevalier 1990) are acts of transgression, constituting a "leap," as Barthes (1974) puts it, over "the wall of antithesis" or the "cuts" separating elementary sign fragments. The logic of these schemes (i.e., analogy) is to establish a *preferred reading* or regulated means of moving across semiotic intervals (see Fiske 1989a, 133–4).

By dissimulating the work of transgression the formulas of reading aim to appear seamless, natural, or ready-made. By combining schemes of transgression and naturalization, language is reduced to the deontological function of *order-words* (see Deleuze and Guattari 1987). Order-words are mythological imperatives designed to govern movements across semiotic intervals. Such narrative mastery does not simply imply that there is only one manner of linking textual fragments but, rather, commands or authorizes certain actions (performative readings) at the expense of others, telling us what we must see or think and how we must act. Like modern exercises of power, the aim of the master narrative is, through the forces of repetition and dissemination, to constitute habits and maintain orderly associations among reading populations (O'Connor 2002).

Master narratives, such as the one noted above, enact a *spatial practice* of interval. They deploy the interval both as a space of transgressive action and authoritarian rule. Naturalizing transgressive space serves to maximize textual authoritarianism and maintain preferred associations while overruling other forms of encounter that might occur there. They want to appear natural in order to remove traces of their intervention. Analogy is, however, only one form of spatial practice that operates through intervals. Montage is an alternative strategy that seems more pertinent to audio-visual media such as film and television. While montage is also a process of assembling fragments (i.e., visual and sound images) it also creates additional possibilities for strategically deploying the interval and for enabling alternative forms of rule. Through the non-discursive assemblage of images, montage produces discursive regimes of enunciation and expression.

Of the diverse mobilities that characterize cinema, it is possible to identify three distinct analytical forms. First, there are *images of motion* that are delineated by what goes on inside the frame as bodies and things change and exchange their relative positions in a set. Second, there are *movements of the camera* that change the set and modulate the frame of reference (e.g., by panning, zooming, and borrowing the momentum of other bodies). And third, there are the *movement-images* that are a consequence of relating movement (of bodies or the camera) to an interval of motion. Instead of simply positing montage as one image following another and requiring external links added by the script or narrative, in montage images act and react upon one another independently of the script or narrative. Through montage shots are selected and assembled, potential openings are introduced, and new technologies and strategies are invented for dealing with the movements through cinematic intervals.

The Interval Close-Up

The close-up is an act of framing par excellence. But framing is not a matter of organizing elements inside an enclosure, like a stage production. It is a special case of *cutting out*, or extracting, a composition unit from the "profilmic material" of the set (Aumont 1987, 36–7). This act of cutting abstracts the image from its spatiotemporal coordinates and its links to those coordinates. The resulting image is affectual rather than actual. An affect-image is thus produced by an act of cutting, but its significance is only realized in the corresponding act of inserting it back into the flow. Through montage the close-up is both a cut-out and an *insert*. This double action produces a primary cinematic interval.

Typically it is the face that constitutes the subject matter of the close-up. Some would suggest that the close-up is a defining element of the cinematic. For example, Bergman suggests "that the possibility of drawing near to the human face defines the primary originality and the distinctive qualities of the cinema" (qtd. in Deleuze 1991, 99). For Eisenstein (1942) "the close-up is the face." Eisenstein's claim suggests that the subject matter of any close-up will necessarily display qualities that are equivalent to the "faciality" traits of a face in close-up. The faciality traits of the cinematic close-up are distinct from images of the face in the "still" (e.g., in a painting or photograph). The still is enclosed by a frame that prevents "spillage" (see Bauman 1988) between the image and its surroundings. This boundary reduces the likelihood of the image extending beyond the frame and being transformed into a stimulus evoking bodily responses (see de Cauter 1993; Falk 1993). But in cinema, what is cut-out is also inserted. The insert is deployed to stake out critical instants, turning points, and to prefigure paroxysms (Deleuze 1991, 89).

Faces are usually taken as a normative reflection of the settings in which people act and perceive. People are typically perceived to have characters and to play social roles: objects are presumed to have real uses and to enter into real connections with people who, in turn, have real relations with one another and with their situations. The close-up makes all these functions disappear. It dissolves the spatiotemporal coordinates (which identify, socialize, and communicate) in order to produce pure qualities (see Deleuze 1991, 100). Supplementing the *actual* relations between people and relations among people, things, and situations, there are also *expressed* relations. For example, standing on a precipice may be connected with the experience of vertigo (as its cause), but this actual connection does not explain its expression (as evidenced by the face in close-up).

Beyond the web of actual relations in the *derived world* of actions and reactions there lies an immanent world of qualities and affects. Alongside actual relations (of persons and precipices) there are expressed, discursive relations. Even if the expressed relation anticipates another actual relation (e.g., a person actually falls over the edge), the expressed remains a *potentiality* of the relation *as it is lived*. The image of the expressed is an affect-image. It *lives* in a virtual world that is distinct from any of its actualizations (in the same way that a quality like redness is not identical with any of the red things that actualize it). What emerges in the close-up is a deterritorialized image of pure potential (Deleuze 1991, 96, 109).

Qualities like vertiginousness can be inserted in the flow of actual relations but they remain ways of living the scene of the precipice.[1] As inserts, affect-images function as thresholds; they occupy intervals between the scenes. They are typically inserted as a means of linking actual situations and the extensions that modify them, where they *qualify* the scene and *motivate* responses. In such cases the power of the affect is harnessed within sensory-motor schemes, where it is made to function as a link between a situation and its response.

The Interval in Large Form

In this montage composition an interval is opened (i.e., inserted) between two different, even opposed, situations. Between these two situations there is a large interstice of *virtual space* (or "irrationally governed inter-state space" [see Bauman 1992, 58]) that is linked by the intermediary movements of action-images. This interval is created to be traversed. It waits to be occupied by heroic actions that invent a means of passage as the affect is subordinated to action. This space is not easily traversed; it is populated with obstacles and other diversionary forces (or temptations [see Bakhtin 1981, 106]). Encounters in the interval take the form of a duel of forces. Typically, the duel takes place in the open with the aim to normalize, discipline, or otherwise *police the public ways* (Virilio, qtd. in Deleuze 1986, 60).

In the large-form, situations embody power. This power is exerted as forces that extend into the behaviour of the characters encompassed by their situations. The force of situations acts on characters as challenges. Characters, in turn, react or respond to the situation with the aim of modifying it, their relation to it, or their relation with other characters (Deleuze 1991, 140). The interval (insert) between the initial encompassing situation and its modified form is quite large, typically spanning the length of the film from its opening to its closing shot. This size of the interval functions not only as a space of reflection but also as a way to measure the "adventure time" (to borrow Bakhtin's expression [1981, 106]) required to acquire an appropriate *habitus*, or *know-how* (see Bourdieu 1993), to respond. Knowing-how takes time. It requires an extensive duration of acquisition (internalization) typically followed by brief moments of actualization (externalization) of the forces thus acquired. The polarities of internalization and externalization are traits of faciality, where one of its facets is the action of seeing (taking in the scene), while the other is the formation of a response.

An action-image is a form of mediation between a given situation and the activity that is mobilized to respond to it. As a whole, the montage formula of the action-image can be simplified as S-A-S, where the element (A) is a moment of reflection between one situation (S) and another. The formula can be modified such that the initial situation (S) motivates actions (A), which restores the initial situation (S), further *degrades* the situation (S-), or *modifies* the situation (S+). En route, this movement encounters counterforces that establish the conditions for a duel or a series of duels, either with a milieu (e.g., a physical duel with a harsh environment), with others (e.g., a psychological duel with a hostile family or bodily duel with an attacker), or internally (e.g., a duel with alcoholism) (see Deleuze 1991, 143–5). The action of the duel is also a relation of forces since it involves acting in response to what other situated forces are doing or are capable of doing.

In the restored form (S-A-S), the resulting outcome is a return to the original situation (S) rather than to a modified one (S+) because the challenges thrown down by the situation are so great that they can only be parried; the force of the response is exhausted in the restoration of the conditions of existence (e.g., the restoration of a threatened identity). This formula is typical of the epic or tragic film, where the action is cyclical and where the initial situation is repeated again and again. Conversely, a character might never develop the know-how to respond to the challenges thrown them by their situation or may simply respond inappropriately. The result is that a problematic situation only deepens or worsens; S-A-S- is the formula typical of the *film noir*.

The more common "Western" formula for the large form is S-A-S+. In this formula a character (hero) must acquire a habitus (a mode of response) sufficient to overcome the demands and challenges of a situation. The process of acquiring heroic forces necessitates a "big gap" between situations, one which is only bridged progressively through the film through "a series of duels that converge on the ultimate duel" (Deleuze 1991, 154). This formula requires that the hero's place is prepared long before the hero comes to occupy it. The hero, only potentially equal to the ultimate challenge, must be prepared; "his grandeur and his power must be actualized" (154). Between the situation and action that changes it the habitus is nurtured and grows capable of a response. Heros are never stationary; they are either internalizing what is in the situation or are acting out this internalized force. The action varies in relation to two poles, one of affective permeation or internalization (S-A), the other of extension or detonation (A-S). Situations permeate the character continuously and deeply, while the character, thus permeated, bursts into action at discontinuous intervals (155). Heroes only act because they see what is in the situation and are affected by it, and only triumph because of the interval or delay that allows them to become capable of action (i.e., for their powers to become equal to the situation). This means that the situation must be given; the hero must either see what there is in the situation and then assemble a response appropriate to it or "take in" what is given and wait for the appropriate moment to formulate a response (an excellent example of this is the development of the character "Johnny" in Dmytryk's classic Western, *Warlock*). In contract to heroes, villains are impulsive. They do not have an interval and are therefore incapable of reflecting or seeing (even their own reflection, as in the many variants of Murnau's *Nosferatu* [1922]).

An exemplar of the large-form action-image is Eastwood's *Unforgiven*. In this film we find the hero (William Munny) withdrawn to a pastoral existence, barely coping with the challenges thrown down by his situation (the death of a spouse, the need of his children, poverty, and the sickness of his animals). He struggles for survival according to the cyclical formula (S-A-S). The powers and qualities of his former life have been held in suspense as his habitus has habituated to the demands of his situation (which itself is the result of a minor duel – a duel with the past, with alcohol, and a wayward lifestyle). His invitation to the challenge comes in the disguise of an open solicitation to revenge the brutal assault of a prostitute. In the bounty offered, the hero sees an opening and the possibility of getting "a new start" for his children. The gap between the assault and ultimate revenge defines the space that the hero will come to occupy. But the hero is not immediately ripe for action: he must discover a habitus of which his situation (and its duels) has deprived him (e.g., he has lost his capacity to aim a handgun, and his horse has habituated to the demands of a pastoral existence). In traversing the large gap between S and S+, he must also find the support of two functional communities: one a fundamental, more or less permanent, moral (or orthodox) community to sanction his actions, the other a makeshift community to provide instrumental support. He must deal with the demands of the former and the failings of the later (e.g., Ned's, rifle proves instrumental in carrying out the long shot, though Ned himself is unable to rise to the challenge; the Kid provides instrumental support for the close shot but has poor eyesight and lacks the conviction to rise to the ultimate challenge).

Parallel to the moral community of the brothel is the false community of Big Whiskey, which is controlled by the heavy-handed sheriff, "Little Bill" Dagget. This pathological community is a disorganized milieu, and so its habits are likewise disorganized. Bodies caught in the disorganized milieu develop "cracked ways of behaving" (Deleuze 1991, 145); their actions are clumsy and gauche and are "inappropriate to their environment" (see Maffesoli 1993a, 10). Following the formula S-A-S, behaviour in the pathological milieu lacks delays or moments of reflection. The affections that permeate its characters are too strong and are manifested in excesses and bad habits. Little Bill, for example, fancies himself a carpenter but builds asymmetrical structures that invariably leak.

In his initial duel with Little Bill, Munny has a fever that leaves him unable to rise to the challenge. His illness, in conjunction with the wounds inflicted by Little Bill, requires the nurturance and support of his makeshift and moral communities. Little Bill's excesses lead him to torture and finally kill Munny's partner, Ned. This event comprises the final affective permeation of Munny, which leads to his explosive action in the ultimate duel with Bill and his false community, a situation in which he is out-numbered and out-gunned but rises to the challenge, formulating the appropriate response, modifying the situation, and establishing a space for the new orthodoxy.

It is typically a pathological community that the hero confronts in the final duel. Pathological and fundamental communities travel along parallel lines that seem to bring them closer and closer together, towards the vanishing point of perspective that marks their final convergence. The way of travel is marked by a series of minor skirmishes, feints, and parries that allow the hero to discover the powers and qualities to face the final duel.

The Interval in Small Form

Once rendered in large form, it is also possible to understand how the force of actions might constitute situations. The small form works with actions and habits that form clichés. The power of the small form is to make actions function indexically[2] – that is, to indicate situations (even very different or opposed situations) that are not given but are directed to exist. Situations are indicated by their habits, that is, by modes of behaviour, gestures, manners, even costumes (see Deleuze 1991). The small form typically follows the formula A-S-A+, where an action (A) discloses a situation (S), which triggers off a new action (A+) (see Deleuze 1991, 160). Here, situations act as media to link together actions at a distance.

In contrast to the large form, where action is premised on seeing and taking in the scene, action in the small form is blind. It follows elliptical paths similar to feeling one's way around a dark room. Its heroes are ready-made with all their qualities and powers. There is little "character development" (see also Bakhtin's discussion of the hero in popular novels [1986, 21]) because characters are constants while spatial environments, social positions, and fortunes constitute missing "independent variables" (see Eco 1985, 180).

In its simplest form, the index can be constituted as an ellipsis between one action and another (as in the contiguous ellipsis form: A ... A+; see Peirce 1955, 108). For example, where a character displays the habitus of a beggar (A) on one occasion only to appear on another occasion dressed in finery (A+) one is directed to the conclusion that the character's situation changed. Indexical actions force the production of events (e.g., new found wealth) even though the event itself is not given.

Complex indexical relations can produce equivocal situations. Here, infinitesimal differences in action or gestures can *simultaneously* indicate two very different or opposed situations, or one situation charged with ambiguity. It is through the construction of equivocity that Chaplin displays his true comedic talent. In *Gold Rush*, for example, the hero finds himself trapped by a storm in a cabin with another prospector, Big Jim. In a classic sequence the starving hero is seen pulling a shoe from a pot of boiling water. Then we see a shot of his bare foot, and then a shot of him sitting down at the table, gently carving the shoe, proportioning out a share of the shoe/turkey to his equally starving colleague, biting the remaining bits of leather off a shoe-nail/bone, and offering his partner an opportunity to divide the nail/wishbone. In this case, a slight difference between two modes of behaviour serves to disclose indexically the opposable situations of feast and famine.[3] The idea of transposing dispositions (clichéd reactions) from one situation to one where you would not expect to find them (like the crowning of the fool in the Bakhtinian carnival) creates the possibility of the comedic effect. The contiguity of habits and characters brings opposable situations into contact as the expressions of actions. Without this virtual expressed element to link them together, actions would be little more than a heterogeneous collection of archaeological remnants lacking a discursive assemblage to hold them together (see Boundas 1993; 1996).

The small form can also be economical from the point of view of production. For example, a shot of a body subject to the play of light and shadow is perhaps more economical than is a shot requiring an actual train to pass before a character. The similar economy of action works for the clever mime that can call forth or express a character or an event with a minimum of gesticulation. By "presentifying absence" (Sartre 1991) such small-form spatial practices bring distance into proximity (see Shields 1992, 189, 192) and link it to appropriate actions. Viewing requires a measure of "cultural competence" on the part of the spectator (see Fiske 1989a) since they must be able to recognize the habitus as an index of the place to which it belongs in order to call forth the appropriate virtual image or get the joke.

The montage of the large and the small represent formulaic deployments of the cinema interval. In the circuits of movement that take place in modernist cinema, the interval appears as a virtual link inserted to bind movements and spaces together. As variations on the theme of "sensory-motor connections" (see Deleuze 1991, 1989) these forms of montage work *non-discursively* to produce discursive regimes of expression that measure the correctness of character or behaviour in relation to situations. Sensory-motor formulae establish their discursive regularities and circuits of meaning by subordinating time (i.e., the interval and the expressed) to space and spatial practices.

In contradistinction to morality, ethics is an analytic that reflects on and short circuits the formation of discursive regularities. Ethical reflection does not produce normal or clichéd responses to situations nor does it assess the appropriateness of action relative to situations. Ethics is an *aesthetic* constituted in the open spaces beyond the circuits and regularities of expression that constitute morality. The space of ethics is deterritorialized, a space of *occupation* rather than habituation. The openness of ethical space does not lend itself to the formation of habits, and situations do not act to encompass it. Ethics is characterized by breaks in the sensory-motor mechanisms. It can be conceived as a failure of the habitus to produce the requisite know-how to respond, or a habitus on holiday. Liberated from the necessity of expressing or disclosing the truth of a situation or action, discourse becomes transformative.

Ethical space is like a sacred site; it is set aside from the everyday. Like a time-out from the ordinary, ethics is divorced from practical aims and the serious business of getting on with things. Ethics constitutes space as any-place-whatever (see also Maffesoli 1993b). Similar to Simmel's (1950, 44) notion of sociability, they are spaces of playful encounters because they represent the "pure form that is raised above all contents" and are "free from the entanglements of practical life." In such spaces, normal circuits of movement are held in suspense as situations and no longer express an interest in practical extensions or morally legitimate actions.

In the open the habitus fails to function normally as the seer and thus fails to produce appropriate extensions. The effect is to create another quality of seeing, closer to the genetic basis of perception itself, or what Deleuze calls *differential perception*. Bakhtin defines the literary equivalent of differential perception as "free indirect discourse"; that is, as a movement of becoming where characters do not simply react mechanically to ready-made or objective situations but, rather, simultaneously constitute the scene for themselves (1984, 52; see also Braidotti 2002 on becoming). Rather than subordinating time to movement through space, ethics reverses this determination. When the habitus fails to translate situations into action, or actions fail to disclose situations, the power of the action-image is likewise suspended and other dimensions of the image are opened.

Time-Image and the Return of the Expressed

The *normal* role of the virtual in relation to the actual is to provide a space of linkage, for, without the virtual, situations and actions would remain disconnected, fractured, and fragmentary. Flashbacks (recollection-images) are inserts that attempt to link virtual and actual within a given perception. However, these inserts always mark the difference between a perception and its expression as a virtual recollection through the use of dissolve-links, by clouding the horizons of the frame, changing from colour to black-and-white, prefiguring the recollection with a close-up of a face in rem sleep (as in Weir's [1993] *Fearless*) or with the use of a voice-off (where the voice is a memory that recounts events in the past). Wyler used the flashback to re-establish broken sensory-motor links in *Seven Year Itch* (1955) in order to challenge the displacing effect of an affect-image (i.e., the nameless object of desire played by Monroe).[4] The power of sound also brings the virtual into perception. Sound-out-of-field is often deployed to link one situation to another by filling the scene with anticipation. The haunting musical score in *Jaws* is exemplary in its virtual qualification of the scene, provoking a sense of anticipation by extending the horizon of the perception with a virtual encompasser. In this case sound proved most effective when its source was not seen (i.e., when it was beyond the frame).

Where flashbacks are inserted to police the scene and the sound-out-of-field is used to structure what comes next, pure optical situations are constituted by disturbances of memory or when memory-based recognition fails to provide appropriate extension (or know-how). This condition (a sociability threshold [Simmel 1950, 47]) is achieved when all practical interest is suspended and the spell of normal interaction is broken or when actions and interactions are no longer conditioned by ready-made structures and situations. The less pre-existing structure there is, the easier it is to reveal forms of sociability as they pass through discourse. As Simmel (1950, 47) argues, any interest expressed in the sociable encounter surpasses the threshold of sociability and transforms it instantly into something qualitatively different.

By breaking sensory-motor connections, time-images produce pure optical situations. Pure optical situations rupture normative temporal demands and time is no longer subordinated to the function of marking pragmatic movements through spatial segments. Similar to Baudrillard's (1990, 44) conception of the crystalline objects "devoid of function or abstracted of use," these pure optical situations do not provoke necessary or utilitarian responses but are open to a multiplicity of responses. The possibility of multiple responses and contingent futures sharing the same universe of probability discounts the governing principle of master narratives. Master narratives rely on the principle of falsification; that is, "any new statement that contradicts a previously approved statement regarding the referent can be accepted as valid only if it refutes the previous statement by producing arguments and proofs" (Lyotard 1984, 26). Narrative mastery invokes singular responses, or "truth," by forming a circuit of meaning. Because sensory-motor formulas express only what is interesting, they are impoverished relative to virtual direct expression. Time-images, in contrast, provoke multiple, and unfinalizable, contingent descriptions as they form circuits with other images from other archaeological planes of the past. Time images are expressed in the discursive form of the questions: what has happened here? how did we get to such a state? (see Deleuze and Guattari 1987). Questions displace action by the necessity of coming up with stories or "fabricating legends" (Deleuze 1989).

Distinct from the voice-off, the voice-in, or cinematic utterance, is a form of virtuality or otherness relative to the actuality of the field. While its powers are derived from the out-of-field, when it returns to the field it takes over its modes of actuality. According to Duras, this kind of utterance is an act of resistance: "torn from its mooring with the visual, it imposes itself on that which resists its independence" (qtd. in Deleuze 1989, 250). For example, the talking comedy took the encounter with the *other* (the other sex, class, region, nation, civilization, etc.) as its privileged object (Deleuze 1989, 230). The more independent the others who pass through the scene, the less pre-existing social structure there is to condition their interactions, and the easier it is to reveal the forms of sociability that pass through their conversations.

It is not conversation which provides the model of interaction, it is interaction between separated people, or within one and the same person, which is the model of conversation. What we might call sociability, or small talk, in a very general sense is not identical with society: it is a matter of the interactions that coincide with speech-acts rather than actions and reactions that pass through them according to a prior structure. (Deleuze 1989, 231)

The talking comedy is defined by the way the speech comes to occupy space. Either everybody talks at once, or the speech of one person fills the space so completely that it reduces the other to vain attempts, stammerings, stutterings, or efforts to interrupt. Speaking instead of acting is essential to the talking comedy. "An actress like Katherine Hepburn reveals her mastery of sociability stakes through the speed of her retorts, the way she disorients her partner and ties him in knots, the indifference to contents, the variety of reversals of perspective through which she passes" (Deleuze 1989, 232). The ordinary madness of family interactions or the intrusion of a stranger can determine the craziness of conversation that spreads the power of voice through the archaeological ruins of a discontinuous visual field that has been deprived of its powers of expression. Welles' *Citizen Kane* (1941) is exemplary in this regard.

Citizen Kane is similar in structure to the small-form where an event has taken place and the ensuing investigation aims to disclose its mystery. In this case Kane is dead, and witnesses to his life offer their recollections in a series of flashbacks. But Welles' assemblage is more complex than this. The investigation is focused on the virtual image of "Rosebud": What is it? To what situation does it refer, and from what situation could it possibly get its meaning? Instead of extending into a response that changes or fails to modify the situation, Rosebud becomes a point of contraction, a starting point for a renewed search and a return to the same point: but it is a return with a difference. Each witness questioned provides an equivalent slice of Kane's life. Each flashback is a leap to a particular region of the past to reconstitute the sensory-motor connections of former presents (i.e., in terms of their situations and habits). This effort of evocation, or summoning up, is aimed at determining which particular region of the past will produce the actual Rosebud. Each time the question is the same: Is this thing Rosebud in this region or not?

The effort of evocation does not result in the formation of serially linked pasts that actualize the truth of the encompassing situation (as in the large form), nor is the action directed towards the piecemeal disclosure of a situation (as in the small form). Instead, each recollection constitutes a continuum on its own, and each refers to a discrete region of the past, all of which are equally coexistent, each containing the whole of Kane's life in one form or another and therefore each equally true (and therefore equally false). Each region of the past possesses its own legendary significance and, therefore, its own contingent future and possibilities. Even when Rosebud is finally disclosed from among the immense collection that was Kane's life, there is no one around for which it holds any particular interest.

Welles was perhaps the first to reverse the subordination of the virtual to the actual. By breaking with the sensory-motor conventions of modern cinema, he was able to create a time-image. This image empties out the realism of response and subjectivity and fills this hollowed-out interstice with the necessity of forging new relations and creating virtual events in a place devoid of events. In Welles' cinema of the question, the meaning of Rosebud is simultaneously relayed into a multiplicity of possible connections and relations, each one incapable of exhausting, by itself, the whole meaning of the term. The whole is equally not an ensemble, linked together by a sensory-motor scheme, but, rather, a collection of fragments lacking an organization that would constitute Kane as an organism, with a variety of functionally integrated parts.

The development of the time-image relates to the crises and failures of the *grands récits* of modernity. The postmodern condition offers little faith in the possibility that the givenness of a global whole, or an all-encompassing situation, could inspire a corresponding system of action capable of modifying it. Similarly, little faith is accorded the possibility that any (small-form) action or series of actions, no matter how great the effort, could disclose the truth of our condition, even partially. There is instead a problem of looking deeper into situations for the possibilities of encounter that hide in the clichéd responses and ready-made formulas of modern strategies of power. Clichés are sensory-motor images that actualize certain forces and necessarily hide others in order to make the things *interesting*. Powers have an "interest" in hiding in clichés as they aim to actualize certain truths at the expense of others. It is only when sensory-motor schemes break that the image is opened to the excesses of seeing and sayings that occupy this particular time interval.

Concluding Remarks

The power of the modern cinema does more that just reflect external situations and their programmatic actions. It has the power to control our seeing and our sayings. The ongoing constitution of modernity is premised on the control of the virtual, in terms of its powers, qualities, and potential expressions. Control does not equal repression. Under modernity the virtual is made use of and deployed in strategic ways to forge relations between actions and situations and to ensure the moral appropriateness of conduct and character in relation to the situations in which we perceive an act. The importance of cinematic sensory-motor links lies in the constitution of cultural cosmologies that form the basis of our perception and orientations to the world. As Shields argues, cultural formations are embodied not so much in learned rules as in bodily dispositions and trained postures; that is, in the more practical paradigms that coordinate group activities and sites (1991, 63).

The development of the time-image reveres the subordination of the virtual to the actual and of time to space. It breaks up the discursive regimes that express sensory-motor links. Being under the time-image means that both *seeing* what there is in situations and the *knowing-how* to respond become open questions. As a form of postmodern ethic, the time-image opens a space to question master narratives and their ready-made truths, norms, conventions, and systems of moral expectation. Its aim is to promote reflection by dislocating the virtual from its snares so that precluded visions, voices, and counter-memories inform our free indirect discourse.

Notes

1 Hitchcock's *Vertigo* (1958) is exemplary in its use of the close-up. In this film there are two worlds: one of affect and desire, one of rules and roles. Repeated inserts show the difference between the two.

2 In Peirce (1955, 108) indices possess three characteristics: (1) they have no significant resemblance to their object; (2) they refer to individuals, single units, single collections of units, or single continua; and (3) they direct the attention to their objects by blind compulsion. Anything that marks a junction or interrupts two experiences regardless of the medium is an index (89–90). For example, "a piece of mould with a bullet-hole in it is a sign of a shot; for without the shot there would have been no hole" (104). The difference between the mould with a hole in it and the one without indicates an action or event somewhere between the disparate experiences.

3 Deleuze (1991, 169) provides the following example of equivocity: "Viewed from behind, Charlie, deserted by his wife, seems to be shaking with sobs, but as soon as he turns round we see that he is in fact shaking himself a cocktail ... the action is filmed from the angle of smallest difference from another action ... but in this way discloses the enormity of the distance between the two situations."

4 In this case the flashback is the voice of normality, which, while on holiday, returns occasionally to restore the situation and its sensory-motor connections. In this sense, the recollection-image serves as a means of *recognition*, reconstituting normality as it extends its force into the bodily dispositions of the main character.

Works Cited

Aumont, J. 1987. *Montage Eisenstein*. Bloomington: Indiana University Press.

Bakhtin, M.M. 1981. *The Dialogic Imagination*. Austin: University of Texas Press.

−1984. *Rabelais and His World*. Bloomington: Indiana University Press.

−1986. *Problems of Dostoevsky's Poetics*. Minneapolis: University of Minnesota Press.

Barthes, R. *S/Z*. 1974. New York: Hill and Wang.

Baudrillard, J. 1990. *Revenge of the Crystal*. London: Pluto.

Bauman, Z. 1988. "Strangers: The Social Construction of Universality and Particularity." *Telos* 78: 7–42.

−1992. *Intimations of Postmodernity*. London: Routledge.

−2000. *Liquid Modernity*. Cambridge: Polity Press.

Boundas, C.V. 1993. "Foreclosure of the Other: From Sartre to Deleuze." *Journal of the British Society for Phenomenology* 24 (1): 32–43.

−1996. "Deleuze-Bergson: An Ontology of the Virtual." In Deleuze: A Critial Reader, ed. Paul Patton, 81–106. Oxford: Blackwell.

Bourdieu, P. 1993. *The Field of Cultural Production*. New York: Columbia University Press.

Braidotti, R. 2002. Metamorphoses: Towards a Materialist Theory of Becoming. Cambridge: Polity Press.

Chevalier, J. 1990. *Semiotics, Romanticism and the Scriptures*. Berlin: Mouton de Gruyter.

Dean, M. 1999. *Governmentality: Power and Rule in Modern Society*. London: Sage.

de Cauter, L. 1993. "The Panoramic Ecstasy: On World Exhibitions and the Disintegration of Experience." *Theory, Culture and Society* 10 (4): 1–23.

Deleuze, G. 1986. *Foucault*. Minneapolis: University of Minnesota Press.

−1989. *Cinema 2: The Time-Image*. Minneapolis: University of Minnesota Press.

−1991. *Cinema 1: The Movement-Image*. Minneapolis: University of Minnesota Press.

−1992. "Postscript on the Societies of Control", *October* 59: 3–7.

Deleuze, G. and F. Guattari. 1987. *A Thousand Plateaus: Capitalism and Schizophrenia*. Minneapolis: University of Minnesota Press.

Eco, U. 1985. "Innovation and Repetition: Between Modern and Post-Modern Aesthetics." *Daedalus* 114: 161–84.

Eisenstein, S. 1942. *The Film Sense*. New York: Harcourt, Brace and Company.

Falk, P. 1993. "The Representation of Presence: Outlining an Anti-Aesthetic of Pornography." *Theory, Culture and Society* 10 (3): 1–42.

Fiske, J. 1989a. *Television Culture*. 1989a. London: Routledge.

−1989 b. *Reading the Popular*. Boston: Unwin.

Foucault, M. 1979. *Discipline and Punish: The Birth of the Prison*. New York: Vintage.

Grosz. E. 1995. *Space, Time and Perversion*. London and New York: Routledge.

Kaplan, A. 1987. *Rocking around the Clock: Music Television, Postmodernism, and Consumer Culture*. New York: Methuen.

Lyotard, J-F. 1984. *The Postmodern Condition: A Report on Knowledge*. Minneapolis: University of Minnesota Press.

Maffesoli, M. 1993a. "The Social Ambiance." *Current Sociology* 41 (2): 1–15.

−1993b. "The Imaginary and the Sacred in Durkheim's Sociology." *Current Sociology* 41 (2): 59–67.

Metz, C. 1974. *Language and Cinema*. The Hague: Mouton.

O'Connor, D. 2002. *Mediated Associations.* Montreal: McGill-Queen's University Press.

Peirce, C.S. 1995. *Philosophical Writings of Peirce.* Ed. Justin Buchler. New York: Dover.

Rose, N. 1999. *Powers of Freedom: Reframing Political Thought.* Cambridge: Cambridge University Press

Rose, N., and P. Miller 1992. "Political Power Beyond the State: Problematics of Government." *British Journal of Sociology,* 43: 173–205.

Sartre, J-P. 1991. *The Psychology of the Imagination.* New York: Citadel.

Shields, R. 1991. *Places on the Margin: Alternative Geographies of Modernity.* London: Routledge.

– 1992. "A Truant Proximity: Presence and Absence in the Space of Modernity." *Society and Space* 2: 181–98.

Simmel, G. 1950. *The Sociology of Georg Simmel.* Trans. Kurt H. Wolff. New York: The Free Press.

Stam, R., R. Burgoyne, and S. Flitterman-Lewis. 1992. *New Vocabularies in Film Semiotics: Structuralism, Post-Structuralism and Beyond.* New York: Routledge.

PART FIVE

RELATIONS WITH THE OTHER

The Marginal Other: Modern Figures and Ethical Dialogues[1]

SUZAN ILCAN

In moral space, the stranger is someone of whom one cares little and is prompted to care even less.

Z. Bauman, *Postmodern Ethics*

Strangers have become the subjects and objects of intense social, cultural, and political exclusion. We need only recall the discontents of a stranger who is refused entry at a state border, or an exiled subject, a native denied cultural membership, a "foreigner" excluded from public service. These strangers, or marginal others, appear everywhere. It is not their image that is at stake here but, rather, the effect that this otherness implies in the development of specific social practices.

In this chapter I explore the notion of the stranger through an analysis of encounters between agents and the stranger informed by ethnographic illustrations taken from northwestern Turkey. Drawing on Bauman's (1999, 1995, 1993) work on strangers and forms of "togetherness," and Cornell's (1995) and Bakhtin's (1986, 1981) notions of ethics and dialogics, I propose three distinct types of encounters with the stranger: monological, analogical, and dialogical. Each occurs in what I define as aesthetic, routine, and ethical spaces, respectively. In the dialogic encounter, and by comparison to the other two encounters, I interrogate the relevance of what may be referred to as a postmodern ethic: an ethic that reflects an attitude towards others that neither deprives them of their difference and distinctiveness nor imposes upon them moral precepts of approval or disapproval. I suggest that this encounter challenges rigid cultural boundaries, fosters voices from the margin, and forms a counter-position to hegemonic practices. Overall, this chapter emphasizes strangeness in an analysis of social encounters and as a basis for understanding what is ethical.

The Marginal Spaces of Strangeness

Episodes of strangeness loom large when entering a new territory, learning a new language, and interacting with unfamiliar groups. They encompass numerous possibilities and occurrences, such as: tourists who either visit or sojourn in another culture, guest workers who search for a place to call home, and numerous others whose aspirations figure as unfamiliar even though they live in a place that they call "home." Strangers are irreducibly other, different, and independent (Grosz 1989, 141). This is why strangers of all kinds, or what Simmel (1950) refers to as "potential wanderers," may interfere with the controlled environments in which they are located. Consequently, they may be relegated to marginal spaces set aside for tourists, migrant ethnic groups, or refugees. Such depictions of strangeness, however, should not imply that there is, as Kristeva (1991, 55) reminds us, only one category of strangeness.

There are many categories of strangers, ranging from members who exist within a social group, community, or culture to group members who see themselves as other in host societies. This being the case, "the 'strangehood' of strangers has become a matter of degree; it changes as one passes from one area to another, and the rhythm of the shift differs between various categories of strangers" (Bauman 1995, 130). The most discerning point is that strangers are not individuals but, rather, a social type, standing alongside other social types such as the relative, the neighbour. Unlike these more familiar social types, strangers have the peculiar characteristic of being at once insiders and outsiders, near and far. As Simmel (1950, 407) suggests, strangers as group members are

> characteristic of relations founded only on generally human commonness. But between nearness and distance, there arises a specific tension when the consciousness that only the quite general is common, stresses that which is not common. In the case of the person who is a stranger to the country, the city, the race, etc., however, this non-common element is once more nothing individual, but merely the strangeness of origin, which is or could be common to many strangers. For this reason, strangers are not really conceived as individuals, but as strangers of a particular type: the element of distance is no less general in regard to them than the element of nearness.

That strangers are both near and far tells us that they are not in "any place" but, rather, are in-between one place and another. As Kristeva (1991, 7) says, the foreigner is someone "not belonging to any place, any time, any love. A lost origin, the impossibility to take root, a rummaging memory, the present in abeyance."[2] Thus strangers stand against an unfamiliar background and are located on the boundary of familiar behaviour. Familiar behaviour is located in and belongs to a space (workplace, prison, school) where certain kinds of relations can be prescribed, expected, or limited.[3] In contrast, a stranger's behaviour must be a form of independence that opposes the aims and requests of the familiar community yet incites from it responses and encounters. Here, the stranger *is* the other. The term "other" ("otherness" or "alterity") refers to what is beyond the frontier of social space. It designates an open space that, in turn, establishes a significant context and frame for those spaces occupied by routine and accepted group relations. It is otherness (the excluded, the outside)[4] that binds space as this or that space. Strangers can therefore only reside on the threshold and at an unfinalizable and unpredeterminable turning point.

Marginal spaces are spaces situated on the periphery of cultural systems of space. They are crtical to understanding a stranger's place in relation to those who belong to centrally placed communities and homes (however imaginary these may be). While these spaces are constituted by the "culture of the marginalized," Shields (1991, 6) adds that these "sites are never simply locations. Rather, they are sites for someone and for something," for specific kinds of persons and for specific kinds of activities. Accordingly, strangers may be regarded as physically close, in the sense that they can be seen or heard, and yet remain at the same time socially and morally remote. The knowledge one has of them may initially seem superficial (in that they appear as blurs) since their presence can only be guessed and approximated. Groups of strangers at bus stops or in restaurants, along with passers-by, constitute brief gatherings, moments now here and then gone. Even though they appear as blurs, however, we should not reduce their importance. They implicate modes of social recognition and spatiality.

In order for strangers to be kept in the category of the unfamiliar, the marginal spaces that they inhabit or bring with them must not transform into spaces in which there are codes of conduct and encounter, such as those of initiations, interdictions, and prohibitions. Such social spaces permit "fresh action" at the same time as they suggest and prohibit other actions (Lefebvre 1991, 73). They also imply a solidarity and continuity of relations between and among a community of people, or a protest against the transitoriness of strangers and the culture of the marginalized. In discussing the scope of Orientalism, Said (1978, 54) emphasizes the poetic character of constructing social spaces or geographical boundaries:

A group of people living on a few acres of land will set up boundaries between their land and its immediate surroundings and the territory beyond, which they call "the land of the barbarians." In other words, this universal practice of designating in one's mind a familiar space which is "ours" and an unfamiliar space which is "theirs" is a way of making geographical distinctions that *can be* entirely arbitrary … All kinds of suppositions, associations, and fictions appear to crowd the unfamiliar space outside one's own.

It is in this way that a conception of strangeness marks not only the limits between the unfamiliar and the known but also the spatial distinctions between the marginal and the social.

Specific types of encounters that characterize relations between agents[5] and the stranger have implications for understanding the role that otherness plays in constituting social spaces and particular interactions and, therefore, disclosing moral and ethical relations. The following section interrogates the perceived "distance" of strangers and the specific kind of contact an agent has with them. This agent, whom I refer to metaphorically as the *flâneur*,[6] relates to strangers monologically by merely acknowledging their presence without taking them or their world seriously. This is not an accidental encounter: it is one that renders strangers as objects. This encounter creates and occurs within *aesthetic* spaces. I present the *flâneur's* vivid imagery of the stranger as a kind of colonial process intolerant to difference and aligned with the modern perspective. Further, I suggest that these modern strolling subjects become strangers to their environments and to themselves.

The Distant Stranger: A Monological Encounter

The distance of strangers (the lack of proximity to strangeness) derives from their perceived "far-away" cultural status and from an agent's moral judgment of them in terms of this distant context. The term "morality" here refers to those overarching and universal beliefs that designate what is appropriate behaviour, calling for a logic of duty and obligation towards others. For strangers to be perceived as distant, an agent must assess them as morally extraneous. In doing so, the agent – as a member of a community upholding moral codes – evaluates them on the basis of their presence. This evaluation enables the agent to maintain her/his identity and centredness by pushing strangers away and into a field of distance.[7] In this context, the agent is a moral figure who imposes value judgments on the stranger.

Those who perceive strangers as distant may be referred to symbolically as *flâneurs*: those inconsequential, non-serious, and semi-detached strollers and spectators (Weinstein and Weinstein 1993, 56), or "pioneer onlookers" (Bauman 1995, 133), who – unlike the hurried, purposeful members of modern crowds – are only interested in observing (rather than disrupting) social phenomena. They may even be inclined to have short-lived contact with them for the sake of achieving certain goals, such as constituting strangers as exotic others (which has similarities to the way that Occidental traveller-writers and colonial discourses represent some non-Western peoples as exotic sexual objects or oppressed victims).[8] The activities of the *flâneur* reflect a colonial process presented and promoted in contemporary societies. These activities render social relations fragmentary, preclude mutual duties between and among people, and detach themselves from the world of social obligations (Ferguson 1994, 26). In what follows, I analyze the *flâneur's* contact with the stranger as being similar to a form of togetherness that Bauman (1995, 49–50) refers to as a "being-aside" togetherness. In this form of togetherness persons are cast *aside* each other. They encounter each other without there being any future consequences in the form of mutual rights or obligations.[9]

Like Bakhtin's hero in the novels of ordeal,[10] the *flâneur* views the distant world of strangers as mere setting and art form. However, unlike the perception of things as works of art that are accessible to those who are able to appropriate them (Bourdieu 1993, 227), this figure is only interested in watching the other from afar. This is because the other (with its own qualities and attributes) "astonishes and fills the subject with wonder and surprise" (Levinas, qtd. in Grosz 1989, 142). Furthermore, since these stereotyped strangers only sensationally please or fascinate the *flâneur* at a distance, they can have no real, long-lasting contact with her/him. Consequently, they are incapable of changing the *flâneur*. Similarly, the *flâneur* does not alter or create their world but only observes it from a distant vantage point. From this point, the *flâneur* enjoys making a sport out of the lives of beggars, vagabonds, or street sellers by both detaching her/himself from their practical concerns and collecting their experiences in a playful manner. As Bauman (1993, 168) states, "strangers, with their unknown, unpredictable ways, with their kaleidoscopic variety of appearances and actions, with their capacity to surprise, are a particularly rich source of spectators' pleasure." Everything in the spectators' field of vision is, however, viewed from one authorial disposition.

The *flâneur's* artistic view of distant strangers imposes a single voice on them. S/he does not take seriously their speaking[11] and acting but, instead, imaginarily decides what sensations these acts offer. The *flâneur*, who may be regarded as both scriptwriter and director (Bauman 1995, 92), observes distant strangers as actors in a play – actors who do not know they are performing for anyone or anything. In this dispassionate observation, there is nothing that accrues or accumulates except that, perhaps, the lust for looking and imagining becomes more affixed and fetishized. No lasting effects emerge from their contact. Consequently, there remains a distance between the *flâneur* and the stranger (between the author and the actor), ensuring that no dialogical or any other kind of encounter is possible. The *flâneur* is able to maintain this distance by transforming the stranger into an exotic other. Within contemporary society, this othering results in a pejorative portrayal of many groups. For example, and as Jenks (1993, 156) illustrates, the cultural representations of the working class and the ghettoized were canonized by the gazing position of the bourgeoisie and of the "people of taste." Distancing, or peripheralizing, the other may also enable the dispassionate observer to recognize her/himself "as the centre." As Mohanty (1991, 73–4) stresses, "it is only insofar as 'Woman/Women' and 'the East' are defined as *Others*, or as peripheral, that (Western) Man/Humanism can represent him/itself as the centre. It is not the centre that determines the periphery, but the periphery that, in its boundedness, determines the centre." Likewise, and in terms established by Charles Baudelaire, the *flâneur* is essentially the modern figure and "the individual sovereign of the order of things who … is able to transform faces and things so that for him they have only that meaning which he attributes to them" (Tester 1994, 6).

In the context of the unplanned and unexpected contact s/he has with these distant strangers, the *flâneur* is socially uncreative but imaginatively productive. The world of distant strangers is a monologically understood and objectified world. It corresponds to a single and unified authorial voice. The *flâneur's* narrative of the other is construed in terms that preclude the other as a partner in the narrative. The outcome of this one-sided story presents the other as a mere *object* of consciousness, not as "another consciousness."[12] In the realm of city life, Weinstein and Weinstein (1993, 56) claim that

> the *flâneur* dehistorizes the city, breaking it apart into a shower of events, primarily sights. He emphasizes synchrony over diachrony, and has no interest in systematizing the fragments of urban life. Each one is an aesthetic object to him, existing to titillate, astonish, please, or delight him. He appropriates the city as performance art, not seeking to know it and certainly not trying to reform it, but merely enjoying it.

Such urban encounters between the *flâneur* and the stranger create and occur within aesthetic spaces that do not spawn mutual obligations or duties. I use the term "aesthetic"[13] here to refer to matters and judgments of taste, attraction, and amusement wherein a subject – in this case the figure of the *flâneur* – is moved by the interest in what can be done with, and experienced by, the stranger. Like Foucault's (1985, 89) "aesthetics of existence," aesthetic spaces take on a brilliance of beauty that is created by spectators able to behold, see, and keep alive the unknown ways and the variety of appearances and sensations that strangers offer. Accordingly, the "pioneer onlooker" is most intrigued by the expressive movements and features that belong to animate bodies. It is in this way that aesthetic spaces embody the poignant gestures of distant strangers and arouse curiosity for the *flâneur*. And it is from out of the initiative one furnishes to things that one also forces these objects to become filled with pleasure in much the same way that artistic perception requires a heightened degree of exhilaration or level of captivation. Consequently, strangers are constructed by the *flâneur* in a zone of distant images, a zone devoid of any lasting contact with, or moral responsibility for, the other.

A zone of distant images is an attribute of numerous places. In the farming community of Arzu[14] and its nearby market setting, located in Turkey's northwestern region of Thrace, distant "strangers" (*yabancılar*) encompass a wide range of groups, including: itinerant merchants, tourists, beggars, and numerous others. These groups are typically known to reside outside the boundaries of social spaces as well as occasionally crossing them. Distant strangers, such as *çingene* (gypsies), represent the paradigmatic Other for most local residents, a representation first drawn to my attention in another northwestern Turkish community in the late 1980s when there were so many situations in which people spoke of what was Other to themselves. Although the *çingene*, who are also referred to as *Romanlar* by local residents, have lived in the region since the early nineteenth century, they are one of the economically poorest groups and are in desperate need of regular employment, adequate housing and health care, and sustained access to formal education. An older villager from Arzu comments on their presence:

The gypsies that you see around here, collecting the vegetables and fruits off the street, all come from *Uzun Köprü* and *Elmali* villages. They visit here from the outside. They arrive with horse carriages loaded with their tents and belongings, and try to earn as much money as they can until their next move. They can't read or write and they live without a book. The ones you don't see here every year, work as street vendors or factory workers in Istanbul.

The itinerant merchants' economic and social status, however, has been and continues to be of little concern to those who do not share their heritage.

From the perspective of local residents, the *çingene* are thought to "live without a book" and only wander to the countryside or from town to town, selling a variety of merchandise ranging from baskets full of fresh spices to flowers, clothing, blankets, and home utensils. In popular village discourses they are not visitors from another country or region (for "another country or region" does not exist); rather, they dwell outside the frontier of social space and therefore embody the very essence of strangeness. These itinerant merchants, who are within reach of most village residents and urban dwellers, are kept at a social distance from those who stroll past them and hence do not establish networks of mutual duties and obligations with them. The strollers, or wanderers, do not take these other "nomads" seriously. They do not foresee them as entering into their "familiar" world as either future kin, neighbours, or marriage partners; instead, they distinguish them in moral terms: as devoid of a religious faith or "fate" and as deficient in acceptable moral behaviour. Local residents would always remind me to "stay away from them" because "they steal." These kinds of judgments separate the onlooker from the other and make the *çingene* morally irrelevant. They are assigned the status of "living without a book" (*kitabsiz yaşiyorlar*), which highlights their absence of traditional, habitual activity as well as their distance from dutiful/faithful behaviour. Similarly, in a central Anatolian community, Delaney (1991, 192) notes that "*çingene* are considered to be sub-human, because they have no Book (Qur'an or Bible) and are thought to be promiscuous, like animals, sharing women in common." It can be said that the figure of the *flâneur* casts *çingene* in an alienated moral disposition since their behaviour is viewed in reference to their divergence from a pattern of commonly accepted conduct characterizing a particular place, neighbourhood, or descent group.

Given the gender divisions of social and pedestrian space, it is primarily male strollers who view itinerant merchants like objects on display. This viewing often occurs in Arzu's (and other villages') nearby marketplace. This place is occupied by a small network of local business and market establishments, state-erected buildings and monuments, a bus depot, a taxi stand, a central mosque, and a main motorway linked to several smaller roads and lanes. It generally attracts a day-time street crowd consisting of town and nearby village residents as well as a multitude of strangers in the form of travelling merchants, beggars, tourists, street musicians, and (occasionally) academic researchers. The territory temporarily occupied by distant strangers evokes interest, curiosity, and the capacity to arouse imagination;

it also provides diversion for strollers, especially for those males who have the opportunity to move through public spaces (i.e., the marketplace environment, streets, and alleys) relatively unconstrained (at least in comparison to females).[15] In their ability to move through and experience the small market setting, strollers frequently marvel at the itinerant merchants' dress and street performances. They amuse themselves by talking about their "strange" (*yabancı*) bright and multicoloured clothing, their seemingly loud voices, and their apparently wayward and nomadic lifestyle. They have a sensational contact with the *çingene* that does not entail any moral responsibility for them since they are not burdened with obligations toward them or with committing themselves to giving anything to them. Such strollers – including wealthy male landowners and business owners – view the *çingene* primarily as an object of aesthetics and as a source of both sensationalism and suspicion, notwithstanding the fact that these others also have a perspective on the strollers themselves (e.g., as strangers, potential consumers, or regulators). Social communication with these stereotyped strangers in pedestrian spaces remains intermittent. Whatever exchange takes place between strollers and the other tends to be one-sidedly aesthetic.

The pedestrian spaces of common walking places are the most spectacular sites, where amusement value overrides most other considerations. In these public spaces made strange, people treat distant strangers as pleasing to the eye or as distasteful, loose, and free (commonly associated with Western women and certain city women who travel about without "appropriate" dress accessories). In all of this gazing, one does not accrue anything: one only plays and scans by immobilizing the least knowable things that draw one's attention. Such playful characterizations usually manifest themselves in the open market, within crowded street cafes populated by local males, and outside village doorways, where itinerant merchants occasionally pass by to sell their goods and services (e.g., their fortune-telling skills). Not only are these common strolling areas known to house objects of pleasure, fear, and mystery,[16] but they have been created as aesthetic spaces by these types of encounters with strangers. In this context, the stroller tends to favour a remoteness between self and other; thus, the other becomes an object of aesthetic judgment while the self becomes constituted as distinct from the other. The figure and activity of the *flâneur* is reflected in the following monological account of a Turkish "gypsy":

She had long slim fingers, I remember, the filbert-shaped nails always tinted with henna, and a brown little face with a wide mouth that always seemed to be laughing. She wore strange, exotic garments of every hue and her shining black hair had twisted through it many vividly hued glass beads. She would tell us about her life in the tents and of her husband, who made baskets to sell to the peasants or sometimes to the rich houses of Istanbul. She gave one the impression that she was sharp as a monkey and oddly alluring, and I used to imagine a fine, swashbuckling husband for her, with swarthy face and gleaming white teeth and gold earrings dangling, flashing in the sun as he moved his leonine head. A tall, muscular man he would be with magnetism to match the strange charm there was about her. (Orga 1988, 22)

In this description, the "gypsy" cannot exceed the limits of her character since she is presented against the firm background of the external world. This novelist's portrayal of the "gypsy" bears a similarity to the way in which the *flâneur's* "spatial practice" retrieves an individual from the crowd by isolating certain features of her/his bodily mannerisms.[17]

What can be projected from the *flâneur's* contact with strangeness is the making of a modern subject – a subject that looks forward with a plan for seeing. The vivid imagery that this figure spawns is a kind of colonial process that renders the other as separate and different. However, since this perception takes into account the stranger's appeal, it is otherness that constitutes the *flâneur* "as the centre." The *flâneur's* supposed centrality is very much in line with the universality of reason and order (and the prospects of freedom and justice) assumed or promised by the modern perspective – a view that relegated magic, mystery, and the obscure to the realm of the irrational and that, on the basis of its rational goal to engineer landscapes and their occupants, justified the colonization and ordering of "strange" land and peoples (Bauman 1992, x; see also Ceyhan and Tsoukala 2002). However, the modern stroller, with his plans for seeing, becomes a stranger to himself. This stranger-*flâneur* treats his native surroundings as an alien site, roams in places not "home" to him, and divides himself from the people he observes by affirming his distance from them. This process involving "a native who becomes like a foreigner" (Shields 1994, 68) is telling of the paradoxes of some contemporary societies, of the decline of the centre and the language of unification. It is full of sites where differences get played out and where a myriad of relations co-exist; that is, where the world is experienced as "simultaneously emancipatory and alienating, promising and in good part providing new freedoms and potentialities, new forms of self-actualization and development, along with new problems and difficulties" (Smart 1993, 115). Such fragmented living seems to be an immutable feature of contemporary times.

With the aforementioned issues in mind, the discussion below deals with how the supposed centredness of the dispassionate *flâneur* can be reshaped, and sometimes supplanted, by other kinds of encounters. In the context of the perceived "nearness" of strangers, I argue that agents encounter strangers in two distinctly different ways. In the first kind of encounter, a "being-with" togetherness, agents impose a prior order on others by analogically defining and situating them. This agent, whom I refer to metaphorically as the *bricoleur*, relates to the other logocentrically within *routine* spaces. By comparing the other to pre-existing and opposing relationships, the agent is exposed to the appeal of others and "subjected" to their call. Here, the stereotyped stranger, the outsider, is active in producing the native "insider." The second kind of encounter with "close" strangers is dialogical. This encounter allows for a dialogue between different points of view, with each view having its own mode of expression and with neither being reducible to the other. In this encounter the participants are in a relation neither of exteriority nor interiority relative to each other; instead, they are mutually implicated in their relation with each other. I present this encounter, a "being-for" togetherness, as creating and occurring within *ethical* spaces. These spaces are created by two subjects who come together, without obligation or sanction, and recognize themselves in each other. Although fragile and unsettled, this type of encounter fragments the tyranny of normative expectations and grants the marginalized an opening to voice their concerns for social change. Overall, analogically and dialogically based encounters are shown to involve negotiations with, and a necessity for, the other.

The Nearness of the Stranger: Analogical Encounters

There is a paradoxical as well as a perceived "nearness" of strangers (near, in the sense of accessibility), wherein one is incapable of keeping away from the space they occupy or share. The social proximity of strangers emanates from more than just their mere sight and impression; they are perceived as near because they can neither be detached from one's view, identity, or play nor be constructed in a zone of distant images. In contrast to the *flâneur's* observation of distant strangers, strangeness is not objectified in the same way since, in order for this to occur, there must be some distance to form a picture of them (Bauman 1993, 148). The nearness of strangers and their ability to be prospective partners in social communication and experience results from the understanding people gain and continue to gain from them as they encounter them. The idea that strangers are in close proximity does not, however, guarantee their full acceptance in one's group or community. As Shields (1992, 195) states, "presence and proximity is no longer an indicator of inside status, of citizenship, or of cultural membership." There are ways of managing or reducing a stranger's near presence and of precluding his/her contact from becoming long-lasting or affective.

In order to live with nearby strangers, yet keep them from regularly entering into one's sphere of immediate social relations and responsibilities, one may move them to the "background," or to the sphere of the invisible. This process requires reckoning them as objects while the person doing the reckoning remains the same. One way to reaffirm the strangeness of strangers and to disregard their close presence is through the "technique of mismeeting." As Bauman (1993, 154) explains:

> By the technique of mismeeting, the stranger is allocated to the sphere of disattention, the sphere within which all conscious contact, and above all a conduct which may be recognized by him as a conscious contact, is studiously avoided. This is the realm of non-engagement, of emotional void, inhospitable to either sympathy or hostility; an uncharted territory, stripped of signposts; a wild reserve inside the life-world. For this reason it must be ignored. Above all, it must be *shown* to be ignored, and to be wished to be ignored, in a way allowing no mistake.

Although techniques of mismeeting are numerous, one of the most pronounced within a variety of social contexts is the avoidance of eye contact.

In communities of northwestern Turkey and elsewhere, it is common for certain people to avert their eyes from those whom they regard as strangers. This is the case if they come from different social classes, descent groups, or neighbourhoods, even though they may live in the same community (or in nearby communities). For example, it is more often the situation for poor farmers than for nearby urban-folk to deflect their look in the face of those who are deemed powerful (e.g., village landlords and military or police personnel). It is also more common for women than for men to avert their eyes in public spaces and in front of "unknown" or unfamiliar men (see also Delaney 1991, 42). At one level, the point of these "mismeetings" is to see the other while pretending not to look and to affirm that nothing will follow the glance of the other. In the case of women, in particular, their avoidance of eye contact not only attempts to obviate future contact with strangers but also to ensure that their occasional dialogues with them remain brief. Women in public spaces should not be seen seeing. This "not seeing" is linked to discourses of female purity and to moral beliefs about appropriate bodily presentation in the gendered organization of public space (Ilcan 1998; Marcus 1992). At another level, the effect of deploying this technique of mis-meeting is to prevent close strangers from gaining knowledge of you and from entering into your social field, with its rules, expectations, and rights (see Bauman 1993, 154). There is no telling, however, when such mismeet-ings will occur, and no guarantee that they will be unobtrusive.

In addition to encounters that keep strangers on the periphery and limit interactions with them, there are other types of encounters with those physically near yet remote. There is what I refer to as an analogical type of encounter that takes place between agents and strangers. In this encounter agents impose a "foreignness" on others. A stranger's outsidedness is made sense of by comparing him/her to other pre-existing and opposing relation-ships. This encounter is similar to what Bauman (1995, 50) calls a "being-with" togetherness. This form of togetherness involves "a meeting of incom-plete beings, of deficient selves; in such a meeting, highlighting is as crucial as concealing, engagement must be complemented by disengagement, deploy-ment of some resources must be paired with [the] withdrawal of others." In this context one develops ways to envision others and to keep one's distance from them. Such disjointed, half-hearted meetings may be accomplished through the use of analogy.

The figure engaged in analogical encounters with strangers may be referred to metaphorically as a *bricoleur*. A shrewd handyperson, the *bri-coleur* compiles a stock of symbolic items and takes from it whatever might be of use in completing the job that s/he is presently doing. The *bricoleur* is on a mission to make sense of the symbolic world through a form of rea-soning that makes differences homologous. The task of the *bricoleur*, as Weinstein and Weinstein (1993, 62) remind us, "is to seek whatever orders of homology and analogy can be discerned in what initially appears to be radically heterogeneous." It is in this way that such a figure is able to view the universe of strangeness as similarity in difference and difference in sim-ilarity while, at the same time, constructing a gap between her/himself and the stranger.

Within the field of Turkish kinship reckoning, the figure of the *bricoleur* attempts to structure the world of near strangers so as to differentiate "us" from "them." In order to comprehend what is other than oneself, one com-mon, calculable scheme consists of placing them in dominant codes of kin-ship reckoning.18 This process relegates particular groups to the status of non-kin. In this cultural framework, non-kin include all those who cannot be categorized as either "close kin" (*yakın akraba*) or "distant kin" (*uzak akraba*). Close kin are those connected to you through immediate ties of blood and marriage, and include consanguines and affines once removed from a person's immediate natal family (e.g., mother's brother, wife's sister, sibling's spouse or children, and so on). Distant kin are those related to you through less immediate ties of blood and marriage. These kin comprise an outer circle of relatives several steps removed from you (e.g., grandmother's siblings, great grandchildren, and so on). Those outside this kin system are of an unknown "origin." They are regarded as *dışarıdan* (those from the outside), or *yabancılar* (strangers).[19]

Descent reckoning plays an important role in assembling and dis-assembling people and groups around the concept of an origin. It bears similarity to the way that some nation-states, such as Germany, use ancestry, or blood ties (the law of blood, or *jus sanguinis*), to grant the children born of native parents the status of German citizenship and, therefore, certain rights and privileges (Ilcan 2002). Identifying one's origins in various communities in Turkey, including that of Arzu, for example, involves the tracing of one's *kök* (one's "roots," or ancestry). *Kök* is the common term used to discuss descent. People trace their lineage to and from their patrilineal ancestors, and in this way *kök* is reckoned exclusively through a chain of father-child linkages. Descending from a common *kök* contributes to the formation of neighbourhoods and groups that may share lifestyles, property, and resources in common. However, not all people who live in descent-based neighbourhoods hold the same rights or privileges. Women who move to such neighbourhoods upon marriage and take up postmarital virilocal residence neither share the same roots nor have the same rights as do other women and men sharing the same descent line. This form of "rootlessness" has contributed to their passionate longings for "home" as outsiders, or strangers. Their perceived stranger status has had many effects on women's lives, ranging from their having to learn and undertake unfamiliar tasks and responsibilities to their inability to inherit or control property, participate in long-standing descent rituals, and move about without being watched by descent members. These women not only loose their familial connection to their homeland and their "roots" but are also believed to suffer from *gurbetlik*, the state of being in a foreign land (see Ilcan 2002). *Gurbet* is a theme in numerous folk songs that tell of the distress and difficulties of being in a foreign land. Voluminous writings on *gurbet* have followed the exiled into an exile literature (*gurbet edebiyati*), a migrant literature (*göç edebiyati*), and the literature of the *Gastarbeiter*. In its common uses, *gurbet* calls forth a sentiment of displacement from one's natal home. This sentiment approaches Kristeva's notion of the "dark origins" so closely associated with "foreigners." In her words, the foreigner does not give the same weight to "origins" as common sense does. He has fled from that origin – family, blood, soil – and, even though it keeps pestering, enriching, hindering, exciting him, or giving him pain, and often all of it at once, the foreigner is its courageous and melancholy betrayer. His origin certainly haunts him, for better and for worse, but it is indeed *elsewhere* that he has set his hopes, that his struggles take place, that his life holds together. *Elsewhere* versus the origin, and even *nowhere* versus the roots. (Kristeva 1991, 29)

Encounters with nearby strangers are created in routine spaces, in spaces of habitual activity. They are spaces where strategies are put into effect and where the outcome is an authoritarian practice of dividing and segregating "outsiders" from those who are on the "inside." In these spaces, nearby strangers are deprived of their specificity, of their past. As a space where analogies are applied and reductions are made, routine space is the locus of strangers transformed into ideological discourse. It is not that this space expresses an outsider's character in any sense: it is simply the space that is created by the intellect's pretentious plan to homogenize her/him. In both kinship and descent reckoning, for example, the *bricoleur* develops a routine to interact with those strangers who are physically near but remote. This routine involves estranging oneself from the other and then devising a conceptual basis from which to make the other more familiar; that is, to make the other an object of one's own reasoning[20] and to include her/him in a familiar habit of reckoning. From within his/her symbolic tool kit, the *bricoleur* takes the pre-existing order of kinship reckoning and administers it to strangers in order to make sense of them and to eliminate their otherness. The *bricoleur*, for instance, reasons analogically that a relative is to a non-relative (a:b) as an insider is to an outsider (c:d) and thus establishes a homology between oppositions (see Bourdieu 1977, 112).

This kind of analogical reasoning, what Derrida (1993, 233) might call "mythological discourse," is used by those "insiders" who are considered to have well established "roots" and a grounded, familial past. It is a reasoning that attempts to govern the other. Like the strategies of hierarchization and marginalization employed to manage groups and populations in contempory societies (see Bauman 2002; Bigo 2002; Rose 1999, Diken 1998; Bhabha 1994), this technique of governing the other involves the *bricoleur* establishing a proximity to strangers while at the same time constructing or increasing a distance from them. This distancing allows "insiders" to have encounters with the other that are characteristically both foreign and familiar. They are foreign in the sense that they are with "outsiders." They are made familiar by having insiders interact with outsiders in the same way that kin are thought to socialize with non-kin; that is, generally, in encounters based upon loose, non-emotional ties and rudimentary commitments. Nearby strangers become, then, the familial foreigners. Since they do not have a recognized, domestic past (as do descent members), their origin is what haunts and plagues them.

The nearness of strangers in the Turkish ethnographic context often silently makes them subjects of a master narrative that can work to reduce their significance or to disempower them from establishing an alternative, oppositional discourse. This does not mean that they are passive or inactive. In fact, their marginal presence initiates actions and incites responses on the part of those who attempt to make sense of them through the *bricolage* process. For example, in-marrying women (known as the "strangers" who come from the outside) have challenged the boundaries of their disposition in village and family hierarchies by transforming routine spaces into extraordinary ones. They have accomplished this by engaging in "mobile habits" and particular female gatherings that allow them to re-vision themselves differently within an embracing context of change.[21] In this way, "the place of difference and otherness ... is never entirely on the outside or implacably oppositional. It is a pressure, and a presence, that acts constantly, if unevenly, along the entire boundary of authorization" (Bhabha 1994, 109). An outsider not only "solicits, beckons, implores, provokes, and demands" (Grosz 1995, 199) but also offers a perspective on "insiders" by locating them as subjects. Quite paradoxical perhaps, it is the *bricoleur* who always remains exposed to the appeals from the margins and to the demands that make what s/he does "subject" to another. What cannot be forgotten is that people on the margins have the potential to limit the *bricoleur's* activity and to rearrange the placement of power, centres, and peripheries.

The Nearness of the Other: Dialogical Encounters

The contemporary world does not just consist of encounters based on modern notions of reason and rationality, such as those exemplified above. It also consists of numerous heterogeneous relations and forms of togetherness that are often unsettled or fragile.[22] Such relations involve encounters with people that are not held together by necessity or by social constraints (e.g., through moral obligations and duties). In fact, there is an increasing disenchantment with modernity defined in Enlightenment terms of progress and universality. We have come to witness challenges to these attitudes, such as:

celebrations of pluralism and uncoordinated diversity; critical assessments of global projects and practices (e.g., Ilcan and Phillips 2003); the displacement of identity and community (Castles and Davidson 2000; Kaplan 1998; Appadurai 1997); and feminist and postcolonial critiques underlining the exclusionary ethos associated with Enlightenment ideals and Western modernism, particularly the lack of gender, ethnic, or cultural specificity (e.g., Phillips, this volume; Parpart 1993; Parla 1985). Overall, these kinds of challenges reveal that any "modernized" continuation of the Enlightenment project will exclude a variety of marginal groups and their life struggles. It is precisely on these ethical and political grounds that there now exists an interest in retreating from grand narratives by decolonizing modern forms of knowledge and power. In line with these concerns, the following discussion highlights a means by which those dislocated or marginalized can be given a voice in and through ethical encounters.

There are ways in which people deal with strangeness or otherness that can permit a dialogical encounter, one that is pluralistic and creative (Bakhtin 1981) as well as conscious (Boddy 1991b, 129). I am referring to a kind of contact with otherness wherein one learns and incorporates from others and sees her/himself in light of the other. This approaches a form of togetherness that Bauman calls a "being-for" togetherness: a type of togetherness that is not concerned with maintaining distance but, rather, with inclusivity and interminability. This occurs when partners come together to form a kind of 'mixture' or an "alloy whose precious qualities depend fully on the preservations of its ingredients' alterity and identity" (Bauman 1995, 51). It is a meeting that involves "safeguarding and defending the uniqueness of the Other" or taking responsibility for the other and learning what needs to be done to exercise that responsibility. In this way, it is not a rationally motivated meeting between people (as is the case between the *bricoleur* and the stranger) since it is not born of reason. It is in fact "*the* scandal of Reason" (52) because it involves an engagement with the other that is bent on living life towards the future and nowhere else. This "being-for" togetherness allows for the opening up to the other or, as Maffesoli (1991, 17) would say, the recognition of oneself in the other.

I would add that this "being-for" togetherness – what can be termed a dialogic encounter – is of an ethical nature if we understand ethics "as a morality 'with neither obligation or sanction,' with no obligation other than coming together and being a member of the collective body." An ethic, then, is something that entices me to acknowledge myself in something that is outside of me (i.e., another person or group) (Maffesoli 1991, 16–17) but that is not based on behavioural rules or on standards used to govern the actions of others. Such an ethic leads agents to recognize themselves in the other and the other in the agent, with neither one ever becoming a function of the other. Here, ethical relations involve being separate from one another at the same time as being together and co-existing with one another.[23] Ethics, so to speak, is a spirit of a people. It is an "attitude towards what is other to oneself" (Cornell 1995, 78) that encourages a reflexive relationship between one and another. The following discussion highlights a specific dialogical and ethical encounter in the Turkish context.

A noteworthy dialogical relationship occurs in the cultural field of magic (*muska, or büyü*) and in specific encounters between Qur'anic and magical points of view. Although denigrated as highly unorthodox, paganistic, and superstitious by the more formally educated and wealthy in the region, magical practices offer a vernacular and informal framework of alternative justice. This framework develops in an emerging social assemblage of encounters and practices that fails to emanate from the authority of orthodoxy and its institutional formalism. The practice of magic attempts to subvert or alter inequitable situations that are the product of *kısmet* (fate), or predetermined destinies.[24] It involves going against the idea of a natural progression of events and longs for another world. It is future-oriented. Specifically, clients (e.g., a wide array of village women and men who long for different life-worlds) take their projects to a *hoca* (religious teacher or spiritual specialist) who then endeavours to configure "fate" more to their liking. In their practice of recoding what is "written" in fixed language (e.g., in religious texts), *hoca*s often borrow Qur'anic prayers to assist their clients' projects. These written prayers are used as entities that not only effect goals (such as shielding clients from misfortune, enhancing future possibilities, and occasionally causing harm) but also expunge any finalized definition of self or other.

The performance of magic is full of parodies and travesties. A central part of executing magic and creating spells, or amulets (also called *muska*), include the varied use and translation of the Qur'anic text by *hoca*s. In the process of performing magic, for example, it is common for *hoca*s to recite or write a *dua* (prayer) from a Qur'anic verse before spells are officially cast. For the "realization" of some specific spells, there is the belief that hand-written Qur'anic prayers – inscribed within amulets – should be placed in social spaces, on inanimate objects, or on people's bodies. For example, saturating an amulet in water, and later having the person (for whom the spell was cast) consume the water in its new symbolic state, are activities believed to bring about the desired change in the person's future behaviour. Such water symbolism is utilized in the performance of love spells (*muhabbet muskası*). It is also employed in sacred texts, applied in mystical poetry, and practised in secularized concepts relating to fate and forms of cleanliness in other parts of Turkey (see Marcus 1992, 145). For the realization of other spells, especially those rare ones that are intended to punish those who have harmed or have been too greedy, there is the belief in soaking amulets (comprised of hand-written Qur'anic verses on paper, clothing, soap) in blood or in reciting Qur'anic prayers at gravesites or in washrooms. These activities are condemned by religious law. In any case, the appropriation of Qur'anic discourse, and the whole spectrum of possible uses to which these words come to light in the magical encounter, highlights a play with and parody of sacred words, what Bakhtin (1981, 71) might call "parodia sacra."[25] It is a process that bears similarity to how the "public secret" – knowing what not to know – in Michael Taussig's *Defacement*, subverts cherished tools and categories of thought "recruited for the pursuit of truth and the unmasking of appearance."

All performances of magical spells comprise a displacement of a "rooted text" in a context in which they are denaturalized from their authoritative seriousness. Only one of these points of view (the one that is parodied [i.e., magic]) is present, while the other exists as an actualizing background for creating and perceiving. These two points of view (magical and Qur'anic) each carry with them their own expression and tone: they are in dialogue with one another, with each view containing its own language that cannot be translated into the other.

Corresponding to the indivisible relationship between the Qur'anic text and magic, both the *hoca* and the client participate with one another in a dialogical encounter. Shared offerings and exchanges between participants are considered to fold the distance between them and to release their privileged identities. On the one hand, the *hoca* plans and metaphysically brings to life a future world for her/his clients based upon their individual experiences and requests. Such future planning involves the *hoca's* expertise and specialized knowledge of Qur'anic prayers and magical spells as well as her/his commitment to bring about the clients' requests. On the other hand, the clients share knowledge and information with the *hoca* (e.g., stories of tragedies, experiences, and wishes for the future). Some women, in particular, request many things from *hoca*s, such as the ritual casting of spells designed not only to remedy their work and marriage difficulties, pregnancy complications, or illnesses but also to challenge their status in familial and economic domains or in local networks of power and authority relations. This alternative justice process, resembling women's rites in numerous pilgrimage shrines scattered all across Turkey, involves a dialogue between the *hoca's* and the client's points of view. Each view has its own concrete expression that cannot be transposed into the other but that nevertheless speaks to, and illuminates, the other's view. This dialogue, related to what Cornell

(1995, 78–80) calls "ethical feminism," offers a way to reimagine the banalities of certain village women. It also provides a basis for subverting, however briefly, the meanings associated with their "fate" as wives, mothers, or dependants and with the strictures of femininity (cf. Boddy's [1988] *zar* spiritual practice; Abu-Lughod's [1990] women's subversive discourses).

In contrast to other transitory encounters, the relationship between the *hoca* and the client is one that endures beyond the moment. It anticipates a future of difference and devises a place for the future. In this encounter one shares knowledge of the metaphysical and the future, and the other shares and expresses the uncertainty of the present and the wishes for the future. In this process, the *hoca* takes it as her/his job to hear the clients' voices and wishes (their own internal discourses) and to take some responsibility for rechannelling these towards new uses. S/he does this by giving their uttering, which often echoes an unhappiness with the present, a potentiality in the future and therefore a place in this "other" world. Accordingly, the *hoca* utilizes and redirects their communication into another field. In order to magically incorporate their voices of change into another field, the laws of this field must be breached with spells cast by the *hoca's* own voice and use of Qur'anic and magical aids. As I was informed by specialists working in the local area, it is only when these two fields operate together that the performance of magic is made tenable. It is within this context that both participants become aware of their capacity to outgrow from within and to expel any finalizing definition of each other. This is because they both interact with one another, with neither one becoming an object for the other (see Bakhtin 1984, 18). Here the *hoca* and client come to identify their capabilities in the souls and wishes of each other. In this orientation one's communication can find itself in intimate contact with someone else's and yet, at the same time, not melt with it, not ingest it, not fade into the other's power. Like Maffesoli's (1996, 16) "the communal being-together" and Shield's (1996) "dialogical verstehen," this encounter is ethical.

In the sphere of magic, people's lives are polemicized, and all of this unfolding takes place through a dialogical encounter devoid of authoritative, universal goals. The *hoca* engages not with voiceless "outsiders" but with active and creative participants. They are capable of standing alongside her/him and of having visions, expressions, and experiences that they could not easily reveal elsewhere. The *hoca* does not, however, become the mouthpiece for their voices; rather, it is the participants who are always battling with the definitions of moral behaviour placed upon them, of determining who they should be, in the mouths and actions of other people. In their engagement with the *hoca* and with magical practices, they come to perceive their own unfinalizability within themselves and render fallacious any firm calculations and definitions of who they might be. It is in this way that encounters with the other can involve a plurality of what Bakhtin (1984) calls unmerged voices, not finalized images of others in the unity of a monologically or analogically understood world. Therefore, this form of encounter is different from that form characterizing the *bricoleur's* relationship to nearby strangers; that is, neither the client nor the *hoca* impose upon each other a pre-given conceptual arrangement or an authoritarian scheme. Instead, the two relate to each other in a way that allows for the creation of two speaking and active subjects who come together unbound by the practicalities and moral "orders" of everyday life. Similar to the "ethics of co-existence"[26] described by Bhabha (1996, 211), this form of togetherness generates an ethical space.

Magic is locally performed in private living quarters where *hoca*s and clients frequently meet, in particular places where animate and inanimate objects carry written spells derived from Qur'anic verses, and near ancient shrines or tombs (*türbe*; Turkish mausoleum) located in the hills. A magical encounter, like a "being-for" togetherness, creates a space of potential transformation. It is a space that permits for the extrication of oneself "from the world of convention, routine and normatively engendered monotony, and transmits her/him into a world in which no universal rules apply" (Bauman 1995, 62). By engaging with magic's alternative cosmology, participants accommodate a future world that produces a different sense of space. This is a world that is not "out there" but one that is envisioned. It is a space reserved for the intermingling of diverse communication that transcends those obligatory beliefs that might otherwise characterize relations between people. Especially when these spaces are invested with subversive or destabilizing relations of power by their visitors, they embrace loci of actions, hopes, and lived situations that distinguish themselves from others. Like the "representational spaces" discussed by Lefebvre, these ethical spaces are qualitative and dynamic. They resemble, on a much smaller scale, the ritual activities surrounding shrines in Turkey (such as the tomb of Susuz Dede in Izmir, which remains completely outside the ambit of the mosque). This is where participants make weekly pilgrimages to the site. They engage in rituals and *dua*s with *hoca*s that seek to subvert troublesome home, fertility, health, and economic issues (see Marcus 1992). These and other similar sites are where participants come together and abandon, for a while, the moral rules of everyday life. In these marginal sites particular minority groups, such as poor women, express their concerns for change and their disenchantment with the moral expectations placed upon them. It is in this way that such a dialogical relation and its parodic features fragment the homogenizing power of local and institutional injustice.

Conclusion

Modern rhetoric so often claims that what lies on the outside, on the margins of the social, poses threats, produces problems, and should be transformed. The analysis presented above suggests that the creation of any singular identity or dominant disposition is both unthinkable and undistinguishable without its difference, its other. The necessity for the other is a point made particularly relevant in my discussion of monological, analogical, and dialogical encounters.

As I have shown, monological encounters construct a distance between self and other at the same time that they enable *flâneur*-agents to recognize themselves as stable and fixed. These modern strolling subjects see others as passive and aesthetic objects to be judged, moved, and scattered about. Paradoxically, however, this strolling subject becomes unknown to his "native" environment. In this wandering game, the *flâneur* is not only animated and captured by the foreign landscape but also becomes a stranger to him/herself, like the European Benjaminian *flâneur*. Different from these encounters in aesthetic spaces, analogical encounters are bent on the *bricoleur's* attempt to homologize those who are on the margins. But in the very technique deployed to make the stranger a familiar (in)difference, interruptions from the other side enter, making the *bricoleur* "subjected" to others. It is in this regard that monological and analogical encounters give weight to the idea that strangeness has become a permanent condition and that contemporary life can neither be fostered nor continued without it. As Bauman (1993, 159–60) reminds us,

> strangehood, so to speak, must be preserved and cultivated if modern life is to go on. None of the essential institutions of modern society would survive a miraculous triumph of "communal togetherness" were it ever to happen; nor would they survive a colonization of the field of mismeetings and civil inattention by personal, emotionally charged relations. Were there no strangers, one may say, they would need to be invented.

This point is not to suggest, however, that all encounters with strangeness develop along the lines of a trajectory that acclaims a singular, discursive identity premised upon encounters with otherness. This chapter proposes the possibility of an assemblage of unmerged differences that permits the establishment of an ethical encounter. This encounter is qualitatively differ-ent from the others: it brings discrete people together in such a way that they come to recognize themselves in the other and to mutually supplement one another, yet they are not bound to each other through rules, moral obliga-tions, or duties. Here, the idea of assimilation is of little value. A dialogical encounter acknowledges the relevance and indeterminacy of another's inter-ests. Although fragile and marginal, it may very well reflect a form of togeth-erness that entails an insistence upon diversity, a recovery of marginalized voices, and a counter-position to hegemonic practices.

Notes

1 I gratefully acknowledge financial support from the Social Sciences and Humanities Research Council of Canada for this research. I would like to thank Rob Shields and Edwina Taborsky for their comments on an earlier version of this chapter. I remain deeply indebted to the women and men of northwestern Turkey, whose thoughts and activities continue to inspire me to think further about moral and ethical encounters.

2 Emine Özdamar's (1994) *Mother Tongue* theatrically explores the social and lin-guistic experiences of exile for Turkish "guest workers" living in Germany. Like Kristeva's (1991, 20) analysis of the marginality of the "foreigner's" speech, she conceives words in a "foreign" tongue as having no childhood.

3 For a parallel view, see Delaney (1991, 172–3) on the limits of crossing boundaries.

4 In *Outside Belongings* Probyn (1996) argues that the notion of the "outside" is one way to think about social relations and to underscore the importance of "relations of proximity." The concept of "marginal spaces," or "strangeness," as defined in this chapter, bears some similarity to her view of the outside in relation to the social.

5 I use the term agent to designate an authorial figure who attempts to define and cre-ate situations as well as construct and objectify others in the process. As discussed later, I depict both the *flâneur* and the *bricoleur* as authorial figures who, from their spatial locations, interact with strangers in distinct ways: the former imaginatively and aesthetically defines the activity of marginal others, without disturbing their behaviour, and the latter makes analogical sense of the strangeness of others.

6 Originally, Walter Benjamin (1983), in his analysis of Charles Baudelaire, linked the figure of the *flâneur* to the urban arcades and galleries of nineteenth-century Paris.

7 This is the content of their sociation with each other since this sociation, in Simmel's (1950, 41) words, "is the form (realized in innumerable, different ways) in which individuals grow together into units that satisfy their interests. These interests, whether they are sensuous or ideal, momentary or lasting, conscious or unconscious, causal or teleological, form the basis of human societies."

8 For more on this see: Ternar (1994, 161); Parpart (1993, 447); Spivak (1992, 54; 1990).

9 Compare this form of "togetherness" with Tester's (1994, 6) "being-with-others."

10 There is no real interaction between the hero and the social world in the novels of ordeal. Secondary characters are transformed into mere setting for the hero and, thus, they do not change the hero. The same is the case for the hero in that s/he

does not transform the world of secondary characters but only reckons it as an "exotic" geography (Bakhtin 1986, 14–16).

11 Kristeva (1991, 20) makes an interesting point regarding the marginality of the "foreigner's" speech. In her words, and from the vantage point of the foreigner, she says: "no one listens to you, you never have the floor, or else, when you have the courage to seize it, your speech is quickly erased by the more garrulous and fully relaxed talk of the community. Your speech has no past and will have no power over the future of the group."

12 See Minh-ha (1991, 189) on the master's monologism.

13 In counter-distinction to my view of aesthetics in the modern sense, Maffesoli (1991) argues that postmodernity emphasizes "artistic will" as its deep source of energy and as the faculty of collective experience. As such, this aesthetic creates an ambience of diverse modes of social situations, experiences, and expressions that reflect ethical functions. Maffesoli refers to these ethical functions as embodying "the ethic of aesthetics: experiencing something together is a factor of socialization." In other words, the aesthetic brings out forms of social affinity and sympathy, and permits one to recognize "oneself in the Other as part of alterity" (16–17). Rather than employing his notion of the aesthetic (the shared sentiment), I have used his understanding of the ethic (the collective bond) (Maffesoli 1996, 20) as a feature of the dialogical encounter discussed later in this chapter.

14 For more detailed ethnographic information on this community, see Ilcan (2002, 1999, 1998).

15 See Delaney (1991, 83) for more on the gendered aspects of strolling or wandering in Turkish village society.

16 However, these monological descriptions of strangers cannot reveal how others initiate actions, encounters, and responses by strollers, nor can they point to a configuration in which the two poles of subjective and objective "shade into each other" (Maffesoli 1991, 14).

17 For a more elaborate discussion of this issue, see Shields (1994, 65) on the link between "crowd practice" and *flâneurie.*

18 The cultural and political significance of kinship reckoning in Turkish society occurs at both local and national levels. See Delaney (1995) for an insightful analysis of the deployment of kinship and descent in Turkish national identity and citizenship.

19 For an expanded discussion on this point, see Ilcan (2002, 1999).

20 This bears similarity to the transposability of what Bourdieu (1993, 65) calls the "habitus."

21 For a further elaboration of these practices, see Ilcan (1998).

22 Bauman (1999) speaks of the uncertainly and insecurity of all forms of togetherness developed in the "multi-network" society.

23 Cf. Boddy's (1991a) discussion of "post-nostalgic."

24 This subversive character of magic bears some similarity to what Boddy (1991b:130) says of the *zar* spirit possession cult in northern Sudan. Not only is the *zar* practice considered as a "subordinate" discourse but the characters of spirits are also shown to subvert local ideals and to parody local meanings.

25 The Latin term *parodia sacra* refers to a parody on sacred texts and rituals. It derives from Bakhtin's (1981) discussion of Cyprian Feasts as an ancient example of the ritual degrading and ridiculing of high powers.

26 Linked to Bhabha's idea of "subaltern secularism" is the notion of the "ethics of coexistence." He argues that the "ethics of coexistence," along with the process of choice, stems from a social space that must be shared with "others." For him, this social space is based on similarity and the recognition of difference.

Works Cited
Abu-Lughod, L. 1990. "The Romance of Resistance: Tracing Transformations of Power through Bedouin Women." *American Ethnologist* 17 (1): 41–55.
Appadurai, A. 1997. *Modernity at Large: Cultural Dimensions of Globalization*. Minneapolis and London: University of Minnesota Press.
Bakhtin, M. 1981. *The Dialogical Imagination*. Austin: University of Texas Press.
– 1984. *Problems of Dostoevsky's Poetics*. Vol. 8 of *Theory and History of Literature*. Minneapolis: University of Minnesota.
– 1986. *Speech Genres and Other Late Essays*. Austin: University of Texas Press.
Bauman, Z. 1992. *Intimations of Postmodernity*. London and New York: Routledge.
– 1993. *Postmodern Ethics*. Oxford: Blackwell.
– 1995. *Life in Fragments: Essays in Postmodern Morality*. Oxford: Blackwell.
– 1999. *In Search of Politics*. Stanford: Stanford University Press.
– 2002. *Society Under Siege*. Cambridge: Polity.
Benjamin, Walter. 1983. *Charles Baudelaire: A Lyric Poet in the Era of High Capitalism*. Yrans. H. Zohn. London: Verso.
Bhabha, H. 1994. *The Location of Culture*. London and New York: Routledge.
– 1996. "Unpacking My Library … Again." In *The Post-Colonial Question: Common Skies, Divided Horizons*, ed. I. Chambers and L. Curti, 199–211. London and New York: Routledge.
Bigo, D. 2002. "Security and Immigration: Toward a Critique of the Governmentality of Unease." *Alternatives: Global, Local, Political* 27: 63–92.
Boddy, J. 1988. "Spirits and Selves in Northern Sudan: The Cultural Therapeutics of Possession and Trance." *American Ethnologist* 15 (1): 4–27.
– 1991a. "Othered and Disoriented in No Man's Land." *Culture* 11 (1–2):63–7.
– 1991b. "Anthropology, Feminism and the Postmodern Context." *Culture* 11 (1–2): 125–33.
Bourdieu, P. 1977. *Outline of a Theory of Practice*. Cambridge: University of Cambridge.
– 1993. *The Field of Cultural Production*. Columbia University Press.
Castles, S., and A. Davidson, 2000. *Citizenship and Migration: Globalization and the Politics of Belonging*. New York: Routledge.
Ceyhan, A., and A. Tsoukala, 2002. "The Securitization of Migration in Western Societies: Ambivalent Discourses and Policies." *Alternatives: Global, Local, Political* 27: 21–39.
Cornell, D. 1995. "What is Ethical Feminism?" In *Feminist Contentions: A Philosophical Exchange*, ed. S. Benhabib, J. Butler, D. Cornell, and N. Fraser, 75–106. New York and London: Routledge.
Delaney, C. 1991. *Seed and Soil: Gender and Cosmology in Turkish Village Society*. Berkeley: University of California Press.
– 1995. "Father State, Motherland, and the Birth of Modern Turkey." In *Naturalizing Power: Essays in Feminist Cultural Analysis*, ed. S. Yanagisako and C. Delaney, 177–99. New York and London: Routledge.

Derrida, J. 1993. "Structure, Sign, and Play in the Discourse of the Human Sciences." In *A Postmodern Reader*, ed. J. Natoli and L. Hutcheon, 223–42. Albany: State University of New York.

Diken, B. 1998. *Strangers, Ambivalence and Social Theory*. Aldershot, UK: Ashgate.

Ferguson, P. 1994. "The *Flâneur* On and Off the Streets of Paris." In *The Flâneur*, ed. K. Tester, 22–42. London and New York: Routledge.

Foucault, M. 1985. *The History of Sexuality*. Vol. 2: *The Use of Pleasure*. New York: Pantheon.

Grosz, E. 1989. *Sexual Subversions*. Sydney: Allen and Unwin.

– 1995. *Space, Time, and Perversion*. New York and London: Routledge.

Ilcan, S. 1998. "Occupying the Margins: On Spacing Gender and Gendering Space." *Space and Culture* 3: 2–26.

– 1999. "Social Spaces and the Micropolitics of Differentiation: An Example from Northwestern Turkey." *Ethnology* 38 (3): 243–56.

– 2002. *Longing in Belonging: The Cultural Politics of Settlement*. Westport and London: Praeger.

Ilcan, S., and L. Phillips. 2003. "Making Food Count: Expert Knowledge and Global Technologies of Government." *Canadian Review of Sociology and Anthropology* 40 (4): 441–61.

Jenks, C. 1999. *Culture*. London: Routledge.

Kaplan, C. 1998. *Questions of Travel*. Durham and London: Duke University Press.

Kristeva, J. 1991. *Strangers to Ourselves*. New York: Columbia University Press.

Lefebvre, H. 1991. *The Production of Space*. Trans. D. Nicholson-Smith. Oxford and Massachusetts: Blackwell.

Maffesoli, M. 1991. "The Ethic of Aesthetics." *Theory, Culture and Society* 8: 7–20.

– 1996. *The Time of the Tribes: The Decline of Individualism in Mass Society*. London: Sage.

Marcus, J. 1992. *A World of Difference: Islam and Gender Hierarchy in Turkey*. London: Zed Books.

Minh-ha, T. 1991. *When the Moon Waxes Red: Representation, Gender and Cultural Politics*. New York and London: Routledge.

Mohanty, C. 1991. "Under Western Eyes: Feminist Scholarship and Colonial Discourses." In *Third World Women and the Politics of Feminism*, ed. C. Mohanty, A. Russo, and L. Torres, 51–80. Bloomington and Indianapolis: Indiana University Press.

Orga, I. 1988. *Portrait of a Turkish Family*. London: Eland.

Özdamar, E. 1994, *Mother Tongue*. Toronto: Coach House Press.

Parla, J. 1985. *Efendilik, Kölelik, Şarkiyatcilik. (Colonialism, Slavery, Orientalism)*. Istanbul: Iletisim Yayinlari.

Parpart, J. 1993. "Who Is the 'Other'?: A Postmodern Feminist Critique of Women and Development Theory and Practice." *Development and Change* 24: 439–64.

Probyn, E. 1996. *Outside Belongings*. New York and London: Routledge.

Rose, N. 1999. *Powers of Freedom*. Cambridge: Cambridge University Press.

Said, E. 1978. *Orientalism*. New York: Vintage.

Shields, R. 1991. *Places on the Margin: Alternative Geographies of Modernity*. London: Routledge.

– 1992. "A Truant Proximity: Presence and Absence in the Space of Modernity." *Society and Space* 10: 181–98.

-1994. "Fancy Footwork: Walter Benjamin's Notes on *Flânerie*." In *The Flâneur*, ed. K. Tester, 61–80. London and New York: Routledge.

-1996. "Meeting or Mis-meeting? The Dialogical Challenge to Verstehen." *British Journal of Sociology* 47 (2): 275–94.

Simmel, G. 1950. *The Sociology of Georg Simmel*. Ed. and trans. K.H. Wolf. New York: The Free Press.

Smart, B. 1993. *Postmodernity*. London and New York: Routledge.

Spivak, G.C. 1990. *The Post-Colonial Critic: Interviews, Strategies, Dialogues*. Ed. S. Harasym. New York and London: Routledge.

-1992. "French Feminism Revisited: Ethics and Politics." In *Feminists Theorize the Political*, ed. J. Butler and J. Scott, 54–85. New York and London: Routledge.

Taussig, M. 1999. *Defacement: Public secrecy and the Labor of the Negative*. Stanford: Stanford University Press.

Ternar, Y. 1994. *The Book and the Veil: Escape from an Istanbul Harem*. Montreal: Vehicule.

Tester, K. 1994. "Introduction." In *The Flâneur*, ed. K. Tester, 1–21. London and New York: Routledge.

Weinstein, D., and M. Weinstein. 1993. *Postmodern(ized) Simmel*. London: Routledge.

Changing Health Moralities in the Tropics: Ethics and the Other

LYNNE PHILLIPS[1]

Great is Sanitation – the greatest work except discovery, I think, that a man can do … We must begin by being Cleansers.

Sir Ronald Ross, *Memoirs*

Though "tropicalism" has been understood recently as a grand narrative directly implicated in the colonial project, this chapter sets out to complicate this story, too, by exploring the competing discourses of health and place employed by a marginalized population in coastal Ecuador. Through a consideration of various responses to the 1990s cholera epidemic, I illustrate how the appropriation of a biomedical perspective by coastal residents is linked to political and economic transformations in the country that have both enabled and limited the credibility of biomedicine for healing the body tropical. In making this case, I argue for the development of a *reflexive ethic* in examining other worlds, an ethic that encourages analysts to remain cognizant of, and responsible for, the colonizing potential of our own desires to map (tropical) Others in particular ways.

A key representation of the Other in discourses of development and health involves the created geography of the "tropics." A product of the colonial imagination, tropical regions and tropical people are an exotic Other that, once "discovered," require conversion to "temperate" ways. In the past, the concept of the tropics went hand-in-hand with the challenge of colonialism to conquer the world; today, in the name of development, the concept still homogenizes large areas of the world (*the* tropics) as an inferior place lacking productivity and morality (Peard 1999; Siemens 1990). As a grand narrative, "tropicalism" contains messages regarding proper conduct for areas of the world that remain resistant to temperate ways, saying more about what is valued in the temperate imagination than about the people who have lived in the tropics for generations.

In this chapter a consideration of how health and illness is understood and acted upon by *campesinos*[2] in coastal Ecuador reveals challenges to tropicalism as a universalizing discourse. This is to not to say that tropicalism is directly "resisted" by local residents or to fail to acknowledge that their subjectivities remain shaped by national and international discourses; rather, we see that the emergence of neoliberal and biomedical practices and beliefs during a critical juncture (an epidemic) generates new forms of knowledge and power that are appropriated in various ways by residents who are themselves concerned to transform health moralities. Taking a reflexive ethical position (Phillips 1996; 1995), I stress our responsibility as researchers to understand the meanings and practices that are put to use by *campesinos* in their efforts to heal the body tropical, without negating our potential role as Cleansers of the Other in our efforts to "understand." It is this position that permits a shift away from dualistic models of discourse and power (dominant/subordinate, us/them, global/local) to reveal the hybridized spaces (Bhabha 1992; Kahn 1995; McDowell 1999) that "tropical" populations and researchers occupy in their encounters.

One of the great challenges for postmodern feminist criticism is to question universalizing forms of analysis and politics (e.g., Butler 1995) without losing "hope" that agency and social change is possible (Benhabib 1995a, 1995b; see also Harvey 2000). Since we inevitably rely on colonial tools[3] to unlearn our colonial ways of knowing, this challenge requires the development of a reflexive ethic that does not permit an exhaustive exploration of discursive disjunctures without also continuously questioning *our* "discoveries" (and not just those of colonialists or development experts). Listening to and talking with people in coastal Ecuador, becoming a student of their histories (what anthropologists call fieldwork), interrupts the temptation to consider them mere victims of and/or accomplices in discursive processes, and it hints at the possibility of a "differently worlded world" (Savigliano 1995).

One could say that I was already well nourished by biomedical reports of disease and illness in the "Third World" when, in 1992, I undertook a new research project on cholera in Latin America. However, I approached the topic of disease in coastal Ecuador with more than a few reservations after spending a month in the "temperate" city of Quito, fully immersed in the often sensationalized media coverage of cholera. Within no time I found myself imagining the coast, where I had been gladly doing research since 1980, as a tropical nightmare, fairly seething with disease and illness. Fears were widespread that cholera would run rampant on the coast, even before any cases had been identified in Ecuador, and, once it was acknowledged that cholera had arrived, it did not take long for this region to be perceived as beyond hope. The tropical heat, poverty, and the undisciplined population combined in the popular imagination to create a portrait of desperation and disorder where cholera would logically breed.[4] The stated preventive measures of the national cholera prevention program[5] appeared to be impossibilities in the coastal context, where potable water and sewage systems are in short supply. This image of the coastal region's "hopelessness" was confirmed by a publicized informal survey conducted in the coastal city of Guayaquil. All those surveyed knew the "rules" about how to keep from getting cholera, but few actually practised them.

How is one to interpret this imagery? Does one argue that the representation of the coast in these terms is simply a product of a long history of highland elitism regarding coastal life? Or is it an example of a more widely held view of the tropics as a geographical space that is in need of "cleansing," of which my views may form a part? Is it, on the other hand, a reflection of the subjectivities of coastal people, an echo of themselves and their environment as "different"?

One way to begin to work through the potential meanings of disease in coastal Ecuador is to consider the disease discourse as a shifting political boundary that limits the agency of those people who live "there" at the same time that it limits the agency of the analyst. This boundary can be understood as a space emerging from the cultural, economic, and political exigencies of being (identity) and place (created geography) (Kirby 1993). A reflexive ethic recognizes the analyst's transformation of this space through her identification of and encounter with people who live in particular places. Thus, local moralities already contain external mappings since the historical views of others have long been part of what that space means to residents; however, in addition, a reflexive ethic acknowledges that part of these external mappings must also include the analyst's reinscription of these boundaries. While such an ethic considers the political processes involved in creating spatial maps as well as "postcolonial others" (Minh-ha 1991, 186; Phillips and Ilcan 2000), it also has the potential to raise our awareness of the responsibility one has to the Other (cf. Cornell's [1995, 84] "ethical feminism"; cf. Ilcan's [this volume] dialogical ethic).

Three Contexts
Neoliberalism
For this research I focus ethnographically on a region located 200 kilometres north of the sprawling coastal port of Guayaquil. When I first arrived in this region in 1980 most land was dedicated to cacao and rice cultivation, but today banana trees blanket the countryside once again, fifty years after the country's first banana boom. *Campesinos* say that everyone had *el fiebre*

(banana fever) in the 1990s, a "sickness" that made them do *cosas brutas* (stupid things), like selling their land to the banana companies.

Changes in the region are related to the extensive implementation in Ecuador of neoliberal economic policies, viewed by many as the cure for Latin America's ailing economies over the last two decades. The proponents of neoliberalism have argued that healthy development occurs when countries privatize social services, eliminate state intervention in the economy, and open themselves to the world market. Though this is an orientation that favours large producers (not small ones) and wealthy consumers (not poor ones), the neoliberal view is that, with sufficient self-discipline and entrepreneurial spirit, everyone will benefit from this prescription in the long run.[6]

As marginalized producers and consumers who have seen many models for development come and go, many *campesinos* in this region are not hopeful about the long run (Phillips 1993). The men have experienced high unemployment and underemployment rates, and their produce has few options in the market. The concentration of land over the last decade has also put considerable stress on women's work in the countryside. Women cook over open fires and wood collection is much more difficult with "all the land being eaten up by bananas." Pigs, traditionally an important source of income for *campesinas* (peasant women), now have to be well guarded because they die from eating the blue plastic bags discarded by the banana plantations. Moreover, the withdrawal of the state from social services extends women's activities and challenges their identities as care givers, since they are the ones considered responsible for people's well-being in a time of decreasing opportunities to live economically viable lives.

A union of agricultural cooperatives (UAC) has been operating in this region since 1974 as a *campesino* organization.[7] A *campesina* women's group (OPW), affiliated with UAC, began organizing health committees here to deal with the problems that developed as a result of a number of serious floods that occurred in the 1980s. This mobilization of *campesinas* took place during the so-called "lost decade" in Latin America, when state support was minimal because of structural adjustment constraints and the neoliberal policies of then president Leon Febres Cordero. It was also during this time that UAC began to transform from a peasant political organization that supported and encouraged a wide variety of *campesino* concerns to a marketing organization ostensibly designed to offer better prices to *campesinos* for their agricultural crops. The two organizations became increasingly intertwined as members of the health committees obtained the right to vote in UAC meetings and to be elected to the executive. *Campesino* engagement with emerging regulatory practices regarding health and illness in the 1990s must be at least partially understood within the context of these transformations under neoliberal rule.

Biomedicine

Spurred on by the advent of antibiotics, biomedical views of health, illness, and healing have been most strongly promoted in Latin America since the Second World War, though there was considerable intervention in tropical areas well before this time (Cueto 1992). The most obvious conduit for these views has been the pharmaceutical industry, the expansion of which has been tremendous over the last three decades. However, more recently, with the support of neoliberal policies that emphasize market de-regulation, bio-medicine has shifted to a more interventionist terrain: it is now proposed as a way of life rather than simply as an option if one becomes ill.

The health committees in this region took on particular significance during the cholera epidemic of 1991. It was within the context of "saving lives" that the health committees went into the countryside, promoting a training program for surviving cholera at home.[8] Stories were widespread about medical doctors refusing to treat patients with cholera symptoms and sending them instead to the local hospital. Rural people do not go to the hospital at the best of times ("it is where you go to die"), but if one died of cholera in the hospital it also meant that a *volorio* (wake) could not be held since the bodies were immediately buried. The poverty of the *campesino* population was also recognized as an important reason for going into the countryside. As one health committee worker put it, "the *sobres* (packages of electrolyte solution) were sold in the hospital for 700 sucres each and when you need 10 sobres and don't have the money, you buy one and then die. So we did not really encourage people to go to the hospital."

Long after the cholera epidemic subsided, the health committee members continued their work in the countryside, receiving training from a new doctor working with UAC. The *equipos* (teams) went into the countryside with a "raising awareness" program, dressed in uniforms of blue and white pinstripes. Women such as Adela, Rosa, and Tomasa, whose voices the reader hears in the remainder of this chapter, spent a considerable amount of time telling *campesinos* about the importance of, for example, boiling water, wearing long-sleeved shirts to prevent malaria, and wearing shoes to prevent parasitosis. The literature distributed by the health committees made clear connections between the health work of the OPW and the political work of UAC. One pamphlet reads: "A strong organization needs healthy bodies." Another reads: "A body needs vitamins just like UAC needs your participation."

The new doctor, Dr Diaz, worked with the health committees and did outreach work in the cooperatives; no other doctors in town took on such work. Uncharacteristically, Dr Diaz also recognized the different interpretations of health problems offered by local residents. "Parasitosis is the real problem here," he told me, "but the *campesinos* will call it diarrhea." As an underpaid doctor who spent time with *campesinos* in the countryside, Dr Diaz stood in stark contrast to other doctors in the area, who simply dismissed *campesino* views as backward and irrelevant. Yet his identity as a social reformer in the area of medicine included a familiar paternalism: *campesino* models of health are important only in so far as our understanding of them enables science and biomedicine to intervene more effectively in people's lives.

"Hello again," his speech began the day I accompanied him on his work with mothers in one cooperative:

> Today we are going to weigh and measure the children. But first I want to say a few words about pre-ven-tion. Because getting sick is not just about taking pills. It's also about what you can do to avoid illnesses. And what do we do? First, what do we do with the foods we eat? We wash them well before we cook them or eat them. And what do we do with our hands? We wash them, before eating. So that there won't be anything on them that might give us parasites. And we should keep our fingernails very clean. [In fact mine were filthy by that time of day and I poked Tomasa to show her and she started laughing. The doctor frowned.] And what do we wear on our feet? Shoes! To prevent any parasites from being on our feet. Good. So now we know that there are things we can do to prevent illnesses. Because it is up to *us* to keep ourselves healthy.[9]

From Dr Diaz's perspective, intervening in rural mothers' worldviews was essential not just for promoting specific practices (such as keeping one's fingernails clean) under the rubric of "cleanliness" but also for encouraging the "correct" morality of self-regulation.

With cholera being defined internationally as a "frightening disease" and a "disease of the poor" – and with poverty and underdevelopment forming a substantial part of Ecuadorian national identity – the extensive proliferation of new health moralities in this and other regions of the country was made possible (Trumper and Phillips 1995). Stories abound, in both the highlands and the coast, about how the country pulled together to "beat" cholera. Indeed, the health committees in this region claim considerable success on this front. All the members, including Dr Diaz, argue that deaths from cholera would have been much higher without their work; in addition, they argue that they have been able to change most people's food preparation practices. "Almost everyone boils their water now," says Adela, the head of the health committees.

> People saw that no one from the committees got sick and they began to think that they ought to take the precautions too. You know that the women of OPW used to be lined up with everyone else at the *dispensario* to get medicine, but not anymore. We don't get sick because we know how to guard our health.

For Adela, at least,[10] the health committees provide a symbol of the efficacy of biomedical regulation.

The Analyst

The priest is giving his funeral sermon to a packed church. "Death, misery and suffering have nothing to do with God," he tells us. "These are not His doing; you need to believe in Him during these times." Pondering his words on our communal walk along the main street to the cemetery, I avoid the holes in the road, one large rat, and numerous deposits of horse manure, noting that the only obstacle that elicits any comment from my companions are the potholes. At the cemetery, in the stifling afternoon heat, people begin crying as a relative of the deceased begins a long, emotional speech. Two boys selling *refrescos* (flavoured ices) drag their stands across the holes and rocks to be closer to the congregation and begin grinding ice. It becomes impossible to hear what the speaker is saying. Rosa, tears streaming down her face, walks over to the refresco stands. I expect her to tell the boys to stop their ice grinding until after the service, but instead she orders two flavoured ices and hands me one. "You eat these?" I whisper to her, trying to hide my horror that an active member of one of the health committees eats "in the streets." "Of course. Don't you?" "No. Well, how do you know it is made of clean water?" I ask. She looks at me a moment, shrugs, and says, "You can give it to the boy if you don't want it." I hold on to the refresco, wondering what to do, and then finally give it to the boy standing beside me, who gladly accepts it. I apologize to Rosa on the way back home, concerned that I have hurt her feelings. "Oh, I suppose I shouldn't eat those things" she says, laughing. Patting her extended stomach, she adds: "It's probably why I have this stomach full of *bichos* (parasites)."

A reflexive ethic is not intended to erase difference but to raise new possibilities for transcending it. The above story moves towards transcending difference by weaving together the analyst and the Other as both subject and object; it creates a new space for both to think about responsibilities differently. This encounter also hints at the colonial tendencies of the analyst – the desire to clarify the "proper" connection one ought to be making in the realm of health and the need to cleanse the Other of contradictions.

Healing the Body Tropical

As cases of cholera continued to be identified in this region, Adela explained to me: "When the epidemic dies down, people think that it's over and they can go back to their old ways. But it's not like that. At least because of cholera, they boil their water now. But they sometimes don't wash the fruit they eat or don't wash their hands ... or they don't wear shoes. There's no good reason for them not to change these habits now, but we continue our work." However, when I visited people in the countryside unaccompanied by health committee members, it became quite clear that changing one's "habits" was a luxury for many. Almost all the women I talked with said that they used to boil their water "but not now." A few women said that boiling the water made it taste bad, or that they had access to a well so that boiling was "not necessary." Most noted that boiling water was just extra work in an environment where there is no running water and little firewood, and where an increasing number of activities must be undertaken to stretch the two dollars (US) a day that agricultural workers are paid. Such views indicate a lack of consensus among local residents about biomedical health strategies as a "natural" alternative to current ones.

On the other hand, however, Ecuador is a country where pharmaceutical solutions to illness already have considerable power in the countryside. In a context where labour-time is consistently being extended to make ends meet, the solution of taking *pastillas* (pills, usually antibiotics) renders other practices of prevention a waste of time. Respiratory ailments (*tos*), malarial infections (*fiebres*) and intestinal infections (*diarrea*) are the ailments for which people are most likely to seek pharmaceutical medication, but high blood pressure (*presion*) and nerves (*nervios*) – problems primarily experienced by women – are also important pharmaceutical targets. A number of homes in the countryside have "peasant medicine chests" implemented by the health committees, which people frequently visit. Campesinas are very keen to have access to vitamins and antibiotics despite their cost. I met countless women who were taking massive numbers of pills a day for their ill-health. "I've just taken twelve, but I have to wait now for four hours before I take any more," said one woman. "Twelve! What for?" I asked. "Oh some are for my anemia, some for my stomach pains, some for my headaches, some for my blood pressure."

The *botiquina* owners obtained their drugs from the *Botica Central*, where drugs were distributed from a small office in UAC. Talking to one woman while she was buying her monthly supply, I asked her what she recommended Vitamin A for. "I think it's for tumours. Or is it for something else?" She asked one of the other women present, who shrugged her shoulders. "Sometimes I get mixed up." "What if I recommend the wrong thing? I am afraid of that. I know these basic things, like aspirin. But some of these pills, I don't know." "Doesn't the doctor give you training in this?" I asked. "Yes, but it is easy to forget and get them confused." This confusion is not surprising in a situation in which pharmaceutical drugs are considered a generic solution to the bodily symptoms of living hard and difficult lives.[11] But it is also an indication that the sign, rather than the intended meaning, of Western medicine is being appropriated by *campesinas*.

In the following story, the analyst encounters the "exotic." The encounter begins with a desire for difference, a desire so powerful that it creates difference through romanticizing an activity identified by the analyst as "really" traditional.

Tomasa's sister brings out a bottle of *puro* (alcohol) from the back room and starts collecting herbs and plants in the garden. An old man suddenly appears and everyone greets him warmly. He enters the house and sits in front of Tomasa's young nephew, who stands as though at attention. Tomasa, her mother, and her sister casually chat on the veranda. I, on the other hand, am spellbound: here, in such an unlikely context, I am experiencing my first encounter with a practising *curandero*. He dips the herbs into a bowl of puro and, starting at the boy's head, rubs the herbs down his arms, neck, chest, back, and legs. The *curandero* pats the boy's head and arms with the leftover puro on his hands. He chants for some time, pointing to the boy's head, then his chest, then his legs. Then he charges the mother 600 sucres, telling her that she should give her son one-half teaspoon of sugar in the morning and a cup of Philips Milk of Magnesia mixed with 7-up at night. Everyone on the veranda nods in agreement. Tomasa, still in her crisp, nurse-like uniform after spending the day giving medical advice and dispensing pharmaceuticals and vitamins to rural women, tells me that it is fortunate that her nephew does not have a more serious case of *susto* (fright sickness).

Here the colonial tendencies of the analyst are quickly interrupted by the hybridization of the space itself: not only does Tomasa inhabit this space quite comfortably but the "traditional" healer himself appears to have no qualms about demanding cash and prescribing the consumption of what appears to be a bizarre combination of "gringo" products. It is only the analyst who appears to be disturbed by the event. It is in this kind of encounter, I believe, that a reflexive ethic emerges: it is precisely because analysts of differently worlded worlds are inspired by the desire to make (logical) sense of what they observe that they also have a responsibility to critically examine this desire – including the almost inevitable temptation to map the world in particular ways – and, ultimately, to put it firmly in its place.

The Politics of Health

I became aware of differences in opinion about the role of UAC and the health committees at a UAC general meeting for executive elections. A slate, consisting almost entirely of people who were already in positions of power in UAC, was put forward for members to vote "for" or "against." A serious disagreement arose about this approach to voting, particularly between members of a cooperative in which I had lived in 1980 and the old guard of UAC. One member, complaining about the tactic being undemocratic, said it was like coming to a soccer game, having only one team show up, and declaring them the winner. Another argued that the meeting had been stacked with members from the health committees who were not members of a cooperative. In the end, the slate won handily.

"No one is for UAC today," says Pancho, the ex-manager of one of the founding cooperatives of the union (a point always emphasized when UAC ignores the criticisms of the *campesinos* who live there). "Only those cooperatives that have someone with a UAC executive position, or where there is an active health committee … ['that Adela can control' interjects Pancho's son], support UAC today." It is both UAC's lack of accountability and its attention to profit-making activities at the expense of social or political activities that draws criticisms. "We always ask for the specifics about what they've done with the money for this or that project and they never respond … all they ever talk about is the market," says another cooperative member.

Indeed, UAC looked considerably different in the late 1990s than it did in 1980. There was no longer a *tienda* selling groceries ("it wasn't profitable," according to one executive member) and no store to sell agricultural *insumos* (fertilizers, etc.). UAC had also begun to operate a massive rice mill built with International Development Bank money. Though the purpose of the mill was to give the cooperative members a fair deal in their rice milling, it was recognized even by the UAC executive that most of the rice they milled was owned by *comerciantes* (town merchants) rather than *campesinos*.

As the above reference to Adela's "control" indicates, the critique of UAC's apparent lack of concern about the needs of the *campesinos* extended to the health committees. Miguel, whose wife is a member of a health committee, explains why:

> The health committees are worked on by Adela before the meetings and the ones who don't agree don't show up. That's why it looks as though our cooperative is the only one ever protesting. Look, most of the decisions that are made by UAC are *hecho en la cama* – ["made in bed?" I asked, looking more than a little surprised, I'm sure] Of course! Adela is Arturo's companion. [Arturo is UAC's manager.] They've got it all covered. These people would die of hunger if they didn't have these UAC positions. They don't have anything to do with growing crops anymore. That's why they are so concerned when people start raising questions.

The health committees, from Miguel's point of view, were simply another way of ensuring control over the direction of the peasant organization. In this sense the strong connection that is made between the health committees' activities of "building healthy bodies" and UAC's claim to be "building healthy peasant organizations" may have worked against the effectiveness of the discourse of cleanliness and self-discipline contained in the biomedical approach to health. For those marginalized from real participation in UAC, consenting to the medical expertise extended by the health committees could be viewed as tantamount to accepting the profit-making orientation of UAC. Thus, while neoliberal perspectives that speak of the need for people "to stand on their own two feet" is an ideology that in many ways appeals to the coastal *campesino*, for most, the concept of being healthy hinges more on the possibilities for economic security than on a desire for cleanliness, and such security has been increasingly difficult to attain. That UAC was seen to be doing nothing to aid in the *campesino's* search for economic security (being more concerned about milling the rice of *comerciantes*) made UAC part of the problem.

Adela, as a member of the UAC executive, was not oblivious to these criticisms:

> Look, I never forget where I come from. My family is from the countryside. My father used to tell me "Don't forget your origins. *Help* the people." And that's what I do. Some people think I'm rich because I wear a clean shirt. But I'll wear the same shirt again – the *same* shirt, but it's

clean, that's all. It doesn't mean that I'm rich. It means I have improved my consciousness about some things. But you know no matter how much you work with some people and tell them they have to change their priorities, they will still walk around in dirty clothes, preferring to waste their money on drinking, not worrying about their health. There's nothing you can do about those people.

For Adela, the linking of the biomedical view and UAC's activities appears to have provided justification for deflecting or ignoring the critiques: "those people" become a disease against which the peasant "body" has to guard itself if it is to remain healthy and strong. Referring to neoliberal approaches to the economy, UAC executive members told me that the organization was constrained to "manage money well" if it was to continue to receive financial support from external agencies. Thus, both UAC and the health committees could neutralize critiques of their work by labelling them attacks from people who fail to understand the dynamics of modern (healthy) organizations.

Not surprisingly, the critics of UAC do not view themselves as undisciplined people unconcerned about their health or their future. The dynamics of "place" explicitly informs their illness discourse. Generally speaking, the ailments that are considered important by most *campesinos* are not thought to be caused by a lack of self-discipline; they are simply "a part of life" in this region. Coughs are usually said to be caused by *polvo* (dust) from the dirt roads in the dry season. Fevers and malaria are related to an upset in the balance of the body (e.g., men working with rice in the wet season, with their feet in the cold water and the heat of the sun overhead). Diarrhea is considered to be a normal part of childhood for *campesinos*. As one woman told me: "Yes my little ones have diarrhea, but it goes. It comes again, but then it always goes. One doesn't have to worry about it much." While biomedical experts might well find these perspectives to be evidence of a fatalistic culture, from the *campesino* point of view they are realistic appraisals of living in the coastal countryside, where diseases, like the market for agricultural crops, move cyclically rather than linearly.

Campesinos in this region are concerned to develop a morality of health but in ways that hint more at the immorality of poverty than at the morality of cleanliness. Illnesses such as *nervios* are specifically constructed around grave concerns about rural men's continued lack of employment and market opportunities and women's extended roles as "keepers of the house" (Phillips 1990). After the cholera epidemic, the only person whom I interviewed in the countryside who claimed that no one in their household suffered from *nervios* or *presion* was also the only one who said that the money they were earning was "reaching better" than in the past. Not too surprisingly, the male household head in this household held an executive position in UAC.[12]

The stories of these *campesinos* reflect complex, hybridized views of health systems that easily disrupt moralities couched in terms of modernity. On the one hand, *curanderos* are hired for the treatment of many illnesses, including *nervios, anemia,* and *presion.* These illnesses sometimes involve symptoms that are considered to be the result of *brujeria,* or witchcraft, a concept that biomedicine would likely consider a major impediment to modernity. On the other hand, people praise the beauty of, but generally ignore, the new "traditional medicine" gardens put in place by the health committees. These impressive gardens contain a variety of different plants for curing aches, pains, and upset stomachs (mint, basil, oregano, sage, yucca, etc.). Yet they are lonely gardens compared to the drug-filled *boticas* located beside them, which are visited by many people. With the cornucopia of pharmaceutical solutions to ill-health, this "new" tradition is simply not seen to be relevant by those seeking help. As one health committee member said to me when we were discussing a plant that apparently helps sore throats, "I don't bother – I just take pills."

Concluding Thoughts

Fictions about the tropics have consistently pit the moral, rational, and industrious temperate zones against the immoral, irrational, and lazy populations of the tropics. This characterization is said to have arisen from the overabundance of resources in the tropics (thereby thwarting industry) and the fact that tropical bodies are "saturated" with disease (causing apparent listlessness). In this sense tropicalism as a universalizing discourse links improper behaviour and inappropriate economies. The rational temperate model of development becomes the logical candidate for enabling the tropics and tropical people to become productive, to become "like us." Anthropological fieldwork is an activity made possible through the very colonialism that produced this discourse on the tropics. The strength of a *reflexive ethic* is its insistence that we examine colonialism's role in our creation of tropical Others, that we consider my judgment – as a kind of cleanser – to be suspect. A reflexive ethic also balances hope for a different future with responsibility – responsibility to ensure not so much "fair representation" but an accountable reinscription of our encounters. My relocation as a participant and as an observer of rural women (as participants and observers of the coastal Ecuadorian situation) shifts the parameters of competing views of the tropics without succumbing to the temptation of creating a romantic counter-resistance to dominant views. For example, we find no "women's voice" here in opposition to the temperate mappings of the tropical landscape; instead, the discourses of modernity crosscut our/their experiences to produce multiple and complex moralities about women's lives – moralities concerning women who may boil their water or wear clean shirts but who, after all, eat on the street or talk to healers to deal with their fears. The health moralities of coastal *campesinos* contain the inequities that have been developing within the region as recent discourses and practices concerning health and development have proceeded. These inequities, it seems to me, have both aided in and constrained the emergence of new moralities in much the same way that the universal message of modernity creates "its own exclusions and its own forms of domination and repression" (Benhabib 1995b, 253).

Combined, neoliberalism and biomedicine in Latin America make a powerful partnership, for their proposal – resolving social problems (such as ill-health and poverty) through individual solutions – is promoted as the only viable one for the future. Latin America's cholera epidemic permitted the implementation of new approaches towards healing the body tropical in coastal Ecuador and held the potential for creating new subjects. However, the effectiveness of the intervention has relied on the assumption that coastal *campesinos* would themselves understand this proposal as a symbol of progress and use it as a basis for transforming their "hopeless" situation. Yet today most coastal *campesinos* are not what temperate mappers would call vigilant about their health: resources seldom allow one to behave otherwise, and one can always take *pastillas* or go to healers if health problems do arise. This, perhaps more than anything, indicates that the neoliberal and biomedical concern for self-discipline has not formed part of the way in which *campesinos* have appropriated these discourses. Far from "hopeless," however, their emerging cleansing strategies suggest hints of other possible interpretations, including a critique of a world where the fever of the market takes precedence over living and where definitions of health hinge on an approach to life that demands constant vigilance. It is, of course, precisely this "misappropriation" of the biomedical discourse by coastal residents that continues to make them the incomprehensible Other to outsiders – and an attractive target for further projects of Sanitation.

Notes

1 An earlier version of this paper was presented in the Department of Anthropology, York University, in 1997. I would like to thank those present for their feedback. I would like to thank Suzan Ilcan, Alan Sears, Patricia Tomic, and Camilo Trumper for their insightful comments on this chapter. I would also like to take this opportunity to thank Lucia Salamea in Ecuador for her insights and friendship.

2 While the term *campesino*, referring to poor rural farmers in Latin America, is employed by academics less frequently today, it is the most common term used by the local inhabitants in this study.

3 Sunder Rajan (1993), in her critical analysis of *sati*, shows how the tropes and conceptual moves of colonialism can be found in the "new" orientalism of postcolonial analyses. Quoting from Arjuna Parakrama's (1990, 8) *Language and Rebellion*, she argues that we "are forced to concede that a 'non-colonialist' (and therefore non-contaminated?) space remains a wish-fulfilment within postcolonial knowledge production."

4 For an account of the flip-side of this connection (i.e., speculation about the relationship between "order" and the impossibility of cholera "breeding" in Chile), see Trumper and Phillips (1996).

5 The key measures refer to refraining from drinking unboiled water, eating in the streets, eating or cooking without washing one's hands, and defecating "in the open air."

6 For critical discussions of the impact of this trend on Latin America, see Gustafson (1994); Jonas and McCaughan (1994); Phillips (1998); and North and Cameron (2003).

7 All names of people and organizations in this chapter are pseudonyms.

8 In 1991-92 the activities of the Health Committee Program included:

   (1) the development of a campaign for cholera prevention, involving consciousnessraising talks, training in the management of diarrhea-related illnesses (consumption of liquids), treating 264 cholera patients, and giving medicines to those who had been in contact with the patients to prevent transmission.

   (2) a parasite elimination program.

   (3) preventive medicine courses (courses on the care and maintenance of generic drugs) for those who had *botiquines campesinos.*

   (4) medicinal plants and vegetable gardens.

   (5) services of the *Botica Central* de UAC, which handled around thirty generic drugs.

   (6) medical attention (committee members learned to give injections and, from a local doctor, learned to recognize many of the illnesses in the region).

   (7) a radio program.

9 It was only after the doctor's speech that I noticed that all the children were wearing shoes, though some had shoes that were far too big for their feet, and the stilted gait of others gave the distinct impression that some of them were unaccustomed to the practice.

10 Adela's evaluation of her health status was unique; other women on the health committees spoke to me about experiencing the same illnesses that other rural women experience (e.g., nerves, high blood pressure). Both Tomasa and Rosa, for example, talked about their bodies constantly aching and sometimes having "a strong pain" in a particular area of their body, symptoms that usually bring women to a *curandero* (healer).

11 No one but Dr Diaz ever talks about malnutrition in the countryside ("they will call it anemia," he says). While there are accessible solutions to anemia (one can take pills), this is not the case for malnutrition. For a discussion of a similar process involving the medicalization of the countryside in Brazil, see Scheper-Hughes (1993).

12 Since conducting this fieldwork I have received a letter (June 2003) from one of the families in the region in which it is noted that the members of the UAC executive have been largely replaced, primarily by the male *campesinos* who were critical of the health committees and the market orientation of the organization in the late 1990s. This transformation complicates my analysis, but I am convinced that it only strengthens the imperative of a reflexive ethic for future analyses.

Works Cited

Bhabha, H. 1992. "Postcolonial Authority and Postmodern Guilt." In *Cultural Studies*, ed. L. Grossberg, C. Nelson, and P. Treicher, 56–68. New York: Routledge.

Benhabib, S., J Butler, D. Cornell, and N. Fraser. 1995a. "Feminism and Postmodernism." In *Feminist Contentions: A Philosophical Exchange.* 17–34. New York and London: Routledge.

– 1995b. "Cultural Complexity, Moral Interdependence, and the Global Dialogical Community." In *Women, Culture and Development: A Study of Human Capabilities*, ed. M. Nussbaum and J. Glover, 135–55. New York: Oxford University Press.

Butler, J. 1995. "For a Careful Reading." In *Feminist Contentions: A Philosophical Exchange*, ed. S. Benhabib, J. Butler, D. Cornell, and N. Fraser, 127–43. New York and London: Routledge.

Cornell, D. 1995. "What Is Ethical Feminism." In *Feminist Contentions: A Philosophical Exchange*, ed. S. Benhabib, J. Butler, D. Cornell, and N. Fraser, 75–106. New York and London: Routledge.

Cueto, M. 1992. "Sanitation from Above: Yellow Fever and Foreign Intervention in Peru." *Hispanic American Historical Review* 72, (1): 1–22.

Harvey, D. 2000. *Spaces of Hope*. Berkely and Los Angeles: University of California Press.

Gustafson, L., ed. 1994. *Economic Development under Democratic Regimes: Neoliberalism in Latin America*. Westport: Praeger.

Jonas, S., and E. McCaughan, eds. 1994. *Latin America Faces the Twenty-First Century*. Boulder, CO: Westview.

Kahn, J. 1995. *Culture, Multiculture, Postculture*. London: Routledge.

Kirby, K. 1993. "Thinking through the Boundary: The Politics of Location, Subjects, and Space." *Boundary 2* 20 (2): 173–89.

McDowell, L. 1999. *Gender, Identity and Place: Understanding Feminist Geographies*. Minneapolis: University of Minnesota Press.

Minh-ha, T. 1991. *When the Moon Waxes Red: Representation, Gender and Cultural Politics*. New York and London: Routledge.

North, L., and J. Cameron, eds. 2003. *Rural Progress, Rural Decay: Neoliberal Adjustment Policies and Local Initiatives*. Bloomfield, CT: Kumarian Press.

Parakrama, A. 1990. *Language and Rebellion*. London: Katha.

Peard, J. 1999. *Race, Place, and Medicine: The Idea of the Tropics in Nineteenth Century Brazilian Medicine*. Durham and London: Duke University Press.

Phillips, L. 1990. "The Power of Representation: Agrarian Politics and Rural Women's Interpretations of the Household in Coastal Ecuador." *Dialectical Anthropology* 15 (4): 271–83.

– 1993. "Cooperatives and Agrarian Transitions: Implications for Neo-liberalism." *Canadian Journal of Sociology and Anthropology* 30 (4): 429–50.

– 1995. "Difference, Indifference and Making a Difference: Reflexivity in the Time of Cholera." In *Ethnographic Feminisms: Essays in Anthropology*, ed. S. Cole and L. Phillips, 21–36. Ottawa: Carleton University Press.

– 1996. "Toward Post-Colonial Methodologies." In *Women, Work and Gender Relations in Developing Countries: A Global Perspective*, ed. P. Ghorayshi and C. Belanger, 15–29. Westport, CT: Greenwood.

– ed. 1998. *The Third Wave of Modernization in Latin America: Cultural Perspectives on Neoliberalism.* Wilmington, Delaware: Scholarly Resources Books.

Phillips, L., and S. Ilcan. 2000. "Domesticating Spaces in Transition: Politics and Practices in the Gender and Development Literaure, 1970–99" *Anthropologica* 42: 205–16.

Savigliano, M. 1995. *Tango and the Political Economy of Passion.* Boulder, CO: Westview.

Scheper-Hughes, N. 1993. *Death without Weeping.* Berkeley: University of California Press.

Siemens, A. 1990. *Between the Summit and the Sea: Central Veracruz in the Nineteenth Century.* Vancouver: UBC Press.

Sunder Rajan, R. 1993. *Real and Imagined Women: Gender, Culture and Postcolonialism.* London: Routledge.

Trumper, R., and L. Phillips. 1995. "Cholera in the Time of Neoliberalism: The Cases of Chile and Ecuador." *Alternatives* 20: 165–94.

– 1996. "Give me Discipline and Give me Death: Neoliberalizing Health in Chile." *Race and Class* 37(3): 19-34.

PART SIX

STYLES AND GENRES OF THE ETHICAL SUBJECT

"Covering Their Familiar Ways with Another Culture": Minnie Aodla Freeman's *Life among the Qallunaat* and the Ethics of Subjectivity

BINA TOLEDO FREIWALD

What grows at the next door neighbour's may look to be growing there,
but the roots of whatever is growing next door may be in your own side
of the yard.   Minnie Aodla Freeman, *Sharing Our Experience*

If you don't put all your identity eggs in one basket, the chances are less
likely that you will kill anyone who looks at them (or who you think looks
at them) as if he wanted to break them. If you don't put all the identity eggs
of the people who are different from you in one basket, the chances are less
likely that you will want to break theirs (or look as if you did).
     Susan Rubin Suleiman, *Risking Who One Is*

Pretext: Here, Now

Freeman's (1978) and Suleiman's (1991) reflections on identity and difference
– on the perils that attend seeing "there" as (always already) an encroach-
ment on "here," and "them" as alien and a threat to the charmed circle
of "us" – were written in the shadow of the Gulf War and the war in Bosnia,
respectively. I read their apt metaphors as timely reminders: affirming
(through the organic tropes) the human longing to belong, contesting any
view of identity as homogeneous or bounded, and recognizing the shifting
and variable nature of identifications. They offer a simple moral: that those
who recognize the complex and shifting grids of affiliation that constitute
their own identity are more likely to grant others the right to theirs. Such
thoughts return to me with added poignancy as I read Jack D. Eller's (1999,
2) *From Culture to Ethnicity to Conflict*, a study that seeks to understand the
"prevalence, virulence, and persistence of contemporary ethnic conflict."
The book has chapters on Sri Lanka, the Kurds, Rwanda and Burundi, and
Bosnia. The last chapter is on Quebec. "Shocked but not surprised" might
best describe my initial reaction to finding Quebec – this place where my

adult life, so far, has unfolded – featured alongside these violent instances of ethnic strife. Shocked but not surprised because Eller openly addresses what are persistent preoccupations but almost-taboo subjects in Quebec: the relationship between an ideology of ethnic nationalism and the project of Quebec sovereignty, and the possibility that the latter might result in a deadly conflict. I was surprised and disappointed, I might add, not to find in Eller's study a discussion of the realities that shaped my early years: the complex dynamics of intra- and interethnic conflict (still far from resolved) in Israel/Palestine.

"Nationalism is the overriding political passion of our time," Jean Bethke Elshtain observes (along with many others), noting that, in nationalism, the human longing for community with others takes on a particular cast that she associates with the twin notions of sovereignty and "the *will-to-sacrifice*." In the logic of nationalistic discourses, power is claimed and sacrifice expected in the name of a nation conceived in the image of a sovereign self: singular, "unified, sharply boundaried" (Elshtain 1993, 168–70). The rhetoric of nationalism thus relies on a triple figuration: imagining the nation as a collective individual (i.e., as a "bounded, homogeneous, and continuous entity"); interpellating (some) individuals as (organic) members of that body politic; identifying those (others) whose exclusion defines and safeguards the integrity of the national body (Handler 1988, 191, 39). Daily, my morning papers (*Le Devoir* and the *Montreal Gazette*, what else?) bring reminders that this is a place of contested belongings, a place "that continually asserts the absolute necessity of an identity," where "identity is an institutional project" (Probyn 1994, 34, 27). The stakes have become even higher since the too-close/not-close-enough referendum vote of 1995 (50.6 per cent to 49.4 per cent for staying in Canada), and then premier Jacques Parizeau's heated response, blaming the loss on "money and the ethnic vote."

One such vote might have been that of Minnie Aodla Freeman, an Inuk from Cape Hope Island in James Bay. It is to her autobiographical narrative, *Life among the Qallunaat* (1978), that I turn my attention in this chapter. Susan Suleiman has noted that theorists of the postmodern subject often create emblematic and utopian figures: Derrida's dancer, Haraway's cyborg, Kristeva's happy cosmopolitan. Freeman's autobiographical persona allows us to pursue what autobiographical writing is perhaps particularly well placed to facilitate: a less lofty, more grounded reflection on "how individuals are categorized and attached to identities, and how identities are invariably produced within the social, political and cultural domain" (Whitlock 2000, 5). Freeman's (1978, 52) is a complex figure: a subject "in the middle," an indigenous autoethnographer of and in the contact zone (to appropriate

Pratt's terms), a translator between and across languages, cultures, and histories in this "invader-settler" society we call Canada (Brydon 1991, 2). Freeman's sustained critique of and dialogue with the indigenous and colonial past and present, moreover, invite us to extend the reflection on the plural histories that constitute the subject to include an interrogation of the role of identitarian discourses within regimes of power. They remind us that the writing and reading of autobiographical narratives can provide "a site for cultural critique and social change," as essentialist notions of identity are challenged and the effects of discourses on subjects are exposed (Bergland 1994, 162). Before turning to Freeman's text, then, some thoughts on nation and self-narration in this place.

At the conclusion of *Le Trafic des langues: Traduction et culture dans la littérature québécoise*, Sherry Simon (1994, 177) reminds us that "la différence culturelle, autant sinon plus que la différence de classe, est la ligne de division capitale qui traverse les populations nationales." I argue here that such fault lines – articulated in the idioms of ethnicity, race, religion, language, culture, history, or region – traverse, and thereby shape, both the autobiographical body and the body politic, for nation and self-narration are inextricable and mutually dependent projects. A sense of national belonging is often central to the making of a self, while life narratives play a key role in the construction and promotion of collective identities: "It is a familiar idea that modernity allows the ordinary citizen to make a national identity central to an individual identity ... It is a slightly less familiar thought that the identity of this nation is tied up with the stories of individuals ... whose stories, in helping to fashion a national narrative, serve also, indirectly, to shape the individual narratives of other patriotic – nationally identified – citizens" (Appiah 1996, 9). The national story, then, is both modelled on the narrative conventions of the life story and offers itself as a model upon which personal identities are to be fashioned.

Both Freeman's autobiography and the Parti Québécois (PQ) government documents I discuss below are subject-constituting projects profoundly invested in the mutual articulation of individual identity and collective identification. I read them together here in order to interrogate those acts of the (affective, social, political) imagination by which selves and communities come to be represented.

The preamble to the "Projet de loi sur l'avenir du Québec" (Bill respecting the future of Québéc), entitled *Déclaration de Souveraineté* (French version) and *Declaration of Sovereignty* (English version), was distributed to every household in Quebec a few weeks before the October 1995 referendum. It was a mass mailing but a personal gesture in each instance for the document specifically addresses itself to the individual reader. Parizeau, premier at the time, writes in the letter prefacing the earlier Draft Bill on the Sovereignty of Québec: "I emphasize that this is your *personal* copy because the initiative of creating a country is not the exclusive concern of a government. Indeed, it must be the concern of each and every citizen of Québec, of the Québec nation as a whole" (emphasis added). The shift from "every citizen" to the "Québéc nation" is telling, demonstrating the power of identity discourses – whether autobiographical or polemical – to effect what appears to be an easy and natural transition from the life of the individual to the struggles of the collectivity. Individual life thus comes to be articulated in double time (individual and collective), assuming the greater, grander, dimensions of a collective saga in which identity is projected across a continuum that stretches from the past of one's ancestors to the future of one's descendants. The *Declaration* (Quebec 1995, 7) announces: "The time has come for us, tomorrow's ancestors, to make ready for our descendants harvests that are worthy of the labours of the past."

The *Declaration*'s collectivist discourse, however, interpellates not only an "I" and a "we" but also a "they" who are not part of "us." At the heart of the *Declaration* – I use this figure advisedly, for the text depends on this idiom to naturalize its claim that "the heart of this land beats in French"[1] – is an elaboration of what constitutes "the very bastion of our identity." Identity, the text affirms (and underscores through the use of italics), is ontologically grounded in being: "*l'etre précède l'avoir. Nous faisons de ce principe le coeur de notre projet*" (10). The English text similarly announces the centrality of this principle through the use of italics: "*to be comes before to have. and this principle lies at the very heart of our endeavor.*" In terms of this document, then, you either *are* or you are not; more specifically, you either are or are not a descendant of those "17th century ... pioneers ... [who have] come from a great civilization ... [maintaining] the heritage of France."[2] National belonging, the *Declaration* intimates, coincides with the identity or being of this particular group and not with any of the others briefly alluded to, such as the "First Nations," "the English community," or "the immigrants": "In order that the profound sense of *belonging* to a distinct people is now and for all time the very bastion of our identity, we proclaim our will to live in a French-language society" (emphasis added).[3]

Language, in the context of this document is, of course, much more than a linguistic or even a cultural marker: it is the identity badge of those descendants of the seventeenth-century pioneers who have benefited, the text concedes, from the "contributions" of the other groups. Thus, while the opening invitation to "the men and women" of this place appears to promise total inclusivity through gender inclusivity, as other categories of identity are introduced this inclusivity comes into question. If, for example, the history of the "men and women" who constitute the collective subject of the *Declaration* is said to range over "four hundred years," what of those with longer or shorter histories on this soil?[4]

"Nous, peuple d'ici" opens the *Déclaration*, affirming the existence of *a* people in whose image the desired nation-state is to be built. Over the past six years in Québéc, the PQ government has been involved in a sustained effort to bring such a project to fruition, an effort that has found one of its most explicit articulations in a document entitled "La citoyenneté Québécoise: document de consultation pour le forum national sur la citoyenneté et l'integration" (<http://pages.infinit.net/andreroy/Forum_citoyen_consultation.pdf>) prepared for a government forum that took place in October 2000. The forum document puts into the official idiom of governance the vision more lyrically expressed in the *Déclaration*. The forum document's gestures towards notions of inclusivity and "vouloir vivre-ensemble" notwithstanding (5), its principal aim, like that of the *Déclaration*, is to affirm the being of a homogeneous national entity, "l'existence du peuple québécois" (18). The document becomes a tour de force of discursive nation-state building, enacting and re-enacting, throughout its fifty-one pages, a rhetorical slippage from "société," to "le peuple québécois" and "nation québécoise," to "l'État du Québéc" (in/through the official discourse, the nation-state has already come into being). It is hardly surprising that the document was met with such outrage and fierce criticism from the very constituency whose concerns it was supposed to address – immigrant groups. In the logic of the forum document, the chief concerns regarding the "nouveaux arrivants" are not the social and material difficulties experienced by immigrants and visible minorities but, rather, their weak sense of belonging ("sentiment d'appartenance"), seen as an obstacle to the realization of an independent nation-state (37). The forum document purports to address the issue of the integration of immigrants, but its language and arguments reveal, at every turn, a different project, one principally interested in making the case against the Canadian state and for an independent québécois nation-state. The identitarian logic of the document ultimately presents a familiar impasse: the appeal to an inclusive notion of citizenship regardless of one's ethnic origin is belied by a narrative of origins that defines the collectivity as descendants "d'une culture et d'une civilisation française originale sur ce continent" (21).[5]

Who, then, is the nation? Whether one accepts Benedict Anderson's analysis of nations as "imagined communities" or supports Anthony Smith's

(1993, 20) thesis regarding "pre-existent ethnic ties," it remains that a key function of any nationalist discourses is to articulate, while naturalizing, its own answer to the question "who are *we*?" It is precisely such certainties that autobiographical writing can help unsettle, for its interrogation of the notion of the unified subject can serve to challenge the founding trope of the nation as "bounded in space, continuous in time, and homogeneous within those spaciotemporal boundaries" (Handler 1988, 50).

Old Trails, New Directions

Autobiographical narratives unfold in the space between two interrogatory and interpellating[6] gestures: between what others think and want of us, and our ensuing quests for self-knowledge and self-realization. "What are you?" people in the South ask Freeman (1978, 62), believing that they already know the answer, and most of the time mistaking her for a Chinese or a Vietnamese. "Who am I?" she asks (140), and proceeds to provide a complex answer. An Inuk among the *qallunaat* (the Inuktitut word for white people), an indigenous subject in a postcontact world, Freeman brings into a particularly sharp focus issues relating to identity and belonging, the convergence of collective history and individual destiny, and the dual imperative to remember while *not* "stay[ing] the same forever" (208).

Freeman concludes *Life among the Qallunaat* with these poignant words: "I miss my dear people who are becoming stranger, even to me, covering their familiar ways with another culture" (217). Freeman's evocative parting gesture invites the reader to reflect on the lessons drawn from a life lived and told across the divides of self and community; colonial history and traditional Inuit ways; *qallunaat* and Inuit linguistic, cultural, and social realities. These are lessons gleaned from living in the middle: between the "Inuk Way" (71) she was born into and a *qallunaat* culture that has made her a stranger in "[her] own country" (21) but that she now embraces as her "adopted home" (46). Lessons about living between longing and affirmation, belonging and alienation; lessons, as well, about the potential of autobiographical acts to document, enact, and effect – for both autobiographer and reader – such migrations and negotiations.

Freeman's closing image – "covering their familiar ways with another culture" – is suggestive in yet another way. It reminds us that autobiographies, as narratives of "resistance to loss" (Gunn 1992, 76), are palimpsests in which the meanings of the past are always already written over by the markings of the present. For Aboriginal and Inuit writers in contemporary Canada, the palimpsest bears the traces of erasure and disfigurement that are the legacy of colonial dispossession. Yet, as Freeman's text suggests, estrangement and self-estrangement are the postcontact realities for Inuit and *qallunaat* alike. The autobiography thus effects a double defamiliarization: Freeman's detailed chronicling of the words and ways of her people and extensive use of Inuktitut, on the one hand, and her representation of *qallunaat* ways and their impact on the Inuit from an Inuk's point of view, on the other, leave the *qallunaaq* reader, no less than the Inuk subject, without the comfort and power of a "pure," "authentic," or exclusive language with which to name the world.

The *qallunaaq*, or non-Aboriginal reader, figures in Freeman's autobiography, and other autobiographies by Inuit and Aboriginal writers, because the palimpsest holds both the memory of the past and the promise of the future. Lee Maracle (1992, 14) offers an apt image for the autobiographer's self, a self who "wolf-like journeys doggedly along old trails with new directions in mind, a self who sees transformation, personal and social as natural and indispensable to growth." The old trails and the new directions are the shared legacy and common responsibility of the autobiographer and his/her readers, Aboriginal and non-Aboriginal alike. This recognition of commonalty, however, tells only part of the story. For the postcontact indigenous subject, the foregrounding of difference is a survival strategy and a means of resistance. The opening sentence of *Life among the Qallunaat* begins: "Whenever a *white* person meets me for the first time" (Freeman 1978, 17; emphasis added). As an Inuk living among the *qallunaat*, Freeman needs both to be alert to *qallunaat* ways – in order to survive in the South – and to guard against their invasive powers. She establishes her particular subject position early on in the narrative by showing Inuit and *qallunaat* to be equally strangers in each other's worlds. Thus, Freeman's initial response to *qallunaat* city reality is speechlessness: she has many unanswered questions, is puzzled by the rules she encounters everywhere, and feels "like a little ant" (17) inside high-ceilinged buildings. However, as she is quick to remind herself and us, often to great comic effect, the *qallunaat* in the South are no less lost when it comes to the ways of her people. White people are forever asking her, "How do you like the weather?" (17), and on her first day in Ottawa her roommates come to watch her unpack, expecting "to be shown sealskin clothing, along with a folding igloo perhaps" (18).

The consequences of such mutual estrangement, however, vary, depending on one's relation to colonial privilege. While the Inuit have had to learn to live among the *qallunaat* and to adapt to their ways (at a high cost to themselves), the same has not been the case for the dominant culture or its institutions. Freeman writes in the concluding pages of her autobiography:

I had met and come to know many *qallunaat* by then and had learned to be cautious with them. Some were nice and kind, but *none wanted to see or understand my native culture*. Some didn't want to know, some didn't have time, some found it too deep to understand or accept. *They all wanted to cover it up with their ways.* (194; emphasis added)

As a chronicler of the ways of her native culture, then, Freeman asks us to read her narrative in the spirit of a critique that "decolonize[s] its .. practice with a more intimate knowledge of the oppressed" (Emberley 1993, 98).[7] However, by using the same palimpsestic image – of one culture covering over another – to figure both colonial violence and her own self-estrangement, Freeman alerts us to the complexities of historical representation and self-narration. As Gayatri Chakravorty Spivak (1990, 59–60) has pointed out, for the postcolonial subject the question "'Who should speak?' is less crucial than 'Who will listen?' ... the real demand is that, when I speak from that position, I should be listened to seriously; not with that kind of benevolent imperialism" that expects from the Other a "representative" and homogenizing self-discourse; "There are many subject positions which one *must* inhabit," Spivak writes, "one is not just one thing" (emphasis added). Freeman, too, does not want kindness or an easy acceptance from her *qallunaat* readers; only their serious consideration of a collective history and a personal story that, to begin with, have to be told in more than one tongue.

Individual Story/Collective History

Freeman was born in 1937 on Cape Hope Island in James Bay and came to Ottawa in 1957 to work as a translator for the federal government. Her autobiography is divided into three parts, which bear these telling bilingual subtitles: "I. *Ottawamillunga*: In Ottawa"; "II. *Inullivunga*: Born to Inuk Ways"; and "III. *Qallunanillunga*: Among the *Qallunaat*." Taken together, the subtitles suggest the life trajectory of a subject who is "multiply organized" (de Lauretis, qtd. in Lionnet 1995, 5). Yes, Part II proudly declares, one is born into a particular collectivity. But this is only one determinant in a tripartite configuration. There is also the collectivity within which one finds oneself – by circumstance, coercion, or a combination of both – for Freeman, it is

Ottawa, where Part 1 of the book opens. And then there is the third factor, which involves agency and choice: Freeman chooses to live "among the *qallunaat*," as the title of her book already announces. What the play of English and Inuktitut in the titles and throughout the book further suggests is that identity and belonging cannot be contained by a single myth of origin or a single tongue: they are plural and not unitary, shifting and not fixed, and can only be voiced in a plurilingual fashion. This "braiding" (Lionnet 1995, 5) of the different identities at the subject's disposal, however, is not a disinterested celebration of heterogeneity; Freeman's plurilingual text uses the languages and traditions that inform and constitute it to mount a sustained critique of colonialism.[8]

To start where the life-story – for this subject – begins: *Inullivunga*: Inuk ways. "I am what I remember," implies the autobiographer, and the reader of Freeman's narrative is invited to ask: why, from among the multitude of memories that make up a past, these particular *collective* remembrances? Some commentators on Aboriginal autobiography have argued that the very premises of the genre – which they consider to be "self-aggrandizement" and "aggressive individualism" (Harry 1985, 149) – are antithetical to the values of Aboriginal cultures. Margaret Harry, for example, claims that Freeman's interest in collective history detracts from the autobiography's focus on her life: "Whenever the autobiographical account threatens to become too personal, too self-centered, Freeman retreats into the relation of anecdotes and traditional tales, thus distracting the reader from the central focus of the work itself and apparently dissipating its theme" (149).[9] Contrary to Harry's dismissal of "anecdotes and traditional tales" as irrelevant to the experience of the narrator-autobiographer, Freeman's evocations of the history and ways of her people prove to be not only inextricable from her self-portrayal but also integral to the shape and movement of her life-narrative as a whole. Emma LaRocqe (1993, xxviii) has observed in her discussion of contemporary Aboriginal writing that "some themes unique to a people dispossessed stand out: a haunting and hounding sense of loss that drives one to reminisce. 'I remember,' many of us write, 'I remember.'" "I Remember" is also the title of a section in Freeman's (1978, 73–4) autobiography in which she recalls the death of her mother when she was barely four years old. This is followed by the section entitled "It Was a Strange Winter," which opens with Freeman's comment: "It was at this time that my father began to encourage me to learn the Cree Indian language" (75). The importance of learning Cree becomes clear when winter approaches and Freeman's family stays behind "right amongst the Indians" (75) in Old Factory River, where her father works for the Hudson's Bay Company store, while the other Inuit families leave for their traditional wintering site on Cape Hope Island.

The beginnings of this individual life, then, are shaped by a private loss magnified by the early stages of collective displacement. In this, Freeman's autobiography illustrates a convergence that marks many life-narratives of racialized subjects, a convergence that foregrounds the emergence of the subject "at the intersection of a person's subjective memory of trauma and collective remembrance of histories of domination" (Thompson and Tyagi 1996, xii). For Freeman, moreover, these experiences of private and collective loss are inextricably bound up with yet another defining moment, that of reaching outside her native tongue to learn another – an other's – language. This proves a mixed bag of blessings and misgivings: it extends the collective circle (creating new alliances), while irrevocably unsettling the comfort of the familiar. In spring, when the first Inuit families return, young Minnie is filled with joy: "There would be so many to play with in my own language ... It was so good to see familiar faces" (Freeman 1978, 77). But from this moment on in the lives of the individual and the collectivity, longing will always be the complement of being, and (self)estrangement the other face of the familiar.

The convergence of personal loss and collective displacement is resonantly captured by another emblematic textual cluster in the autobiography. Its signifier is a date, the year 1957. In 1957 Freeman turns twenty, and it is in that year, as she informs us in the opening sentences of her autobiography, that she comes to Ottawa as a translator for the federal government; this, then, is literally where the narrative begins. We do not learn the full significance of this date, however, until the autobiography's second beginning, in a section entitled "The Story of My People," which opens Part II of the book. Tellingly, Freeman's (1978, 70) account of that history opens not with a birth but a death, the death of her mother's father, "grandfather Weetaltuk," who was the leader of his people on Cape Hope Island for fifty years and who "died in 1957 at the age of ninety-eight." His passing has disastrous consequences for his people, ushering in a new phase of colonization: the group he had led becomes disorganized, no longer capable of fighting "the [qallunaat] intruders who were so anxious to relocate them" (70). The community is moved by the Department of Northern Affairs to Great Whale River, with promises of jobs and better housing – promises that never materialize: "Every able-bodied person from James Bay was set back by this move. They were taken advantage of when their leader died."[10]

Grandfather Weetaltuk's death comes up again twice in the last part of the book, and it does so in a manner that foregrounds the centrality of the event to both the personal story and the historical narrative. In the first episode, the messengers who come bearing news of Weetaltuk's death have also been sent to discuss the marriage arranged, according to custom, at Freeman's birth. Although Freeman has been called home for that purpose (from the hospital in Windsor where she had first been a patient and then a student nurse and translator for other Inuit patients), the marriage never takes place, and she is urged by her grandmother to leave home again. "Home was just Meant to be a Memory" reads the title of this key section, whose significance is further signalled by the fact that, at fourteen pages, it is the longest section in this book comprised mostly of one- to two-page sections. The section suggests that Freeman's exile from her home and land – which will become permanent from this point on – is only partly due to her grandmother's disapproval of the groom-to-be. Much more serious is the threat posed by the void left after the leader's death, leaving the community vulnerable to the *qallunaat's* invasive ways. Freeman interweaves her younger self's musings with factual information about what came to pass:

> I wondered what would happen now to the Cape Hope Islanders. Would they choose another leader or just drift apart? Or would the government move them to another settlement? (The government wasted no time and moved them to Great Whale River. There the group was no more. Such a proud people just mingled in with the other crowds who had to rely on an alien culture for survival). (184)

Grandfather Weetaltuk's death indeed seals Freeman's fate as an exile from her familial and collective home. For a while she works as a babysitter for a family, away from home. She is profoundly unhappy, longing "to go home" (198) and hopeful, when her father comes to visit, that he will take her back with him. Two section titles tell the whole story: "Father, Please Take Me Home" (200), and, when he doesn't, "Father Had His Own Reasons" (200). She is heartbroken when he leaves, and only "years later [finds out] why he did not fight to take me home" (201). The explanation, given as the autobiography is nearing its end, eloquently demonstrates the imbrication of the personal in the collective/historical as it effects a double closure, bringing to a close both Freeman's search for answers to personally compelling questions (why did her grandmother send her away? why didn't her father take her home?) and her quest for the historical truth of her people:

> After grandfather Weetaltuk's death, the James Bay group had no leader, no one who kept them together ... At this time, too, the *qallunaat* from the Department of Northern Affairs were asking the James Bay group to

move to Great Whale River. Father felt at the time that nothing was right at home, there was no solid base. Everything was in upheaval. There was no security left among them, and father did not want me to come home to that. As father put it, "Our home was *nalunartuq*," hard to understand, future unknown, solid security missing. *It was as though my group had dispersed into nothing*, the proud people were no more ... So, father did have reasons for not taking me home. (201; emphasis added)

Although the group might have dispersed into nothing, grandfather Weetaltuk's legacy lives on in his granddaughter's narrative: "Even though I know that the Cape Hope Inuit are no longer there, I still think Weetaltuk lives on" (184). He lives on in her evocations of the language, history, and traditions of her people. He lives on through a resisting memorial discourse that is not static or nostalgic but a dynamic force that effects significant narrative and ideological work.

Grandfather Weetaltuk's Legacy: The Uses of Collective Memory

Freeman ends Part I of the autobiography with a section entitled "The Situation Was Familiar." The situation that has become familiar to her is being manipulated by Ottawa officials and the media. In this episode she is made to pose for a photograph without being asked or informed about its context. Later, she sees her picture in the paper with the caption "Eskimos buying [savings] bonds, keeping up with progress" (65). Freeman writes:

I felt sick. I had no idea what bonds were. My parents had never even heard about them, let alone buy them ... I felt sick because I was being used to show the *qallunaat* in the South how well the Inuit are treated in the North ... *never were there photographs that showed the truth about my people's lives.* (65; emphasis added)

As Heather Henderson (1988, 66) has observed, in her autobiography Freeman "sets out to provide the *qallunaat* in the South with her own true 'photographs' of the Inuit in the North." These textual representations constitute the bulk of Parts II and III – which deal with her life before her arrival in Ottawa – but are also central to her account of her life in Ottawa in Part I.

"To truly heal," writes Mary Carpenter (1997, 226), an Inuvaliut from the Western Arctic, "we must say our truth." Such a saying of personal and collective truths drives Freeman's autoethnographic practice in *Life among the*

Qallunaat. Writing in and of the contact zone, the autoethnographer's interest goes beyond "the retrieval of a repressed dimension of the *private* self" to include the recreation of an indigenous "*collective* identity through the performance of language" (Lionnet 1995, 39). The orientation of such a practice, however, is not towards the production of "authentic" autochthonous representations. Autoethnographic writing, Pratt (1992, 7) writes, is dialogic (and often bilingual), involving "partial collaboration with and appropriation of the idioms" of the dominant colonial culture; it comprises those instances in which "colonized subjects undertake to represent themselves in ways which *engage with* the colonizer's own terms" (7). Engaging both the dominant and indigenous cultures , such writing also *addresses* itself to both, albeit to different ends. As an autoethnographer, then, Freeman is an observer of and commentator on multiple, intersecting, realities: traditional Inuit life, Inuit life in transition, the *qallunaat* experience in the North, the Inuit experience in the South, and *qallunaat* life in the South. Her deployment of a collective memorial discourse – grandfather Weetaltuk's legacy – in turn fulfills multiple functions in her text: creating a complex autobiographical persona; validating an Inuk perspective; preserving a collective culture; and presenting a nuanced and sustained critique of colonial practices and history, with a view to imagining a different future.

A collective memorial discourse plays a central role in the narrative construction of Freeman's character. Remembering how things are, or were, "in my culture" (Freeman 1978, 21), serves, for example, to alleviate the estrangement and isolation that Freeman feels in Ottawa (the subject of the first part of her book). An unsettling first ride on a crowded bus during rush hour becomes more bearable when she conjures up the familiar image of a sled ride: "When I traveled with my family, the sled would not move if it was too full; the dogs could not budge it without help" (25). Invoking the past also assists Freeman in making sense of the unfamiliar present. Confused and almost immobilized by a barrage of rules she encounters at the women's residence and at work – "rules and more rules that made me feel I could not move unless I was told" (17) – she regains agency not through nostalgic or idealizing retrospection but by bringing her knowledge of another culture to bear on the new one. While realizing that "rules are things we Inuit children were never brought up with: we ate when we were hungry, slept when we were tired, came and went with the weather" (17–18), she also recognizes that the traditional way has its own structure and rules: "My culture has rules, too, but I learned them when my bones and brain were soft, so they were easily embedded and put there to stay" (71).

Remembering allows Freeman to draw on the knowledge passed on to her by her people and to use it for survival in the South; this is particularly critical since, as Freeman observes, the *qallunaat* have depended on the Inuit to help them survive in the North but extend no such consideration to Inuit in the South: "The department has taken families out of the North to employ as translators" but gives them no training or assistance in "how to survive in the South" (63). When she finds herself manipulated by officials and the media in Ottawa, Freeman can figure out "the whole set-up because I had grown up with the great politicians of my people and had known, seen and experienced their way of handling the community ... I began to learn that *qallunaat* too had politics" (65).

Remembering also serves to counter one of the greatest threats faced by a colonized people, the danger that their culture and self-knowledge – devalued and dismissed by the dominant power – will dissipate and disappear, to be replaced by internalized colonial constructs. Freeman's experience in Ottawa allows her an insight into the ignorance and arrogance that subtend the colonial project:

> my image of the *qallunaat* collapsed. I used to think they knew everything, were capable of anything, could change all things from bad to good. And most of all, I thought they knew all about the Inuit. All of the *qallunaat* who had come to my land had that attitude. But here all they knew was that it was cold in the North, that Inuit rub noses. (24)

This is an empowering realization for Freeman – one that sustains, in turn, her resisting narrative. Her memorial discourse, a "countermemory" (Thompson 1995, 60), exposes colonial ignorance, its erasure and devaluation of that which it does not understand. Her re-membering – which involves "both the act of memory and the restoration of erased persons and texts [or other cultural practices] as bodies of evidence" (Gilmore 1994, 27) – allows for a sense of individual and collective identity and worth, while also effecting, in the reader, a re-cognition, a different understanding of colonial history.

Freeman (1978, 86) reflects on her grandfather Symma's predictions that "one day our land will be full of *qallunaat*, that no one will know the other, that there will be unrest among the Inuit," and concludes: "Certainly *qallunaat* are becoming many in our land and *the Inuit are losing touch with each other*" (emphasis added). Recalling and recording the ways of her people becomes a way of re-establishing such contact, of preserving the collective self-knowledge of a people whose culture has been an oral one.[11] Remembering in order to counter and challenge colonial devaluation and erasure,

Freeman's narrative addresses both the uninformed *qallunaaq* reader and the Inuk subject who runs the double risk of forgetting and internalizing another's construction of the self. Comparing electricity in the South to the Inuit *"quillik* – the seal oil lamp," Freeman comments: "Though I realize how lucky I am [to have the comfort of electricity], I will never cease to believe that my ancestors were smart and resourceful" (30).

What's in a Name?

Throughout the autobiography, Freeman's extensive use of Inuktitut words, embedded in linguistic and cultural translations/explanations, adds a further dimension to her dual project of producing a postcontact Inuk subjectivity and pursuing a critique of colonial history. The centrality of language to the survival of a people and their culture is a key issue for Inuit and Aboriginal writers. *The Cree Language Is Our Identity* is the telling title of a volume containing the La Ronge Lectures of Sarah Whitecalf, a Cree from the Moosomin Reserve in Saskatchewan. When Freeman meets an Inuk child in a St Boniface, Manitoba, hospital, she observes: "[he had] forgotten his language completely. This was as sad as any illness. How will he communicate with his parents when he goes home?" (45). Emma LaRocque (1993, xv) is clear in her indictment: "The issue is not that Native peoples were ever wordless but that, in Canada, *their words were literally and politically negated*" (emphasis added). In *Geniesh: An Indian Girlhood* Jane Willis (1973) has recorded an experience that has marked many in her generation: on first arriving at the residential school, the Cree children were presented with its rules: "Rule number one … There will be no Cree spoken in this school. Anyone caught speaking it will be severely punished" (46). Not only were Inuit, Indian, and Métis children in residential or public schools not allowed to speak their Native languages, adds LaRocque (1993, xv–xvi), what is less known "are all the ways our words have been usurped, belittled, distorted and blockaded in Canadian culture."

Language figures centrally in Native and Inuit autobiographies, as these narratives articulate both the profound threat to identity posed by the dominant colonial cultures (both English and French) and strategies of linguistic and cultural resistance. Already at Willis's (1973, 46) residential school the children fight back: "This [rule prohibiting use of Cree] was a rule we absolutely refused to follow. By refusing to speak either Cree or English when any of the staff were around, we were able to escape punishment." Autobiographies like An Antane Kapesh's (1976), Jane Willis's, and Freeman's document the ways in which those silenced words have been reclaimed, restored, and revalorized. Their boundary-crossing strategies include the mixing of generic and cultural codes drawn from Aboriginal oral traditions and Western literary forms, the thematization of the experience of living in/between two (or more) languages and cultures, and the use of Aboriginal languages. Willis and Freeman incorporate Cree and Inuktitut, respectively, into their English texts, while the primary language of Kapesh's narrative is Montagnais.[12]

What are the uses of a native tongue? As noted earlier, one of Freeman's primary objectives in *Life among the Qallunaat* is to tell her people's truth – which I understand in the sense of "making of truth rather than its revelation" (Whitlock 2000, 204). A first truth is already signalled by the bilingual title: the life of a people is inextricable from their language(s), and any truthful representation of it has to pass through those idioms.[13] The title also reminds us that naming, of both oneself and the other, figures centrally in processes of colonization and decolonization. As Hertha Dawn Wong (1992, 37) has observed in her study of Native American autobiography, "nothing is so fundamental to self-construction as one's name(s)." Jane Willis uses her Cree name, Geniesh, in the title of her autobiography. Alice French, a Nunatakmuit Inuk, signs both volumes of her autobiography "Alice French" but entitles the first *My Name Is Masak* (1976) and opens the second, *The Restless Nomad* (1992), with these observations:

> In school I was Alice, an Inuit girl being educated. Now, going down the steps with my father, I felt like one who had been lost, having been so long away from home, going back to a way of life I had almost forgotten.
> My name is Masak ... Among my people, the Inuit, our names are very important. Unless you know who you are, or what name you are called, you are displaced and homeless, so it was important that my father call me by name. His mother's name had been Masak also, so *it was reassuring when he called me Masak. I felt as if I was going home.* (French 1992, 1; emphasis added)

Since home is not only the familial home but also the home of one's people, the naming of that collectivity is as fundamental to one's self-construction as is one's proper name. In *Life among the Qallunaat*, Freeman draws on this insight to great rhetorical effect. Two emblematic narratives stand juxtaposed as we open Freeman's book. On the one hand, the hegemonic scripts of the Library of Congress classification, which reads "Eskimos-Canada-Biography," and the Foreword by Alex Stevenson, Former Administrator of the Arctic, who speaks paternalistically of his department's policy "to help the Inuit cope" with change (Freeman 1978, 9). In sharp and ironic contrast stand Freeman's title and her chosen epigraph, a gloss on the word "*qallunaaq* (singular); *qallunaat* (plural): literally 'people who pamper their eyebrows'; possibly an abbreviation of *qallunaaraaluit*: powerful, avaricious, of materialistic habit, people who tamper with nature" (13). It is in the space between these two scripts that Freeman's life and story unfold. In telling that story, she counters colonial interpellation by refusing the "self-recognition" (Gilmore 1994, 20) it seeks to elicit. "Non-recognition," Leigh Gilmore has argued, is a powerful strategy of resistance: the subject can refuse "to speak when spoken to in the language of address" (20). Freeman refuses the colonialist meaning of "Canada" as a benevolent protector, offering instead her view of these invader-settlers as "qallunaat." And she refuses the official interpellation of her as "Eskimo": "To me the word 'Eskimo' means nothing" (88). The word means nothing to her as a self-designation, but it is replete with the meanings of cultural othering: "It is an Indian word – *escheemau* – that the *qallunaat* tried to say at one time. It is a Cree word: *Escee*, sickening, can't stand it; *mau*, human. At first encounter Cree Indians were sickened by the sight of the Inuit eating raw meat" (88). Using the autobiographer's prerogative to have the last word, Freeman quickly adds: "Today, the Inuit still eat raw meat and it's still *yam yam* as far as I am concerned" (88). As a strategy of resistance, moreover, nonrecognition involves not only deconstructing and refusing othering interpellations but also authorizing indigenous self-interpellations. Free-man thus proceeds to address us in her language, explaining: "The Inuit, too, gave themselves an identity ... The Inuit differentiated themselves from the animals of nature, not from other races. *Inuk* means one human; *Inuuk* means two humans; *Inuit* means many humans. Inuk can also mean alive as opposed to dead" (88).

Self-interpellations, Freeman knows, are as much a product of history – and as such *subject to change* – as are the living beings they hail. Concluding her etymological foray into naming, she writes: "Today, of course, the Inuk identifies himself as Inuk, different from any other race he has encountered since the days when just he and the animals of his land lived in the north" (88). One of the great strength of Freeman's narrative lies in her ability to avoid the twin pitfalls of essentializing and othering. As her etymological glosses on the words *Inuk* and *qallunaat* suggest, the intended effect is not to cast the *qallunaaq* as the Inuk's Other but, rather, to foreground the extend to which the *qallunaat's* appearance in the North has had an impact on the Inuit. Her bilingual narrative speaks directly to the condition of post-colonial and heterogeneous societies – societies in which language no longer serves simply as an agent of conservation, entering, instead, into relations of exchange and appropriation, and participating in processes of cultural redefinition and negotiation (Simon 1994, 29).

"Who Am I?"

When Freeman is in the South, her Inuk identity is invisible to the people around her, who project onto her their idea of the Other. She writes with her characteristic cutting humour:

> I have been taken for many nationalities. Some people ask, "what are you?" Some try to guess. Some take a long time to come around to the question. Some open up a subject about their world travel and talk on and on about China. At one time their questions got out of hand. They asked me what I thought of the Vietnam war. I did not know what to say about this because I had never known war. The only enemy we have in the North is the bitter cold winter or some summer weather, which can suddenly turn on us and prevent our fathers from hunting. (Freeman 1978, 62)

Mis-recognition unsettles one's sense of self – Freeman comments, only half in jest, "in fact, I have been taken for one [a Chinese] so often I was beginning to think that I knew them" (48) – but it also lends particular force and vitality to an ongoing interrogation of identity. About half way through the autobiography, Freeman articulates her narrative's most compelling questions: "Who am I? What am I doing here? What will become of me?" (140). Her sense of self-estrangement has many sources. As a young person, she first comes to self-knowledge in the alienating context of the residential school. Moving back and forth between two very different cultures, ways of life, and value systems leaves her with many unanswered questions:

> I felt mixed up. My mind suddenly became aware of me ... When will I need all this that I am learning? Everything that I did seemed to be so childish, and yet grown-up duties that I saw and did seemed to be too much. According to my culture, I was now a woman ... In my culture, at that age of fourteen to sixteen, I was supposed to be married, having learned the skills and endured the duties. But here in school, I was neither a woman nor a child. I was certainly at the *makkuttuk*, the soft age, a teenager's growing pains. (140)

Two key sections in Freeman's book – entitled "Caught between Two Lives" (38) and "I am in the Middle" (52) – address her predicament directly. She is caught between two lives because her world has been irrevocably altered by the *qallunaat's* arrival and because, by the time she arrives in Ottawa at the age of twenty, she has lived in both cultures and is now faced with a difficult choice between the two. "I keep telling myself," Freeman writes, "that I have been born twice, once to grow and *learn* my own culture, and again to *learn qallunaat* culture. Once I was asked which way of life I preferred. I said that I did not really know, and that it would take years to explain my choices and preferences. They both have good and bad, wonderful and sad, easy and hard times" (71; emphasis added).

For Freeman, living outside her culture of birth has defamiliarized the very idea of a culture of one's own; culture, she recognizes, is acculturation, an experience of learning, of immersion and participation in a surrounding environment. Her decision to stay in the South, in her "adopted home" (46), rather than return to her native "land and home" (195), attests to the complex subject position she occupies. To the extent that her decision is in acknowledgment of the colonial dislocation and subsequent disintegration of her people, it is an indictment of the forces that have victimized her and her community. However, by deciding to stay in Ottawa Freeman is also opting for the greater personal freedom that *qallunaat* culture offers, allowing her, with her grandmother's blessing, to avoid an undesirable arranged marriage dictated by traditional Inuit custom. A further blurring of boundaries occurs as we realize that, although in one way Freeman's choice to live in the South means a break with the traditional way of life, in another way it is continuous with the values of that culture. Freeman recalls her father's counsel that one "should have a chance to learn different things and to meet different people" (39).

Caught between two lives, Freeman's response is *not* to choose one life over another but "to be two people" (39): to enjoy the "freedom" and "private life" (39) the South offers, and when at home among her people, "[to] involve myself in other chores and mind my elders" (40). Her decision is in recognition of who she has *become*; with every new thing learned, she writes, "I felt a little change in me" (27). When she meets another Inuk in Ottawa, for example, she is so happy to see him "not only because he was Inuk but because he knew Inuk ways. His reawakening of the Inuit in me made me realize how alone I was" (29). But it also makes her realize that her "'Inukism' was slowly disappearing, being buried deeper and deeper" (29). More than anything, Freeman's experience across cultures makes her realize that an identity is not an innate quality. As a translator, she knows that words are inextricable from particular experiences and perceptions, but she also knows that they are objects of exchange. As a translator, she studies the people around her (52) with the same attentiveness she applies to words, recognizing in them the same relational, context-bound, and potentially migratory qualities exhibited by language.[14]

The work of translation, Sherry Simon (1996, 167) writes, "at once elicits and confuses the link between self and community, recognition and estrangement." Sameness and difference, Freeman realizes, appear in complex combinations and permutations. Travelling across Canada as a translator for the government, she meets other Inuit who are "strange to me and I was strange to them," but with whom she shares a common predicament of being "in the middle" (Freeman 1978, 52). In the section entitled "I Am in the Middle," only the first paragraph deals with Freeman's situation; the rest of this longer section details the multiple positioning of others. Freeman realizes that there is more than one way of being "in the middle" and that such a condition could be experienced in its multiple inflections by a single individual. Her own experience, she notes, helps her recognize others in similar situations: "Being in the middle I also studied the young women in the North," finding that the Inuk woman "is also in the middle, between the Inuk man and the qallunaaq man" (56). While the Inuk man notices "what she can do and not what she looks like" (56), the *qallunaaq* man seduces her with flattery and drinks. The tragic aftermath is sadly predictable: pregnancy, venereal disease, rejection by the *qallunaaq* man, rejection by the Inuk man, "suffering in her mind" (57). The Inuk man, too, is caught in the middle, "caught between his desire to go hunting and the demands of the clock" and waged work (52). Here, too, the consequences are disastrous: debt, loss of traditional hunting skills, drinking and gambling, marital breakdown.

Not only the Inuit, but also "the *qallunaat* in the North" are "in the middle, between their jobs in the North and their authorities in the South" (53). Freeman's view of identity as positional and contingent allows her to perceive structural similarities across lines of gender, "ethnic" origin, and power. *Qallunaat* in the North come to understand how "the Inuk lives," understand the "full meaning of his language," and see their common humanity: "To him the Inuit are human after all" (55). Faced with his Southern bosses' "big plans" (55) of expansion and exploitation, however, the *qallunaaq* living in the North wants to speak out but worries that what he says "will affect his job which he cannot afford to lose ... No matter how he feels and how much he understands the Inuk way, he chooses to be quiet and to sit back and listen. *He is now Inuit*" (56; emphasis added). "Qallunaaq" and "Inuk" thus assume a provisional sense – which exists *alongside* the historical determination – a sense that attaches itself not to origins but to one's familiarity with a social world and one's position within it. As a subject living "in the middle," Freeman recognizes that it is not the solidity but the precariousness and multifariousness of identity that are the more common experiences, and properly so. She reports a telling exchange with a woman who had followed her son, the school principal of the residential school, from England: "'I left my old home, all my friends, so I am a stranger here,' she said. 'At least you are at home,' she commented. I told her that I was not really home either. I tried to tell her where my home was, but she had no idea" (210). This is perhaps the ultimate estrangement: to be among people for whom your home does not even exist as an idea.

A postcontact reality, Freeman suggests, is one in which the subject is always-also a stranger among strangers. But her perspective is also a profoundly critical and political one: "Stranger; how odd is the meaning of that word and yet that is what I was in my own country" (21). When a piano teacher insults her with offensive comments about ungrateful "natives," she responds with clearly directed anger: "For the first time, I felt a hint of hate growing inside me; I did not have to take this stranger's attitudes in my land and home" (195). An episode towards the end of the book captures this subject position. On her first day as supervisor at the school she used to attend, Freeman enters the playroom, and "the noise of many languages came to my ears. Some were speaking their own Indian language and some, English" (212). While her non-Native colleagues doubt her ability to deal with the students and are surprised at her success, Freeman knows differently:

They didn't realize that I had some advantages over them. I spoke four languages, two of which all the children understood. I also knew some of the girls' parents, some of their sisters and brothers had gone to this same school with me. I said nothing, and I had no time to explain long stories. *They had no time to listen either.* They never realized that *they were strangers more than I.* Some were from England, from Scotland, from Toronto, from Woodstock, Ontario, and even one from the United States. (215; emphasis added)

Freeman uses her autobiographical narrative to give voice to that silenced self, to make those who could never find the time take notice and listen. And she does so through a form of writing that "challenges its own indigenous, conventional models as well as the dominant structures and institutions of the colonizer" (Mehrez 1991, 259).

Grandmother's Legacy: "One Can't Plan to Stay the Same Forever"

The subject Freeman constitutes through her autobiographical narrative is not only a multiple but also a changing one. Affectively, it is a subject who has known loss, loneliness, and longing. One of the first sections of the book is entitled "Many Reasons for Loneliness" (Freeman 1978, 22), and Freeman's parting words are: "I miss my dear people" (217). The sense of being alone, however, is ultimately mitigated by the recognition of others who similarly live "in the middle." And longing is never a nostalgic desire for a return to the unchanged landscape of the past; rather, it often serves the narrative function of an active re-membering, of contesting and disrupting colonial dismemberment. In one example, Freeman, seeking refuge from the alien urban landscape, finds a place behind Parliament Hill, near the water: "There all the memories of home would come to mind" (26). Although tears are shed, the moment leads not to the past but to the present, and to a critique of colonial arrogance and self-deception: "I would wonder why *qallunaat* stressed to Inuit people that they keep their houses clean, when the water right in their backyard looked so filthy" (26). As Singh, Skerrett, and Hogan (1994, 17) argue, memory – both collective and individual – "is a function, not an entity." It can be a function, moreover, in the service of change; in memorial narratives, writers explore "how individual memory is inseparable from collective memory, which is *continually subject to change*" (vii; emphasis added). Memorial narratives, particularly by ethnic and postcolonial subjects, seek not only to document but, indeed, to effect change; their interrogations of public memory "are a reminder that all memories – individual, family, ethnic, or racial – are socially constructed and allow for their reconstruction in *narratives in quest of change* and new meaning. Narrative recollects in its aspiration to a new 'story,' a new history" (vii; emphasis added).

Significantly, the two sections that address Freeman's crucial decision to effect change in her life by staying in the South – sections that are symmetrically positioned at either end of the autobiography – also foreground change as a vital force in the lives of individuals and the community. The world described in "Caught between Two Lives" (Freeman 1978, 38–40) and "Home Was Just Meant to Be a Memory" (180–93) is a world in which little stays the same: when a prearranged match turns out to be undesirable, new plans have to be made; when the community finds itself leaderless and vulnerable to colonial manipulation, new strategies of survival are devised. Such change, however, does not have to entail individual or collective disintegration. On the contrary, the inevitability of change and its regenerative potential are taken by Freeman's grandmother to be the cornerstones of life. When Freeman is harassed by a jealous *qallunaaq* wife who wrongly accuses her of having an affair with her part-Native husband, Freeman decides to leave the family (with whom she had been staying as live-in help), recalling the wise counsel of the woman who raised her: "like grandmother always said, some things don't stay the same forever, and one can't plan to stay the same forever. Grandmother was always right when it came to human nature" (208).[15]

With grandmother's evocation of "human nature" we've come full circle: to the here and now, to Suleiman's basketfuls of identity eggs, to Freeman's multiple signature in the essay from which I quoted at the opening of this chapter. In that essay-letter to "Dear Leaders of the World" concerning the lessons of the Gulf War, Freeman (1993, 189) calls upon them to "lead us into a peaceful world" by recognizing that boundaries are more permeable than the identity "purists" would have us believe and that our very survival depends on people from different cultures "meet[ing] half way." Such a meeting half way would take place at the half way, in the middle, in the place of translation where differences can speak to each other in the idiom of a shared humanity. At the conclusion of *Life among the Qallunaat*, Freeman (1978, 194) reflects: "[the *qallunaat*] always wanted me to be different, a novelty, and they refused to see that I was a plain human being with feelings, aches, pain, joy, happiness, gratitude, and all the other things that every other being was capable of having." Freeman's essay-letter makes it clear that finding such a meeting-ground is every individual's responsibility. She signs the letter "Minnie Aodla Freeman, an Inuit first, very Canadian, and most of all a woman who cares about what's happening in the world" (Freeman, 1993, 189). The signature suggests a view of identity premised on three epistemological and ethical imperatives: a recognition of the plurality of identity; a rejection of a hierarchy of identities (as "Inuit," "Canadian," "woman," "citizen of the world," all receive an equally strong emphasis: "first," "very," "most of all"); and a conviction that, since "everything is inter-connected" (188), caring about the well-being of others is fundamental to selfhood. Difference, Freeman's signature suggests, is not identity's Other but one of its vital signs.

Such a commitment to thinking through and sustaining difference, Diana Brydon (1995, 16) has proposed, is one way of imagining the community that is Canada, a community attentive to "the differences that make Canada Canada, *and* the differences that continue to challenge that national formation of an immigrant, capitalist culture on usurped land." If our worst fears – that the "all-too-familiar tank is moving in from the horizon"

(Lecker 1996, 51) – are to be averted, here as elsewhere, it will have to be through political action premised on a more paradoxical, less binary, conception of identity. Many today are writing in an attempt to articulate such a vision in terms that are both global (in the idiom of human rights, for example) and specific to a place and the histories that constitute it. Jean Bethke Elshtain (1993, 171) speaks of a "politics *sans* sovereignty," a vision she finds articulated by Central European leaders like Adam Micknik and Vaclav Havel, one that is premised on a view of identity as "an on-going, lifelong process of becoming," and grounded in principles of human rights and an ethic of responsibility and accountability to others. Such an understanding regards difference as an inflection of the human, but it also reserves the right to judge, for all is not always well: "What we require is a complex moral universe, a world of ... particular ties *and* universal aspirations" (173). Brydon (1991, 196) similarly writes of a search for a new globalism that "simultaneously asserts local independence and global interdependencies," and seeks to define differences in ways that "do not depend on myths of cultural purity or authenticity but that thrive on an interaction that 'contaminates' without homogenising." Here and now I take comfort in these voices and, closer to home, in the thousand signatures endorsing a very different kind of declaration that reads, in part: "Nous rejetons tout nationalisme qui fait la promotion d'une identité fondeé sur l'ethnicité. Nous [toutes et tous] ... partageons une meme patrimoine de droits et de responsabilités" ("Nous sommes toutes et tous Québécoises et Québécois," *Le Devoir*, 16 January 2001, A2). A *patrimoine* imagined in the idioms of rights and responsibilities, of democratic principles and civic solidarity, is a fine heritage indeed to carry into the future. Here or anywhere.

Notes

1 "cette terre bat en français et que cette pulsation signifie autant que les saisons qui la régissent, que les vents qui la plient, que les gens qui la façonnent" (Québec 1995, 8).

2 "At the dawn of the 17th century, the pioneers of what would become a nation and then a people rooted themselves in the soil of Québec. Having come from a great civilization, they were enriched by that of the First Nations, they forged new alliances, and maintained the heritage of France" (Québec 1995, 8).

   The French text reads: "À l'aube du XVIIe siècle, les pionniers de ce qui allait devenir une nation, puis un peuple, se sont implantés en terre québécoise. Venus d'une grande civilisation, enrichis par celle des Premières Nations, ils ont tissé des solidarités nouvelles et maintenu l'héritage français" (Québec 1995, 8).

3 "Notre langue scande nos amours, nos croyances et nos rêves pour cette terre et pour ce pays. Afin que le profond sentiment d'appartenance à un peuple distinct

demeure à jamais le rempart de notre identité, nous proclamons notre volonté de vivre dans une société de langue française" (Québec 1995, 10).

4 The *Declaration* appeals: "The time has come to reap the fields of history. The time has come at last to harvest what has been sown for us by four hundred years of men and women of courage, rooted in the soil and now returned to it" (Québec 1995, 7). A direct challenge to this version of history can be found in the words of Alanis Obomsawin, Abenaki filmmaker, singer, and poet from Quebec. Talking about the purpose of her films, she explains: "The basic purpose is for our people to have a voice ... We cannot do this without going through the past, and watching ourselves and analyzing ourselves, because we're carrying a pain that is 400 years old. We don't carry just our everyday pain. We're carrying the pain of our fathers, our mothers, our grandfathers, our grandmothers - *it's part of this land*" (qtd. in LaRocque 1993, xxvi–xxvii, emphasis added).

5 A similar internal tension is evident in former Québec premier ministre Lucien Bouchard's (2001) resignation speech (11 January 2001). On the one hand, there is Bouchard's characterization of himself as accountable to all Quebecers, and his affirmation of the democratic principles of *l'État québécois* in the spirit of "générosité et d'ouvertures à toutes a à tous, sans égard à leur origine ethnique et culturelle" (1). On the other hand, we find Bouchard's reiteration of his mission, as leader of the PQ, to bring about Québec's souvereignty – clearly not the wish of *all* Quebecers – a national project conceived and advanced not in the name of the aforementioned ethnic and cultural diversity of the citizenry but, rather, to respond to what are seen as the aspiration of "le peuple québécois" (2).

6 My use of the term draws on a modified understanding of Althusser's (1971, 176) view of the individual subject as pre-appointed by "ideological configuration[s]." Recent theorizations recognize that the sites of identity formation and self-representation are multiple and changing, and that there exists a dynamic relationship between ideology and agency, dominance and resistance. Theorists of autobiography have elaborated a view of the subject as a "site of excessive and oppositional solicitations and markings" (Gilmore 1994, 20), as occupying shifting positions within the grid of assigned or interpellated identities, and moving "within and against the rules" (S. Smith 1991, 189). In such a view, subjects are participatory agents in institutions and discourses of powers, and thus potentially capable of mediating, contesting, and transforming those systems (Gagnier 1991, 10–11). Identities, Himani Bannerji (1995, 28) has written, are constructed within a given "history and social organization of ruling" but can also be "deconstruct[ed] and reconstruct[ed] in an oppositional context."

7 Given the tone and subject-matter of the autobiography, it is not surprising that non-Inuit readers have felt compelled to reflect on their own position and implication in this power dynamics. In some instances, however, the discussion betrays the very problems the critic tries to address. Margaret Harry's (1985, 149) essay, for example, starts out bemoaning the lack of interest in reading and publishing Aboriginal writing in Canada – which she attributes to ignorance and stereotyping – but then proceeds to legitimate the Southern reader's discomfort with Freeman's choice of "techniques of Inuit narrative rather than those of the dominant culture." Harry even goes so far as to suggest that "Indian and Inuit autobiographies be written to conform to white literary conventions" (150)! Robin McGrath (1997, 229) acknowledges that the non-Inuit reader's lack of familiarity with the culture might make it

difficult to recognize certain patterns, but she still finds fault with the autobiography for becoming too abstract and "disconnected from the foreground of dates, places, events and people that we usually associate with biography or autobiography."

Julia Emberely's suggestive reading of a passage from Freeman's autobiography presents other difficulties. Emberely chooses to conclude *Thresholds of Difference* with a reading of a section from the autobiography entitled "Silly Cry." In it Freeman recalls the time she was reduced to tears and silence by her *qallunaaq* roommate's insistence that she wear the baby-doll pajamas Freeman received as a gift and had been keeping in a drawer. The roommate finds Freeman's behaviour incomprehensible and accuses her of failing to show appreciation for the girl who had given them to her. While the young Freeman could only respond with tears and silence to her roommate's barrage of questions and exclamations, Freeman the autobiographer not only voices the "unsayable" but, indeed, reverses "the investigator/investigated relation of exchange between herself and a *qallunaat* woman" (Emberely 1993, 169). Re-enacting that scene for the *qallunaaq* reader, Freeman sets the record straight: explaining her response at the time, pointing out her *qallunaaq* friend's ethnocentric blindness, and reaffirming her right to live by her values and beliefs. While Emberley perceptively argues that Freeman's text "describes its own silencing" (152), her interpretive practice enacts its own kind of silencing. Ultimately, Emberely is less interested in Freeman as a subject than as one subjected and contained by an "Inuit gender formation" (167); less interested in Freeman's representation of "the unspeakable knowledge of the investigated subject" (168) – for which Emberely would have had to engage with the rest of the autobiography – and more concerned with registering her discomfort with "Freeman's moralism" (168), concluding that Freeman "writes in a narrative and technological form the limits of what she can say given the gender containment to which she is subject" (169).

8 As Sherry Simon (1994, 27) has observed in *Les trafic des langues*: "The transgressive potential of the plurilingual text lies in its contestation of national and cultural boundaries, its foregrounding and interrogation of one's relation to the collectivity and to collective identities" (my translation).

9 Such an approach appears to me misguided in several respects: it betrays a reductive reading of Freeman's complex text; it displays an ethnocentrically and historically limited view of the genre; and it ignores the rich traditions that inform contemporary native expression. As Hertha Dawn Wong concludes in her study of tradition and innovation in Native American autobiography, "Speaking one's life is not a new phenomenon; people have been speaking their lives since they discovered their voices, themselves, and their communities" (20).

10 On Inuit relocation in the Eastern Arctic, see Tester and Kulchyski (1994).

11 This is a sentiment often expressed by Inuit and Native writers and artists. In *Inuit Women Artists: Voices from Cape Dorset*, a volume that brings together artwork and personal narratives by Inuit women artists, Pitaloosie Saila (1994, 164–5) concludes a text she entitles "What I Remember" with these words: "The drawings I do are my heritage to my children, my grandchildren and future generations. I draw what I have seen or heard; I draw about my life. I draw so the Inuit traditional way of life can be preserved on paper, and it is only when I draw that it will be shown." In her introduction to *Inuit Women Artists*, Freeman (1994, 17) reiterates this point: "Both Inuit and *qallunaat* alike should speak of them [the Inuit women artists] more often and should talk about their names and works. As we look into the future, not many people will have seen all the traditional scenes that these women hold in their

minds ... It is because these artists have seen and felt and lived these experiences that they are so good at their art. They have handled the equipment traditionally used for making the Inuit way of life comfortable. They carry in them the very survival techniques that have brought them to this day."

12 The publishing history of Kapesh's text, however, raises troubling issues. The autobiography first came out in a bilingual Montagnais-French edition published by Leméac in Ottawa. Sadly, it was superseded in 1982 by a unilingual French edition published by Éditions Des femmes in Paris (as compelling a case as any for the need to decolonize feminist practices). The violence of this editorial decision is all the more inexcusable given the utmost importance that Kapesh attaches to her language. Her very opening words are: "Dans mon livre, il n'y a pas de parole de Blanc" [in my book, you will not find the White man's words]!

13 A helpful study of postcolonial writers' use of European and indigenous languages is Zabus (1991).

14 My understanding of the significations that cluster around the figure of the translator in Freeman's text is thus different from Henderson's (1988, 68) reading of Freeman's character as "condemned to remain on the border between two worlds" and as embodying "the schizophrenic split between Inuit and *qallunaat*, North and South, past and present."

15 Freeman echoes this conviction – a conviction that has perhaps been her most valuable strategy of survival – in her dedication. Dedicating the autobiography to her family, Freeman passes on to them the wisdom of a people who have prevailed: "Teach, learn, care and love while you can / for nothing ever stays the same."

Works Cited

Althusser, Louis. 1971. "Ideology and Ideological State Apparatuses: Notes towards an Investigation." In *Lenin and Philosophy*. Trans. Ben Brewster, 127–85. New York and London: Monthly Review Press.

Appiah, Anthony K. 1996. "Introduction." In *The Seductions of Biography*, ed. Mary Rhiel and David Suchoff, 9–11. New York: Routledge.

Bannerji, Himani. 1995. *Thinking Through: Essays on Feminism, Marxism, and Anti-Racism*. Toronto: Women's Press.

Bergland, Betty. 1994. "Postmodernism and the Autobiographical Subject: Reconstructing the 'Other.'" In *Autobiography and Postmodernism*, ed. Kathleen Ashley, Leigh Gilmore, Gerald Peters, 130–66. University of Massachusetts Press.

Bouchard, Lucien. 2001. "Allocution á l'occasion de la démission du premier ministre de Québéc." http.//www.premier.gouv.qc.ca/premier_ministre/ (Site officiel du premier ministre du Québéc). 11 January.

Brydon, Diana. 1991. "The White Inuit Speaks: Contamination as Literary Strategy." In *Past the Last Post: Theorizing Post-Colonialism and Post-Modernism*, ed. Ian Adams and Helen Tiffin, 191–203. New York: Harvest Wheatsheaf.

– 1995. "Introduction: Reading Postcoloniality, Reading Canada." *Essays on Canadian Writing* 56 (Fall): 1–19.

Carpenter, Mary. 1997. "Stories: 'Skeleton Woman,' 'Woman of the Sea.'" In *Echoing Silence: Essays on Arctic Narrative*, ed. John Moss, 225–30. Ottawa: University of Ottawa Press.

"La citoyenneté Québécoise: document de consultation pour le forum national sur la citoyenneté et l'integration." <http://pages.infinit.net/andreroy/Forum_citoyen_consultation.pdf>.

Eller, Jack David. 1999.*From Culture to Ethnicity to Conflict: An Anthropological Perspective on International Ethnic Conflict.* Ann Arbor: University of Michigan Press.

Elshtain, Jean Bethke. 1993. "Sovereignty, Identity, Sacrifice.*"* In *Reimagining the Nation,* ed. Marjorie Ringrose and Adam J. Lerner, 159–75. Buckingham: Open University Press.

Emberley, Julia. 1993. *Thresholds of Difference: Feminist Critique, Native Women's Writing, Postcolonial Theory.* Toronto: University of Toronto Press.

Freeman, Minnie Aodla. 1978. *Life among the Qallunaat.* Edmonton: Hurtig Publishers.

– 1993. "Dear Leaders of the World." In *Sharing our Experience,* ed. Arun Mukherjee, 186–9. Ottawa: Canadian Advisory Council on the Status of Women.

– 1994. "Introduction." In *Inuit Women Artists: Voices from Cape Dorset,* ed. Odette, Leroux, Marion E. Jackson, and Minnie Aodla Freeman, 14–17. Vancouver: Douglas and McIntyre (for The Canadian Museum of Civilization).

French, Alice. 1976. *My Name is Masak.* Winnipeg: Feguis.

– 1992. *The Restless Nomad.* Winnipeg: Pemmican.

Gagnier, Regenia. 1991. *Subjectivities: A History of Self-Representation in Britain, 1832–1920.* New York: Oxford University Press.

Gilmore, Leigh. 1994. *Autobiographics: A Feminist Theory of Women's Self-Representation.* Ithaca and London: Cornell University Press.

Gunn, Janet Varner. 1992. "A Politics of Experience: Leila Khaled's *My People Shall Live: The Autobiography of a Revolutionary."* In *De/Colonizing the Subject: The Politics of Gender in Women's Autobiography,* ed. Sidonie Smith and Julia Watson, 65–80. Minneapolis: University of Minnesota Press.

Handler, Richard. 1988. *Nationalism and the Politics of Culture in Quebec.* Madison: University of Wisconsin Press.

Harry, Margaret. 1985. "Literature in English by Native Canadians (Indians and Inuit)." *Studies in Canadian Literature* 10(1–2): 146–53.

Henderson, Heather. 1988. "North and South: Autobiography and the Problems of Translation." In *Reflections: Autobiography and Canadian Literature,* ed. K.O. Stich, 61–8. Ottawa: University of Ottawa Press.

Kapesh, An Antane/André, Anne. 1976. *Je suis une maudite sauvagesse: Eukuan nin matshimanitu innu-iskueu.* Trans. from the Montagnais by José Mailhot in collaboration with Anne-Marie André and André Mailhot. Ottawa: Leméac.

LaRocque, Emma. 1993. "Preface or Here Are Our Voices – Who Will Hear." In *Writing the Circle: Native Women of Western Canada,* ed. Jeanne Perreault and Sylvia Vance, xv–xxx. Edmonton: NeWest.

Lecker, Robert. 1996. "The Writing's on the Wall." *Saturday Night,* July/August, 15–25, 51.

Lionnet, Françoise. 1995. *Postcolonial Representations: Women, Literature, Identity.* Ithaca and London: Cornell University Press.

Maracle, Lee. 1992. "The 'Post-Colonial' Imagination." *Fuse,* 16 (1): 12–15.

McGrath, Robin. 1997. "Circumventing the Taboos: Inuit Women's Autobiographies." In *Undisciplined Women: Tradition and Culture in Canada,* ed. Pauline Greenhill and Diane Tye, 223–33. Montreal: McGill-Queen's University Press.

Mehrez, Samia. 1991. "The Subversive Poetics of Radical Bilingualism: Postcolonial Francophone North African Literature." In *The Bounds of Race: Perspectives on Hegemony and Resistance,* ed. Dominick LaCapra, 255–77. Ithaca and London: Cornell University Press.

Pratt, Mary Louise. 1992. *Imperial Eyes: Travel Writing and Transculturation.* London: Routledge.

Probyn. Elspeth. 1994. *"Love in a Cold Climate": Queer Belongings in Québec.* Montreal: Concordia University GRECC.

Québec, gouvernement du. 1995. *Déclaration de souveraineté.* In *Projet de loi sur l'avenir du Québec, incluant la déclaration de souveraineté et l'entente du 12 Juin 1995.* Québec: Éditeur officiel du Québec.

Québec, government of. 1995. *Declaration of Sovereignty.* In *Bill Respecting the Future of Quebec, including The Declaration of Sovereignty and the Agreement of June 12, 1995.* Québec: Québec Official Publisher.

Saila, Pitaloosie. 1994. "What I Remember." In *Inuit Women Artists: Voices from Cape Dorset,* eds. Odette Leroux, Marion E. Jackson, and Minnie Aodla Freeman, 161–5. Vancouver: Douglas & McIntyre.

Simon, Sherry. 1994. *Le Trafic des langues: Traduction et culture dans la littérature québécoise.* Montréal: Boréal.

– 1996. *Gender in Translation: Cultural Identity and the Politics of Transmission.* London: Routledge.

Singh Amritjit, Joseph T. Skerrett, Jr., Robert E. Hogan. 1994. "Introduction." *Memory, Narrative, and Identity: New Essays in Ethnic American Literatures.* Boston: Northeastern University Press. 3–25.

Smith, Anthony. 1993. "The Nation: Invented, Imagined, Reconstructed?" In *Reimagining the Nation,* ed. Marjorie Ringrose and Adam J. Lerner, 9–28. Buckingham: Open University Press.

Smith, Sidonie. 1991. "The Autobiographical Manifesto: Identities, Temporalities, Politics." In *Autobiography and Questions of Gender,* ed. Shirley Neuman, 186–212. London: Frank Cass.

Spivak, Gayatri Chakravorty. 1990. "Questions of Multi-Culturalism." In *The Post-Colonial Critic: Interviews, Strategies, Dialogues,* ed. Sarah Harasym, 59–66. New York and London: Routledge.

Suleiman, Susan Rubin. 1994. *Risking Who One Is: Encounters with Contemporary Art and Literature.* Cambridge, MA: Harvard University Press.

Tester, Frank James, and Peter Kulchyski. 1994. *Tammarniit (Mistakes): Inuit Relocation in the Eastern Arctic, 1939–63.* Vancouver: UBC Press.

Thompson, Becky, and Sangeeta Tyagi. 1996."Introduction: Storytelling as Social Conscience – The Power of Autobiography." In *Names We Call Home: Autobiography on Racial Identity,* ed. Becky Thompson and Sangeeta Tyagi, ix–xvii. New York: Routledge.

Thompson, Dawn. 1995. "Technologies of Ethnicity." *Essays on Canadian Writing* 57 (Winter): 51–69.

Whitlock, Gillian. 2000. *The Intimate Empire: Reading Women's Autobiography.* London: Cassell.

Willis, Jane. 1973. *Geniesh: An Indian Girlhood.* Toronto: New Press.

Wong, Hertha Dawn. 1992. *Sending My Heart Back across the Years: Tradition and Innovation in Native American Autobiography.* New York/Oxford: Oxford University Press.

Zabus, Chantal, 1991. *The African Palimpsest: Indigenization of Language in the West African Europhone Novel.* Amsterdam: Rodopi.

"A Network of Relations": Ethical Interdependence in Bronwen Wallace's Talking Lyric

BRENDA CARR VELLINO

> From as early as I can remember it was my grandmother, my aunt, my girl friends, my women friends, female teachers and mentors who spoke the world for me ... When my grandmother demanded to know the last name of any of my friends, when she located that friend within her matrix of who married who etc. ... she was celebrating a network of relationships which constituted her world ... the essence of my narrative style – has come from these women's lives and the stories they told. What I try to do is to recreate their voices, their view of things, their way of telling a story.
>
> B. Wallace, *Two Women Talking*
> In memoriam: 1945–1989

At the heart of Bronwen Wallace's poetics is a profound sense of the way our lives take shape in narrative relation to other people's stories and their reciprocal responses to ours. As a result, she developed a poetic voice that was immediate, down-to-earth, and always caught in the act of offering up a good story. Her distinctive gesture is the direct address of the talking lyric, calling a community of readers into narrative filiation and response-ability. Significantly, she attributes her talking lyric to forms that, for her, constitute female popular knowledge and culture – gossip and storytelling.[1] In a number of essays and interviews, Wallace frequently honours a genealogy of female and familial storytellers that produced in her an aesthetic that uncloses the bounded lyric form – the Keatsian and New Critical well-wrought urn – opening it to myriad collaborative voices. She recounts the way her narrative poetics developed around the kitchen sink with her multigenerational womenfolk and around the kitchen table with her working-class menfolk (Wallace 1992, 173–6). Two overlapping communities of gender and class, then, inform the ideological horizon of her poetic practice. A third significant community of filiation is ecological, that of the earth itself. The speaking subject of her poems comes to being in webbed communities – fragile, contingent, and interdependent.

Such a relational conception of the human offers the grounds for an ethical subjectivity – accountable for and responsible to the other's well-being, both human and non-human. Wallace's longstanding experience in female and feminist communities such as Kingston's first-stage Interval House for women and children at risk from domestic violence, provides a context for her wider ethical engagement.[2] Perhaps because women's social experience has been lived out through the legal, medical, economic, cultural, and domestic construction of their bodies, "the body" and its inscription is central to any feminist theorizing. Wallace is no exception. Her relational subject is an explicitly embodied and embedded subject who seeks accountability to her own particular history as it intersects the embodied histories of those she encounters. From her deep attentiveness to the vulnerable body, which we share with others, grows Wallace's ethical engagement with the body's world.

In the discussion that follows, I draw upon poems from Wallace's last two volumes – *The Stubborn Particulars of Grace* (1987) and *Keep That Candle Burning Bright* (1991) – to develop my claim that she makes an important intervention into the self-enclosed traditional lyric through fashioning a talking, embodied, communal, and popularized lyric. I show how this intersects the larger philosophical project of refashioning the individualist subject of Western public discourses. Through an extended close-reading of a suite of poems testifying to her experience as a social worker at Kingston's Interval House, I explore the ethical possibilities of a relationally constructed and embodied poetics. Following this, I engage the way she expands upon Flannery O'Connor's maxim that "possibility and limitation mean about the same thing" to offer a poetics and ethics of limitations.

Wallace's relational subject is resonant with the refashioned self called for by recent moral philosophers and ethicists (such as Alasdair MacIntyre, Paul Ricouer, and Emmanuel Levinas) as well as that conceptualized by ecologists like Gary Snyder. In the cultural realm, numerous statements of poetics by female, environmentalist, and minority poets reflect the urgent need to rethink the lyric as a form that can carry the weighted questions of social embodiment and historical accountability. An alternative lyric modality simultaneously requires new poetics and revisionist models of human subjectivity informed by, but not subordinated to, postmodernist critique.

Attentive to the "interbeing" of life-forms (Nhat Hanh 1991, 96), human subjects, poet, and readers, Wallace's relational subject finds a formal analogue in her hybrid lyric form, which weaves literary, visual, musical, and documentary media together to break down hierarchical categories of elite and popular culture.[3] By invoking a range of intertexts and forms from celebrated photographs of the contemporary grotesque by Diane Arbus to short stories by American writer Flannery O'Connor; from the music of Joni Mitchell, Ferron, and

Emmy Lou Harris to that of Elvis, Bob Dylan, Van Morrison, the Beatles, and the Talking Heads; from Marxism, grass-roots feminism, anthropology, popular science, and social work to newspaper tabloids, gossip, and womens' conversations, Wallace shows the co-implication of cultural representations and popular media with literary and social discourses. Such a porous weave of discourses opens the lyric to self-reflective engagement with its status as a form subject to historical process and, consequently, to new articulations of ethical subjectivity.

In *Keep That Candle Burning Bright*, a suite of poems dedicated to Emmy Lou Harris, Wallace invokes the popular idiom of country music at the juncture of lyric to further democratize the form, opening up the possibilities of poems as public space. This volume also becomes a site for extending Wallace's (1992, 208) long-standing redeployment of the elegy form to articulate a "feminist way of dying." Finally, while she is often skeptical and provisional about the possibilities of lyric transcendence, she explicitly offers her conversational poems as "small stratagems" (1987, 33), rituals of provisional healing and grace, "speaking to the wounded place in all of us" (1992, 208). Inevitably, such claims necessitate renewed engagement with humanist categories and seeming universals, which she persistently risks. These are questions that are studiously avoided by most of her postmodern academic respondents.4 Rather than dismissing them, I suggest that, in order to negotiate a rapprochement between ethics and postmodernism, we need to revisit the categories and vocabularies of Western political and moral philosophy as these are implicated in literary criticism.5 It is my contention that, through her talking poems, this fierce, gentle, and humble poet from Kingston, Ontario, makes a substantial contribution to our crucial conversations around the subject of ethics and an ethical subject for the late twentieth-century.

Unclosing the Lyric: Towards a Communal Form

A story of yours got this one going,
so I'm sending it back now, changed of course,
just as each person I love
is a relocation, where I take up
a different place in the world.

B. Wallace, "Bones," *Stubborn Particulars*

In "Appeal," and "Benediction," the framing poems for *Stubborn Particulars of Grace*, Bronwen Wallace establishes the primacy of the conversational, storytelling mode to her poetics. The particulars of daily life spun out in gossip and anecdote around her grandmother's Sunday table provide the material and aesthetic ground out of which she writes. If there is a heroic figure and gesture in her poems, it is that of the ordinary storyteller – poet, blood relation, friend, and reader – offering and affirming narrative connection in the twin acts of telling and listening. Wallace's "female narrative form" is constructed by "virtuoso feats of jump-cutting ... digression, interruption, free association, cross-weaving, speculation, re-examination" (Lee 1989, 13). Her talking lyric is driven by an unruly, non-linear, conversational logic of interpolated stories and overlapping plot-lines. As she puts it, "a story of yours got this one going" (Wallace 1987, 80). While this form gives the appearance of spontaneity, like other free verse poems it borrows from the extra-literary mode of everyday conversation to create an artful imitation that serves as a "formal analogue" (Holden 1986, 33). Wallace is not alone in exploring the "contemporary conversation poem" (33); what interests me, however, beyond the fact of such artful spontaneity, which turns on the convention of the speaking voice, are the uses to which Wallace deploys the conversational form.[6]

Jonathon Holden suggests that the conversation poem establishes its moral authority or "ethos of the speaking voice" by the oxymoronic effect of the ordinary poet in the act of brilliant conversation (33–7). I would like to suggest instead that Wallace's genealogical strategy of "evoking other voices," her reconstruction of poetic voice as "only one voice in a huge community" (Wallace 1992, 211), offers a significant intervention into the construction of a solitary speaker and monologic voice associated with the traditional lyric.[7] In her role as columnist for the *Kingston Whig Standard*, Wallace cast her essays, like her poems, in a conversational mode, a matrix for understanding the writer-reader transaction as an exchange of mutually implicated and communally defined knowledges: "Writing this column has also helped me to appreciate how much my readers' response contributes to my work, how much I use what people tell me about a poem or a column in writing the next one ... The conversation expands, grows more complex. It could go on for quite a while" (201). In her theory of poetry as a conversational transaction, she joins a chorus of poets and lyric theorists who follow Charles Olson's (1985, 606) call to shift poetry away from the "lyrical interference of the individual as ego," which was set forth in his 1950 manifesto "Projective Verse." Recall the conventions once associated with "pure lyric" in the theory and practice of both the Romantics and the New Critics, which include the following: *brevity* and condensation of form; *unity* of vision and form constellated around a single speaker, feeling, image, and/or situation; representation of inner life or *pure subjectivity*; the "cry of the heart" overheard by the invisible reader; *intensity* of emotion and language; a *ritual*, quasi-religious function embodied in the nightingale's pure *song*, producing epiphany-like *insight* into the *transcendent* and sublime; and self-enclosure, *timelessness*, and *universality* of the aesthetic object. Not surprisingly, "pure lyric" is often taken to be the perfect embodiment of the literary and the most typical example of high culture.[8] One only has to consult any literary handbook on "lyric" to confirm that this mode is still accepted wisdom for the teachable poem. However, contemporary theorists, such as those who appear in *Lyric Poetry: Beyond the New Criticism* (1985), have pointed out that such conceptions have, disturbingly, positioned poets as aesthetic escape artists. The equation of lyric with pure transcendence ironically renders poetry socially irrelevant or therapeutic, solely in the personalist mode. This effectively disables poetry for social engagement and intervention (Coniff 1988, 48).[9]

In the wake of the cataclysms of the twentieth century, poets like Dorothy Livesay, Denise Levertov, Adrienne Rich, Gary Snyder, Carolyn Forche, Di Brandt, Dionne Brand, Lillian Allen, and George Elliot Clarke have, with increasing urgency, sought to refashion a popularized poetry of social relevance, a lyric that can carry the weight of the historical, social, and political.[10] Similarly, critics are beginning to offer theories of these new poetic modes, which they are variously calling postmodern lyric, dialogic lyric, radicalized lyric, anti-lyric, collage lyric, intertextual lyric, process lyric, and engaged lyric.[11] Rather than seeing such rearticulations of lyric form as being about the "death of poetry" and the failure of lyric, I suggest that we are witnessing a revitalization of lyric, contingent upon its capacity for the dialogic already implicit in its origins as an embodied form. The somatic register, and indeed the ritual register, of the sung lyric signals a fundamentally social form that invokes a community of listener-participants.[12] For Bronwen Wallace, the revitalization of poetry depends on a renegotiation between poem and world; her talking lyric enacts a deliberate re-placing of the poem in the public sphere, an invocation of diversely webbed communities within the hybrid form of her conversational poetry. In short, Wallace's construction of a talking lyric opens the form to possibilities for intersubjective conversations that are at heart deeply ethical.[13]

Because of its connection to non-literary discourses such as journalism and diverse social idioms or speech genres celebrated in Bakhtin's theory of dialogism (Monroe 1987, 32), the interweaving of narrative into the lyric is celebrated by a number of recent critics as essential to rendering it socially and communally relevant.[14] Susan Stanford Friedman (1994, 15) notes that it has become commonplace among postmodern theorists to critique narrative as "regressive representationalism" invested in the "tyranny of the symbolic order"; however, in concert with her, I suggest that narrative, along with subjectivity, agency, and voice, is a category that needs renewed attention.[15] She reminds us of the "turn to narrative" by many minority women and writers of colour – a move that underscores the important function of narrative as a mode of social knowledge, memory, and testimony. Narrative becomes a central strategy by which new knowledge is created and old knowledge is disrupted or shifted (16–17, 25). Rather than seeing narrative and poetry as discrete genres in binary opposition, as does Jonathon Holden (1986, 38) when he cautions that the conversation poem risks collapsing into the flatness of prose, the prose poem may be seen as a productive site of aesthetic conflicts and negotiations that plays out more broadly based social struggles constellated around class and gender (Munroe 1987, 18). The ideological implications and possibilities of prose are embedded in the history of two of its primary forms; consider the rise of the newspaper and novel which coincided with new communities of bourgeois and women reader and writers (Munroe 22–23). In the prose poem's contradictory self-definition, "it rejects literature's (especially poetry's dream of itself as pure other set apart in sublime isolation ... from the more prosaic struggles of everyday life" (19). Because of its discourse-crossing status, the prose poem offers a special potential for provoking questions that disturb the boundaries between the aesthetic and the socio-political (21). Its dialogic openness to a variety of discourses and forms of elite and popular culture, as well as all registers in between (32), invites access and incites community. In her "Nightwork," for example, Wallace interconnects the work of a snowplow operator, baker, nurse, doctor, burger flipper, and a telephone operator who all constellate in an "imagined community" around a woman in labour.[16]

Significantly, there is a correspondence between Wallace's reconception of a relational lyric subject and refashionings of the individualist subject of the public sphere in Western democracy called for by recent ethicists. The proceedings of the 1984 Stanford University conference entitled *Reconstructing Individualism: Autonomy, Individuality, and the Self in Western Thought* (1986) point out that "unproblematic individualism" has increasingly been questioned by contemporary experience and radical changes in human knowledge. Reciprocally, there is an overlapping array of discourses, disciplines, representational forms, and contexts that are similarly committed to refashioning modes of subjectivity more conducive to just encounters between the self and the other, both human and non-human. These would include political, moral, and environmental philosophy; sociology and psychoanalysis (particularly object-relations theory); eco-feminism; earth-centred spiritual practices, particularly Aboriginal wisdom traditions, "engaged Buddhism" like that practised in Thich Nhat Hanh's "order of interbeing"; and "green" theology such as that articulated by Rosemary Radford Ruether.[17]

Traditionally the terrain of political and moral philosophy, ethics is a discursive field that reintroduces us to questions of moral agency and accountability to justice claims. At the juncture of literature and ethics, questions have typically focused on abstract universal social effects and moral functions such as whether texts demonstrated good or bad moral characters and whether literature somehow improves readers. Not surprisingly, ethical questions fell on hard times with the demise of thematic criticism; however, several special issues, such as *Yale French Studies'* "Literature and the Ethical Question" (1991) and book-length studies by Tobin Siebers (1988), J. Hillis Miller (1987), and Wayne Booth (1988) signal what would seem to be a promising "return of ethics." Claude Nouvet (1991, 2) offers important questions on the conjunction of literature and ethics:

> Firstly, how does ethics come to question literature and literary analysis? Specifically, how, when, and where does ethics intervene ... and become an unavoidable question? Secondly, how do literature and literary analysis come, in turn, to question ethics? And again, specifically, how do literature and literary analysis rethink notions which either ground an ethical discourse or traditionally belong to the field of ethics?

I wish to distinguish my engagement with the ethical question in literature from both Miller's notion of ethical encounters with the textual other, by which he means submission to the heterogenous play of language, and from Wayne Booth's benevolent pluralist model of the ethics of fiction. These concepts, in my view, have a limited capacity to account for the urgent claims of negotiating uneven power relations in our increasingly inequitable world.

In reconsidering the scope of compelling ethical questions for literature, I wish to propose that we first need to consider the traditional circumscription of ethics in the wider discursive field. We need to look more closely at socio-political discourses around atomistic individualism, individual rights, and private morality as well as at legal codes regulating and maintaining an abstract common good that is grounded in a conception of the universal subject. Seyla Benhabib (1987, 81) critiques the abstract, "disembodied," and "generalized" other of moral philosophy, who theoretically stands in for all others but in actuality fails to account for women and other minorities. While Benhabib acknowledges the necessity of generalizable notions of human integrity and worth in ethics and rights discourse, she offers an alternative model of the self as a historically embodied "concrete" other. This is reinforced by her notion of "interactive universalism," which "regards difference as a starting point for reflection and action" and the "moral point of view as a contingent achievement of an interactive form of rationality rather than as a timeless standpoint of legislative reason" (81, 87, 92; Benhabib 1992, 6). In concert with Benhabib, a number of contemporary social theorists and philosophers offer parallel concepts for more just social relations: Alasdair MacIntyre's notion of narrative subjectivity, Paul Ricouer's notion of reciprocal self-esteem and solicitude for the other, and Emmanuel Levinas's notion of the face to face as the paradigmatic ethical encounter.

Alasdair MacIntyre's narrative or relationally constituted self most closely resonates with Wallace's refashioning of poetic subjectivity and voice in the conversational lyric. He suggests that human life unfolds as lived narrative with unpredictable turns, formal constraints, and multiple plot options (MacIntyre 1981, 216). The properties of the narrative mode itself imply two key factors that link narrative to ethics – relationality and accountability. To relate a story is to imply a kinship of listeners; to give an account is to imply accountability and intelligibility:

> I am not only accountable, I am one who asks others for an account, who can put others to the question. I am part of their story, as they are part of mine. The narrative of any one life is part of an interlocking set of narratives ... Without the accountability of the self those trains of events that constitute all but the simplest and barest of narratives could not occur; and without that same accountability narratives would lack that continuity required to make both them and the actions that constitute them intelligible. (218)

For MacIntyre, as for Wallace, narrative is fundamentally a form that enables and enacts community. This further facilitates the conception of a historical, socially embodied, and ethical identity: "I can only answer the question 'What am I to do?' if I answer the prior question 'Of what story or stories do I find myself a part?'" (216, 221, 222).[18] Paralleling MacIntyre's rearticulation of narrative selfhood, Bronwen Wallace opens these questions into the public space of her poems and her newspaper columns in the *Kingston Whig Standard*. As a public intellectual, she contributes to and popularizes the conversations around what constitutes the self in ethical relation; indeed, she constructs her readership as a public, a community of citizens who engage in public debate and have the capacity to exercise public opinion (Habermas 1991, 398–9). Such popularized moral philosophy is crucial for it is in the public domain that the self imagined and upheld by social institutions and popular culture has been most "persistently individualist" (Heller and Wellbery 1986, 12). The normative hero of Western social discourse appears as a key player in interlocking public narratives: "Modern definitions of the self and psychology, of ethical responsibility and civic identity, and of artistic representation and economic behaviour all rest on the notion of an individual whose experience and history, whose will and values, whose expressions and preferences are essential constituents of reality" (1). Through her invention of a talking lyric, Wallace not only offers the possibility of a democratized form but also an ethical one contingent upon a relational and embodied subject.

Testimony at the Interval: "We Are That Close"

> When I write of disrupting or changing history, I begin with the assumption that people can change, that we are not totally determined by, bespoken by the culture in which we live.
>
> Bronwen Wallace, *Two Women Talking*

In what is perhaps her most moving, powerful, and compelling poem – "Intervals" – Bronwen Wallace uses poetic testimony to call her readers into ethical awareness of extreme-limit experiences of domestic abuse. The poet/speaker of "Intervals" echoes, but is not identical with, Wallace's own experience as a worker at Interval House in Kingston, Ontario. Across the five numbered sequences of the poem – "Entry," "Free Speech," "ECU: On the Job," "Short Story," and "Departure" – Wallace modulates between subjects of focalization: the poet/speaker as Interval House worker, the women and children who are survivors of domestic violence, variously (dis)engaged witnesses, and the reader-witnesses. This narrative strategy of multiple focalization, coupled with fluid negotiation between voice registers and first-, second-, and third-person pronouns, effectively constructs a relationally constituted ethical subject.[19] By her direct address to the reader, Wallace takes "us" behind the closed doors of those we see as "them": Her conversational voice draws us to see our complicity with, and our corresponding need to become witnesses against, configurations of power that are tacitly sanctioned by the silences in social memory.

Holocaust survivor Elie Weisel suggests that ours is an era in which we are inventing a new testimonial literature. According to Shoshana Felman, testimony functions to instigate a crisis in public knowledge by bringing formerly occluded extreme-limit experiences to social memory (Felman and Laub 1992, 53–4). These most often include indignities to the human body and integrity of being, such as those witnessed in Holocaust narratives or Latin American *testimonios* like that of Guatemalan writer Rigoberta Menchu.[20] Incest and physical abuse narratives such as those offered in Elly Danica's (1988) *Don't: A Woman's Word* and Bronwen Wallace's "Intervals" sequence expand the horizon of testimony to include explicitly gender-based trauma endured in "private" domestic and family contexts.[21] While testimony theory most frequently addresses those experiences with direct implications for altering the social memory of collective public history (e.g., the Holocaust), women writers frequently follow an axiom of feminist thought that troubles the false distinction between the private and the public spheres. Wallace, herself, actively disrupts the containment of gendered violence in the domestic realm by consistently linking private and public spheres in her poetic testimony. Sequence 1 of "Intervals" probes a map of both the intimate and public spaces of the city – parks, restaurants, and suburban homes – a seeming comfort zone, "innocent and reassuring," now defamiliarized as "an edge like any other; / its dark, the border territory between houses where violence holes up in men's hands" (Wallace 1987, 59–60). In tandem with public spaces, she implicates public media and discourses as conditions of possibility for individual non-engagement: for example, a television newscaster functions as an illusory interval "between you and the damage, a voice / over the shots of bodies, letting you look / up from the screen / to the square of street outside / and back to the weather" (59). The five numbered sections of Wallace's poem draw on a variety of public discourses – from media, to documentary, to film, to human rights, to narrative – to suggest the ways in which these too are constitutive of social reality, part of the stories that provide and limit meaning for our lives.

In her introduction to *Against Forgetting: Twentieth Century Poetry of Witness*, Carolyn Forche (1993) addresses the dilemma of the artist who seeks to testify to extreme-limit experiences. She reminds us that the "crisis of witnessing" is at once an aesthetic and ethical dilemma for there are the inevitable dangers of aestheticizing indignity even as a poet seeks to give them voice and form. The extremity of experience itself fosters a second crisis in language and form, which is wrenched by an attempt to engage the unwitnessed and unsayable (41–2). Following Adorno's ethical challenge to a formalist aesthetics in the aftermath of Auschwitz, Forche argues that extremity necessitates new forms of poetic thought (42).[22] The aesthetic, the literary, and the poetic cannot remain unchanged by the cataclysms of history. "Shattered, exploded, or splintered narrative" frequently embodies the impress of extremity; bearing only partial witness, such traumatized form and wounded language is scored by the silences, the unspeakable indignities, the stammering tongues (42–3). Indeed, it may be argued that the Modernist and Postmodernist preference for fragmented forms such as the lyric sequence in the wake of the First and Second World Wars stands as evidence that the literature of the twentieth century at large bears the impress of extremity in its formal properties.[23]

Bronwen Wallace's "Intervals" is such an exploded form; its implied narrative movement from "Entry" to "Departure" jumpcuts across numbered segments and between scenarios, speakers, and focalizers. Within each sequence, narrative and imagist fragments proceed by collage and apposition. In Sequence 2, through interspersed and italicized fragments of definitions, Wallace offers the interval itself as a tenuous, liminal mid-space between danger and provisional safety, knowing and ignoring, inaction and agency.[24] She begins with the primary meaning of "interval house" as a first-stage shelter for women and children survivors of domestic abuse, then moves to consider dictionary variations, evoking an open space or pause that lies in-between:

The distance between persons
in respect of positions, beliefs, etc.
or between things in respect of their qualities
the difference of pitch between two
musical sounds

a gap

a 24-hour crisis line (Wallace 1987, 63)

This last cluster of definitional fragments asks us to be attentive to the dissonance between an interval in its spatial register as a marker of distance and difference between persons and in its temporal register as one compelling urgent action. As a space-time juncture, the interval signifies relations that occur in the gaps between subjectivities. This liminal space is one of limit and possibility within which ethical choices to cross, bridge, or close the intervals between us are confronted. Wallace offers the interval as a multiple marker of the wound in language, form, and social relations – a crisis and limit of knowing and reciprocity between "us" and "them." Testimony at the interval becomes a crucial speech act that traverses this wound, this knowledge gap, and brings it to social memory.

In Sequence 2, Wallace (1987, 62–3) offers the wound both as literal marker of domestic violence and a repressed silence in the social body: "the wound shut off from the eye, from the brain / going on, going on alone / behind sheets and sheets of anaesthetic." Sequence 2 is ironically entitled "Free Speech" to underscore the limit of legal and human rights codes for survivors of abuse who appear in cameo vignettes: Sylvia, deaf and with rotted teeth; Ruth, with broken jaw wired shut; and seven-year-old Marilyn, left for three days with her arm crushed in a wringer washer (60–2). These narrative fragments are collaged with the definitional variants of interval. Any simplistic notion of free speech as an individual right is provisionalized by the social conditions that limit and constrain. Conversely, the exercise of free speech in the act of testimony is reframed from an individual right to a communal responsibility. These formerly unacknowledged traumas become a juncture between indignities to the physical body and social amnesia in the body politic. They echo other anaesthetized images found in the "Intervals" sequence – the voice-over commentary mediating "between you and the damage" of the evening news; "the TV's blue light spreading into the street and inside / the people, frozen by it"; and the slaps and punches on the soundtracks of Old Westerns or Three Stooges films (60, 66). These disembodied images are counterpointed with the persistent physicality of contrasting body imagery – lungs, heart, brain, cells, DNA, genetic codes, tissue, wound, bruise. These exemplify Albert Camus's injunction that the artist as "freedom's witness" must testify "not to the law, but to the body" (qtd. in Felman and Laub 1992, 109). Wallace uses body imagery as an interval or a place of negotiation between the body of the woman-survivor, that of her speaker/safe house worker, and that of the reader-witness. Against the impulse to disembodiment evidenced by the discourses of popular culture and media, Wallace offers embodiment as the grounds for ethical encounters between the self and another.

When considering testimonial advocacy such as Wallace undertakes in "Intervals," it must be noted that speech acts of witnessing are never simple or uncomplicated. In "speaking for" the other, writer witnesses risk redeploying an imbalance of representational and social power in which the trauma survivor is reified as victim and stripped of her agency. As Carolyn Forche (1993, 37) notes, "humility brings the poet before an ethical tribunal, a place where the writer must recognize the claims of difference, the otherness of others, and the specificities of their experience. Witness, in this light, is problematic: even if one witnessed atrocity, one cannot necessarily speak about it, let alone for it" In "The Problem of Speaking for Others," Linda Alcoff (1991–92, 7, 20–1, 22, 27) suggests the following helpful strategies:

accountability to one's location as constitutive of our analysis, investments, and speech; consideration that one's situation is never entirely separate from the other's in the delicately webbed histories and discourses in which we are mutually constituted; attentiveness to configurations of power as the grounds for any speaking; and sustained reflection on the probable outcomes of our words on the material contexts and persons involved. These guidelines provide a model for ethical humility in the always vexed circumstance of advocacy witnessing. Wallace herself mentors such testimonial self-vigilance when she acknowledges the limits of her knowledge and vision as an Interval House worker. In an interview with Peter Gzowski, she discussed her unexamined assumptions before working at the shelter:

> I thought what most people thought, which was that people who got involved in that were sick people ... that it just happened to, you know, maybe women on welfare or to people who drank ... And that it was cut and dried, that people who stayed in that situation were just idiots ... By listening very carefully to the women at Interval House ... [I realized] That they weren't totally victims and they weren't totally passive. That they were trying to work their way through this situation. (Wallace 1992, 22)

In Sequence 3, "ECU: On the Job," Wallace (1987, 63–4) evokes the film technique of an extreme close-up to delicately probe the reciprocal relation between the shelter worker and a woman survivor:

> If I were to place my hand on the side
> of her head, the bruise at the left temple
> would exactly fit the palm, the heel
> curving over her left eye, where the rim
> of the heel of her husband's shoe has left
> a gash marked out by the doctor's stitches,
> which I follow now
>
> . . . .
> ... her bruise
> is the only currency between us.
> I carry it home like a paycheque,
> my fingers smelling of ointment and blood,
> and when someone asks me how it went today
> it is the bruise that spills from my mouth
> uncontrolled, incurable ...

Here the worker undergoes a crisis of witnessing that interrogates the normalizing construction of this exchange as her "night's work ... our daily bread bought with it" (64), while tenderly probing the bruise as a juncture where she and her partner are also implicated in their gendered bodies. The wound "becomes the dark between us in the bed at night" (64). The worker becomes the body's witness as an uncontrollable testimony spills from her mouth. Similarly, in "Bones," the poet-speaker notes a transference between one scene of witnessing and another, which exemplifies our co-implication in the crisis of the body's indignity:

Everywhere I went, my work experience
drew me through confessions I couldn't stop,
and I couldn't stop talking about them
so you had to listen
but, being you, in that way that listening
can be active, when the listener re-enters
the country of her own damage
from a new direction. (Wallace 1987, 81)

Like the students in Shoshana Felman's course on Holocaust testimony who compelled their roommates and friends to listen to midnight outpourings of their own anguished testimony, it appears that the worker is subpoenaed as a witness to an atrocity within which she seemingly becomes interpellated (Felman and Laub 1992, 47–8). Carolyn Forche (1993, 17) reminds us of the way in which literary testimony resonates with its legal counterpart as a speech act of judicial witness, but the question remains: before what court of law is the evidence produced and to what ends? It would appear that something like a court of ethical appeals against indignities suffered in body and spirit is invoked. The aim seems to be an overwhelming, even reflexive urge to bring these to social memory so that they might be redressed and vindicated. The act of witnessing becomes a reconstructive ethical act that wrests language from the limit of the unspoken and sets itself in opposition to the very conditions that annihilate the body (45). Registering both the intimate and public body, testimony provides a therapeutic and ethical function, rendering specific violations of human rights intelligible in the almanac of history, while in the telling itself the subject may experience provisional healing in the act of public grief, witness, and redress.

Such a powerful internalization of the bruise or trauma resonates strongly with Emmanuel Levinas's model of the ethical encounter between oneself and another who is not me. Displacing the autonomous hero of Western democratic discourses, Levinas argues that the primary act of being is found in the "face to face" encounter with the other, one which inevitably summons an ethical response of vigilance on her behalf. The radical significance of the face to face situation is that it is the other's vulnerability that seizes the self as a kind of hostage and calls her to lay down the sovereignty of her ego (Levinas 1989, 85):

> To expose myself to the vulnerability of the face is to put my ontological right to existence into question. In ethics, the other's right to exist has primacy over my own, a primacy epitomized in the ethical edict: you shall not kill ... The ethical rapport with the face is asymmetrical in that it subordinates my existence to the other. (24)

What are the implications of Levinas's profound reflection for an ethics of literary representation? Jill Robbins asks whether there can be a textual equivalent for the face of the other. In Levinas's theory, to see is also to hear, to be summoned by the voice of the other (Robbins 1991, 137–42). I suggest that the speech act that deliberately constructs textual encounters with the other in order to make claims for social justice may call the reader to response-ability in a parallel way to Levinas's face of the other. Paul Ricouer (1993, 140) asks if reading itself compels an encounter with the other in a kind of ethical experiment: "in what way does narrative, which is never ethically neutral, prove to be the first laboratory of moral judgement?" Adapting this, I suggest that the imagined face and voice becomes an interval of reading where ethical criticism can take place. To encounter a voice is also to engage the social contexts that produced the other in all her complexity. As Henry Giroux (1993, 20) notes, the reader is always confronted by ethical decisions: "Here I stand ... here and now I face an other who demands of me an ethical response."

Like other contemporary poets, such as Denise Levertov and Gary Snyder, Wallace's concern with ethical interdependency leads her to environmental concerns. Her practice of an ecological poetics is most manifest in her body imagery, which persistently reminds us of the material, biological, and chemical elements that we share with human and non-human others.[25] Wallace (1987, 64–5) probes beneath the surface of the woman's bruised head in "ECU: On the Job," to open up the layered complexities of agency and survival that occur in the brain and connect us at the cellular level to a possible future:

the brain is adding hydro to food
to first and last month's rent, phone bills
and cough medicine, trying to make ends meet
while it keeps the heart
pumping the blood to her wound,
food for the new cells,
pushing her slowly into the future

. . . .
... a future
which includes us all, exactly
as the child growing in the salty fluid of the uterus
includes everything our cells remember
of the long swim in from the sea.

Our future. Though it may be no more
than the last few years of this century
already so full of horrors.

Here Wallace deftly negotiates a kind of provisional universal that implicates this woman's future with our future and the future of the planet. She deploys an evolutionary image, a cellular memory of our pre-human genealogies, to compel recognition of an ecological self accountable to its embeddedness in webbed human and biotic communities.[26] This move is integral to Wallace's refashioning of a relational and interdependent subject. Expanding notions of selfhood open up further possibilities for understanding our mutual determination and ethical accountability.

While this may seem to skirt dangerously close to a conventional humanist universal that masks and denies difference and particularity, Wallace (1992, 177–8) takes great pains to nuance a working definition of commonality:

the voice of the narrative poem ... is somewhat collective. I say *somewhat* collective, because I recognize that it is also private, specific to a particular person in a particular place, at a particular time. I say *collective* because I want to convey that it is emphatically not "universal," in the sense of Universal Human Experience ... but we do have a collective experience – collective as in a choir or political movement – in which the whole grows from, but does not transcend, its separate parts.

Elsewhere, in *Keep That Candle Burning Bright: Poems for Emmy Lou Harris*, she uses the choir as a central image for relational selfhood or a notion of the individual embedded in a community in which everybody plays or sings a part (1992 203, 211):

> Of course, when I'm listening to Emmy Lou Harris, I'm listening to a whole lot of other people at the same time, like Gram Parsons, Rodney Crowell, Kitty Wells, Chuck Berry, Merle Haggard, Dolly Parton and at least two busloads of church choirs. All that proves is that nobody sings alone, although it is equally true that nobody, not even Emmy Lou Harris, will ever sing "Sweet Dreams of You" the way Patsy Cline did ... This is what I mean when I say that all lives weave that way, in and out, between all that we share and all that we don't, manners and mystery, History and the moment I get called on, as you do, to be nobody but me. (Wallace 1991, 17)

Like MacIntyre, Wallace also reminds us that narrative itself is a relational mode that depends, at least in part, on what is held in common. Further, testimonial speech acts assume a shared stance against indignities to the body. Without a provisional universal that modulates between particular contexts and shared values, ethical claims for justice would be impossible. As Gayatri Spivak suggests, we need to simultaneously uphold and submit to "persistent critique" those categories which we "cannot not want" or need (Spivak and Winant 1990, 93).

In the implied narrative movement of "Intervals" from "Entry" to Departure," Wallace invokes a process of reader initiation, a journey guided by an alternate cartography to the tourist-map of the city with which the poem opens. This unfolding journey involves a descent into dangerous knowledge that alters our previous frames of reference and stereotypical assumptions. It is one function of testimony to bring knowledge to a crisis, to unhinge prior cognitive categories and frames (Felman and Laub 1992, 53–4). In Sequence 4, "Short Story," Wallace offers us a vignette focalized around a reader surrogate in the persona of a "friend" who overhears spousal abuse in the upstairs apartment. This sequence turns on the way we use pronouns as distancing devices, similar to the interval maintained by third person narrative voice, and the voice-over damage control of the TV newscaster: "This isn't one to be told / in the third person, / though we keep on trying to" (Wallace 65). To her friend's strategies for coping with "what she doesn't know," her explanations for the way "those people" want to live, the poet/speaker answers by challenging binary categories that maintain an illusion of separate non-implicated identities:

(this story about *them*, about *those* people)
so that we who hear it can forget
how little is ever really possible
for any of us, botched
failed things to whom it may come only once
and never clearly, that moment
when the voice that tries to sing
through all our stories rises, briefly,
first person singular,
cries *yes* and *now* and *help*
help me. (67)

Here, Wallace shifts the register from the distancing third person to the collective "us," comprised of individuals who experience an interval of acute
vulnerability, limitation, and failure that compels us to cry out to the community in the "first person singular." She effectively deploys an allegory in
which pronouns are the protagonists that bridge the interval between persons. Wallace further compels a shift to a relationally constituted self with
the "middle voice" strategy of the second-person pronoun typical of much
of her poetry and used in the opening sequence of "Intervals"(Dorscht
and Savoy 1991, 6). This ambiguously marks the speaker's self-talk and direct
address to the reader ("your own childhood, your life running on automat-
ic" [Wallace 1987, 59]). As Bina Freiwald (1991, 116–17, 129, 128) notes, the
"elasticity of the second person," along with Wallace's shifts between singular and collective pronouns, gives formal expression to "the mutual embeddedness of life and story with other life-stories, and the dialogic quality of
the conversational mode" as the matrix for intimate address between speaker and reader.

Throughout "Intervals," Wallace implies that the reader has a powerful
ethical function as a co-witness in the testimonial transaction. In an interview from *Arguments with the World*, Wallace (1992, 213–14) reframes our
conventional understanding of confessional poetry as an outpouring of inti-
mately tortured but self-enclosed images in the tradition of Lowell, Plath,
and Sexton to consider a form that compels relational engagement:

When we tell intimate things about ourselves we are in some way asking
for, if not absolution, at least support, inclusion … a healing gesture from
the other person … It's part of what I was saying about wounds and damage – it's another way of opening yourself up to the other person … For
me, it's a request placed on the reader to stand in a certain relation to the

speaker ... We tell each other about our lives recognizing that we're going to be inextricably connected as long as we're human beings on this earth.

It is the reader's task to confer significance, to witness the cognitively dissonant, to render the unsaid intelligible, to participate in creating new categories of knowledge, to confirm that the testimony matters in our public memory. This textual exchange is an interval of ethical bridging in which the reader is called to respond.

Most profoundly, Bronwen Wallace's "Intervals" leaves the reader with an uncompromising sense of our co-implication as women and men in an ongoing history of gendered violence, along with an urgent need to act for our collective future. In a series of refrains that echo across three of the sequences, she moves us from *hearing* voices on the crisis line ("for all they have time to tell me before something stops them"), to *seeing* the survivor's bruise in intimate detail ("Something as small as that. / The time we have left/to see it"), to *doing* or undertaking urgent action based on our intimate connection:

We are that close.

Each of us, who are only
the work of our lungs as they empty
and fill themselves,
the back, the arms
the cells need, the brain
where all this happens all the time.
All of it and only that.

We are that close
The time we have left
to do it. (68)

The cumulative repetition of the "time we have left" emphasizes both urgency and hope, the balance of a future that hangs on our present ethical choices and investments. As Shoshana Felman notes, "the literature of testimony is not an art of leisure but an art of urgency" (Felman and Laub 1992, 114).

Wallace repeatedly positions the women and children survivors, the advocate witness, and the readers as co-witnesses in a mutual present upon which our future depends. Here as elsewhere Wallace upholds her deep belief in the capacity for mutually determining personal agency and social change: "I begin, always, with the power of the personal, the private, the unique in each of us, which resists, survives and can change the power that our culture has over us" (Wallace and Moure 1993, 79). This vision extends in "Change of Heart" to a man who "beat my friend unconscious":

> I'd like to make it
> his voice, coming to you
> as the one witness you can trust
> but instead, there's only mine. (Wallace 1987, 74)

Yet she imagines "the night it hit home: / this was it, his one and only life," with the result that he made of the memory of the woman's screams a way of "speaking to the muscles / that control his hands, to the stammer he thinks of as his changed heart" (74–5). Such a nuanced exploration of this possibility for personal and transformative agency refuses any reductive analysis in which the male perpetrator of violence is outside of the ethical community. Wallace characteristically disrupts one-dimensional responses that limit agency, hope, and the conditions for change. Agency, or the will and capacity to act on rational thought, has been the definitive gesture of the political and economic subject of Western humanism. In tandem with reconstituting this subject as relational, agency itself shifts from self-contained individual acts to those that have consequences and reverberations in the concentric narrative communities in which we find ourselves embedded.

"The Smaller Stratagems. Whatever Works": Towards an Ethics of Limitation and Healing

I'm writing to the wounded part of each person, men as well as women. The power of feminism is the power of the victim who has recognized a way to use her damage. There's a great line in an Adrienne Rich poem about knowing that her wound came from the same place in her as her power ... It's the denial of our damage, our limitations, our vulnerability, our mortality that's got us where we are.

Bronwen Wallace, *Arguments with the World*

Fundamentally, the effect and intent of Wallace's relational poetics is spiritual. Borrowing Flannery O'Connor's maxim that "possibility and limitation mean about the same thing" (poignant words from a woman who lived with lupus), Wallace offers a poetics of limitations, failures, and losses that seeks to effect healing in individuals and the body politic. Not only does she attend to the wounded and imperfect body throughout her writing life but she also reanimates the elegy tradition to significantly rearticulate Western conceptions of death as a violent and final ending or as so transcendent as to be unreal. In Wallace's lexicon this is reconfigured through reflection on a "feminist way of dying," an understanding she came to after caring for a friend who died of cancer at age thirty-three. In the last year of her own life, Wallace wrote a suite of poems for Emmy Lou Harris, *Keep That Candle Burning Bright*, that embody her feminist philosophy of dying. This new formulation extends her notion of narrative community, positing an ecological understanding of death as meaningfully carried forward in the lives of the living. Wallace (1992, 211) established a practice of starting her poetry readings with a poem by a Canadian writer who had died, such as BP Nichol or Gwendolyn McEwen, to convey her awareness that community "includes the dead as well as the living." She writes of how country music great Gram Parsons blooms "from his dying" in Emmy Lou's cover rendition of one of his songs "as each of us blooms / from the deaths that nourish us and let us go, the deaths we survive" (1991, 36). Death, perceived by many to be the greatest limitation, is reconceived as a place of possibility:

One of the things I really notice as I get older is … how important it is to develop a feminist understanding of death and dying in the face of denial and technological nightmare that the medical profession is built on – denial of the body. There's so much power in the body. If we could learn to attend to that power, we would learn not to fear what our bodies do. It's connected to how we see the body of the earth; by denying that we're part of the body of the earth, we're going to kill it. (1992, 208)

Here, key elements in Wallace's philosophical and poetic vision are brought together: refashioning a relational self involves a double move of revaluing both the powers and limits of our embodied existence as these are implicated in the ebb and flow of the earth's cycles. Wallace also revisits the long tradition of poetic meditations on mortality, along with the conventional elegy form; she suggests the ongoing necessity of examining the meaning of death for our lives, while historicizing death in the twentieth-century particulars of ecocide, megadeath, and technological intervention.[27]

Against the grain of a culture of "getting over" death, Wallace (1991, 18) approximates a talking lyric country lament in *Keep That Candle Burning* to show us the wisdom of "hurtin'" songs singing the sorrow side of life, and a voice "that sings on, using its breaking to do it."[28] In the tradition of country blues, Wallace offers her own version of talking lyric, crossing elitist boundaries between high and low culture to offer stories for the road, traded over coffee at the truckstops on the highway of life, lyrics to live and die by. Country itself is already a complex border-crossing form, drawing upon and intermixing musical styles and modes from diversely constituted communities with particular racial, working-class, and regional southern roots: gospel, blues, and American folk forms like Celtic fiddling, Appalachian hillbilly blue-grass, waltz, and ballad. It is a music of grit and survival that connects to my own ancestral lineage, particularly one tough granny, Sarah Bishop, who single-handedly raised eight children on welfare in a two-room house during the Depression era in Alabama. The iconography of country invokes a kind of allegory of the rootlessness and displacement experienced by the subjects of twentieth-century capitalism in North America, along with a call to reground in and seek out new forms of community.[29] From the staple images of country music – truckstops, truckers, cowboys, rodeos, drifters, on-the-road-again songs, hurting songs, drinking songs, break-up songs – Wallace creates poem parables, enigmatic gems that provide wise words, "equipment for living" (Burke 1989, 513–14).

Wallace's poetry of awkward embodiment – "singing for everything i couldn't be" (Wallace 1991, 10) and "ordinary moving" (Wallace 1987, 101), facilitates a negotiation between the stubborn particulars of daily life and mystery. It is the invocation of the imperfect body, the out-of-tune voice – those "noisy, untidy selves we've lost out there somewhere," the partial gesture of connection that renders her poems so powerful (Wallace 1991, 11). In their ordinariness, commonness, and banality, limitations find a place, a voice, to feel at home in and with:

> Why not sing for what we can't do, instead of all this booming and bragging, most of us stuck in the back row anyway, squawking and gimped-up. What if some tuneless wonder's all we've got to say for ourselves? Off-key, our failings held out, at last, to each other. What else have we got to offer, really? What else do we think they're for? (32)

Here the conventional lyricism of the song is brought to earth and reborn as off-key "talking country blues" singing for "what we can't do."[30] Humorous and humbling acceptance of failings is the groundnote for community formation. This rewrites an ethos of individual mastery that attends the performance of both the lyric poet, the musician, and, dare I say, the literary critic.

One section of *The Stubborn Particulars of Grace*, entitled "Nearer to Prayers than Stories," not only signals another genre-crossing impulse of Wallace's talking lyric but also asks us to reconsider the possibilities of lyric's ancient roots in communal ritual. Gestures and phenomena that now seem to belong to an unfashionable quasi-religious discourse circulate: miracles, grace, blessing, benedictions, saints' relics, and personal talismans. In fact, the poet/speaker seeks to come to terms with the "practical particulars of grace" at the Sunday dinner table, and the possibility that she "could say for myself, just once, / without embarrassment, bless, / thrown out as to some lightness / that I actually believe in" (Wallace 1987, 110–11). With the decline of organized religion, the extended family, and ethnic heritage as meaningful categories for multigenerational and mixed lineage descendants of New World immigrants, is there a way in which we still need rituals that structure and confer meaning on significant passages of life and ground us in accountability to something other than ourselves? Is it possible that we need to revisit what I wish to call the gifts of lyric: the register of communal ritual, beauty, and myth that can offer wisdom, healing, and connection; opportunity for self-reflection on inner-life process; contemplation of "large" philosophical and spiritual questions; and a matrix for engagement with the somatic register through attentiveness to sound and musicality? Lyric's historical relation to the mnemonic in its sound devices and the performative speech act points to possibilities for lyric as a form that is potentially non-dualistic in its attention to inner life, embodiment, and social memory.

True confessions of a former card-carrying postmodernist: I pose the above in the form of questions because they are ongoing for me. Among other writers – like Di Brandt, George Elliott Clarke, and Joy Kogawa – Bronwen Wallace's practice has compelled me to re-examine the contemporary suspicion of categories like the aesthetic, the beautiful, and, particularly, the transcendent. While we need to remain attentive to the dangers of unmitigated transcendence, which has been so frequently counterposed to the stubborn particulars of daily life and history, perhaps contemporary poets are showing the way for a non-dualistic negotiation between the spirit, heart, and social registers. Do we need both/and strategies rather than playing one at the expense of the other? Rather than the song being elevated above the struggle or the struggle dragging the song through the mud, is there a balance to be found? Like her provisional universal, Wallace asks us to reconsider the possible benefits of a category such as provisional transcendence.[31]

In *Stubborn Particulars*, imagery of the illumined body – bones rendered translucent in an X-ray scan – recalls the preciousness of life sustained in this moment:

what he sees; how their deaths
quicken the air around them, stipple their bodies
with a light like the green signals
trees send out before leaves appear.
. . . .
but doesn't it come to the same thing
for all of us? So frail, how could we bear
this much grace, when it glances

off the odds and ends we've no idea
what to do with ... (Wallace 1987, 40)

This is the language and iconography of transcendence recast. No longer in
some elsewhere or "upthere," grace glances like light off the odds and ends
of daily life, the stubborn particulars through which each of our fragile bodies moves. Mystery – the uncanny, grace-grounded, indwelling in the here
and now, incarnate in our biotic and human communities. As Wallace says,
foreshadowing her own closing chapter, "What about ... the woman who
accepts her death and in doing so enriches her life? The whole idea that the
body must be transcended – both the human body and the planet's – where
has that gotten us?" (Wallace and Moure 1993, 22).

Wallace's relational subjectivity, her lyric community midwifed in the
talking lyric form itself, and her commitment to provisional healing, leaves
her vulnerable to criticism from postmodernists like Rachel Blau DuPlessis
(1990, 153, 190n.): "One sees a moving and serious reconsideration of gender
in feminist 'humanist' poetries – combined with an attention to wholeness,
healing, lyric transcendence, and affirmation that is not a uniformly plausi-
ble, though it is always a repetitively narratable, sequence. If one, could
retain that passionate, feeling ethics without the uniformities of telos..."
What such critics have failed to notice with respect to much of what gets
panned as a nostalgic relapse is that this is not the old humanism. Most
accurately, Wallace is a posthumanist humanist. Her emphasis on the dignity of all life forms, including the non-human, does not allow for a collapse
back into prepostmodern humanism. Similar to a number of current
thinkers, like Cornell West and Susan Stanford Friedman, Wallace reanimates former categories of subjectivity, agency, community, and, most
importantly, ethics. Her attentiveness to complex registers of identity, contexts, and construction of knowledge/power indicates implicit incorporation
of some of postmodernism's important questions. Feminists and minority

writers have argued that we cannot do away with notions of subjectivity and agency, standpoint and commitment, but, instead, must renegotiate these, submit them to the lens of self-reflexive critical thinking, and re-circulate them in the context of living practice and ongoing exchange. Wallace's popularized talking lyric, her relational and embodied subject, and her ethical poetics contribute to conversations about poetry, ethics, and community that we cannot live without.

for a moment in there, maybe two or three milliseconds, your body moves to the beat my thought set up, just as my hand writes by what it hears of you, out there somewhere. You should almost say that, for a millisecond anyway, we both consent to this, with our whole selves, every strand alight and quivering. (Wallace 1991, 43–4)

Acknowledgments

I wish to offer my deep appreciation to Bronwen Wallace for a poetry of vision, honesty, integrity, beauty, grit, and humour; she continues to be one of my most valued teachers. My heart's gratitude to Robin Buyers for introducing me to Wallace's writing many years ago. Ongoing thanks to several generations of students for thoughtful seminars and essays on Wallace's work. I am especially grateful to SSHRCC for research funding, to Naomi Watson Laird for her research assistance, to Barbara Gabriel for her fine editorial eye, and to Andre Vellino for sharpening my mind and softening my spirit.

Notes

1 See Susan Stanford Friedman's (1994, 23–5) "Craving Stories" for an important discussion of women writers of the long poem who braid narrative and lyric together in order to better probe large questions of subjectivity, myth, and history.

2 I wish to distinguish Wallace's ethical vision from an essentialist feminist ethic of care, nurture, and connectedness.

3 Mukherjee and Schudson (1991) take up discussion of the democratizing effects of cultural studies, along with changing notions and functions of "culture," in their excellent introduction to *Rethinking Popular Culture*.

4 In the special Bronwen Wallace issue of *Open Letter*, Eric Savoy (1991), Susan Rudy Dorscht (1991), and Barbara Godard (Di Michele and Goddard 1991) each recuperate Wallace for postmodernism and poststructuralism in a manner that does not account for those unruly elements that resist such critical domestication. Savoy's (1991, 96) focus on a "poetics of absence," a "constantly elusive signified," and the "gap of nonrecovery" is particularly persistent in its appropriation of Wallace's practice for postmodernism. Interestingly, Wallace (1992, 206–7) herself was wary of approaching writing solely through a postmodern frame. Mary Di Michele, in

conversation with Barbara Godard, argues that Wallace was writing "beyond post-modernism" to foster community (Di Michele and Godard 1991, 55).

5 Susan Stanford Friedman (1991, 465, 474, 478, 479) provocatively argues for a "recuperative analysis" that renegotiates questions of humanism, ethics, agency, authorship, selfhood, experience, intention, and meaning while being informed by the problematizing method of postmodernism. Such a both/and practice of critique without dismissal seems essential to any ongoing practice that undertakes an ethical engagement with the social body and the body's world.

6 See Donna Bennett (1991, 71) on Wallace's recasting of the meditative lyric as the "stream of conversation poem."

7 The notion of the "solitary scribbler" in a lonely garret is not limited to the lyric poet. Indeed, as Linda Brodkey (1987) demonstrates, this is a writer personae embodied both through the elevated Romantic figure and the alienated artist of Modernism. She reminds us that this is "only one story about writers and writing" (55). One only has to look at the ongoing urgent work of Pen International on behalf of state-tar-getted writers like Ken Saro-Wiwa and Salmon Rushdie to understand the powerful political and social significance that writers embody in parts of the world other than North America and England.

8 For a discussion of lyric conventions, see *The New Princeton Encyclopedia of Poetry and Poetics* and Perloff's (1982) "From Image to Action." Perloff notes that "the equation of poetry with lyric is almost axiomatic in contemporary criticism" (415). Kevin McGuirk (1996) further reminds us that lyric has often been taken to be interchangeable with the aesthetic, the sublime, the civilizing, and high culture, as is the case in Matthew Arnold's *Culture and Anarchy*.

9 Hosek and Parker (1985) is a good starting place to find discussion of the limits of lyric. See also Coniff (1988), Perloff (1985), McGuirk (1996), Nielsen (1996), and Norris (1992).

10 See Levertov (1981); Rich (1986, 1993); and Clarke (1993) for examples. Consider also the increasing popularity of cross-medium performance forms of dub poetry, rap, and spoken word, which suggests that poetry continues to matter in public culture, even as it keeps on changing to accommodate new audiences.

11 For critics interested in new formulations of lyric, see McGuirk (1996), Nielsen (1996), Perloff (1985), and Norris (1992).

12 Dorothy Nielsen (1996, 5) reminds us of the historical legacy of the somatic register in lyric through the physicality of voice, meter, and rhyme, while Roland Greene (1991) calls attention to the lyrics' roots in ritual and performance.

13 Alasdair MacIntyre (1981, 210–11) expressly reads conversation as a form of "enacted narrative" that is central to every human transaction but that is "so all-pervasive a feature of the human world that it tends to escape philosophical attention."

14 To challenge my own argument against the traditional lyric, in contrast to pervasive contemporary criticism of lyric monologism, Monroe (1987) provocatively reminds us of the "dialogical nature of all language" to argue that dialogism is "a constitutive feature of poetry as well as prose" (35n).

15 Susan Stanford Friedman (1994, 18–22) recalls that, while lyric and narrative are seen as regressive forms in contemporary American criticism, for French critics like Kristeva the poetic is seen as a transgressive mode with the capacity to disrupt the symbolic order. This demonstrates how crucial it is to historicize any theory as a narrative from a particular context in order not to misapply them to our own.

16 Benedict Anderson (1991) writes of nations as "imagined communities," but this is

also a provocative notion for other social identity groupings (e.g., workers and/or women).

17 For psychoanalytic reconceptualization of the bounded self, see Chodorow (1986) and Gilligan (1986). For green Buddhism and eco-theology, see Titmuss (1995); Halifax (1990); Nhat Hanh (1991); and Ruether (1992).

18 Similarly, Paul Ricouer (1990, 114) upholds "narrative identity" as a crucial link between the agentive subject and the "ethico-juridicial subject." Our capacity to evaluate our actions as worthy of esteem (as in narrative analysis of character) is the condition for reciprocal evaluation of the other as a capable and accountable subject who merits respect (118). This notion is developed in Ricouer's (1993) invaluable *Oneself as Another*. Wayne Booth (1993, 78, 89, 93) also argues for "the social self" constituted by "multiple affiliations" and comprised by a polyglossic, "character-rich assemblage."

19 I am indebted to Bina Freiwald's (1991) excellent discussion of Wallace's use of narrative voice and pronouns.

20 Felman and Laub (1992) offer the first well developed theory of holocaust testimony. Many of their insights may be applied to testimonials by other types of trauma survivors.

21 Judith Herman (1992, 7) documents the way in which public knowledge of psychological and somatic trauma (such as shell shock and hysteria) have a peculiar history of "episodic amnesia." We need only recall the way Freud's oedipal and electra complex theories were born out of his about-face on the earlier clinical discovery that hysterics were survivors of sexual abuse. Witness a parallel backlash against the possibility of traumatic memory by current advocates of "False Memory Syndrome." Each of these cases suggests the way that testimony – the bringing to light of the formerly hidden – threatens the structures of social memory.

22 Adorno's (1973) famous pronouncement that "after Auschwitz, it is no longer possible to write poetry" was a much larger indictment of the role of culture in the Nazi regime, typified by the notorious practice of having Jewish musicians play chamber music while their comrades were marched to the gas chambers. He later revised this verdict to suggest that it is in "art alone that suffering can still find its voice, consolation, without immediately being betrayed by it" (qtd. in Felman and Laub 1992, 33–4; Adorno 1982, 312). John Beverly (1993, 98–9) entends Adorno's assertion that "for thought to be true to today ... it must also be thinking against itself" to argue for a postliterary practice typified by the Latin American *testimonio*.

23 I am thinking here of such exemplary works as Eliot's "The Wasteland"; however, I am not suggesting that such a formalist response to the crash of established certainties posed by the First World War is identical to the post-Auschwitz view held by Adorno and others that the aesthetic is contaminated by its complicity in atrocity.

24 See Susan Rudy Dorscht's (1991, 101–3) reading of the interval as the gap between ideology and experience – "what we have been given and what we require."

25 Slack and Whitt (1992, 572) argue for a "non-anthropocentric alternative" in cultural studies. *Rethinking Individualism*, as broad-based a project as it is, demonstrates the way that much contemporary refashioning of subjectivity is limited to self/other relations between humans. For further evidence of Wallace's deliberate construction of a biotic or ecological self, see her poem devoted to Koko the talking gorilla (Wallace 1987, 85), "Rhythm and Genes" (Wallace 1991, 41), and numerous essays in *Arguments with the World* (1992). While the conjunction of environmental and feminist commitments could lead one to read Wallace as an

eco-feminist, she does not invoke the central axiom of conflated violation of woman and the earth so much as she draws upon notions similar to deep ecology's concept of the earth as a life-web and biotic community in which each living being requires biospecies equality (Halifax 1990, 25, 34). See Janet Biehl (1991) for a critique of eco-feminism.

26 It is important not to over-idealize community as an answer to contemporary ethico-political dilemmas. I take Iris Marion Young's (1990, 300) points on the tendency of community to suppress difference and promote falsely hegemonic unity; however, I find she overdetermines her suspicion of reciprocity and identification with others in the name of a postmodern critique of the "metaphysics of presence" (311). I do not wish to meet her charges of "hopeless utopianism" with "hopeless skepticism," but I would suggest that her model of political action is severely limited. This is typified for me by her version of contemporary city life, a transaction of mediated relationships between "strangers who do not understand each other." This model offers a kind of relativistic individualism that cannot account for the way we are socially and filiatively constituted.

27 Like many critics, I am struck by Wallace's sustained engagement with elegy, which makes it seem as though she were somehow intuitively preparing for her early death. While fuller discussion of Wallace's refashioning of the elegy form will have to wait, I suggest that some features of the modernist anti-elegy and female elegy discussed by Ramazani (1994) Schenck (1986) are relevant to her work. Wallace, by her disquietingly persistent meditation on death in both SP and KCBB, refuses the tidy consolation of Freud's "normal mourning," which Ramazani identifies with the pattern of traditional elegy. However, unlike Wilfred Owen, whose anti-elegiac images of screaming shells replace funeral choirs, Wallace works elegy into her theory of community. This is more in keeping with Bowlby's argument that prolonged mourning is a means of remembering the lost one and sustaining the capacity for relation in their absence (qtd. in Gilligan 1986, 244–5).

28 Freud (qtd. in Ramazani 1994, 11) himself noted of pre-First World War mourning rites, "We showed an unmistakable tendency to put death on one side, to eliminate it from life. We tried to hush it up." Such banishment of mourning has only escalated with privatized and sanitized mourning rituals and the tendency to see grief as a pathology, weakness, or self-indulgence that must be gotten under control. Poetic elegy remains one of the few venues for a public articulation of grief and resistance to cultural denial (Ramazani 1994, 11–5).

29 For a discussion of country music, see the article by Akenson (1992) and Lewis (1993), particularly MacKay's reading of spurned love lyrics as displaced laments for lost community by musicians with working-class and southern regional roots (in Lewis 1993, 301). Interestingly, Wallace side-steps questions of gender stereotypes associated with country music by invoking Emmy Lou Harris, a female precursor central to the 1970s upsurge in women's country. See Lewis's "Conflict and Contradiction in Country Music" for a discussion of buddy songs, honky-tonk queens, and rodeo angels (in Lewis 1993, 112–15). Wallace seems most interested in country as a form preoccupied with community.

30 I am indebted to Dennis Lee's cover notes on KCBB for the term "talking country blues."

31 For a sustained reflection on the need to re-engage categories of the aesthetic and the literary, see Levine (1994) and Brooks (1994).

Works Cited

Adorno, Theodor. 1973. "Meditations on Metaphysics." *Negative Dialectics*. Trans. E.B. Ashton, 361–8. New York: Seabury.

–1982. "Commitment." In *The Essential Frankfurt School Reader*, ed. Andrew Arato and Eike Gebhardt, 3000–18. New York: Continuum.

Akenson, James E. 1992. "Social and Geographic Characteristics of Country Music." In *America's Musical Pulse*, ed., Kenneth J. Bindas, 45–52. Westport, CT: Praeger.

Alcoff, Linda. 1991–92. "The Problem of Speaking for Others." *Cultural Critique* 20 (Winter): 5–33.

Anderson, Benedict. 1991. *Imagined Communities: Reflections on the Origin and Spread of Nationalism*. London: Verso.

Bennett, Donna. 1991. "Bronwen Wallace and the Meditative Poem." *Queen's Quarterly* 98, 1 (Spring): 58–79.

Benhabib, Seyla. 1987. "The Generalized and the Concrete Other." In *Feminism as Critique: On the Politics of Gender*, ed. Seyla Benhabib and Drucilla Cornell, 77–181. Minneapolis: University of Minnesota Press.

–1992. "Introduction." *Situating the Self: Gender, Community, and Postmodernism in Contemporary Ethics*, 1–19. New York: Routledge.

Beverly, John. 1993. *Against Literature*. Minneapolis: University of Minnesota Press.

Biehl, Janet. 1991. *Rethinking Ecofeminist Politics*. Boston: South End.

Booth, Wayne C. 1988. *The Company We Keep: An Ethics of Fiction* Berkeley: University of California Press.

–1993. "Individualism and the Mystery of the Social Self." In *Freedom and Interpretation*, ed. Barbara Johnson, 69–101. New York: Basic.

Brodkey, Linda. 1987. "Picturing Writing: Writers in the Modern World." In *Academic Writing as Social Practice*, 54–81. Philadelphia: Temple.

Brooks, Peter. 1994. "Aesthetics and Ideology: What Happened to Poetics?" *Critical Inquiry* 20 (Spring): 509–23.

Burke, Kenneth. 1989. "Literature as Equipment for Living." In *The Critical Tradition*, ed. David Richter, 512–17. New York: St. Martin's.

Clarke, George Elliott. 1993. "Renaissance of Poetry: the Idea that Words have Meaning and Consequence is Back in Style." *Ottawa Citizen*, 2 December 1993, A19.

Chodorow, Nancy. 1986. "Toward a Relational Individualism: The Mediation of the Self through Psychoanalysis." In *Reconstructing Individualism: Autonomy, Individuality, and the Self in Western Thought*, ed. Thomas Heller and David Wellbery, 197–236. Stanford: Stanford University Press.

Coiniff, Brian. 1988. *The Lyric and Modern Poetry*. New York: Peter Lang.

Danica, Elly. 1988. *Don't: A Woman's Word*. Charlottetown, PEI: Gynergy.

di Michele, Mary, and Barbara Godard. 1991. "'Patterns of Their Own Particular Ceremonies': A Conversation in the Elegiac Mode." *Open Letter* 7th ser., 9 (Winter): 36–59.

Dorscht, Susan Rudy. 1991. "Writing at the Interval." *Open Letter* 7th ser., 9 (Winter): 100–11.

–and Eric Savoy. 1991. "Introduction." Spec. Bronwen Wallace issue. *Open Letter* 7th ser., 9 (Winter): 5–9.

DuPlessis, Rachel Blau. 1990. "Otherhow: Poetry and Gender: some Ideas." In *The Pink Guitar: Writing as Feminist Practice*, 140–56. New York: Routledge.

Felman, Shoshana, and Dori Laub. 1992. *Testimony: Crises of Witnessing in Literature, Psychoanalysis, and History*. New York: Routledge.

Forche, Carolyn, ed. 1993. "Introduction." *Against Forgetting: Twentieth Century Poetry of Witness*, 29–47. New York: Norton.

Freiwald, Bina. 1991. "'This Isn't One to Be Told / in the Third Person': Wallace's Life-Stories." *Open Letter* 7th ser., 9 (Winter): 112–33.

Friedman, Susan Stanford. 1991. "Post/Poststructuralist Feminist Criticism: The Politics of Recuperation and Negotiation." *New Literary History* 22: 465–90.

– 1994. "Craving Stories: Narrative and Lyric in Contemporary Theory and Women's Long Poems." In *Feminist Measures,* ed. Lynn Keller and Cristanne Miller, 15–42. Michigan: University of Michigan Press.

Gilligan, Carol. 1986. "Remapping the Moral Domain: New Images of the Self in Relationship." In *Reconstructing Individualism: Autonomy, Individuality, and the Self in Western Thought*, ed. Thomas Heller and David Wellbery, 237–52. Stanford: Stanford University Press.

Giroux, Henry. 1993. *Living Dangerously: Multiculturalism and the Politics of Difference*. New York: Peter Lang.

Green, Roland. 1991. *Post-Petrarchism: Origins and Innovations of the Western Lyric Sequence*. Princeton: Princeton University Press.

Habermas, Jurgen. 1991. "The Public Sphere." In *Rethinking Popular Culture*, ed. Mukherjee and Schudson, 398–404. Berkeley: University of California Press.

Halifax, Joan. 1990. "The Third Body: Buddhism, Shamanism, and Deep Ecology." In *Dharma Gaia: A Harvest of Essays in Buddhism and Ecology*, ed. Allan Hunt Badiner, 20–38. Berkeley: Parallax.

Heller, Thomas, and David E. Wellbery. 1986. "Introduction." In *Reconstructing Individualism: Autonomy, Individuality, and the Self in Western Thought*, ed. Thomas C. Heller, David E. Wellberg, and Morton Sosna, 1–15. Stanford: Stanford University Press.

Herman, Judith. 1992. *Trauma and Recovery*. New York: Basic.

Holden, Jonathon. 1986. "The Contemporary Conversation Poem." In *Style and Authenticity in Postmodern Poetry*, 33–44. Columbia: University of Missouri Press.

Hosek, Chaviva, and Patricia Parker, eds. 1985. *Lyric Poetry: Beyond the New Criticism*. Ithaca: Cornell.

Lee, Dennis. 1989. "Bronwen Wallace's Work Crackled with Energy." *Globe and Mail*, 26 August. C18.

Levertov, Denise. 1981. "On the Edge of Darkness: What Is Political Poetry?" In *Light Up the Cave*, 115–29. New York: New Directions.

Levinas, Emmanuel. 1989. *The Levinas Reader*. Ed. Sean Hand. Cambridge, MA: Basil Blackwell.

Levine, George. 1994. "Introduction: Reclaiming the Aesthetic." In *Aesthetics and Ideology*, 1–39. New Brunswick, NJ: Rutgers.

Lewis, George H. ed. 1993. *All that Glitters*. Bowling Green, OH: Bowling Green State University Press.

"Literature and the Ethical Question." 1991. Special Issue, *Yale French Studies* 79.

MacIntyre, Alasdair. 1981. *After Virtue: A Study in Moral Theory*. Notre Dame: Notre Dame University Press.

McGuirk, Kevin. 1998. "'All Wi Doin': Tony Harrison, Linton Kwesi Johnson, and the Cultural Identity of Lyric in Postwar Britain." In *New Definitions of Lyric*, ed. Mark Jeffreys, 49–75. New York: Garland.

Miller, J. Hillis. 1987. *The Ethics of Reading*. New York: Columbia University Press.

Monroe, Jonathan. 1987. *A Poverty of Objects: the Prose Poem and the Politics of Genre*. Ithaca: Cornell University Press.

Mukherjee, Chandra, and Michael Schudson. 1991. "Introduction." *Rethinking Popular Culture*, 1–61. Berkeley: University of California Press.

Nhat Hanh, Thich. 1991. *Peace Is Every Step: the Path of Mindfulness in Everyday Life.* Toronto: Bantam.

Nielsen, Dorothy. 1998. "Ecology, Feminism, and Postmodern Lyric Subjects." *New Definitions of Lyric*, 127–49. New York: Garland.

Norris, Keith S. 1992. "Openmouthed in the Temple of Life: Denise Levertov and the Postmodern Lyric." *Twentieth Century Literature* 38, 3 (Fall): 343–52.

Nouvet, Claude. 1991. "Foreword." *Yale French Studies* 79: 1–2.

Olson, Charles. 1985. "Projective Verse." *20th Century Poetry and Poetics*, 3rd ed., ed. Gary Geddes, 596–608. Toronto: Oxford University Press.

Perloff, Marjorie. 1982. "From Image to Action: the Return of Story in Postmodern Poetry." *Contemporary Literature* 23 (4): 411–27.

– 1985. "Postmodernism and the Impasse of Lyric." In *The Dance of the Intellect: Studies in the Poetry of the Pound Tradition*, 172–200. Cambridge: Cambridge University Press.

Ramazani, Jahan. 1994. *Poetry of Mourning: The Modern Elegy from Hardy to Heaney.* Chicago: University of Chicago Press.

Ricouer, Paul. 1993. *Oneself as Another.* Chicago: University of Chicago Press.

Rich, Adrienne. 1986. *Blood, Bread, and Poetry.* New York: New Directions.

– 1993. *What Is Found There: Notebooks on Poetry and Politics.* New York: New Directions.

Robbins, Jill. 1991. "Visage, Figure: Reading Levinas's Totalitiy and Infinity." *Yale French Studies* 79: 135–49.

Ruether, Rosemary Radford. 1992. *Gaia and God: An Ecofeminist Theology of Earth Healing.* San Francisco: Harper.

Savoy, Eric. "The Antecedents of It: A Poetics of Absence." *Open Letter* 7th ser., 9 (Winter): 88–99.

Schenck, Celeste. 1986. "Feminism and Deconstruction: Re-Constructing the Elegy." *Tulsa Studies in Women's Literature* 5 (1): 13–27.

Slack, Jennifer Daryl, and Laurie Anne Whitt. 1992. "Ethics and Cultural Studies." In *Cultural Studies Reader*, ed. Lawrence Grossberg, Carrie Nelson, and Paula Treichler . New York: Routledge.

Siebers, Tobin. 1988. *The Ethics of Criticism.* Ithaca: Cornell.

Spivak, Gayatri with Howard Winant. 1990. Interview: "Gayatri Spivak on the Politics of the Subaltern." *Socialist Review* 3: 81–97.

Titmuss, Christopher. 1995. *The Green Buddha.* London: Wisdom.

Young, Iris Marion. 1990. "The Ideal of Community and the Politics of Difference." In *Feminism/Postmodernism*, ed. Linda J. Nicholson, 300–23. New York: Routledge.

Wallace, Bronwen. 1987. *The Stubborn Particulars of Grace.* Toronto: McClelland and Stewart.

– 1991, *Keep That Candle Burning Bright and Other Poems: Poems for Emmy Lou Harris.* Toronto: Coach House.

– 1992. *Arguments with the World: Essays by Bronwen Wallace.* Ed. Joanne Page. Kingston: Quarry.

– and Erin Moure. 1993. *Two Women Talking: Correspondence 1985–87.* Ed. Susan McMaster. Toronto: Living Archives of the Feminist Caucus of the League of Canadian Poets.

Memory, Identity, and Redemption
Notes on the Culture of Autobiography

FRANCESCO LORIGGIO

Redeem
The time. Redeem the
The unread vision...
T.S. Eliot

But, I would ask, to whom does identity no longer matter?

Paul Ricoeur

Towards the end of the 1970s Christopher Lasch described American social behaviour of the time as a kind of grass-roots disenchantment with progress. "Having no hope of improving their lives," he contended, "people ... convinced themselves that what matters is psychic self-improvement: getting in touch with their feelings, eating health food, taking lessons in ballet or belly-dancing, immersing themselves in the wisdom of the East, jogging, learning how to 'relate,' overcoming the 'fear of pleasure'" (Lasch 1979, 29). Together with other things, at the heart of this retreat from "the political turmoil of the sixties" into "privatism" and "personal preoccupations" lurked a penchant for confession and autobiography. Lasch was harsh about the new turn of events. In *The Culture of Narcissism,* the book from which the above quotations are taken, and in *The Minimal Self* (1984), its sequel of a few years later, no phenomenon escapes suspicion: from the sexual revolution, to the rekindling of the Cold War under the Reagan presidency, to feminism, to the bureaucratization of procreation and family planning, social mores are always symptomatic, are always available to further diagnosis. Scratch the veneer of self-justification the decade wraps itself in, and the celebration of the emotions will actually reveal itself to be a flight from feelings; the freedom of open marriages a refusal of commitment; the care for the body anxiety over physical decline, old age; and self-awareness, precisely, narcissism or its accompanying tic, the belief that survival comes before all else. There you have – Lasch insists – the human condition North-American style during the 1970s and the 1980s.

Anyone whose business is literary criticism might rightly wonder how Lasch would have responded to the current fascination with life stories and autobiographies, or to the heavy incidence of confessionalism and/or other autobiographical markers within critical writing. Would he treat them as a protraction, an after-effect – perhaps now restricted to the campus and to the campus sphere of interest – of the state of affairs he deplored in the 1970s and early 1980s? Or would he revise his own assessment of the earlier decades? What would he think of books such as Gloria Anzaldua's *Borderlands*, Frank Lentricchia's *The Edge of Night*, Nancy Miller's *Getting Personal*, or collections such as *The Intimate Critique*, which mix criticism and reflections of a very personal nature?

Lasch's works are a good place in which to begin a discussion of autobiography and the web of considerations – historical, cultural, and ethical – it inspires. For *The Culture of Narcissism* and *The Minimal Self* put autobiography against a background that produces an eerie sense of déjà vu, cultural uncanniness that is critically quite embarrassing, perhaps even disturbing. No doubt about it, in these two books Lasch is speaking about the phenomenon, about the word that has dominated the intellectual debate of the last quarter of a century, about *postmodernity*. The references to the retreat from the political gives the issue away right from the start. And yet Lasch steers the actuality of his topic towards unexpected swerves. In his two books there is little trace of the sophistication academic critics have come to expect from the debate on the postmodern. Bluntly stated, *The Culture of Narcissism* and *The Minimal Self* do without some of the pivotal theoretical patronages of the contemporary intellectual world a bit too blatantly for our comfort.

The accounts that literary critics have most commonly looked up to have more frequently adumbrated postmodernity or autobiography in terms of *grands récits* and *petits récits* – of the demise of the former and the proliferation of the latter. On its own the emphasis on the *récit* part of the formula sends us back to one of the most obsessive leitmotifs of contemporary philosophers – the centrality of language and linguistics. Indeed, autobiography owes a good chunk of its fortune, these days, to the fact that for a whole sector of literary theory it has been *the* test case with which to settle *the* question. Deconstructionists, particularly, just haven't been able to avoid confronting themselves with works that seem to promote authorship, voice, and subjectivity, besides mimetic representation. What better specimen on which to verify the axiom whereby, when all is said and done, it is always textuality, language, or rhetoric that prevails? In an essay that anticipates the gist of quite a lot of criticism about autobiography, Paul De Man (1979, 926) suggests that the autobiographist's exaltation of the self might be better understood as an effacement. Since autobiographical texts, or texts with strong autobiographical proclivities, rest on personification, on a paradoxical marshalling of prosopopoeia, since voice and face are conferred to the narrating "I" by means of a trope, attributes are simultaneously granted and withheld, are instituted and unmasked as very public constructions. Autobiographies are the exception that reasserts the rule, writing that illustrates how literariness operates.

By contrast, the parables Lasch would parlay into criticism are about vogue, fashion, human conduct. The locale in which they situate their analyses is the laboratory of everyday sociology – Main Street America. And the narcissism they allude to is John Doe's or Jane Doe's – yours, mine, and everyone else's. Lasch's two books are unabashedly straightforward psychohistory, empirically compiled portrayals of people's demeanour in North America circa 1975 to 1985. As such, the correspondences they vehicle for us install extremely insidious dilemmas into the debate on postmodernity.

If Lasch's reportage-narratives are credible, if, however unphilosophical they may be, they are an appropriate rendering of the ferments we associate with the postmodern, then the theories that have announced postmodernity are in double jeopardy. Either they are depictive theories, the late-twentieth-century props of a realism that, in spite of appearances, has no explanatory power (it is coterminous with the late twentieth century, with all the culture of the period, it tells how the times are, not why they are as they are). Or, should postmodernist theories be deemed to be explanatory, then they are self-contradictory (by refusing any representational responsibility, they would be without any "out-there" to explain; by legitimizing the kind of observations Lasch comes up with, they would be explaining by citing as proof that which they should instead be interpreting). This is, I believe, the preliminary monkey wrench that affects all the pieces of the philosophical apparatus that supposedly has made the intellectual climate of these last decades run. But the parallels that Lasch's books, in their down-home, un-Parisian candour, allow to surface also raise problems with the details, with some of the individual issues.

In *The Minimal Self*, writing your memoirs is like being witness to the barest of stories – the story of a self that has perdured against all odds and dare not ask for anything more. It is doomsaying from the side of survival, a slightly less nervous variation on the imagery of disaster that takes hold of the American mind and finds responsive chords almost everywhere, from groups protesting nuclear testing, to environmentalists uncertain about the future of the planet, to religious sects awaiting the arrival of Judgment Day, to individuals just discontented with the daily grind or the ominous ubiquity of the government and its agencies. That is, Lasch's rehearsal of postmodernity is complete: along with autobiography and the staple items, it manages to accommodate also the then still incipient apocalyptic strain of theory. In so doing, it deranges *avant la lettre* other facets of the conventional wisdom about postmodernity. Not only because Lasch's is a narrative that promises resolution, which verges on closure and thus exposes the well-roundedness of the story high theorists have tried to keep discreetly fragmentary (in typical postmodern theory, the apocalyptic theme is not stressed with quite the same insistence by the thinkers who have concentrated on narcissism, the precession of simulacra, and the like). The analogies between Lasch's books and those of the lineage criticism has monumentalized and enshrined, of the Lyotards, the Foucaults, or the Baudrillards, are analogies between low theory – or perhaps, as we would say today, a cultural studies approach – and high theory, between genres and traditions of thought. Echoes of American pragmatism run through Lasch's predilection for analyses that linger on the actions of individuals, on the social, public consequences of the decline of ideologies and the revival of apocalyptic discourse, rather than on the pre-eminence of signs and sign systems. And it *is* disconcerting, it *does* increase the level of hermeneutic suspicion to suddenly realize that, after all, the powerful, captivating exhortations about the end of the subject, the end of humanism, the end of history fit together historically with the experience of the Holocaust and the messianism of fundamentalist religious sects.

Most important, the analogies between Lasch and the theories of the postmodern extend also to the omissions. Although for different reasons, *The Culture of Narcissism, The Minimal Self* and De Man's article assign to autobiography an equally negative role. In the picture Lasch paints, the American people of the post-Vietnam era have finally reached that stage in history where decadence begins. As citizens of other major Western nations, they too now suffer from a surfeit of history; events have become the nightmare from which they would like to wake up so that forgetfulness may begin. Writing of yourself and apocalypticism reinforce each other: worrying about disaster – imminent or perpetrated – leads to the withdrawal from public life, to an atomistic, ultra-individualized society; the social paralysis, the more serious, massive dropping-out that goes with the loss of interest in the affairs of the *polis,* with the mass-introspection of the 1970s and the 1980s, is best epitomized by the fear of potential catastrophes or the anguish, the anxiety, about the catastrophes of the past, distant, and near. For De Man the infinite multiplication of *petits récits,* the retreat from History writ large that the rehabilitation of autobiography might be made to signal would not be such a bad epilogue did it not conceal too conspicuous a literary and ideological pitfall. In dealing with autobiography, Demanian criticism must unveil the unabated and unmastered susceptibility for representation, not the desire for *self-representation*. The personal is always an epiphenomenon; the moment you surrender to it, you transform yourself into an embodiment of something else, of mechanisms that require "reading" in order for them to be explicit. With classical postmodernism, the postmodernism closely allied to deconstructionist philosophy, there is no tension between the narrated "I" and the codes overriding it. The "I" has no option beyond acknowledging its grammaticality: as soon as it steps outside the public domain, it forfeits all semblance of autonomy. But autonomy is an obligation, a traditional illusion that De Man finds well worth losing.

Understandably perhaps, considering the assumptions presiding over them, neither of these emplotments of autobiography, attitudes towards history, and the imagination of disaster can permit itself to contemplate any significant variables in the elements with which it operates. The American citizenry that *The Culture of Narcissism* or *The Minimal Self* portray is too innocently homogeneous, too zealously beholden to the analytical tools of traditional twentieth-century sociology. Lasch collapses the determining conceptual category into the notion of class and assigns to the *middle* class – white and male, despite his many nods to feminism – the role of the protagonist of Americana. Race and ethnicity don't appear at all in the psycho-history he sketches out, either as forces in American society or as criteria through which to filter research. Hence the request for autobiography can be blamed on a coy, spoiled-child, glutted boredom with a tradition ultra-familiar and too easily accessible, a malaise akin to the late-modern American fondness for Geraldo, Oprah, docu-dramas, pills, drugs and therapy, which needs to be diagnosed and set right. Lasch never stops to inquire about where, exactly, autobiographies are coming from, whether they may be written from within a pluralized horizon, by African Americans or Chicanos or women or immigrants differently positioned in the American society by status and its allotment of cultural power, suffering not from too much history but from not enough. He never asks whether such a positioning counts as data, or whether proceeding from such data would not give an altogether different weight to the apocalyptic dimensions of the sociological or philosophical prologues that autobiography is often charged with proving or confirming. Having denied the texts any *specific* sociocultural provenance, he can neglect the consequences that are attached to them and that would quickly seep into the history with which he surrounds them.

The narrating "I," whose profile De Man outlines in his essay is equally general, an Ur-subject with only a linguistic identity, whose requisites and stipulations are ministered to by grammar and textuality. Unable to countenance the possibility that narrators may be differently marked, may initiate their tales with different pasts, different burdens and different agendas, and may long for or be striving towards different outcomes, Demanian deconstruction skips over the rest. Its emplotment of autobiography, history, and literature is predictable and without choice. The encounter with textuality, with the great equalizer of defacement, occurs always *after*, as a conclusion, never at the beginning, when it can be configured as a struggle, an event that the "I" has already allowed for, and in coming to grips with which he or she is positing other venues and other ventures or even other inklings of the times (i.e., more mixed and more complex versions of postmodernism than the vulgata of earlier decades offers).

In what follows I explore some of the current alternative collusions of autobiography – especially Western minoritarian autobiography, the autobiography of those residents of the West who are in deficit relation with history, and, especially, the ethical ramifications of its emergence. As in these introductory comments, my concern will be not individual autobiographies, not the single texts, but the notion of autobiography and the kind of other disciplinary or critical sponsorships it elicits within the contemporary ethos.

Unlike Lasch, studies of self-writing quite often dwell on the positive, "active" ingrediency of self-writing. Elizabeth Bruss (1976) and Albert E. Stone (1982) have entitled their books on the genre, respectively, *Autobiographical Acts* and *Autobiographical Occasions and Original Acts*; Nancy Miller's (1991) opening essay in *Getting Personal*, whose subtitle is *Feminist Occasions and Other Autobiographical Acts*, explicitly equates autobiographies with "cultural criticism." In feminist critical texts the personal re-emerges as part of the response to the final entrenchment of theory within academia. By its presence in a discourse about literature or – as more frequently happens – about theory itself, the intrusion of the writer's voice, of his or her here and now, casts doubt on the process through which theorists achieve their authority. The target is not the "aboutness" of theory, its specific contents; rather, it is its form, its exasperating rationality, its dry sense of control, its being addressed to abstract, disembodied model readers, all of which feminist critics have seen as the avatar of masculinity, of the power of the male, a writing for which any recourse to personal experience or any personalized bond a writer might wish to establish with readers would be a deplorable impropriety. In this respect, the question is not the peculiar properties, the specific message or value of this or that theoretical school. In "Me and My Shadow," a landmark article of autobiographical criticism now republished in *The Intimate Critique*, Jane Tompkins (1993, 33) quotes excerpts from works by Michel Foucault, Félix Guattari, and Harold Bloom that she had begun to read and then candidly divulges that she couldn't finish any of the texts. Another article in the same collection, by Linda Robertson (1993), reports, with high dosages of irony, on an after-the-lecture reception for John Hillis Miller. Going still further, Susan Koppelman (1993), also a contributor to the anthology, ignores altogether the usual etiquette and academic circuits of criticism and writes about literature in letters she sends to the readership of friends and acquaintances she has forged for herself throughout the years.

Of course, as criticism autobiography has its share of skeletons in the closet, some of which are palpably textual. How private must the allusion be in order for it to qualify as autobiographical, to effect a break, a suspension in the rhythm of a theoretical or critical reflection – to be noticeable? Do you have to mention the body, to confess that you've been wanting to go to the bathroom as you've been writing, as does Tompkins (1993)? Or do you have to talk about your father's penis, as does Nancy Miller (1991). Do works of autobiographical criticism not have to be distinguished, with some appearing to be more interesting than others? And will this not finally serve to reinstall authority, to reabsorb such texts into the academic juggernaut? How much – if any – autobiography should a teacher encourage from students? By reappropriating the emotional and the personal as female, isn't a critic essentializing? But the overall, accumulated stakes are higher than this – much higher.

Autobiographical criticism clearly rejects the modern (and postmodern) heroic, epic version of the critical gesture. In one fell swoop it conjoins and relativizes the meanderings of some of the genealogies that theory has most usually taken for granted. It demonstrates how obsequiously the critic has reconciled the idea that a text is like a "catalyst" (T.S. Eliot 1953, 26) or a "pudding" (Wimsatt 1954, 4) or a "crystal" (Lévi-Strauss 1958, 254) – and is therefore accessible to anyone who has at his or her disposal the right prosthesis, the right methodologies – with the idea that the text is oracular, obscure, ineffable and, therefore, accessible to the exegesis of interpreters capable of surpassing themselves, being endowed with special individual skills. As it is for anyone aspiring to become a scientist or a writer, aspiring to become a critic is, in modernity, to agree to intellectual purgation, to a secular asceticism whose first law is the denouncing of a series of fallacies (intentional, affective, and so on) and that culminates, by the second half of the twentieth century, in the abrogation of subjectivity. Ever since (at least) Mallarmean symbolism and its revisitations by modernist writer-critics or postmodernist philosopher-critics-writers, only if you know how to let go of your personality do you deserve authority. On the strategic superiority of anti-biography, there has been little disagreement in recent Western high culture. Michel Foucault's (1977, 138) celebrated lines about the "murmur of indifference" with which queries concerning authorship should be met ("What matter who's speaking?"), or about the need to mask the self, to desire anonymity (Foucault 1988), neatly clinch T.S. Eliot's (1953, 25) equally celebrated dictum about the need to embrace tradition and the effects of such an embrace: the right aesthetic fire is that which converts the artist's progress into "a continual self-sacrifice," a "continual surrender." Academic criticism has bought into these itineraries, and most emphatically and eagerly into those components that could be best bureaucratized, domesticated into a disciplinary routine and the proper institutional confection (two classes a week for three years, enrolment paid in advance, and you get the stamp on your transcript). Whereas a Verlaine or a Rimbaud relinquishes his identity ecstatically – at the coffee shop or at the opium den – future critics do so by learning to rejoice in the death of the author, are initiated into the critical vanguard through the university's less intimidating *via negativa* – by writing papers that are adequately objective.[1]

Autobiographical criticism and the criticism that focuses on autobiography with the intent to retrieve it append the history of ordinary peoplehood to the three-pronged saga of self-denial, which sanctions the apotheosis of the scientist, the *artiste*, and the literary theorist – the heirs of the priest. In such texts as *The Intimate Critique* the intellectual is just your everyday man or woman who happens to be a critic. A discrete, unobstreperous unpacking, this umpteenth shedding of the aura draws the debate about literature away from its usual gravitational pulls. Despite the deliberate ad hocery and/or the reluctance of some of the proponents to indulge in theoretical speculation, in the lingo they repudiate, the rehabilitation of the personal or the private is not without theoretical purchase: it brings back into the limelight all the irritants connected with action that modernity has sought to repress, to keep on the sidelines, or, at any rate, away from centre stage.

One of these has to do with the metaphorics of late-twentieth-century literary theory. In reading autobiographical criticism we enter the structure-agency controversy through the door reserved for literature and literary studies. The performative bent of the essays in *The Intimate Critique* or *Getting Personal* reminds us of a famous observation of Charles Sanders Peirce (1932, 189), that lithium can be defined in terms of atomic weight or by enumerating the steps required to obtain it chemically, "what you are to *do* in order to gain a perceptual acquaintance with the object." And it reminds us that the duality Peirce so limpidly discerned has been beclouded but not interrupted by the most notorious recent outbreak, the tug-of-war between Jacques Derrida and John Searle, or by literary studies' co-optations (massively in favour of the French philosopher). When Nancy Miller (1991) says that women writing autobiographical criticism overcome the "anxiety about feminine exposure" (23) by accepting being authors of a "personal spectacle" (24), by "making a spectacle of gender" (22), by, so to speak, "making a scene," her remarks have to be taken at face value as a transposing in the vocabulary of literary criticism of some of the underlying corollaries of the agency-oriented camp.

Autobiographies are speech acts, and a critical perspective that, in grappling with such writings, puts into relief the relevance of action and borrows its tropes from drama would seem as à propos as one whose metaphors are text- or language- or grammar-based. The many uses and abuses of the concept of subject and of subjectivity in literary studies today are indicative of preferences. They do not exhaust the resources criticism has at its disposal. Such concepts as that of person, individual, and character, which other periods have found valuable, could also apply on those critical occasions that now depend exclusively on the concept of the subject, and they would carry with them other theoretical or critical traditions (Rorty 1988, 78–98).

Any restressing of action and agency resuscitates with new urgency the question of the singularity of the lives that self-writings narrate. No matter how it is described in detail, autobiography differs from other genres in so far as it is about specific individuals – the individuals writing it – who cannot be replaced by anyone else. Modernity's rebuttal – that autobiographies are written and, as written, are constituted by devices public in nature, that individuality must be constructed to be noticed, and that this calls upon supplementary operations (themselves rule-laden and rule-bound) – is a valid one, though not without reproach. Ultimately, it dilutes individuality into originality, confusing it with the same paradoxical privilege it has inevitably, from modernism to postmodernism, bestowed on writers and scientists (a text and the events and characters it narrates are "estranged," "defamiliarized," in the vocabulary Russian formalists have bequeathed to criticism, by proper manipulation of collective, "impersonal" conventional strategies). And this, when it comes down to it, cancels out individuality, reduces it to an after-effect, a receptacle, an instantiation of codes and norms.

The resistance to theory that the last decades have been witnessing does not reflect, as Paul De Man (1986, 8ff.) claimed, a reaction against the importation of linguistics in the literary domain; rather, what is questioned is the privilege certain theories have accorded to a certain linguistics, to certain principles, which have come to stand for the study of language *tout court*. From the Russian formalists to structuralism to poststructuralism, the paramount slogan of criticism has been the one drafted by Saussure: there are basic units of language and these units are constantly re-utilized in verbal communication and combine with each other in codified fashion. Be it the well sutured structure, be it *différance* or the play of signifiers or the trace or iteration, much of the conceptual armamentarium of literary theory presupposes lengthy disquisitions about signs or phonemes. But theory might have found an equally profitable departure in the cogitations about the expressive, creative aspects of verbal communication that a linguist such as Wilhelm Von Humboldt embarked upon in the nineteenth century, or in the notion of utterance Mikhail Bakhtin developed seventy years ago in polemic with the Russian Formalists.

If you start with language as *energeia,* as activity (Von Humboldt 1988: 49), with uttered language (Bakthin 1993), the unit of analysis is no longer determined by rules of linguistic or textual segmentation, by grammar, or by phonology. The repeatability of the elements will still be indispensable to any form of communication, but communication also obeys a second dynamic. As uttered, language is language exchanged by users. The units are always functional to some *particular* exchange: they may be large, small, simple, complex, as short as one word, or as spread out and as sprawling as a novel. They last until the individual users have said or written all they have to say, have finished their thought on the subject at hand. Moreover, the units situate themselves within a temporal rhythm, the rhythm of the exchange to which they belong: they may appear in the guise of a question or in the guise of an answer, come before or follow another unit. While each utterance may be grammatically similar to the other items of the sequence, to some degree it is always a once-for-all occurrence that escapes the stern determinism of abstract codifications. Here is how Bakhtin (1986, 105) describes it:

> The two poles of the text. Each text presupposes a generally understood (that is conventional within a given collective) system of signs, a language (if only the language of art) ... Everything behind each text that is repeated and reproduced, everything repeatable and reproducible, everything that can be given outside a given text (the given) conforms to this language system. But at the same time each text (as an utterance) is individual, unique, and unrepeatable, and herein lies its entire significance (its plan, the purpose for which it was created) ... With respect to this aspect, everything repeatable and reproducible proves to be material,

a means to an end. This notion extends somewhat beyond the bounds of linguistics or philology. The second aspect (pole) inheres in the text itself, but is revealed only in a particular situation and in a chain of texts (in the speech communication of a given area). This pole is linked not with elements (repeatable) in the system of language (signs), but with other texts (unrepeatable) by special dialogic ... relations. [It] is linked with the aspect of authorship and has nothing to do with natural, random single units.

To submit either of these alternatives to the interrogations and the quandaries the other deposits on a text would be thus to mix apples with oranges, to imply that there is only one justifiable theoretical faith, only one true road to interpretation. At the very least the hypothesis that frictions may co-exist within literature, that literature may admit contrasting attitudes, should be recognized at this late stage of the game.

In more or less direct conjunction with the polemic on singularity or the emphasis on agency and action, autobiography and autobiographical criticism let reverberate anew another critical *topos,* which pertains to the theoretical status of the emotions. Briefs against neutrality and impersonality have been held at various intervals during the last one hundred years, principally within projects aiming to detach the humanities from the straitjacket of models taken from the natural sciences. At their widest, most comprehensive compass, the parameters of the emotions overlap with those of ontology: Dasein, in Heidegger's (1963, 173) *Being and Time,* is always disclosed "mood-wise," manifesting itself as anguish or dread. It is due to their proximity to ontology that the emotions, within anti-scientistic philosophy, have always been coupled with practice and have been invoked, in effect, whenever it has become necessary to dissever practice from theory. In some of the works of the younger Bakhtin (1993, 13) – pages that, read today, speak trenchantly to current criticism's tendency for performing autobiography while discussing it – actions are unique, "once-occurring event[s] of Being," and thereby "something ... no longer thought of, but something that *is,* that ... is being actually and inescapably accomplished through me and others (accomplished *inter alia* also in my deed of cognizing) ... that is actually experienced, affirmed in an emotional-volitional manner." To act is to act "participatively," to be involved personally ("everything is given to me as a constituent moment of the event in which I am participating" [33]), hence passionately.

The syllogism is best rounded out by Charles Taylor, who touches all the bases and ties the many loose ends neatly together. Texts such as *Sources of the Self* (1989) and *Human Agency and Language* (1985) – exemplary for an understanding of new millennium – ground much of their reflection on an analysis of the emotions. They are obliged to do so because philosophy would be for nought if it didn't honour the commitment to examine every-day life that a number of the century's cultural strands, from existentialism on, have assigned to it. "How can we ever know that humans can be explained by any scientific theory *until* we actually explain how they live their lives in its terms?" asks Taylor (1989, 58). More specifically, philosophers cannot slide over these questions because many of the properties human beings exhibit in conducting their everyday business – our aspiration to dignity and fulfilment, our sense of how we are seen by others, and so forth – "are essentially bound up with the life of a subject of experience" and arouse "strong evaluations" that are inconceivable without the inducements and instigations that stem from feelings and passions (Taylor 1985, 54). Language and culture do impinge on the full gamut of the emotions, do bind individuals to other individuals, and do add further ethical caveats. But they require, in turn, carriers, vehicles, some embodiment that brings us back to the life of the sentiments. To echo the title of one of Taylor's essays, humans cannot but be "self-interpreting animals." Or, better, translating and distilling further the resonances of Heidegger's or Bakhtin's or Taylor's endeavours, autobiography is the mode of being by which and through which humans attain agency, proceed towards action. You always autobiographize in the book of your mind, you automatically arrange previous works and days in a narrative pattern before venturing that always subsequent gesture, which is always unrepeatable and new, which may prolong but also negate and rewrite time past. And you always do so with fear and trembling or a sigh of relief.

I don't want to belabour this more than I already have. The intersection where theories of self-interpretation, the emotions, and action converge is a very busy one.[2] I suppose I could summarize most of my argument thus far by saying that, in stressing the positive ingredients of autobiography, through its predilection for action and its subsidiary conceptual or literary analogies, autobiographical criticism corroborates a trademark commonplace of these last few decades, the one that proclaims the personal realm to be the same as the political and blurs the borders between the private and the public. Lasch and the deconstructionists dissolve the duality in favour of the public or of the code. It is language and rhetoric that (for a De Man, a Barthes, or a Derrida) "thinks" individual lives and individual stories. Or (for Lasch) there can be valid, political, positive action only where there is wide consensus, where the individual is at one with the broadest imaginable collectivity. What I have been maintaining is that in order for borders to be blurred, they must first be assented to, receive some ratification, and that once you agree that there is an antinomy between public and private you concede that any accentuation may just as easily go in the direction of the private, that the private, the personal, and the autobiographical are viable theoretical categories.

This is true, I would submit, across the board, on all levels of the debate about autobiography. And it modifies a number of the premises of the tradition of the modern or the postmodern. Emotions are steeped in language but are not depersonalized for being so: if I am suffering, it is not irrelevant that you sympathize with me or that you will be able to tell about my suffering, but it is my suffering. Life is always "in quest of narrative," in Paul Ricoeur's (1991) apt phrase. It is always being emplotted in the mind. But Hannah Arendt or Bakhtin would be quite warranted in noting that Ricoeur's approach to autobiography restates the usual twentieth-century platitude about the indivisibility of theory and praxis. Prompted by mental narratives that obey conventional generic wisdom, actions convert into unique events. The repercussions, the subsequent actions they beget, in being carried out, may be unexpected besides being unrepeatable. A "natality principle" is ensconced in every action since every action is potentially a new start: "To act in its most general sense, means to take an initiative, to begin ... The fact that man is capable of action means that the unexpected can be expected of him, that he is able to perform what is infinitely improbable" (Arendt 1958, 177, 178).

The force of narrative logic, which may at the outset propel my actions towards a certain *telos*, has no dominion over the consequences, the other actions those initial actions originate, and, thus, constantly relocates me and my decisions. In so far as a sense of self is the mandatory preamble of action, in so far as the self is "reflexively understood by the person in terms of his or her biography" (Giddens 1991, 53), human beings *rewrite* – rather than *write* – their lives. Mental, everyday autobiographies precede or follow activity. They are always accommodating new, unforeseen occurrences. Between life and life-writing there are straddlings, discontinuities, intermittent teeter-totterings. And this further complicates their relation. As narrations, mental autobiographies are modelled on the repertory of story-lines a culture keeps in its archive. As purveyors of specific, particular agencies, they are recapitulatory-inauguratory narratives, hence – it could be concluded – themselves a variety of action, even if, perhaps, one of those Bakhtin (1993, 13) dubbed "cognizing" actions.

In a similar vein, talk of form, of rhetorical strategies or the iterability of signs only serves to underscore the qualities that make a written autobiography a verbal product or text or literary work. It doesn't establish the *sort* of product, of text, or literary work an autobiography is. Were you to concede that prosopopoeia is the genre's master trope, and effacement the feature that attests to the text's literariness, you still wouldn't have quite shut the door on the reverse operation. Autobiography intertwines the singularity of the life being depicted with the story of the writer: it is the narrative in which "the hero, the narrator and the author can be identified by the same name" (Blasing 1977, xi; see also Lejeune 1975, the source of the equation). On this basis, it can with equal right be thought of as the text that refuses to be an allegory, whether of writing or of any other operation: just as the person whose masking tropology discloses remains *that* person, with all its other non-public, non-collective properties, so autobiography is literature that resists literature.

I am not proposing that criticism should turn the tables on the theories that have envisioned the autobiographical "I" as being pervaded by and absorbed into public, impersonal arrangements, precepts, and models. Like everyone else, I am aware that in late modernity declarations of individuality are, willy nilly, declarations of membership in some group or other. There are, at the historical level, connections between the collective and the particular peculiar to our portion of the century that haven't yet been hashed out critically. How are you yourself and a male or a female, an African American or Italian Canadian, a homosexual or a heterosexual, a labourer or a doctor, an adolescent or a senior citizen? My point is that, on these questions, criticism's obsession with the debunking of representation has been less of an advantage than has been presumed. We still aren't as clear as we might be about the distinguishing traits of types, archetypes, and stereotypes or of the concomitances between them, or about how each of these notions comes to bear upon an individual's self, now, in the pluralized, polyethnic, and multicultural environment of which we are part.

For all its sophistication, advanced theory hasn't gone much beyond Erich Auerbach's (1959, 11–76) early statements on the workings of the trope known as *figura*. In the Christian worldview the German scholar recounts, the individual earthly, historical destiny is enmeshed with Providence's emplotment of history, which exists as a perfect mimesis of immutable heavenly designs: the Tree of Knowledge foreshadows the Cross, the story of Moses that of Christ. Criticism has merely detemporalized and secularized these connections, with language or literature or fiction and the various models harking back to them substituting for Providence and myth. The continuous search for recondite motivations has expounded away and neatly diluted the historical salience of the cultural revolution that had as its centrepiece the individual. But today – and for several decades now – individuals have also been assuming general categories to construct their private unique identities. You can present yourself as African American, lesbian, Italian American, and so forth by adopting some of the signs – haircuts, lifestyles, dress codes – particular groups ascribe to themselves or are ascribed by others. By the same token, public images – types, archetypes, stereotypes, *figurae* – perdure in so far as individuals recycle them, reactivate them in their lives or in their writings or films or videos or research monographs. And this exposes the culture reproduced by public, conventional, statal, or other institutional-collective means to the vagaries, the improbabilities, of private lives, of individual talent. Traffic is two-way and loop-like: from public to private and from private to public, from the impersonal to the personal and from the personal to the impersonal, with one feeding on the other. Nonhuman archeologists or anthropologists researching our world would probably concur with the semiotician Youri Lotman (1977, 8–9; 1990) that, from the perspective of humanity, culture – the sum total of all individual, unrepeatable written utterances – is an example of "I-to-I" communication, a large auto-biography, the repository of the vicissitudes of the species.[3] In the light of the recursivity that governs the relation between the private and the public realms, it isn't a *boutade* for the creator of Madame Bovary to profess that "Madame Bovary, c'est moi." The many resistances autobiography opposes to literature don't prevent it from being a suitable metaphor for literature – no less valid, in any event, than the concept of text or the notion of literariness are for some of its features.

As might be surmised, the third theme I referred to earlier grafts onto this debate. The tensions between the singular and the collective, the private and the public, are played out, in autobiography, against an apocalyptic setting whose presence, in turn, lays bare some of the whys and wherefores of culture. The individual's willingness to take cover in group identity is sanctioned – at least in some measure – by the enlarging of the horizon of reproduction that has occurred in the last century, especially its last few decades. The availability of always new media has increased our awareness of one of the degrees-zero of culture, whereby cultural activity is a struggle for permanence. Going to the group or going on paper are part and parcel of the same desire. In writing about your life, you register emplotted recollections. Unlike the implicit stock-taking that goes on in the mind, or the reassessments and re-evaluations that prompt or inhibit action, the words you consign to the page are remembrance twice over, memory *of* the past and memory *for* the future.

As records of personal, private histories that depend on and contribute to collective history, autobiographies recapitulate a function of literature that antecedes and supersedes most of the issues criticism has lionized in the last few decades. A survey of the criss-crossings between culture, literary texts in general, and genres such as autobiography during the last fifty years would vindicate John Searle's (1977, 200) conviction, contra Derrida (1977), that the phenomenon of iteration, the reusability of the rules on which communication is founded, is an altogether different affair from writing, the technical reproducibility of signs. Written works – all of them, of whatever genre and style – inscribe, have the capacity to fix, to outlive human beings, to protract meanings beyond the bound of their single carriers. Before it is narrative or not, traditional or not, avant-garde or not, culture is a Vichian commixture, textuality in which the imagination cohabits with history under the tutelage of Mnemosyne. Poets, recites *The New Science*, are the first historians of nations because memory has three aspects: "memory when it remembers things, imagination when it imitates or alters them and invention when it gives them a new turn or puts them into proper arrangement and relationship" (Vico 1984, 313–14).

Vichianly intended, culture is always ethically charged because it must pay proper homage to time and entropy, the other-than-human forces constantly knocking at its door. The extent to which it is affected by temporality – just as it fends time off – is probably best brought home by the wistfulness that surrounds ruins, or by the outrage that greets censorship or vandalism, any action that hastens the always impending amnesia, the Alzheimer syndrome of the collective mind. Unattended, manuscripts, film footage decay; the statues in the squares suffer pollution, erode, slowly lose pieces, change appearance. And politicians and the powers that be can doctor artifacts, undo their basic, intrinsic monumentality. You can have tow trucks pull away the disgraced leader's mausoleum. You can include the name in the encyclopedia and then erase it as soon as the bearer is in prison or in exile. One day, Milan Kundera writes, official pictures show Clementis, the Czech party bureaucrat, next to Gottwald, the party leader, on the balcony, facing the crowd below. Four years later, Clementis has been charged with treason and hanged, his image airbrushed: all that remains of him in the pictures is the cap he placed on Gottwald's head (Kundera 1994, 3).

That nether side is built into culture. Regardless of the material employed or of how much mechanical reproduction has further decelerated their slow mortality, texts are always written in a country church yard, etched on faded urns. They are an elegy, a necrology as well as a eulogy: in celebrating someone's life or past events of your own, you mourn their passing; in mourning, you celebrate. The unstated preliminary counsel of art and signs in general is: "The world we evoke is not there or belongs to another era. We permit you only to act as if you are recollecting it." Kundera's reaffirmation of the political value of cultural memory, his conception of the writer as participating in "a struggle against forgetting," (ibid.), is supplemented by the epigraph that opens one of Edmond Jabès's (1991, n.p.) books: "écrire, maintenant, uniquement pour faire savoir qu'un jour j'ai cessé d'exister; que tout, au-dessus et autour de moi, est devenu bleu, immense, tendue vide."

For the view that I have been defending here, the metaphorization of the Holocaust, which in the North America of the late twentieth century has gone hand in hand with the resurgence of autobiography, rather than an excuse for navel-gazing is an attempt to work through the apocalyptic propensities intrinsic to culture. By not appreciating this, you overestimate the capacity of modernity to reduce the sense of ontological insecurity. Some high theory has seemed content to resolve the problem of the coincidences with history by pointing to the proliferation of simulacra. Such whistlings in the dark notwithstanding, risk remains a major motif of current thought.[4] The advances in military know-how, the pluralization of society, the growth of the world's population, the daily incidence of mobility have increased – and not decreased – the vulnerability of individuals and/or groups. In narrating our epoch, you are constantly invited to establish causalities between the multifarious existence of risk-enhancing tools and that of the many sign-making devices: the vertiginous growth of the industry of cultural reproduction can be seen – without forcing the debate on culture, I would submit – as a kind of obscure counterbalancing technological stock response to the always more ingenious, more elaborate and all-inclusive capacity for destruction. Not to mention the inherent fragility of the simulacra: the paper on which we send those faxes, the diskettes on which we save those articles, the videotapes we watch deteriorate very rapidly. Were some unthinkable cataclysm to obliterate New York, the drawings on porcelain or ceramic artifacts would probably still be readable in the debris long after documents on paper have biodegraded and plastic materials all shrivelled up. The narrative of loss that postmodernism has tried to repress, to wish away, has actually kept returning in always more obtrusive formats. Many of us (not all) copy excessively to protect ourselves from excessive obsolescence as well as to express our right to consume or to exploit the accessibility we have been afforded by technology. More than a society of spectacle, ours, here in the West, Andreas Huyssen (1995) has intimated, is a society of the museum: the main goals and the overall modus operandi of that institution (conservation through selection, permanent exhibits but continuous readjustment and updating of the items) have come to stand for good number of the psyco-social and ideological undercurrents of the age.

Significantly, to overlook the complicities between autobiography, risk, culture, and memory would be to disregard some of the core patterns of

North American culture. The after-the-bomb scenarios popular culture has devised in the Mad Max film cycle or in the Terminator series or in minor one-film blockbusters such as Kevin Kostner's *Waterworld* elevate self-reliance to the rank it has in the Western. They are populated by characters – marauding mercenaries, reluctant bad-good-guys, or plain simple folk – who are first of all excellent *bricoleurs*, with a knack for creating formidable weaponry and useful gadgetry out of the detritus of nuts, bolts, sheet metal, and rusty bric-à-brac the Explosion or some other global disaster has deposited on the burnt out or submerged planet. The history these fictions unfurl is gloomy but, like the biblical, original Apocalypse, also chiliastic, almost as if the yearning for a new start could not be experienced without some shuddering, or as if the forlorn panorama were a projection of the desire for a clean slate, for some pioneering, primordial phase of the kind epitomized by the frontier, Wild West days. In the United States autobiography has been the genre of the "frontierization" of literature from the Puritans on. Lest it be forgotten, the American intellectual who most eloquently and most explicitly called for the closing out of the "overpaid accounts" to the muses of "Greece and Ionia," for the emergence of a truly nativist American culture, was the author of "Song of Myself" (Whitman 1950, 157). Nor are other exemplary twists to this narrative about culture, annihilation, and national identity lacking in the North American continent. In the 1970s, while Lasch was chastizing the despondency of his compatriots, a few miles up north Canadian nationalist critics were discovering that survival in the face of a harsh environment or a resisting indigenous population was the underlying archetype of English-Canadian poetry and fiction, the recurring image that condensed and refracted the cultural history of the country (Atwood 1972). On the other side of the English-French divide, *la survivance* is to this day *the* rallying cry of francophone Québécois, who view their culture as being at permanent risk and the preservation of the Québécois identity as an unfinished project.

This is why those critics who, in reacting to multiculturalism, today berate minority groups for their sometimes protective posturings, for having smuggled the criterion of self-interest in matters cultural, end up with narratives that are invariably ambiguous and/or contradictory. Both as a critical occasion (in texts that highlight the writer's professional affiliation, his or her critical allegiances) or as a political occasion (in those cases in which the writer's minority status, whether imputable to gender, ethnicity, or race, is one of the subjects covered), the autobiographical impulse pays tribute to the same prerogatives dominant perspectives enjoy and that dominant groups can afford to expect as a right of citizenry. In the 1970s, the 1980s, and the 1990s, by consigning your story to paper you are doing what others are doing when they retrieve hitherto unknown women writers or when they plead for a canon broad enough to house minoritarian texts: you are asking to share in officialdom, in that machinery of perpetuation that, in as much as it is public and collective and does the remembering for you, grants you the power to turn off some of the words, some of the images gurgling in the mind. Autobiography is writing that, by and large, would rather not have been written, or that is written so that the writer may forget.

Culturally and politically, the attempts to delegitimize autobiography by relegating it among the pathological genres of the age is a confirmation of privilege no less than an exorcising ritual. Stoicism and understatement are good medicine, provided they are medicine for everyone else but you: those who protest the "broken polity" (Hughes 1993, 3ff.) don't see themselves as complainers who are also vying for air time and who could be cured by learning to grin and bear it; they are social critics. The popularity of the autobiographical mode, its traditionally low ranking in literary gradings, and its current re-evaluation can all be attributed to this doubleness. Self-writing is the textual site where, in compliance with the rules and regulations that ensure the longevity and perdurability of official cultures, the onus for the inscription of minority groups is continuously displaced, is transferred away from school syllabi, state-wide exams, textbooks, the reading required for acculturation and on to the individual. If you want to be inscribed – or just to inscribe – you have to go private, to do it yourself and to hope in the benevolence of the market. Vice versa, it is with all these political and cultural encumbrances, with all this freight – as the most demotic and most constrained of modes, the mode practised by people who, as individuals, cannot forget, are condemned to remember, and perhaps to remember passionately, emotionally – that the autobiographical mode has been espoused by minority writers. When you write about yourself as a member of a group, you are writing *about* autobiography and the autobiographical, about their meaning.

At most what would seem to be in order, now, in the twenty-first century, would be some distinguishing among the subgenres to which the overlappings between autobiography, culture, and risk can give rise. A prophetic or, in any event, future-looking element runs through American Puritan or American nativist autobiographical texts. Residues of it can be detected in the apocalyptic strains of the 1970s and the 1980s, where, for all its private discomforts, individual destiny is never entirely severed from history writ large, from a collective destiny always all-embracing, with everybody equally affluent and majoritarian. In twentieth-century immigrant texts, the past needs always to be confronted, even when it is to be surpassed, when the slant is towards eulogy more than towards elegy. Carrying a celebratory plot are all the immigrant autobiographies that endorse the metamorphosis they narrate: Mary Antin's (1912) enthusiastic account of her Americanization, of her progress from Russia into the new land, the new culture, the new citizenship still emblematically recapitulates this subcategory. Elegiac plots narrate an incomplete and more sober metamorphosis, one that coincides with the separation from a "there" or a "then." The poetics of these plots has been perhaps most trenchantly voiced by the Italian-Canadian poet Pier Giorgio Di Cicco. His poetry recodifies the usual negative stereotype about Italians being too melodramatic and stretches the scope of its emendations to encompass the cultural and political uses of memory. Sentimentality, he admonishes, "is what the proud fear" (Di Cicco 1986, 5). In a world more and more suspicious of all-purpose formulas, in which "life is one foolishness or another" (14), the emotions can be a "choosing." And this goes – on the same grounds – for memory: to immigrants, it too may be "like a film too maudlin to pity," and yet "the best thing [they] have to feel human about" (1979, 10).

As with singularity and unrepeatability, the implications of this are momentous. Once again, autobiography picks up on material usually catalogued under the rubric of "postmodernism" and changes – or at least irrevocably contaminates – its valence. The apocalyptic strain, the sense of an ending that high theory has accepted in euphoric tones, is triggered now by real historical risks, by ontological insecurity (members of immigrant groups) or by the push for a new beginning ("frontier" mentality). In either case, whether it leads to the retrieval of the past or to its disavowal, the yearning for inscription, to fix some identity, clashes with the irreducible anti-essentialism of postmodernist thought. However public and conventional and provisional the identity autobiography constructs, it must be believed for it to function until the sequel, the next re-emplotment of events into a cohesive narrative, occurs.

Here is where the ethical vocation of autobiographical texts discloses itself most transparently. Risk personalizes the pathos of inscription. It's my survival, as a body and as a cultural being, that is at stake when I seek comfort in the secular mightiness of the word, in the mediological, durational, public, conventional properties of written language. The historical (as opposed to existential) poignancy of the lines by Jabès quoted above is conveyed perhaps with greatest concision by the Native American writer Leslie Marmon Silko (1977, 2): "[Stories] aren't entertainments. Don't be fooled. They are all we have, you see, to fight off illness and death. You don't have anything if you don't have stories." But once a text is fixed by a medium, once it enters the public domain, it partakes of another dynamic, which, too, is summed up emblematically by autobiography.

The unarticulated story, the story left in the mind, is an incomplete, truncated one. It yields no endurance, no respite from the anxiety of finitude. Autobiographical inscription revitalizes the relation between writer and reader without discrediting the self-oriented pulls of the writing. In surviving by fixing, I survive for you as well as for myself, and if I fail for you I also fail for myself. Just as the individual is constituted by the group but is the carrier of the group and helps constitute it with his or her own personal story, so autobiography cannot do without the interlocutors whose lives it can help shape (for the story to be successful, you have to have readers who acknowledge the inscription, who, by reading it, release it within, appropriate it for, history). Texts are never only memoranda that groups or individuals send to themselves. We are right when we most commonly think of stories, poems, essays, reportages, communiqués in relation to "I-You" communication, the intraspecies or intragroup type of communication that is addressed to others. But autobiographies append to this unimpeachable axiom the proviso whereby "I-You" communication builds upon, rather than negates, "I-I" communication.

Autobiographical writings of all stripes circulate within a space that can be always pluralized. Human culture comprises the communication among groups, group cultures, the communication among individual members. To listen to Lotman (1985), even the single brain is amenable to internal division and thus to "I-You" commerce: in bicameral neurology, lateralized functions are asymmetrical to each other. Is such a space a postlapsarian space, the space succeeding Eden or some initial unfragmented condition? Is it a pre-utopian space, the space that is a prelude to unhindered, ideal conversations founded on shared general principles? Is it the intermediary, mediating space of hybridity, of cultural mixture, or perhaps of the new realignments of fellowship, the new social amalgamations that our age seems to be edging towards? Perhaps all that really can or should be asserted, critically, is that pluralism is an inalienable constituent of all versions of human interaction, of those that fall prey to the myth of Babel and of those that refashion the myth into polyphony or dialogism. Contrary to all appearances, "I-You" communication, dialogue, is not synonymous with the transferring of speech: it entails translation and interpretation – hence different individuals, different ideologies, different frames of mind – rather than the full, unadulterated reception of data. Bakhtin, the father of polyphony, summarized all of this with the term "extralocality," the outsidedness of each person to the other, without which there would be, not exchange of messages, opinions, words, texts but, rather, the continuous corroboration of a code or of a single perspective.

This is how I would reformulate what is, in recent political philosophy, the suggestion most relevant to the many imbrications between culture, autobiography, memory, and the *Zeitgeist* – the view that politics must make room for the appeal for recognition coming from groups and individuals (see Taylor 1994). That my personal or group identity is dialogical, that it is guaranteed by my fellow human beings (who can know aspects about me and my story I can't know myself – what the back of my head looks like, how I was born, how I will die – and for whom I act as a guarantor), that this cannot be denied, amplifies rather than reduces the role of self-representation. You don't have to be a card-carrying supporter of liberal individualism, or of group solipsism, to realize how socially useful individuality or group identity can be. I will not be able to fulfill my responsibilities towards you unless I am able to detach myself from you. "We raise new questions for a foreign culture, ones that it did not raise itself; we seek answers to our own questions in it ... Without *one's own* questions one cannot creatively understand anything other or foreign." It is Bakhtin (1986, 7) again, and his words could very well have been pronounced on behalf of autobiography and the autobiographical instance in literature and culture. Can I really recognize you if I have no inscription from you to offset my perception of you? If I do not grant you your right to inscribe yourself or do not grant your self-inscriptions access to the public sphere, who, outside of me or my own community, will recognize my representations of myself? Would I not be depriving myself of an additional backdrop against which to refract and to bolster *my* identity? And would I not be depriving you of a service if I did not develop the capacity to autobiographize, to narrate my story? To construct a narrative that would enable me to differentiate myself from you, and, therefore, to offer you the chance to develop *your* questions, to refine your perceptions of yourself?

Let me close with an illustration that is not from an autobiographical work but that is about autobiography. In *La Sarrasine*, a film by the Italian-Canadian director Paul Tana, there is a sequence near the beginning that presents the young, illiterate wife of a Sicilan tailor as she is learning to write by jotting down in a notebook the verses of a Renaissance epic that her husband slowly and magniloquently enunciates for her. This scene – surely one of the most compelling scenes of writing in recent cinema – is expanded upon by the film. As the story unfolds, the notebook becomes a diary. Ninetta, the Saracen woman of the title, will confide to it her thoughts, painfully writing word by word, or occasionally commenting on events via voice-over devices, as if reading from her journal. When the tailor accidentally kills a Québécois merchant (the film is set in the Montreal of the early 1900s) and is imprisoned, she has to resist pressures to move back to Italy. Upon her husband's suicide in jail, to avoid being repatriated against her will by a freshly arrived brother-in-law, Ninetta hides in one of the rooms of the dead merchant's emporium. She is found there by the latter's widow, who has herself resisted the advice of her father and her priest and decided to reopen her husband's business. In running away, Ninetta inadvertently leaves behind the notebook. The film doesn't spell out what the Québécois woman understood of the diary (her father had travelled to Italy and could have translated for her), but the diary is returned to Ninetta, and the viewer is left with the impression that it produced some tacit solidarity between the two characters, that having come across it did permit the Québécois woman to know more about her own plight, and that her subsequent gesture did strengthen Ninetta's conviction to stay in Canada.

In locating autobiography within the history of the genres of the century, the breadth of Ninetta's claims should not be minimized. As with "narcissism" – or words like "belonging," "ghetto," and "victim," which recently have been the object of unflinchingly denigratory semantics, of a rhetoric always somehow beyond inquiry – in dialogue the impulse to inscribe the self, to set its story down, is primary and not necessarily negative. Wittingly or unwittingly, in writing that story, you are crossing the line that separates self-designation from self-exhibition. The current decades may very well be the historical phase in which narcissism acquires a new cultural meaning, in which, like survival, narcissism is a moral imperative, a civic duty, one of the prerequisites of citizenship. To love your neighbour, you must be able – or be enabled – to love yourself, to reclaim or maintain your self-esteem, your dignity. The moment autobiographies circulate publicly, are candidates for admission into collective archives, the complex labour by which personal memory aids and abets and is aided and abetted by cultural memory, by group mnemonics, unleashes the process that redeems it. In autobiography you arrange your recollections in a narrative pattern and you deliver them to the refractions of others. But redemption is the dialectical aftermath of an initial effort, of the struggle to retain biographical continuity. It is not forthcoming if you cannot also look into that darkling mirror that is your history. Just as "I-You" communication puts space in the forefront (there is a hiatus between me and my interlocutor that I must somehow negotiate), the "I-I" communication on which "I-You" communication hinges activates time, a most unpostmodern dimension.

In this perhaps lies the last theoretical moral that autobiography can pass on to literary studies. Constantly inherited and invented (invented from group or archival material, inherited because someone endeavoured to reinscribe them in his or her own personal story), identities are temporal pauses during which persons catch their breath and prepare themselves for dialogue. Fixed (in print or other media) autobiographies are the notification of such pauses, telling how such pauses have been achieved. They thus put a damper on the glorification of flux, of movement, of the continuous, nonstop, infinite dissemination and permeability of meanings and beliefs that has been the most conspicuous and appealing exercise of classical postmodernist theory. Are the autobiographies of minority writers or the autobiographies written by critics after the decline of the *grand récits* postmodern or not, then? In order to answer this question we may have to start by putting some distance between postmodernity (the period, the chronological entity) and postmodernism (the critical movement), which has provided only one of the filters through which to look at the last fifty years or so, albeit the most influential one.

Notes

1 T.S. Eliot's "Tradition and the Individual Talent" already supplies all the links. Both modernist and postmodernist theorists have contested science's self-proclaimed familiarity with Truth but not its "objectivity". See Eliot (1953, 24): "It is in this depersonalization that art may be said to approach the condition of science"

2 Various substantial disciplinary and interdisciplinary projects now are focusing on issues of relevance for the study of autobiography. Some of the most interesting ones lie outside of the territory of both "traditional" literary theory and the Althusser-Derrida-Foucault-Lacan quaternary that sets the limits of high theory. Thus the immunologists or the physiologists who tell us that cells react to bacteria by recognizing them as the "non-I" or that organs do the same with transplanted organs, the anthropologists who adopt epidemiological approaches to culture (see Sperber 1996), the sociologists who work with the notion of complexity and conduct biology-sensitive reassessments of subjectivity (Morin 1980) provide unblinkering insights. To say that subjectivity is linguistically constructed doesn't explain how it is that an individual (and by using this term I am already introducing some conceptual slippage) is able to deploy the pronoun "I." Would that individual be able to deploy the pronoun properly without some prior capacity to engage in self-reflexion, in self-reference?

Even the projects within the disciplinary confines most adjacent to literary studies, and that literary studies would find congenial, have been many and differently nuanced. Just to pursue one of the threads that runs through some of the things I have been saying, Paul Ricoeur's (1991) perceptive canvassing of the way life is emplotted in the mind would be supported by the work of Roger Schank (1990) in Artificial Intelligence, which also posits that the human way of knowing and/or self-knowing is primarily narrative. Both would have to be checked against such philosophers as Charles Taylor (1989) and Amélie Oksenberg Rorty (1988), who have done much to clarify the meaning of the notion of self or of such other notions as character, person, individual and subject. But all of them would have to be further collated with the traditions (American pragmatism, for one) or individual thinkers (Mikhail Bakhtin, Hannah Arendt) who have put a heavy premium on the relation between self, action and beliefs.

Finally, while I have been downplaying the specifically literary co-ordinates of autobiography, the issues they raise about genre or literary and cultural history are not extraneous to the interdisciplinary give-and-take. How autobiographies are different from diaries or memoirs, whether they can be written in poetry as well as in prose, in the third person as well as in the first person, whether autobiographies published before Romanticism are autobiographical in the sense in which the term is used today: these rubrics, which are typically literary, do help to better pinpoint the preoccupations of philosophers or sociologists (particularly the preoccupations about narrative) and should be part of any debate.

3 Lotman's (1990) most detailed survey of the semiosis of autocommunication is found in "Autocommunication: 'I' and 'Other' as Addressees." Of his very elaborate exposition I would underline two basic tenets: (1) that with autocommunication the sender and the receiver are the same, although in different moments in time and with different attitudes and ideologies; (2) that with autocommunication the message acts as the code sender and receiver share. Needless to say, this inversion of the normal functions of message and code is of great suggestiveness for the study of autobiography. It puts the genre under the aegis of temporality and again forces us to rethink the relation between the notions of iteration, repetition, and inscription.

4 On this, too, I can only be stenographically brief. Ontological risk is a topic that looms large in the sociology of modernity (see Giddens 1991; but also Beck 1999). Within the discourse with which other social sciences have addressed the question of modernity, worthy of note, besides the classical texts of Mary Douglas (e.g., Douglas and Widavsky 1982), is the work of the Italian anthropologist Ernesto De Martino, which is entirely devoted to the exploration of the apocalyptic situation in its various forms and kinds (psychopathological, cultural, individual, collective, etc.). Unknown outside Italy, De Martino used the notion of "loss of presence" to describe the disorientation, the crisis that befalls individuals when they are no longer guaranteed by the culture and the cultural institutions of the society they find themselves in and that would otherwise, in different circumstances, provide them with the wherewithal that fixes beliefs and fosters the capacity to act. The very language with which his texts are imbued, the connotations it sediments on such terms as "presence" (which, for De Martino, becomes meaningful within a historical, sequential context) would be sufficient to earn him a larger readership than he has had (see De Martino 1973 and 1977). The only substantial writing about him in North America of which I am aware is that of Saunders (1993).

Works Cited

Antin, Mary. 1912. *The Promised Land*. Boston: Houghton Mifflin.

Arendt, Hannah. 1958. *The Human Condition*. Chicago: Chicago University Press.

Atwood, Margaret. 1972. *Survival: A Thematic Guide to Canadian Literature*. Toronto: Anansi.

Auerbach, Erich. 1959. "'Figura.'" In *Scenes from the Drama of European Literature: Six Essays,* 11–76. New York: Meridian.

Bakhtin, Mikhail. 1986. "Response to a Question from the *Novy Mir* Editorial Staff." In *Speech Genres and Other Late Essays*. Trans. Vern W. McGee, 1–9. Austin: University of Texas Press.

- 1993. *Toward a Philosophy of the Act*. Trans. Vadim Lapunov. Austin: University of Texas Press.
Beck, Ulrich. 1999. *World Risk Society*. Malden, MA: Polity.
Blasing, Mutlu Konuk. 1977. *The Art of Life: Studies in American Autobiographical Literature*. Austin: University of Texas Press.
Bruss, Elizabeth W. 1976. *Autobiographical Acts: The Changing Situation of a Literary Genre*. Baltimore: Johns Hopkins University Press.
De Man, Paul. 1979. "Autobiography as De-Facement." *Modern Language Notes*, 94: 919–30.
- 1986. "The Resistance to Theory." In *The Resistance To Theory*, 3–20. Minneapolis: University of Minnesota Press.
De Martino, Ernesto. 1973. *Il mondo magico*. Torino: Boringhieri.
- 1977. *La fine del mondo*. Torino: Einaudi.
Derrida, Jacques. 1977. "Signature Event Context." *Glyph* 1: 172–96.
Di Cicco, Pier Giorgio. 1979. *The Tough Romance*. Toronto: McClelland and Stewart.
- 1986. *Virgin Science*. Toronto: McClelland and Stewart.
Douglas, Mary, and Aaron Wildavsky. 1982. *Risk and Culture*. Berkeley-London: University of California Press.
Eliot, Thomas Stearns. 1953. "Tradition and the Individual Talent." In *Selected Prose*, ed. John Hayward, 21–30. Harmondsworth: Penguin.
- 1974. "Ash Wednesday." In *Collected Poems, 1909–1962*. 93–105. London: Faber and Faber.
Foucault, Michel. 1977. "What Is an Author." In *Language, Counter-Memory, Practice*, 113–38. Ithaca: Cornell University Press.
- 1988. "The Masked Philosopher." In *Politics Philosophy Culture*, ed. Lawrence Kritzman, 321–30. New York: Routledge.
Giddens, Anthony. 1991. *Modernity and Self-Identity*. Stanford: Stanford University Press.
Heidegger, Martin. 1963. *Being and Time*. Trans. John Macquarrie and Edward Robinson. New York: Harper and Row.
Hughes, Robert. 1993. *The Culture of Complaint*. New York: Warner Books.
Huyssen, Andreas. 1995. "Escape from Amnesia: The Museum as Mass Medium." In *Twilight Memories: Marking Time in a Culture of Amnesia*, 1–35. New York: Routledge.
Jabès, Edmond. 1991. *Le Livre de l'hospitalité*. Paris: Gallimard.
Koppelman, Susan. 1993. "Excerpts From letters to Friends." In *The Intimate Critique: Autobiographical Literary Criticism*, ed. Diane P. Freedman, Olivia Frey, and Frances Murphy Zauhar, 75–80. Durham and London: Duke University Press.
Kundera, Milan. 1994 [1980]. *The Book of Laughter and Forgetting*. Trans. Michael Henry Heim. New York: Harper.
Lasch, Christopher. 1979. *The Culture of Narcissism*. New York: Warner.
- 1984. *The Minimal Self*. New York: W.K. Norton.
Lejeune, Philippe. 1975. *Le Pacte autobiographique*. Paris: Seuil.
Lévi-Strauss, Claude. 1958. "La Structure des Mythes." In *Anthropologie structurale*, 226–55. Paris: Plon.
Lotman, Youri. 1977. *The Structure of the Artistic Text*. Trans. Donald Vroon. Ann Arbor: Michigan Slavic Contributions.
- 1985. "L'asimmetria e il dialogo." In *La semiosfera*, 91–110. A cura di Simonetta Salvestroni. Venezia: Marsilio Editori.

– 1990. "Autocommunication: 'I' and 'Other' as Addressees." In *Universe of Mind: A Semiotic Theory of Culture*, 20–35. Bloomington: Indiana University Press.

Miller, Nancy. 1991. *Getting Personal: Feminist Occasions and Other Autobiographical Acts*. New York: Routledge

Morin, Edgar. 1980. *La Méthode*. Tome 2: *La Vie de la vie*. Paris: Seuil.

Oksenberg Rorty, Amélie. 1988. *Mind in Action*. Boston: Beacon.

Peirce, Charles Sanders. 1932. *Collected Papers*. Vol. 2. Ed. Charles Hartshorne and Paul Weiss. Cambridge, MA: Harvard University Press.

Ricoeur, Paul. 1991. "Life in Quest of Narrative." In *On Paul Ricoeur. Narrative and Interpretation*, ed. David Wood, 20–33. London and New York: Routledge.

Robertson, Linda, R. 1993. "Social Circles: Being a Report on J. Hillis Miller's Campus Visitation." In *The Intimate Critique: Autobiographical Literary Criticism*, ed. Diane P. Freedman, Olivia Frey, and Frances Murphy Zauhar, 81–92. Durham and London: Duke University Press.

Saunders, George. 1993. "'Critical Ethnocentrism' and the Ethnology of Ernesto De Martino." *American Anthropologist* 95 (4): 875–93.

Schank, Roger. 1990. *Tell Me a Story: A New Look at Real and Artificial Memory*. New York: Scribner's.

Searle, John. 1977. "Reiterating the Differences: A Reply to Derrida." *Glyph* 1: 198–207.

Silko, Leslie Marmon. 1977. *Ceremony*. New York: Viking.

Sperber, Dan. 1996. *Explaining Culture: A Naturalistic Approach*. London: Blackwell.

Stone, Albert E. 1982. *Autobiographical Occasions and Original Acts. Versions of American Identity from Henry Adams to Nate Shaw*. Philadelphia: University of Pennsylvania Press.

Taylor, Charles. 1985. *Human Agency and Language*. Cambridge: Cambridge University Press.

– 1989. *Sources of the Self*. Cambridge, MA: Harvard University Press.

– 1994. "The Politics of Recognition." In *Multiculturalism: Examining the Politics of Recognition*, ed. Amy Gutman, 25–73. Princeton: Princeton University Press.

Tompkins, Jane. 1993. "Me and My Shadow." In *The Intimate Critique: Autobiographical Literary Criticism*, ed. Diane P. Freedman, Olivia Frey, and Frances Murphy Zauhar, 23–40. Durham and London: Duke University Press.

Vico, Giambattista. 1984 [1948]. *The New Science*. Trans. T.G. Bergin and M.H. Fisch. Ithaca: Cornell University Press.

Von Humboldt, Wilhelm. 1988. *On Language*. Cambridge: Cambridge University Press.

Whitman, Walt. 1950. "Song of the Exposition." In *Leaves of Grass and Selected Prose*, 157. New York: Random.

Wimsatt, W.K. 1954. *The Verbal Icon*. N.p.: University of Kentucky Press.